Linguistic
Meaning

Linguistic Meaning

Volume 1

Keith Allan
Monash University

Routledge & Kegan Paul
London and New York

First published in 1986
by Routledge & Kegan Paul plc

11 New Fetter Lane, London EC4P 4EE

Published in the USA by
Routledge & Kegan Paul Inc.
in association with Methuen Inc.
29 West 35th Street, New York, NY 1001

Set in Times 9 on 11 pt
by Columns of Reading
and printed in Great Britain
by The Guernsey Press Co Ltd
Guernsey, Channel Islands

Library of Congress Cataloging in Publication Data

Allan, Keith, 1943–

Linguistic meaning.
Includes bibliographies and indexes.
1. Semantics.   2. Meaning (Philosophy)   3. Speech
acts (Linguistics)   I. Title.
P325.A424   1986   401'.9   85–14525

British Library CIP Data also available
ISBN 0-7100-9587-2 (v. 1)
ISBN 0-7102-0699-2 (pbk. : v. 1)
ISBN 0-7102-0697-6 (v. 2)
ISBN 0-7102-0698-4 (pbk. : v. 2)

Words are the tokens current and accepted
for conceits, as moneys are for values.

(Francis Bacon *Advancement of Learning* II.xvi.3)

To Grace, Roanne, and Sophie
For all they've had to put up with

Contents

Volume 1

Chapter 1   Beginning an account of linguistic meaning: speaker, hearer, context, and utterance (1)

Chapter 2   What is meaning? (75)

Chapter 3 Meaningful properties and meaning relations (140)

Chapter 4   Lexicon semantics (214)

Chapter 5 The semantic interpretation of sentences: a study of Katz's semantic theory and post-Katzian semantics (274)

Volume 2

Chapter 6 Prosody and meaning (1)

Chapter 7   Informational aspects of the utterance (59)

Chapter 8   Speech Acts (164)

Chapter 9   Epilogue: on linguistic meaning (281)

Figures and Tables

Figures

Tables

Volume 1

Preface

Whoever thinks a faultless piece to see
Thinks what ne'er was, nor is, nor e'er shall be,
In every work regard the writer's end,
Since none can compass more than they intend.
(Alexander Pope *Essay on Criticism*, 253-6)

This book presents a coherent, consistent, and comprehensive account of linguistic meaning, centered around an informally presented theory of meaning. It is intended for graduate and undergraduate students of linguistics, or any linguist curious about what a theory of meaning should seek to accomplish and the way to achieve that aim. It came to be written (like many textbooks, I suppose) because I could find no satisfactory text for my own students to use when tackling the problem of linguistic meaning. There are many good books which touch on a part of our theme – indeed, several have appeared since I began this ms; but none offers a comprehensive theory of linguistic meaning; and in tandem, no two of them present a consistent theory of meaning (they would probably use different terminologies to boot). Originally, I had intended to make an historical survey of theories of meaning, because it happens that there is a diachronic as well as logical progression from studies in lexical semantics to theories of sentence meaning to theories of utterance meaning. But there were other things that it seemed necessary to include as well – like a study of prosodic meaning, a sorely neglected area; consequently, the book which these words preface has turned out to be far more comprehensive than the book I first envisioned. Its rapid growth began with my identifying the primary task of a theory of linguistic meaning as presenting a rational model of the steps a hearer must take in order to understand the meaning of a speaker's utterance. This equates the primary task of a theory of linguistic meaning with describing a theory of speech acts; and a theory of speech acts presupposes a theory of semantics and a theory of prosodic meaning, as well as a proper treatment of the co-operative principle, context, and background information – all of which needed to be discussed in the book. The second task of a theory of linguistic meaning is to identify what meaning is, to explain the relationship between sense and denotation, and explicate the nature of meaningful properties and meaning relations; and these too needed to be included. Furthermore, it seemed inadequate to offer the reader a critical appreciation of other people's theories without also presenting a coherent alternative to the hypotheses objected to.

And so the book grew. Just how, can be gauged from a look at the contents list (which will also reveal that not every topic which could be included, has been). In consequence, only the most intensive (and at the same time extensive) course could expect to go through the book in one year. I use its contents over four years of study. The advantage of presenting so much material within the confines of a single work is that the student who studies only one part of the book can, if he or she so wishes (or is so directed), see how that part fits into a coherent framework. For exactly this same reason, it also liberates the teacher from worries about the way in which some particular topic – say, speech acts (ch. 8) or prosodic meaning (ch. 6) – is to be seen as part of a coherent theory of linguistic meaning.

As the book grew to meet the goals newly set for it, so did the publisher's deadlines slip by, and I have to thank Peter Hopkins of Routledge & Kegan Paul for his understanding and generosity in this matter. I should also like to thank the many students, friends, and colleagues who have, wittingly or unwittingly, been helpful to me in writing this book. There are too many for me to thank each one here, but I should like to express especial gratitude to Sue Favret, Rodney Huddleston, Jerry Katz, Junzo Kusunose, Adrienne Lehrer, John and Heidi Platt, and Anna Siewierska – though none of them can be blamed for any part of what follows. Finally, I must thank my wife Grace, who got so exasperated at sharing me with a book, that she eventually decided to study her rival and offer a nonlinguist's comments on it. All this travail and effort will be well justified if *Linguistic Meaning* can inspire its readers with an interest in the theory of meaning, and, better still, an enthusiasm to extend our knowledge about it.

K.A.
Melbourne, April 1984

Acknowledgments

Grateful acknowledgment is made for permission to quote from the following copyright sources. Figures 7.1–7.3 are from R. de Beaugrande *Text, Discourse, and Process: Toward a Multidisciplinary Science of Texts* 1980 © Ablex Publishing Co.; D.L. Bolinger, 'The atomization of meaning', *Language* 41, 1965 © the author and the Linguistic Society of America; Figures 2.4–2.5 are from P. Kay & C.K. McDaniel 'The linguistic significance of the meanings of basic color terms' *Language* 54, 1978 © the authors and the Linguistic Society of America; Figure 2.3 is from W. Labov 'Denotational structure' *Papers from the Parasession on the Lexicon* ed. by D. Farkas, W.M. Jacobsen, & K.W. Todrys © Chicago Linguistic Society; Tables 3.1–3.2 are from C.E. Osgood & T.A. Sebeok (eds) *Psycholinguistics: A Survey of Theory and Research Problems* 1954/ 1965 © Indiana University Press; Table 3.1 and Figure 3.1 are from C.E. Osgood, G.J. Suci, & P.H. Tannenbaum *The Measurement of Meaning* 1957 © University of Illinois Press.

The principal symbols and conventions

Symbols other than the ones listed below may be used from time to time with values that will be made clear within the co-text.

S	speaker
H	hearer
U	utterance
L	language
C	context
W	world spoken of
PA	perfunctory face-maintaining verbal acknowledgment
E	language expression
*E	E is ungrammatical or unacceptable
?*E	E is seemingly ungrammatical or unacceptable
??E	E is of very dubious grammaticality or acceptability
?E	E is of dubious grammaticality or acceptability
Σ	sentence
NP	noun phrase
N$_\emptyset$	uninflected noun
VP $\rightarrow$ V (NP)	a verb phrase has for its immediate constituent(s) a verb and optionally a noun phrase
Γ	variable for a category node
λ	variable for a lexicon item
Φ	prosody of U

1 (C)V(C)	1 stress
Tones:	` fall, ´ rise, ˆ rise-fall, ˇ fall-rise, ¯ level
/	disjuncture

Keys: high key / mid key / low key

P	proposition
P,Q	variables for propositions
A → B	A implicates B
A ⟷ B	A and B have the same meaning
A & B	A and B
A v B	A or B
$\begin{Bmatrix} A \\ B \end{Bmatrix}$	A or B
~A	not-A
x ∈ F	x is a member of F
F ⊂ G	F is a subset of G
F ∪ G	F is the union of F and G
F ∩ G	the intersection of F and G
F = (G ∪ G′)	F equals the union of G and its complement set

Categories such as Bird, Tomato, Traitor are written with an initial capital letter

×‹	boundary between two information constituents (ch. 7)
[P]	preparatory condition (on illocutionary act, ch. 8)
[S]	sincerity condition (ch. 8)
[I]	illocutionary intention (ch.8)
[E$_S$]	executive condition on speaker (ch. 8)
[E$_U$]	executive condition on utterance (ch. 8)
[E$_C$]	executive condition on context (ch. 8)
§8.5.3.2	refers to ch. 8 section 5.3.2
(6.3.7)	refers to the seventh example in section 6.3

italics are regularly used for cited forms and for book titles; they are
   sometimes used in examples to pick out significant expressions

SMALL CAPITALS are used for emphasis within the text

'single quotes' are regularly used for quotations and the titles of articles

"double quotes" are regularly used to enclose meanings; sometimes
   lexemes; and sometimes as 'scare' quotes

Phonetic symbols have IPA values, e.g. English /biid/ = *bead*; /bi·t/ =
beat; /θɪŋ/ = *thing*; /ˈplɛʒə/ = *pléasure*; /æt/ = *at*; /tʃəətʃ/ = *church*;
/dʒʌdʒ/ = *judge*; /hɒt/ = *hot*, or in Cockney /ʔɒʔ/ = *'o'*; /jɔɔ/ = *your*;
/pɒt/ = *put*; /buu/ = *boo*; /ɪə/ = *ear*; /ðɛə/ = *there*; /ʃaɪ/ = *shy*; /kaʊ/
= *cow*; /kɔɪ/ = *coy*; /pɛɪ/ = *pay*; /gəʊ/ = *go*.

Chapter 1

Beginning an account of linguistic meaning:
speaker, hearer, context, and utterance

> Pity the poor analyst, who has to do the best he can with meanings that are as elusive as a piece of wet soap in a bathtub.
>
> (Dwight Bolinger *Aspects of Language* 1975:205)

1.1 Introduction

We are in a hall, waiting for someone to speak. He goes up to the microphone, opens his mouth to say something, but before any sound comes out collapses from a heart attack. We may presume that at the moment he collapsed, the would-be speaker had formulated some language expression which he was about to communicate to his audience: but it died with him. The point of recounting this sad tale, is to demonstrate that no matter what language the speaker may have in his head, it is of no consequence to anyone else – including the linguist – until he has uttered it. Thus, the source for linguistic data is the speech act: where a speaker S makes an utterance U in language L to hearer H in context C. This is not to deny that a whole range of language expressions which could be uttered never are;[1] but these are only interesting because they could potentially be uttered; and they are only recognizable to someone other than the person who thinks them up, when they ARE uttered: after all, linguists deal in language, not telepathy.

Our concern in this book is to examine ways of accounting for linguistic meaning, and a large part of that task will be accomplished by describing a set of procedures for assigning meaning to any utterance U (in language L) made by speaker S to hearer H in context C. In this context we examine what is to be understood by the terms S, H and C, and the reasons why speaker, hearer and context cannot be ignored in a comprehensive theory of linguistic meaning; then, to complete preparations for describing procedures for assigning meaning to any utterance U, there is an introductory discussion of the contributions to meaning of the various constituents of U.

1.2　The properties ascribed to speaker S and hearer H[2]

1.2.1　S and H as hypothetical men-in-the-street[3]

In giving an account of linguistic meaning both S and H are taken to be model persons, and not any actual, real-life speaker and hearer. We ascribe to S and H the sort of capabilities and judgment attributed to the 'reasonable man' in law;[4] they are the hypothetical men-in-the-street who adopt whatever practice is customary under the prevailing circumstances; they have no personal idiosyncrasies, and they are not omniscient, nor clairvoyant, nor foolish. We assume that each attributes to the other these same properties. In this way, we hope to guard against such individual quirks as a speaker who consistently uses *left* when he means "right" – not because it is intrinsically uninterest- ing, and despite the fact that an account of such behaviour could be given, but simply because it takes us too far out of our way. Except perhaps for recognizable slips of the tongue, as when the usher says *Let me sew you to your sheet*, or anyone says *Women have had to fart very hide for their rights*, we are not interested in what S intended to say (which would take us into psychology) but only in what he does say – i.e. in his utterance U. Nor are we interested in what H thinks he heard – but, once again, only in U. Our aim is to make explicit in an abstract model each step in H's reasoning which, given that S utters U in context C, leads H to determine S's meaning in U. This goal is justified because, having ascribed to S and H the qualities of reasonable men (see n.3), what H reasonably takes to be S's meaning IS the meaning of U. But note that our theory of meaning will not pretend to be a psycholinguistic theory of utterance interpretation: it will not try to model actual mental processing, conscious or unconscious. A real hearer may in fact determine S's meaning in a completely different way from the way proposed in our abstract model. Even if our model happens to correlate exactly with a real hearer's psychological processing, he might have available certain cognitive strategies to short-circuit the process, and strategies such as these would be totally irrelevant to a theory of linguistic meaning.

We take it for a descriptive norm that S and H are individuals interacting as a dyad. It is in any case very rare for a single utterance to be made by speakers in unison, though not so unusual for writers to do

it; but when it occurs there is no correlative effect in the meaning of U. On the other hand, it is very common for S to address an utterance to more than one hearer: we show in §8.9 that on most such occasions S's meaning in U is the same for each hearer and, for theoretical purposes, we may proceed as though H were any individual among those hearers. Sometimes, however, S intends his utterance U to mean different things to different hearers; on these occasions, U has as many meanings as U communicates to the different hearers. It also happens that U may be overheard by someone for whom it wasn't intended. None of these situations involving more than one hearer presents a problem for a theory of meaning based on the descriptive norm that S and H form a dyad in which a speaker S addresses his utterance U (in language L) to a hearer H in context C.

1.2.2 The importance of being reasonable

We have ascribed to S and H the qualities of reasonable men. There is (normally) a mutual expectation that S and H will behave reasonably towards one another, and will co-operate with one another, in their language interchanges as in other kinds of social behaviour. The primary function of language is communication, i.e. the deliverance of meaning from S to H; ordinarily, if H perceives a noise S makes to be linguistic, he reasons that S has produced it with the intention of communicating something by making use of the conventions of some natural language. We may call this the communicative presumption.[5] Because S wants to communicate with H he will use language that he expects H will understand. It is well-known that speakers use different varieties of language with different hearers: this is one way in which S co-operates with H in the language interchange. But being a reasonable man, S co-operates with H in other ways, too. For instance he normally speaks using sufficient volume not to be inaudible, yet not so loudly as to discomfort H; he tries to ensure that his utterance is not irrelevant to its context, that it is clear enough to be understood, that it is concise and straightforward enough not to waste H's time unduly, and honest enough not to mislead him. Thus, although (2.2.1 and 2.2.2) mean more or less the same, it would normally be unreasonable for S to use the former in place of the latter.

(2.2.1) There is a male adult human being in upright stance using his legs as a means of locomotion to propel himself up a series of flat-topped structures some six or seven inches high.

(2.2.2) There is a man going upstairs.

And we recognize the following discourse as abnormal just because it is not reasonable:

> INTERVIEWER: A stitch in time saves nine. What does that mean?
> SCHIZOPHRENIC: Oh! That's because all women have a little bit of magic in them. I found that out. And it's called, it's sort of good magic. And nine is a sort of magic number. Like, I've got nine colours here you will notice. I've got yellow, green, blue, grey, orange, blue and navy. And I've got black. And I've got a sort of clear white. The nine colours, to me they are the whole universe; and they symbolize every man, woman, and child in the world.
> (Sherry Rochester and James R. Martin *Crazy Talk* 1979:94-5)

Although we can understand the words and sentences the schizo-phrenic uses and recognize a disjointed thematic progression, we cannot get to grips with his meaning because there is an absence of reasonable coherence.

The communicative presumption includes a presumption that S has some purpose in saying what he does; e.g. S intends to inform H of something, or to promise H he will do something, or he is requesting H to do something, or maybe S is just making conversation. It is the presumption that S's utterance is reasonable and intended to make sense, that leads H to look for nonliteral meanings when the utterance cannot be understood literally. Suppose, e.g., S says,

(2.2.2) I don't like being a tax inspector, but it's my bread and butter.

Here, 'bread and butter' cannot be interpreted literally as "bread with butter on it"; so, presuming that S is observing the reasonableness condition, H seeks a nonliteral interpretation in terms of the idiom *bread and butter* meaning "source of income". Or take a case where S drops a plate and comments *Clever!* Whatever S's tone of voice or facial expression, H knows that a literal interpretation of S's utterance is at odds with the context, because dropping plates does not count as a clever act; moreover, H knows that S must know this too – i.e. that it is mutual knowledge.[6] Now, either S is making a totally inappropriate and unreasonable remark, or he is presumed to have some reasonable purpose in uttering 'Clever!' after dropping a plate. It is part of S's and H's knowledge of English usage that when people are being ironic about their own actions, or sarcastic about other people's, they often say the opposite of what they mean; so if S was being ironic, then by

'Clever!' he actually meant "Not clever!" – which is almost certainly the correct interpretation, because it is a comment the context warrants.

Without the communicative presumption we could not begin to cope with nonliteral usage, because we would have no convention for deciding whether S was speaking nonliterally or just talking nonsense. Nor should we be able to recognize that if S says e.g. *Women have had to fart very hide for their rights* he has slipped his tongue into a spoonerism; as it stands this utterance is nonsense; but given the presumption that S intended to communicate a reasonable and interpretable statement, H can figure out what S presumably meant to say.[7] And, of course, the presumption that S is being reasonable, and that he has some purpose in saying what he does, is equally important in the interpretation of straightforward, literally meant utterances. E.g. if S says *What's the time?* H presumes that S wants to know what time it is and that was his purpose in asking the question. Now, it is true that people may have more subtle purposes than this, e.g. S might have asked H the question in order to strike up a conversation; or if they are travelling to a rendez-vous with someone else, as a means of obliquely asking H whether he thinks they will arrive on time. Whatever S's purpose may be, it can be presumed that he does have some reason for uttering U, and H's understanding of U will often involve his recognizing that purpose.

Because the communicative presumption gives H to believe that S will have some reasonable purpose in uttering U, he will normally be willing to expend some effort in trying to figure out S's meaning, so it is co-operative of S to make H's task as quick and easy as possible. We have already seen that S should not unnecessarily risk confusing H by using e.g. (2.2.1) instead of (2.2.2), or (2.2.4) below instead of (2.2.5):

(2.2.4) Never imagine yourself not to be otherwise than what it might appear to others that what you were or might have been was not otherwise than what you had been would have appeared to them to be otherwise.

(Lewis Carroll *Alice in Wonderland* 1965:84)

(2.2.5) Be what you would seem to be.

Although this principle applies in general, it need not do so provided S has good reason for the form his utterance takes. E.g. in (2.2.4) it was Lewis Carroll's purpose to amuse his readers by having the Duchess (whose utterance this is) violate a co-operative norm and seek to confuse Alice.

While speaking of reasons for prolixity, compare (2.2.6) with (2.2.7).

(2.2.6) Help!

(2.2.7) I wonder if by any chance you wouldn't mind helping me?

Where speed and efficiency are at a premium, for instance if S were drowning, the brief (2.2.6) is entirely appropriate as a request for H's help, and (2.2.7) would be correlatively inappropriate. The ritualistic prolixity of the request in (2.2.7) demonstrates S's extreme deference towards H, and would be most appropriate where S has reason to think that H might feel unduly imposed upon by a simpler request, and where (2.2.6) would be unacceptably curt.[8] In any event, it is co-operative of S to use the appropriate form of request so as to correctly indicate to H the nature of the request; and unreasonable for him to do otherwise.

It would be unreasonable of S to make utterances that contain internal contradictions, e.g. *My brother is an only child.* Generally when people say things like this, or

(2.2.8) The green door is brown,

And they are not known to be insane, or tripping out, etc., H will presume S intends the utterance to be understood as sensical, and he will look behind the apparent contradiction for a meaning – e.g. for (2.2.8), "the door which was said to be green is in fact brown". We saw earlier, in the quote from the schizophrenic, that S cannot as a rule talk nonsense and be thought reasonable. The exception, if it is an exception, is when S has a comic purpose, cf.

BILL:	My lords, ladies and other National Assistance holders – tonight the League of Burmese Trombonists presents a best-seller play entitled:
ORCHESTRA:	TIMPANI ROLL. HELD UNDER: –
PETER:	The Terror of Bexhill-on-Sea or . . .
ORCHESTRA:	THREE DRAMATIC CHORDS.
HARRY:	The Dreaded Batter Pudding Hurler.
ORCHESTRA:	CLIMAX. THEN DOWN NOW BEHIND: –
BILL:	The English Channel 1941. Across the silent strip of green-grey water – in England – coastal towns were deserted, except for people. Despite the threat of invasion and the stringent blackout rules, elderly gentlefolk of Bexhill-on-Sea still took their evening constitutionals.

F.X.:	EBB TIDE ON A GRAVEL BEACH.
CRUN:	Ohh – it's quite windy on these cliffs.
MINNIE:	What a nice summer evening – typical English.
CRUN:	Mnk yes – the rain's lovely and warm – I think I'll take one of my sou'westers off – here, hold my elephant gun.
MINNIE:	I don't know what you brought it for – you can't shoot elephants in England.
CRUN:	Mnk? Why not?
MINNIE:	They're out of season.
CRUN:	Does this mean we'll have to have pelican for dinner again?
MINNIE:	Yes, I'm afraid so.
CRUN:	Then I'll risk it, I'll shoot an elephant out of season.
BOTH:	(Go off mumbling in distance)
BILL:	Listeners who are listening will, of course, realise that Minnie and Henry are talking rubbish – as erudite people will realise, there are no elephants in Sussex. They are only found in Kent North on a straight line between two points thus making it the shortest distance.

(Spike Milligan *The Goon Show Scripts* 1972:23f)

The communicative presumption extends to the Goon Show scripts (and those of its artistic successor Monty Python) and leads H to seek a reason for their linguistic unreasonableness: he finds it in S's intention to be comic.

Unnecessary prolixity, self-contradiction, uttering anomalies and non-sequiturs are not the only ways in which S might be unreasonable. It is often unreasonable for him to state the obvious: e.g. if I tell you that you are reading this book, then I am unreasonably wasting your time. Stating the obvious is not always unreasonable; e.g. S can be teaching H a procedure by demonstrating it so that H can perceive it for himself, but at the same time S may describe the actions being carried out in order to reinforce H's perception of them. Tautologies like (2.2.9-10) also state the obvious:

(2.2.9) My neighbour, who is a woman, is pregnant.

(2.2.10) The prime minister is the prime minister.

If H knows the meaning of *pregnant* (and it would be unreasonable of S to utter (2.2.9) to him otherwise) he can be expected to know that 'my neighbour is pregnant' necessarily implies the neighbour is a woman; in consequence the appositive clause 'who is a woman' is redundant. H will be predisposed to look for a purpose behind S's including it in the utterance, and would be wasting his time (since I cannot think of any context, other than a discussion like this one, in which this tautology might naturally occur). Unlike e.g. *The Prime minister is Mr. Gladstone*, (2.2.10) apparently states the obvious. However, such a sentence may be used with heavy stress on 'is' to imply that there is something very special about being prime minister, cf. *After all, the prime minister IS the prime minister*. Turning to questions: unless S is sanctioned to quiz or test H's knowledge, S should not normally waste H's time by asking H questions to which H has reason to believe S already knows the answers. This is why a question such as (2.2.11) can be used as an insult:

(2.2.11) Do you know that 2 plus 2 equals 4?

Assuming that S and H are over the age of eight, then S will know that $2+2=4$, and he will know that H will know it too, and also that H will know he knows H knows it (i.e. S knows that H knows it will be mutual knowledge). S thus speciously adopts the role of quiz-master; and because the equation $2+2=4$ is regarded as a very basic item of knowledge, S's question amounts to "Do you know even the simplest things?" which is, of course, insulting.

We have seen that S and H are expected to be reasonable in their participation in language interchange. H can reasonably presume that S's utterance U is intended to communicate something to him, and he will therefore make the effort to understand U, no matter how unreasonable it might appear at first sight.[9] For his part, S can expect H to be able to reason out his meaning, and S is constrained to co-operate in making this task as quick and easy as possible – consistent with getting his meaning across. In the following text we see the interlocutors co-operating to achieve a mutual understanding.

(2.2.12)

E: OK. Now we need to attach the conduit to the motor. The conduit is the covering around the wires that you . . . were working with earlier. There is a small part . . . oh brother.

A: Now wait a s . . . the conduit is the cover to the wires?

E: Yes and . . .

A: Oh I see, there's a part that . . . a part that's supposed to go over it.

E: Yes.

A: I see . . . it looks the right shape too. Ah hah! Yes.

E: Wonderful, since I didn't know how to describe the part.

(Barbara Grosz 'Focusing and description in natural language dialogues' 1981:88)

Here we see E struggling to describe the conduit while A searches for something in the setting which seems to match what E is trying to describe.

It is usual for S to describe things in a manner which he judges will enable H to identify what he is talking about as speedily and as easily as possible. Thus S should not use only the absolutely minimal description possible in the context of the utterance, any more than he should be too prolix. For instance, to answer the question *What tool should I use?* with *The red-handled one* might be all that is absolutely necessary were a screwdriver required and this happened to be the only red-handled tool in sight; but it would be preferable to answer *The red-handled screwdriver* because this description, consisting of the generic name and a salient attribute of the object, gives H a larger number of significant parameters by which to recognize it. Because in the situation described there are not several red-handled screwdrivers to choose from, to answer *The red-handled screwdriver with the small chip on the bottom and the loose handle* would waste H's time with unnecessary details of insignificant attributes of the tool.

Consider the following interchange.

(2.2.13)

E: Remove the pump and the belt.

A: Is this thing with the flanges on it the pump?

E: Point at "the thing with the flanges on it" please.

A: I'm pointing at the thing with flanges on it. These little ribby things are flanges.

E: Yes, the thing you are pointing at is the pump. The little ribby things are cooling fins.

(Grosz 1981:89)

Here one can see alternative descriptions of a single object offered in an attempt to achieve mutual understanding. Notice how the apprentice, A, relies on appearance to describe and identify what is being spoken of, whereas the expert, E, gives a functional description.

Being reasonable involves both S and H being co-operative; and being co-operative requires each of S and H to be reasonable. In the next section we examine the other semantically relevant co-operative conditions on S and H, some of which we have touched upon already.

1.2.3　Being co-operative is being polite (mostly)

1.2.3.1　Paying attention to H's 'face'

Speaking to others is a social activity, and like other social activities (e.g. dancing, playing in an orchestra, playing cards or football) it can only take place if the people involved, S and H, mutually recognize that certain conventions[10] govern their actions and their use of language, and also their interpretations of the actions and utterances of the person they are speaking with (i.e. their interlocutor). Each interlocutor is held responsible for his actions and language use, and hence his observation of (or violation of) the conventions of language interchange.

If communication is to proceed smoothly, then S and H have to co-operate with one another. A very large part of their co-operative behaviour can be explained in terms of mutual presentation of 'face' (cf. Erving Goffman 'On face-work: an analysis of ritual elements in social interaction' 1955, Penelope Brown & Stephen Levinson 'Universals in language usage: politeness phenomena' 1978). Face is the public self-image that S and H must have regard to; we don't just 'lose' face in the eyes of our co-interactants, we also maintain it, and enhance it. A moment's thought should confirm from everyday experience that virtually every time S opens his mouth he needs to take care that his utterance will either maintain, enhance or threaten H's face in just the way he intends to affect it, while at the same time maintaining or enhancing his own face. It should also be obvious that this contributes to utterance meaning, recall the saying *It's not what he said, it's the way that he said it*. A satisfactory theory of linguistic meaning cannot ignore questions of face presentation, nor other politeness phenomena that maintain the co-operative nature of language interchange.

Face is composed of two co-existing aspects: (i) 'positive face' is the want of a person that his attributes, achievements, ideas, possessions, goals, etc. should be desirable to at least certain others; (ii) 'negative face' is the want of a person not to be imposed upon by others.[11] In a given context these two aspects of face can lead to tension if the satisfaction of one constitutes an infringement upon the other: e.g. there are times when to be ignored is a worse fate than to be noticed but criticized, and times when the balance leans the other way. Although both verbal and nonverbal acts affect face, we shall only be interested in the face affects of utterances. The face affect of an utterance is calculated against the sum of three pragmatic factors: D rating, P rating, and R rating.

D rating is based on the social distance between S and H, and determined on such parameters as their comparative ages, sexes, and socio-cultural backgrounds.

P rating is based on the asymmetric relation of H's power over or inferiority to S in the context of utterance: e.g. if S is a police constable and H is a doctor, then in the doctor's surgery H will have a superior rating to S, and when policeman S stops doctor H for speeding, H will have an inferior rating to S's.

R rating is based on the relative ranking of a particular act within the context of utterance: e.g. to ask H the time is less onerous than asking to borrow his car; but in an emergency it would not be onerous for S to ask to borrow H's car to drive him to the hospital.

The greater these ratings are, the more polite (= less face threatening) S should be in order to be co-operative. Knowing how to use a language correctly means being able to assess these values accurately and correlate them with certain language expressions, ways of speaking, tone of voice, etc. in order to produce an utterance that has the intended face affect. This is something non-native speakers often fail to achieve, and therefore they unintentionally cause offence. Also the norms from one language community do not necessarily all carry over into other communities, even among speakers of the same language. The face affect of the utterance is correlated with the sum of the values attributed to *D*, *P*, and *R*, so a low score on one component offsets a high score on another. If the score is too high for the linguistic strategies used in the utterance, H may be insulted, if it is too low, H may be flattered. It may appear that the safest procedure would be to flatter H except when you want to insult him; but by convention we anticipate that people who flatter expect something in return, just as people who insult incur a debt to repay; in consequence there is a constant inclination to maintain face all round: as Brown and Levinson 1978:66 put it, 'normally everyone's face depends on everyone else's being maintained.'

Brown & Levinson show convincingly that different linguistic strategies are conventionally used to mitigate different degrees of face threat in verbal acts. They identify four basic strategies to mitigate the face threatening content of U where (based on the sum of *D*, *P*, and *R* ratings) the message in U is (1) least face threatening to H, (2) less face threatening to H, (3) more face threatening to H and (4) most face threatening to H. We may crudely demonstrate these with examples of S seeking some change for a slot machine.

1 least face threatening to H, S should utter it bald on record i.e.

come straight out with it (e.g. *Got any change?* macho to a macho close friend)

2   less face threatening to H, S should utter it with attention to H's positive face (e.g. *Hey Harry, have you got any change?* politely to a friend)

3   more face threatening to H, S should utter it with attention to H's negative face (e.g. *I'm sorry to trouble you, but do you by any chance have change of a dollar?* to an apparently ladylike stranger)

4   most face threatening to H, S should utter it off the record i.e. be indirect (e.g. *It's so embarassing, but I don't have enough change!* to the big boss S is trying to impress)

Now if S should use strategy (3) to his spouse instead of (1) or (2), he would appear very distant, treating her too much like a distant acquaintance instead of an intimate; this is because use of a high numbered strategy will mislead H into thinking that the face threat is greater than it was, and so one of the D, P, or R values is higher than it should be. Thus the strategy S uses to mitigate a face threatening act should be the one appropriate to the degree of face threat; too high a numbered strategy is usually just as bad as too low a numbered strategy.[12]

The conventional nature of face affect strategies is also demonstrable from exchanges of greetings. When people's paths cross, they may choose to hurry past one another avoiding eye-contact and speaking; or they may choose to meet. Meeting is potentially a face threatening situation, and so common that there are conventions for coping with it. Meeting rituals involve co-operative nonverbal acts such as smiling and shaking hands, and the uttering of certain verbal formulae. These verbal formulae are examples of what Malinowski has called 'phatic communion':[13] their function is to communicate S's co-operative attitude toward H, not to trade information. The meet-and-speak convention is strong in most, if not all, cultures, because greetings attend to H's face wants (and by reciprocation, to S's face wants too); thus a person who says nothing on meeting another will be thought unfriendly, unco-operative, and even downright rude. Exchanges of greetings, such as the following from Hausa (a Chadic language spoken in and around the north of Nigeria) show similar patterns in many cultures:

A: *Ranka ya daɗe.*   "May your life be a long one."
B: *Yauwa, sannu!*   "Well, hello!"
A: *Lafiya?*   "How are you?"
B: *Lafiya lau.*   "Very well, thanks."

A:	*Ina gajiya?*	"Are you weary?"
B:	*Ba gajiya.*	"No. I'm fine."
A:	*Yaya aiki?*	"How's work?"
B:	*Aiki da godiya.*	"Good."
A:	*Ina gida?*	"How's the family?"
B:	*Lafiya. Ina labari?*	"Well. Any news?"
A:	*Labari sai alheri.*	"Things are going well."
B:	*To madalla. Sai an juma.*	"So, thank god. See you later."
A:	*Yauwa. Sai wana lokaci.*	"OK. See you sometime."

S attends to H's positive face wants by asking after his well-being and that of his family, and generally expressing interest in how things are going for him, closing with a friendly promise to see him again. S attends to H's negative face wants by not burdening H with his problems. If S walks up to H and says without greeting

(2.3.1.1) I'll come straight to the point . . .

he is felt to be being brusque. The reasons are that the failure to greet is a threatening act (because S fails to attend to H's face wants), and this is compounded by S employing a bald on record strategy appropriate to the mitigation of only the least threatening acts while uttering words which typically serve to introduce a fairly serious face threat to H. All told, S is giving H a rough ride with (2.3.1.1). To maintain H's face, so far as possible, S should have opened the conversation with a greeting and perhaps a remark about such non-face-threatening matters as the weather or traffic conditions,[14] cf.

(2.3.1.2) Hi, how are you? Lousy weather isn't it? What I wanted to ask you about is . . .

This at least makes the pretence of allowing H to reply, even if the delivery is so rapid as to preclude one. It is polite (i.e. face-saving) to invite one's interlocutor to speak and occasionally to give him the chance to speak; note the criticism inherent in *He never lets me get a word in edgeways* – which complains of the affront to S's positive face if S feels his own utterances are undervalued, and to his negative face if he feels imposed upon.

1.2.3.2 Attending to H's positive face

There are many other ways than greetings and partings[15] in which S seeks to affect H's positive face. To maintain or enhance it S will take a complimentary interest in H, his attributes, achievements, ideas, possessions, and goals: crudely put, S tries to make H feel good. To this end, S will avoid open disagreement with H (while being careful not to toady); and he will try to get on side by accommodating[16] his language usage so as to treat H in a manner calculated to please; and S may offer H invitations and other minor services in order to express a friendly and co-operative attitude. Acts maintaining or enhancing H's positive face are favours which H is expected to repay in some way – perhaps only with his company, but possibly with something more tangible like a job appointment. Nonetheless, owing a favour is not a face threat of the same magnitude; nor is it even so bad as having one's positive face wants ignored altogether.

Consider some of the linguistic effects of co-operative attention to H's positive face. Straight out compliments are generally determined from the content of the utterance, and there is little else worth saying about them here. However, it is worth noting a couple of pragmatic strategies for complimenting H. Where there is some social distance between S and H, but not a great deal, compliments often involve hyperbole and exaggerated stress, cf.

(2.3.2.1) What a fanTAStic BLOUSE that is!

Close acquaintances, on the other hand, may compliment through understatement:

(2.3.2.2) Not a bad idea of yours, to eat here.

It is, of course, complimentary to someone to go along with their expressed or implied point of view, i.e. to show empathy. Thus when someone is speaking, his interlocutor co-operatively makes a perfunctory face-maintaining verbal acknowledgment such as *Uh-huh*, *Right*, and *Yes* to S's positive propositions; and to the negative ones either agrees *No* with the proposition, or *Yes* in support of S's attitude.[17] There are also more elaborate verbal acknowledgments expressing empathy or sympathy, whose function is still primarily co-operative, cf.

(2.3.2.3)
    A: I had a flat tyre on the way home.
    B: Oh God, a flat tyre!

(2.3.2.4)
    A: My hubby was up all last night with a sore toe!
    B: Was he? You poor thing.

Questions like the one in (2.3.2.4.B) do not really expect answers, their main function is to indicate empathy. So far as is possible, one avoids disagreeing with what one's interlocutor says; in consequence we find sequences like the following:

(2.3.2.5)
A: What is she, small?
B: Yes, yes, she's small, smallish, um, not really small but certainly not very big.[18]

The co-operative convention is to agree with your interlocutor so far as you can, perhaps by spelling out the common ground, and then to disagree.

Sometimes, critical remarks and other attacks on H's positive face are excused by an introductory clause in which S humbles himself, cf.

(2.3.2.6)
a. I've probably misunderstood you, but . . .
b. I may be missing the point, but . . .
c. I'm not sure this makes sense, but . . .
d. This is just nitpicking, but . . .
e. I don't want to rush you, but . . .

Then there are the prevarications like

(2.3.2.7)
a. Don't get me wrong, but . . .
b. I don't want to offend you, but . . .[19]

And there are apologies for disagreeing,

(2.3.2.8)
a. I'm sorry, but I can't agree with you.
b. Forgive me, but I don't agree with you.

It is usually less of an affront to plead inability to comply with someone's face wants than to express unwillingness to do so. This is particularly clear when refusing an offer, because to do so is a serious face threat to the person making the offer. Direct refusals can be used to hurt, and are therefore generally avoided; compare

(2.3.2.9)
A: Wanna come to a movie tomorrow?
B_1: No I don't.
B_2: I'm sorry I don't.
B_3: (I'm sorry) I can't.

B_3 is better than B_2, which is better than B_1. B_1 is bald on record, and with the right tone of voice might be acceptable between very close friends but would be very insulting to a mere acquaintance. Where the *D* or *P* rating makes the refusal a most-face-threatening act, it will tend to be made off record, cf.

(2.3.2.10)
    A: Wanna come to a movie tomorrow?
    B: I'm sorry, I have to wash my hair.

Here the refusal has to be inferred from B's apology and what is obviously meant to be taken as an explanation of B's inability to comply with A's request.[20] The strategy of blaming an unco-operative act on causes supposedly beyond S's volition is employed to excuse negative face affronts as well as positive face affronts like this one.

We now turn to ways in which S may accommodate his language usage to affect H's positive face. Perhaps the grossest accommodation possible arises in a multilingual situation, where S chooses which language to use in making his utterance. For instance, given a triad comprising two English-speaking Poles and an Englishman who doesn't speak Polish, the Poles may choose to speak English with one another out of politeness to the Englishman.[21] A Nigerian university teacher will normally use standard English in class, because that is what is expected of him; but he will use either a vernacular language or pidgin English to a garage mechanic unless he wants to be branded hoity-toity. Similar to language accommodation is dialect and accent accommodation; however, S needs to be careful not to be thought to be mocking H if he converges towards H's dialect and accent. A clear example of dialect accommodation is where a Londoner uses standard English dialect and an RP accent when lecturing in a British university (because he feels it is expected of him); switches to cockney when conversing with a London cabbie, converging toward the cabbie's dialect and accent; and adopts a mid-Atlantic way of speaking with post-vocalic *r*s and /ɑ/ instead of /ɒ/ when in America.

Many people may only be able to use one dialect of one language and so they cannot accommodate to different dialects, let alone another language. But these people will still have the ability to use different styles or varieties of their language so as to affect H's positive face. Take an example of such stylistic variation from Tamilnadu in south India: when speaking to a landlord a Harijan (an 'untouchable') 'may mumble and speak in unfinished sentences as if shy to express foolish thoughts [, which] contrasts sharply with the same man bargaining with less powerful but still high caste persons' (Brown & Levinson 1978:191). Presumably the Harijan deliberately uses these different styles to meet H's expectations of him in the different utterance contexts; and by thus accommodating himself to H's positive face wants, he maintains H's positive face.[22]

The style of language S uses will be responsive to the degree of formality in the context of utterance. Martin Joos in *The Five Clocks* 1961:11 has identified five levels of formality: frozen, formal, consultative, casual, intimate. The ordinary speaker will not recognize firm boundaries between these various degrees of formality, but he will respond to a range between frozen and intimate styles. To take an example: at lunch before a board meeting Ed and Max might be on casual christian name terms; but when conducting official business in the board-room Ed would address Max as 'Mr. Chairman' if Max were chairman of the board, because the official business of a board meeting is customarily conducted in a frozen style. Note that it is not simply their presence at a board-meeting which demands use of the frozen style; if Ed were to utter an unofficial aside to Max during the course of the meeting, he would quite properly use a casual style. Politeness strategies for formal contexts are the same as those used to mark social distance, D; but they are influenced by the relative status P of S and H. The reason for this is that a large difference in status between S and H typically corresponds with a high D rating, which in turn corresponds to a high formality rating. Where S is inferior to H (i.e. where H's P rating is high) he will tend to accommodate to H's expectations by ensuring that his language use diverges from H's. Examples are the bumbling speech of the Harijan addressing a landlord, cited above; the use of higher than normal pitch among some speakers of Tamil (a Dravidian language of south India) and in Tzeltal (a Mayan language of Mexico);[23] the use of UNRECIPROCATED deferential terms of address such as English *sir, madam, Your Highness, Miss X*, etc. If, on the other hand, S is superior in status to H, he can choose either to maintain the power differential by ensuring that his language use diverges from H's; or he may lower the D rating, choosing to be informal and show solidarity with H by using in-group markers that demonstrate convergence to H's language usage and consequently his concern to enhance H's positive face wants. Where S and H are of similar status and there is a low D rating, informal in-group language is the regular mark of solidarity. It is marked by the use of colloquialisms, slang (including swearing), diminutives, contractions, ellipsis, the use of first names, nicknames, and such address forms as *baby, boy, brother, bud(dy), dad(dy), darling, dear, duckie, ducks, fella(s), gorgeous, grandad, guys, handsome, honey, luv, Mac, marra, mate, mum(my), old boy, sexy, sis(ter), sweetheart,*[24] etc. cf.

(2.3.2.11)
   a.   Wotcha think? Worth a quid, Frankie boy?
   b.   Liz darling, when have I got to see those bloody conservationist
       people?

As the *D* rating or formality increases, so the language used gets closer
to the standard English found in textbooks – or the closest regional
approximation thereto.

In more formal styles, the jargon of hobbies, trades, and professions
marks the solidarity of in-group members (in addition to being thought
necessary for the pursuit of the said hobbies, trades, and professions).
Slang is an important in-group marker within informal contexts, and
the reason it changes so rapidly is that membership of the in-group is
volatile and new groupings invent their own slang (cf. Glendon F.
Drake 'The social role of slang' 1980). Close friendship is often marked
in informal contexts by unserious bandying of insulting expressions, cf.

(2.3.2.12)
   FIRST YOUTH: Hullo, congenital idiot!
   SECOND YOUTH: Hullo, you priceless old ass!
   THE DAMSEL: I'd no idea you two knew each other so well!
                 (Quoted from a *Punch* cartoon by Stern 1965:323)

Context and tone of voice are what distinguish the true insult *You
stupid bastard* from its joking use between close friends.

A change from S's normal manner of addressing H marks a
meaningful change from S's normal attitude to H. Thus, familiars who
normally use in-group forms to one another may switch to formal or
high *D* forms in order to express withdrawal of intimacy; e.g. when S is
very angry with H and uses 'Mr. Higginbotham' instead of 'Fred'. The
same strategy is used in many languages; for instance, when a Japanese
speaker feels some tension toward a friend he will switch from
(2.3.2.13) to (2.3.2.14) according to Sachiko Ide in 'Japanese
sociolinguistics: politeness and women's language' 1982:376.

(2.3.2.13)

Kimi	wa	soo	iu	kedo, . . .
in-gp.-you	topic	so	in-gp.-say	though

"Although you say so, . . ." [Friendly, informal]

(2.3.2.14)

Anata	wa	soo	ossyaru	kedo, . . .
out-gp.-you	topic	so	out-gp.-say	though

"Although you say so, . . ." [Distant, quite formal]

In some languages, though not in English, acquaintances who normally address each other formally may use an informal mode of address to mark the withdrawal of respect; the English counterpart is communicated prosodically (i.e. via the tone of voice), and perhaps by the use of such informality markers as diminutives and swearing.

In many circumstances S will underplay his own attributes, ideas, possessions, and achievements, belittling his own positive face in order to enhance H's. In short, he will be modest. Japanese has a number of S-humbling devices which have no exact counterpart in English, cf.

(2.3.2.15)

Watashi ga	iku	
I	in-gp.-go	"I'm going" [Friendly, informal]

(2.3.2.16)

Watashi ga	mairu.	
I	humbly-go.	"I'm going" [Humble]

There are also S-humbling prefixes which may be affixed to certain Sino-Japanese nouns,[25] e.g. *gu* literally "stupid", *syoo* literally "little", *setsu* literally "bad": *gu-sai* means "my wife" with a humble connotation (but not "my stupid wife"); and *setsu-bun* is an explicitly modest version of "my (written) work". In English, S's modesty is counted a laudable trait, particularly in conversational interchange among strangers or mere acquaintances; but there are few formulae to rely on in expressing it. The honorific *Sir* and *Madam* used to clients and customers, and in formal letters, are remnants of self-humbling before H; so are those phrases like *Your humble servant* that once ended formal letters; the off record *Yours faithfully* is still used for this purpose in Britain. The only general S-humbling strategy open to English speakers is to avoid mentioning himself, as in the (b) samples below:

(2.3.2.17)
  a. It appears to me that the world is in recession.
  b. It appears that the world is in recession.

(2.3.2.18)
  a. I believe that both women and men should take care over their appearance.
  b. Both women and men should take care over their appearance.

(2.3.2.19)
  a. I can have it ready for you Monday.
  b. It'll be ready Monday.

(2.3.2.20)
   a.   I've brought you some flowers.
   b.   Here are some flowers.

(2.3.2.21)
   a.   I do my best.
   b.   One does one's best.

Comparable strategies are reported in Athapaskan languages (of western north America)[26] and Japanese.[27] Yet the most prevalent means of self-humbling in English is to say something self-deprecatory; e.g. when the hostess invites you to the dinner table and says *It's not much I'm afraid* you recognize that she is being modest, and does not intend the observation to be taken literally. Here is another example of self-deprecation:

   A: To get back to skiing. Have you done much?
   B: No. Um. Done a fair bit of mountaineering though. Not really
        mountaineering but sort of mucking around on Ruapehu and
        Tongariro and that. Um. I've climbed up Ruapehu twice and
        sort of skied down from the top. Which didn't really involve
        much skiing, y'know. Sort of go down from the top all the way
        down. Sort of all over in about half an hour. And ah . . . since
        then I've gone down twice in the weekends.[28]

Note how B deprecates his abilities and achievements as a mountaineer (he claims only to 'muck around' on mountains) and a skier (going down a mountain doesn't involve much skiing, he says). In this way the speaker allows for the possibility that H would do much better than him, and thus he offers no threat to H's positive face.

S's attention to H's positive face will lead him to offer (or deny) minor services to H. Society is maintained by people co-operating with one another, helping one another; one individual does things for another as part of the social contract so that when he needs help himself, he can expect the debt to be repaid by another member of the society. Thus there is a social obligation to give one's interlocutor what he wants – within reason. This kind of obligation is relevant to the analysis of the meaning of sentences like (2.3.2.22)

(2.3.2.22) You need my help, Cynthia.

We recognize this as an offer of help even though the offer is not made explicitly; we do so because of S's social obligation. Provided the co-operative principle is being observed and S has it within his power to help, then for S to assert that H needs his help is tantamount to his accepting the obligation to help H. Assuming that if H needs help he wants help, this is a positive face affect. As readers may judge for themselves, for S to utter (2.3.2.22) and then refuse to help would be a severe affront to H's face and therefore an act of hostility.

S tries to make H feel good by taking a positive interest in H's attributes, achievements, ideas, possessions, goals, etc. while downplaying his own. He uses language in a way calculated to please H by being deferential where necessary, and otherwise either politely keeping his distance or expressing solidarity. Whatever the social distance between S and H, there are certain formulae that S may use to establish togetherness with H by appealing directly to him in the course of the narrative. One that is widely used is the phrase *y'know* as in 'Which really didn't involve much skiing, y'know' (quoted above), or *Well, you know, I've been, y'know, thinking about buying a, y'know, new car for ages*. Another such phrase used in south England is the tag question with a first person subject, cf.

(2.3.2.23) Well, I was walkin' down the street, wasn't I, when this geezer comes over and gives me a shove.

(2.3.2.23) also exemplifies the historic (or narrative) present, which is another device for bringing H into the thick of the story. In Australian English and the American Valley Girl dialect (named for California's San Fernando Valley), declarative sentences are often uttered with a high rising terminal reminiscent of (but not identical with) the question intonation. This seems to function (rather like *y'know*) as a check that H is following the narrative, by seeking nonverbal or verbal acknowledgment from him (cf. §6.5.3). It is a part of the co-operative endeavour to be friendly towards H and make him feel good. Maintaining H's positive face is also effected by fulfilling social obligations towards him, and rendering minor services (e.g. laughing at his jokes). For X to fulfil an obligation or render a service to Y incurs a debt that Y is expected to repay – if only by the expression of gratitude. The debt is incurred because in fulfilling his social obligation or rendering the service there is an imposition on X that threatens his negative face, and which therefore needs to be counter-balanced. Thus, to try to maintain face all round, Y must not impose unduly upon X – but that is a matter for the next section.

1.2.3.3 Attending to H's negative face

Whereas the maxim 'be polite' is usually interpreted as enjoining S to pay attention to H's positive face, it is equally important for S to pay attention to H's negative face by not imposing on him. The maxim 'don't impose'[29] regulates behaviour such as not performing acts offensive to the interlocutor like striking him, staring at him, avoiding his gaze, standing too close or too far apart from him. Of more interest to us, however, are linguistic impositions of which there are four categories.

(i)   Attacks on H's positive face, e.g. insults to his self image and the people or things dear to him (including his ideas and beliefs).

(ii)   Straightforward impositions on H's person, possessions, time, etc. such as S requiring H to carry out some act, or asking H for the use of his possessions or ideas.

(iii)   Requiring H to expend unreasonable effort in order to understand what S means in uttering U because it is uncomfortably loud, inaudible, incoherent, irrelevant, abstruse, or otherwise unreasonable.

(iv)   Wittingly misleading H into erroneous beliefs and assumptions.

In the previous section we saw that attacks on H's positive face can be ameliorated by S humbling himself, cf. (2.3.2.6); prevaricating, cf. (2.3.2.7); apologizing for the affront, cf. (2.3.2.8); or pleading force of circumstance, cf. (2.3.2.9). All these are methods of ameliorating the imposition in order to minimize the ill-effect; and because they exist they are expected to be used on occasions when S issues a threat to H's positive face; failure to ameliorate the threat is assumed to be deliberate – a further twisting of the knife, as it were. Failing under appropriate circumstances to state congratulations, regrets, condolences, apologies, thanks, etc. (a class of speech acts that in §8.5.2.5 we call 'acknowledgments') will count as affronts to H's positive face.

Turning to straightforward impositions on H: generally, the imposition occurs when H is to carry out some act at S's behest. Bald on record impositions use the imperative, i.e. S tells H to carry out some act, cf.

(2.3.3.1)
    a.   Tell me your name.
    b.   Go to bed!
    c.   Don't get lost.

Typically such imperative impositions are coercive and they are appropriate only when S has a higher P rating than H. However, many languages, including English, have five classes of exceptions to this constraint.

(i) Where it is mutually recognized that for H to carry out the act will satisfy some want of his, e.g.

(2.3.3.2)
  a. Have a good time!
  b. Turn right at the next junction, and it's first on the left.
  c. Heat the milk and stir in the sugar. Add a pinch of salt.
  d. Let me carry that.

(ii) When the matter is urgent and there is no time to be lost on niceties, cf.

(2.3.3.3)
  a. Help!
  b. Look out!
  c. Don't move, there's a snake by your foot!

(iii) In invitations like *Come in, sit down, and have a cup of tea*.
(iv) In supplications where H is mutually recognized (in the context of utterance) to be in a dominant position and able to do something to S's benefit:

(2.3.3.4)
  a. Grant me this, oh Lord.
  b. Forgive me for interrupting you professor, but I wonder if you can help me?
  c. Leave me alone; don't beat me any more.
  d. Excuse me.

(v) Between intimates mutual coercion may be acceptable with respect to minor acts and services; thus, provided the tone of voice is not too imperious, S can issue imperatives such as *Shut the door*.

In interrogative impositions S asks H to carry out some act while pretending to give H the option to concur in carrying out the request, thus giving (or appearing to give) him the right to reject the imposition and save his negative face. This is why it is more polite to ask *Will you pass the salt?* than to tell someone *Pass the salt!*.[30]

Declarative impositions come in two kinds. Firstly there are the off record impositives, sometimes called 'indirect requests', where H is left to infer that S wants him to carry out some act. In the more direct among these indirect requests S actually says what he wants to be done, e.g. *I'd like these letters typed as soon as possible, Janis*. Here S doesn't explicitly ask or tell Janis to get the letters typed, but typically the context will be such that Janis is obliged to carry out the act at S's behest. The more indirect sort of indirect request might occur when S says *It's stuffy in here* and looks meaningfully at the closed window. Since stuffiness is unpleasant, H has a social obligation to relieve it by opening the window – always provided he is in a position to do so. The other kind of declarative impositive is the very mildest kind of imposition, and is mostly not thought of as an imposition at all. Whenever S offers an unsolicited opinion or piece of information which he expects H to adopt, he imposes on H. However, this kind of imposition only becomes objectionable when H feels that S is foisting unwanted opinions and information upon him; particularly if there is a suggestion that S is concomitantly seeking to enhance his own positive face wants at the expense of H's negative face wants.

There is a variety of strategies and devices for ameliorating impositions. We begin with the strategy of impersonalizing the imposition by omitting explicit reference to H carrying out the act. The imperative standardly omits explicit reference to H, cf.

(2.3.3.5) Give me that book this instant!

Where S does explicitly refer to H, as in a declarative command like

(2.3.3.6) You will give me that book this instant!

S is interpreted as being more coercive, more threatening, than when employing the corresponding imperative. The same is true where the imperative is accompanied by a vocative, provided that H is the only possible addressee (i.e. the vocative is not used to pick H out of a crowd), cf.

(2.3.3.7)
   a.   You, give me that book this instant!
   b.   Give me that book this instant, you!

Notice that with a supplication addressed to a stranger, an impersonalized vocative address form such as *sir*, *madam*, *mate*, *Mac* is more polite than *you*, compare

(2.3.3.8) Excuse me, sir.

(2.3.3.9) Excuse me, you.

Off record, indirect, requests may omit explicit reference to H, cf.

(2.3.3.10)
   a.   I'd like these letters typed as soon as possible, please.
   b.   Hey, I need some help over here. [sc. "Come and give me a hand"]

    c.   It needs a bit of salt adding. [sc. "Put a bit of salt in it"]
    d.   There's the washing up to be done. [sc. "You do it."]

Impersonalization can also be achieved by deleting a second person agent from a passive clause; for instance

(2.3.3.11) This child has been beaten far too severely

can be used to avoid directly accusing H, while at the same time implying that H is the culprit. If one can conceive that the very act of addressing H is an imposition on him,[31] then the imposition can be ameliorated by not addressing him directly as an individual, but including him among a number of people spoken of: this strategy will explain the deferential connotation of the use of second person plural forms to address singular addressees in many languages,[32] e.g. French:

(2.3.3.12)

a.	Vous	êtes	très	gentil
	out-gp.-you	are	very	kind	[Formal]
b.	Tu	es	très	gentil
	in-gp.-you	are	very	kind	[Informal]

Even more obviously impersonalizing is to address H in the third person as a mark of deference, e.g. in Polish

(2.3.3.13)

a.	Co	mama	robi?
	what	mother	is-doing
	"What are you doing, mother?"		[Deferential]
b.	Co	robisz,	mama?
	what	you-are-doing	mother
	"What are you doing, Mum?"		[Nondeferential]

Another means of ameliorating the imposition is for S to suggest that he will share in carrying out the act, cf.

(2.3.3.14)
    a.   Come on now, let's put our toys away.
    b.   Shall we put our toys away?
    c.   In the next chapter, we seek to answer the question 'What is meaning?'

This is an expression of solidarity with H in bearing the burden of the act. Instead of sharing in the imposition, S can propose to swap an imposition on H for a favour towards H, cf.

(2.3.3.15)
- a. You scratch my back, and I'll scratch yours.
- b. Could you tell me your name if I tell you mine?

Sometimes, S may seek to evade personal responsibility for the imposition; e.g. when the policeman says

(2.3.3.16) I must ask you to blow into the breathalyzer, madam.

The same strategy is used by the child who has to explain the condition of his uncle's Ming vase, but does not dare admit responsibility for dropping it (the damage to the Ming vase is an affront to the uncle's negative face, of course):

(2.3.3.17) It went and broke!

Responsibility for opinions and pieces of information is sometimes evaded through impersonalizing, compare the (a) and (b) sentences in the following;

(2.3.3.18)
- a. It is thought that a dingo is unlikely to remove the clothes from a baby before eating it.
- b. I think it unlikely that a dingo would remove the clothes from a baby before eating it.

(2.3.3.19)
- a. They say that Idi Amin is a cannibal.
- b. Idi Amin is a cannibal.

In using the (a) sentences, S pretends to report what other people think and say, instead of imposing his own opinions and purported facts on H.

Another kind of strategy altogether is for S to minimize the imposition and perhaps joke it off; this is probably only possible in informal contexts. Cf.

(2.3.3.20)
- a. Could you do me a big favour and lend me your pen? ['Big' must be ironic, and mean "small"]
- b. I wonder if you could do me a little favour?
- c. Tell me just one thing.
- d. Could I borrow that old heap of junk you call a car? Just for an hour or two?
- e. Would you give me just a taste of that cake?
- f. OK if I tackle these cookies now?

The jokiness of some of these is presumably intended to stroke H's positive face, and to that extent offset the imposition which affronts his negative face.

Imperative impositions presume that H will accept the imposition and carry out the act demanded. Interrogative impositions, on the other hand, purportedly give H the option of rejecting the imposition; and for this reason they are reckoned more polite. The less certain S sounds about H's acceptance of the imposition, the more polite his utterance will be counted. Consider how imperious and even threatening (2.3.3.21) is because of S's brash confidence in the imposition:

(2.3.3.21) I'm sure you won't mind lending me your car for the weekend, Harold?

In consequence, the more tentative and hesitant S is, the more he ameliorates the imposition. This is seen in the fact that a subjunctive makes a politer request in (2.3.3.22) than the indicative in (2.3.3.23):

(2.3.3.22)
   a. Would you have a look for me?
   b. Would you have this in leather?

(2.3.3.23)
   a. Will you have a look for me?
   b. Do you have this in leather?

Being pessimistic about the likelihood of H complying is obviously going to be politer than being optimistic, thus (2.3.3.24) is more polite than (2.3.3.25):

(2.3.3.24) You wouldn't have change of a dollar would you?

(2.3.3.25) Would you have change of a dollar?

However, this is a tricky matter since a negative attitude when offering an invitation would be less appropriate than a positive attitude, because it both reflects on the sincerity of the offer and insults H by seeming to doubt he would be polite enough to accept.

(2.3.3.26) You wouldn't like to come to dinner on Friday, would you?

(2.3.3.27) Would you like to come to dinner on Friday?

As every reader will know from personal experience, the potential face threats of certain acts have to be carefully balanced against one another if we are to maintain good relations with our co-interactants.

The particular ameliorative devices we have been looking at are generally called 'hedges';[33] the more elaborate the hedging and the more hesitant the delivery of the utterance, the politer it will seem; consider the following, in which the hedges are emphasized.

(2.3.3.28)
a. *Perhaps* you could help me.
b. *I wonder if you might* help me?
c. You *couldn't perhaps* lend me your car for an hour or so?
d. I, *um, suppose you, um wouldn't by any chance be able to, um*, lend me your car for an hour or two?

Hedges are also used to back off from opinions and assertions, cf.

(2.3.3.29)
a. *Perhaps* John's in the loo.
b. You could leave work early, *maybe*?
c. *It's possible that* Henry can't speak either English or German like a native.
d. She's *sort of* pretty.
e. It was a *kind of* bang.
f. She's *not exactly* small. But small*ish, I guess*.

In addition to being tentative about imposing on H, S can come right out and apologize for the imposition, cf.

(2.3.3.30)
a. *I'm sorry to trouble you*, but do you have the time?
b. *Forgive me for bothering you*, but do you have a pen?
c. *I'm sorry to have to tell you that* your mother has died.

The most frequently used ameliorators are those which purport to ask whether H objects to the imposition S is putting upon him. Perhaps the best known of these is *please*, meaning "if it please(s) you". Although this seems to question H's willingness to accept the imposition, it is in fact impossible for him to ever seriously respond *No, it doesn't please me* or *I won't because it doesn't please me to*.

(2.3.3.31)
a. Please keep off the grass.
b. Please remember to water the petunias, darling.
   Could you please post this letter?
d. Wouldn't you post this letter for me, please?
e. It's ten o'clock, gentlemen, please. [Publican announcing closing time.]

f.   Jeeves, it's getting stuffy in here; please. [sc. Open a window, Jeeves.]
g.   What's your name, sir, please?

It may be seen from these examples that *please* occurs with requests (presumably the publican in (e) is asking his customers to drink up and leave the premises). Where S wishes to foist his assertions onto H, he may ask permission (supplicate) as in, e.g.

(2.3.3.32)
a.   Let me tell you about Jack and Diane.
b.   Let me tell you what I think.

Another way for S to ameliorate assertions is to establish whether H wants him to go ahead and make the assertion, cf.

(2.3.3.33)
a.   If you'd like me to I'll tell you all about the Valley of the Kings.
b.   Do you want me to tell you what I think?

Alternatively, S may hedge his imposition by questioning whether it is possible for H to accept it, cf.

(2.3.3.34)
a.   Come tomorrow, then, if you can.
b.   Your wife's asked me to give her a lift home, if that's OK with you.
c.   Caspar Milquetoast has been married six times, if you can believe it!
d.   Ariadne wants to stay, if we can have her.
e.   Would it be possible for you to lend me your car for an hour or two tomorrow?

Then there are the tag questions that purportedly seek H's consent, cf.

(2.3.3.35)
a.   Let's go to a movie, shall we?
b.   Don't get lost, will you?
c.   Sit down, will you?
d.   Sit down, won't you?

The meanings of these tags are discussed and compared in §8.8 and I'll say no more about them here.

There is one last strategy to ameliorate straightforward impositions, that is to pretend that H has already accepted the imposition or is in receipt of the impositive information, cf.

(2.3.3.36)
   a.   How old did you say you were? [It is not necessary for H to have
        said anything about his age]
   b.   You do know your skirt is see-through, don't you?

We now turn to impositions of the third type, those which require H
to expend unreasonable effort in order to understand what S means in
uttering U because it is, e.g. uncomfortably loud, inaudible, incoherent, irrelevant, abstruse, or otherwise unreasonable. Impositions of
this type have already been discussed in §1.2.2. Certain conventions for
avoiding these particular impositions were described by H. Paul Grice
as 'maxims of the co-operative principle' in his 'Logic and conversation'
1975. Grice identified four categories of maxims that serve as reference
points for language interchange; three of them are appropriate here.
Because I have somewhat different intentions from Grice I shall
reinterpret each of the Gricean categories in terms of a single maxim,
and refer to these jointly as the co-operative maxims.

The maxim of 'quantity': S should give no more and no less
   information than is required to make his message clear to H.
The maxim of 'relation': S's utterance U should not (in general) be
   irrelevant to the context in which it is uttered, because that might
   make it difficult for H to comprehend.
The maxim of 'manner': where possible, S's meaning should be
   presented in a clear, concise manner that avoids ambiguity, and
   avoids misleading or confusing H because of stylistic ineptitude.

Grice clearly says that observation of or violation of the maxims has
meaningful implications (what he calls 'conversational implicatures' cf.
§3.9) which we can identify as the implications of the face affects
caused by the observation or non-observation of the maxims. The
maxims should be seen not so much as rules to be obeyed, but as
reference points for language interchange. They might be compared to
the compass points North, East, South and West, that serve as
conventional reference points by which we may tell which direction a
traveller is going, and by which the traveller himself may decide which
direction he ought to take to arrive at his destination. By convention, a
traveller takes the shortest route in journeying from A to B; but he
may violate that convention if he has some good reason for doing so.
Similarly, a speaker may violate – or, more exactly, exploit – the
conventions (i.e. maxims) of the co-operative principle in order to
communicate a certain meaning. For instance, a pun or 'double
entendre' trades on the exploitation of the maxim of manner by being

shamelessly ambiguous; consider the following interchange from Shakespeare's *Henry IV Pt.2*, II.iv.110.

> *In a tavern: Sir John Falstaff, the Hostess, Doll Tearsheet (a whore).*
> *Enter Pistol.*
> PISTOL: God save you, Sir John!
> FALSTAFF: Welcome, Ancient Pistol. Here Pistol, I charge you with a cup of sack.[a] Do you discharge upon mine hostess.[b]
> PISTOL: I will discharge upon her, Sir John, with two bullets.[c]
> FALSTAFF: She is pistol proof sir; you shall hardly offend her.
> HOSTESS: Come, I'll drink no proofs nor no bullets: I'll drink no more than will do me good, for no man's pleasure I.[d]
> PISTOL: Then to you, Mistress Dorothy; I will charge you.[e]
> DOLL T: Charge me![f] I scorn you, scurvy companion. What! You poor, base, rascally, cheating, lacklinen mate! Away you mouldy rogue. Away! I am meat for your master.[g]
> PISTOL: I know you, Mistress Dorothy.[h]

(The superscript [a-h] are referenced in the glosses given in footnote 34.)

Such ambiguity is licensed because it is entertaining to H. This is something that Grice overlooked.[35] S's ability to make what he is talking about interesting to H is just as important as his ability to make it clear, concise and unambiguous – perhaps more so. Although subject matter is an important ingredient here, we all know that there are people who are boring no matter what they are saying, and others who are amusing and interesting to listen to whenever they open their mouths. It is especially important that S should be entertaining when engaged in phatic communion with H, because then it is the fact of speaking which is important (to maintain the social accord) rather than the content of what is said. But even in an academic paper, S should not only be succinct in presenting his argument, he should also endeavour to present it in such a manner that it will hold H's attention.

In 'Logic and conversation' 1975:52, Grice offers an instance of a deliberate and meaningful flouting of the maxim of quantity, which goes something like this. Professor Levin has been asked to write a testimonial for a former philosophy student applying for a position in the philosophy department at another university. The testimonial reads:

Dear Sir,
    Mr. Feinstein's command of English is excellent, and his
    attendance at classes has been regular.

                                  Yours etc.

The qualities praised in this testimonial are not the qualities primarily sought in a philosophy teacher, and Professor Levin presumably knows this, and knows that the reader of the letter will know he knows it, too – which is exactly why Levin has flouted the maxim of quantity. Because Feinstein was his student, Levin knows what he is like as a philosopher, and he has pointedly refrained from commenting on the matter in his testimonial. The only reason for this deliberate omission will be that Levin has nothing positive to say on the matter; and rather than come out and say 'Feinstein is no good at philosophy' he has left it to be inferred from his violation of the maxim of quantity. It is part of folk wisdom to 'read between the lines' – which is an exhortation to look out for transgressions of the maxim of quantity such as Professor Levin's.

It is not only S's presumption about the mutual knowledge existing between himself and H in the context of utterance that determines how he will exploit the maxim of quantity, but also the purpose behind the interchange. In an academic paper it will be valued for S to be as succinct as possible; but in chatting to a close friend or relative on the phone, where the purpose of the conversation is largely to maintain social accord, S will often be deliberately prolix because he might otherwise appear curt and in an unsociable hurry to bring the conversation to an end.[36]

The maxim of relation can also be exploited, for instance by someone changing the subject without warning so as to indicate that they find the topic under discussion embarrassing. Irrelevance can be, and often is, used for comic effect, as we saw in §1.2.2. An accidentally irrelevant remark may elicit the comment *Not that that's got anything to do with the price of fish*, which issues a gentle chiding (either from H or from S to himself). A remark which S fears may seem irrelevant, though it isn't intended to be, can be excused by a formula such as *This may be a red-herring, but . . .*, or *I'm not sure that this is relevant, but . . . .* This kind of formula is the one most used to try to ameliorate what S fears might be construed as unreasonable (linguistic) behaviour on his part.

The fourth category of linguistic impositions listed at the beginning of this section corresponds to the spirit, though not to the letter, of Grice's maxim of quality: it is that S should not wittingly mislead H into erroneous beliefs and assumptions.[37] In other words S should be sincere in what he says and have reasonable grounds for saying it; thus he should state as facts only what he believes to be facts, he should make offers or promises only if he intends to carry them out, he should pronounce judgements only if he is in a position to judge, and so forth.

In our society we generally take what people say at face value (which is why we are likely to get caught out on April Fools' Day). There are conventionally recognized exceptions, of course: for instance a politician speaking as a politician is expected to be insincere much of the time; but as your next door neighbour discussing with you what to do about a fence between your two properties, he is expected to be as sincere as anyone else. Within our society, lies are regarded as unco-operative because they mislead H without benefitting him in any way; indeed, if H were to act as though, say, U expressed a truth instead of a falsehood he might make a fool of himself or worse, and so cause affront to his own face. However, so-called 'white lies' mislead H in a way that S believes is to H's advantage; e.g. if S knew that H's beloved spouse died in lingering agony at the site of an auto accident he might tell H that the spouse died instantly, in the belief that the white lie would cause H less distress than the truth.

Because of the value placed on S's sincerity, S may feel the need to protest the sincerity of any utterance he thinks H might doubt – as in the emphasized parts of the following.

(2.3.3.37)
 a. *You might not believe this, but* Harry has been married six times!
 b. Harry's been married six times, *if you can believe it!*
 c. *Would you believe that* Harry's been married six times?
 d. I'll go tomorrow, I promise. *I really mean it.*
 e. *Swear to God* I'll remember to go tomorrow!
 f. *Honestly*, I'd like to know why you think that?

The emphasized expressions in (2.3.3.37) signal to H that incredulous though he may be about the main point of S's utterance, it is nonetheless sincere and not intended as an affront to his negative face.

In summary: if S intends to maintain H's negative face he needs to observe the maxim 'don't impose'. This overriding maxim can be subcategorized into four more particular maxims governing the four categories of imposition on H's negative face:

Don't attack H's positive face.

Don't impose on H's person, possessions, or time by asking him to do things for others, or by using or abusing his possessions, and so forth.

Don't require H to expend unreasonable effort in trying to understand U.

Don't wittingly mislead H into erroneous beliefs or assumptions.

Contraventions and prospective contraventions of these maxims should be ameliorated in the ways discussed above unless S deliberately intends to affront H's negative face.

1.2.4 The co-operative principle

The co-operative principle holds whenever S and H mutually recognize S's observance of the communicative presumption, the reasonableness condition, and the normal conventions pertaining to face affects within the language community. S observes the communicative presumption when he makes an utterance U in language L to H in context C such that H can reasonably presume S intends to communicate something to him by means of U. This implies that U has meaning; and for H to determine the meaning of U in context C is for H to succeed in recognizing what he presumes S intends to communicate through his speech act. Since it is one of the chief aims of this book to propose an abstract model of what is necessary for H to determine the meaning of U, we must give due regard to the significance of the communicative presumption.

The communicative presumption presupposes the reasonableness condition by presuming that S has some reason for uttering U (rather than keeping quiet or uttering something different). S further observes the reasonableness condition if he has some reason for selecting the particular form of U – e.g. a reason for choosing to say *Pass the salt!* rather than *Can you pass the salt?* when he wants the salt passing. In determining the meaning of U, H seeks the reasons for S's having uttered U in the particular form U takes; he does so on the presumption that S is observing the reasonableness condition. Our theory of linguistic meaning must necessarily presume the same.

Our theory must also take account of the normal conventions pertaining to face affects within the language community because, as we have seen, utterance meaning is in part determined in response to these conventions. There is a general presumption in language interchange that S will be polite except where he intends to affront H's positive face, and that he will not normally impose on H without good reason lest he affront H's negative face; moreover, S will generally be maintaining or enhancing his own face through what he says and the way he acts. Although the ways in which face affects are achieved do vary somewhat from one language to another, we have seen that similar linguistic devices and strategies are used in unrelated languages and cultures.

Were there no communicative presumption, reasonableness condition, or conventions pertaining to face affects – which together constitute the co-operative principle – it is difficult to see how communication would be possible. Without the co-operative principle, there would be no ground rules for deciding whether or not S's utterance U (made to H in context C) makes sense, or what value should be put on it. Conversely, S would have no ground rules for getting his message across to H. We have glimpsed babel in the quote from the schizophrenic in §1.2.2 above: because the schizophrenic violates the co-operative principle we have no way of ascertaining what he means; normal interpretative procedures do not apply, and therefore normal communication breaks down. Were there no co-operative principle, H would have no way of determining the meaning of S's utterance U. In consequence it is axiomatic to our theory of meaning that S observes the co-operative principle (and is recognized by H to do so) when S utters U in language L to H in context C.

No satisfactory account of utterance meaning can be given unless we assume that S observes the co-operative principle. Provided the co-operative principle itself is not violated, the various maxims can be; and when they are violated, there is a consequential effect on the meaning of the utterance. For instance, if the maxim 'be polite' is violated but the co-operative principle is being observed, then H will assume S intends to affront his face – and the affront is part of the meaning of his utterance.[38] Suppose, though, such an affront was not intended. Suppose that instead of saying *Do you think you could open the window?* a nonnative speaker of English says to a fellow train-traveller, a stranger and native English speaker, *You must open the window*. The latter (H) will be affronted; but he might recognize that S is a foreigner whose affront is perhaps an unintentional result of a poor command of English, and therefore excusable. Unintentional face affects are nonetheless face affects; they are meaningful, but they are generally less meaningful than intentional face affects.

This concludes what we have to say about speaker S and hearer H. They are both reasonable men who mutually recognize and observe the co-operative principle. They observe the reasonableness condition and have the ability to exploit it on occasion. S will observe (and H will make) the communicative presumption with respect to S's uttering U in the language L to H in context C. Like all other speakers of L they will know the normal conventions pertaining to face affects within their language community. S knows how to exploit these to convey a particular message to H, and H will know how to interpret S's utterance U in relation to them. What H reasonably takes to be S's meaning in U is, so far as we are concerned, the meaning of U; thus if we describe an abstract model for H's reasoning of the meaning of U, we have a model of utterance meaning.

1.3 Context

1.3.1 The three categories of context

We have said that linguistic data arises when speaker S makes an utterance U in language L to hearer H in context C. The term 'context' is used here (as in everyday speech) to mean any one or more of three different kinds of things. The first of these we shall discuss is the physical context or SETTING of the utterance U. Setting is defined on the spatio-temporal location of the utterance, i.e. on the particular time (moment) and particular place at which S utters U and the particular time and place at which H hears or reads U.

The second sense in which 'context' is customarily used is to describe THE WORLD SPOKEN OF in U. More often than not, the world spoken of (which we symbolize W) is the real world familiar to all of us; but e.g. in George Orwell's *1984* the world spoken of is a fictional world such as Orwell imagined would exist on earth in the year 1984: it is not to be confused with either the real earth world of 1984, nor with the world of 1948 in which Orwell wrote the book. Of course, most of our everyday conversation is about the world around us at the moment of speaking – i.e. W includes the setting of the utterance U: but that does not make these two categories of context one and the same thing; setting could be described as the world spoken IN whereas W is the world spoken OF.

The third category of context we shall discuss is TEXTUAL ENVIRONMENT. The textual environment is provided by the TEXT in which U appears, i.e. the set of utterances of which U is a member and which together constitute a cohesive semantic unit. Text should not necessarily be thought of as a static, perfected unit; in conversational interaction it is a dynamic ongoing construction – this may add to the difficulties defining text but it does not radically alter them. In the written medium a text can be thought of as the paragraph containing U, the episode containing that paragraph, the chapter containing that episode, or the book containing that chapter. Corresponding expansion in the notion of text can be imagined for an utterance which occurs in conversation. The text in which U occurs will usually help define the world spoken of in U.

The notion of textual environment is not usefully restricted to utterances but is applicable to any language expression E within U, given that E is an utterance constituent that may be of any length from morph (a constituent of a word) up to the whole of U, cf. §1.4.2. Under the heading of textual environment we shall refer to CO-TEXT as well as to text. The co-text of a language expression E consists of the language expressions that co-occur with it in the text containing E.[39]

In summary, context C consists of any one or more of three things: the setting, or spatio-temporal location of the utterance U (and consequently of S and H); W, the world spoken of in U; and the textual environment of U and of the language expressions within U.

1.3.2 Setting

Setting is defined on the spatio-temporal location of the utterance: in the simplest case this entails a dichotomy between the time and place at which S is located when making the utterance U, and the time and place at which H is located when he hears the utterance U. The dichotomy is obvious, if, say, S writes a letter to H: normally, S's utterances within the letter will be made earlier than and in a different place from H's reading those utterances.[40] The dichotomy holds in principle even in face to face dialogue (still the commonest kind of communication even in modern industrial societies) and all languages recognize it when the setting is spoken of. I will refer to these two categories of setting as either S's zone or zone 1 and H's zone or zone 2. All languages have 'deictic' expressions to denote things within the setting: deictics that fall within S's zone include first person pronouns, and demonstratives *this* and *here*; deictics which fall within H's zone include second person pronouns, and demonstratives *that* and *there*. The pronouns identify S and H, respectively; however, it is noticeable that the demonstratives have spatial rather than temporal orientation towards zone 1 and zone 2. Although tense systems are universally oriented on S's moment of utterance[41] no temporal expressions correspond closely and conventionally with the dichotomy between S's zone and H's zone to parallel the spatial locatives, *here and there*. The reason is that in face to face interaction S and H are easily perceived to occupy separate spatial locations (*I'm here*, *you're there*); however, there is no time gap between them, and no readily perceivable time gap between S's making the utterance and H's hearing it: hence, there are no temporal locatives to parallel spatial locatives which typically differentiate S's zone from H's zone.

The dichotomy between zone 1 and zone 2 is generally complemented by a third category of setting for people and things outside of both S's and H's zones, which we will call zone 3.[42] The deictic expressions used of zone 3 include the third person pronouns, but standard English uses the same demonstratives for zone 3 as for H's zone; however, some nonstandard English dialects use *yon*, and many languages have different spatial locatives for each of the three zones in the setting. Compare the (b) and (c) sentences in (3.2.1-2):

(3.2.1)
    a.   *This here* tree under which I am sitting
    b.   *That there* tree under which you are sitting.
    c.   *Yon* tree under which he is sitting.

(3.2.2)
    a.   Watashi ga suwatte-iru *kono* isu.   [Japanese]
        "This here chair on which I am sitting"
    b.   Anata ga suwatte-iru *sono* isu.
        "That there chair on which you are sitting":
    c.   Anohito ga suwatte-iru *ano* isu.
        "Yon chair on which he is sitting"

Although this three-zone subcategorization of setting is perhaps the commonest among the languages of mankind, minor variations occur when different perceptions of the categories of setting get encoded in standard expressions within different language communities.

Although there are often syntactic constraints on the use of one zonal deictic rather than another, these are usually offset by S being able to express his point of view in assigning a person or object to a particular zone; however, even this is normally governed by conventions. One such convention, in some languages, is the honorific use of a third person pronoun when addressing H – zone 3 being at a greater distance from S than zone 2. On occasion S can even speak about himself in the third person in order to distance himself as speaker from himself in some other role, e.g. when President Nixon said of himself 'The President should not become involved in any part of this case'.[43] Compare the meanings of (3.1.3-4):

(3.2.3) Ah, so you're here!

(3.2.4) Ah, so you're there!

In (3.2.3) S includes H within zone 1 (S's zone) but in (3.2.4) he locates H outside of it. The flexibility of zone boundaries is such that (3.2.3) can be a legitimate utterance if H has arrived in the same country as S, even though they remain 2000 kilometers apart; whereas (3.2.4) can legitimately be used if H is sitting only a metre away from S! The actual physical location of somebody or something is less significant than the way S chooses to perceive that location in relation to himself or to H. For instance, of a particular mole on his foot S might say (3.2.5) on one occasion and (3.2.6) on another:

(3.2.5) Here on my foot there's a mole.

(3.2.6) There on my foot there's a mole.

In (3.2.5) S counts the mole very much a part of himself; in (3.2.6), on the other hand, he distances himself from it by using the initial 'there' which places it in zone 3. Concomitant with drawing money from his pocket or purse S would be more likely to say *Here's the money* than *There's the money*; while the latter would be more appropriate where the money is in his hand outstretched towards H.

The relative locations of S and H are significant to the choice of other adverbs, too; consider the situations where it is appropriate for S to say to H *I'm coming up* instead of *I'm coming down*, to say *I'm coming in* instead of *I'm coming over*, and so forth. The primary senses of the verbs *come* and *go* also have their source in zones of the setting: *come* being used for movement towards S's and H's zones, whereas *go* is used for movement towards zone 3. Compare the meanings of the following:

(3.2.7) I'm coming. [sc. towards H's zone]

(3.2.8) Are you coming? [sc. with S or towards S's zone]

(3.2.9) Are you going? [sc. yonder, towards zone 3]

(3.2.10) I'm going. [sc. yonder, towards zone 3]

It is impossible to order H to **Come there!* and it is odd to say *I'm going here* unless 'here' is identified by e.g. pointing a finger at the place or jumping into a particular seat concomitantly with uttering 'here' – because either of these acts puts the place indicated within S's zone. A sentence like *Max came to tea at Ruth's* therefore requires either that S is or was also at Ruth's, or that S is telling the story from Ruth's point of view (so that he adopts Ruth's zone as his own).

Consider now the use of personal pronouns and their correspondence with the three zones of setting. There may be one speaker or (in the written medium) more than one: there may be one or more hearers; and there may be one or more third persons; so the personal pronouns can always be either singular or plural. However, languages may have different pronouns for conjunctions of people (or things) from different zones in the setting. For instance, Ilocano, a language spoken in the Philippines, has the following pronouns:[44]

co	"S"	zone 1
mo	"H"	zone 2
na	"3rd singular"	zone 3
da	"3rd plural"	zone 3
mi	"S & 3rd person(s)"	zones 1 and 3
yo	"H & 3rd person(s)"	zones 2 and 3
ta	"S & H"	zones 1 and 2
tayo	"S & H & 3rd person(s)"	zones 1 and 2 and 3

Few languages have such a comprehensive system, though many distinguish between so-called inclusive *we* "S & H" and exclusive *we* "S & 3rd person(s)". English *we/us* is mostly ambiguous between them, but the abbreviated '–'s' in *Let's* is necessarily inclusive, cf. *Let's go to a movie* which must refer to S and H, not to S and anyone else.

The features of setting which contribute to the use and interpretation of personal pronouns are similar to those which may help determine appropriate forms of address: they include the sex of S and H, and S's perception of the social distance and relative power rating between himself and H. H's perception of S in the setting may well affect his judgement of U's credibility – which is part of the meaning of U. The setting is usually what determines the language and variety of language used, and often the topic of discourse: for instance, certain expectations are in force when an utterance is made in church, in a disco, in court, in a class room, in a restaurant, in the home; although such expectations need not be lived up to, they are an important consideration. The language appropriate to supporting one's team at a football game is not necessarily appropriate to praising one's god in a church; and to use inappropriate language is meaningful. Setting also typically establishes whether the medium of the utterance is the spoken or the written language; though the difference between them has few direct implications for the analysis of meaning, written language does typically allow a greater degree of semantic (as well as structural) complexity. The setting will often determine genres and hence how we should be prepared to tackle the world spoken of in U; a textbook, a poem, a novel, a prayer, a commercial, a serious conversation, passing the time of day, will each be interpreted from a different set of presuppositions – e.g. we expect a textbook to offer facts and well-grounded opinions, but we don't expect this of a novel. Thus the setting will often contribute to determining S's intentions in uttering U, and hence the meaning of U. And we should not completely ignore the peripheral contributions to meaning from paralinguistic phenomena as the physical distance maintained between S and H in face to face communication, their posture, facial expressions, gestures, and direction of gaze – all of them features of setting.

1.3.3 The world spoken of, W

The central notion within the general notion of context is the world spoken of:[45] (i) only when the world spoken of includes the setting, does setting fall squarely and uncontroversially within the linguist's domain; (ii) the most important function of co-text is to determine exactly what world is being spoken of. The world spoken of, W, is the world revealed in the utterance U: it may be S's version of the real world of his and my and your experience; or it may be the world of S's dreams, or a deliberately created fictional world; it may be a mix of fact and fiction; or it may be S's report of someone else's world. Provided S pays at least some attention to the co-operative principle, almost any utterance U made in language L will evoke a world. Take, for instance, a decontextualized sentence uttered by a linguist wishing to exemplify a point (such as this one):

(3.3.1) Almond Eyes ate her Kornies and listened to the radio.

(3.3.1) evokes a world in which there is a female (we know this from the possessive 'her'); since she is listening to the radio, it is probable that she is human, and therefore that 'Almond Eyes' is a nickname. At some time in the past Almond Eyes was eating Kornies while listening to the radio, so 'Kornies' must be some kind of food (the name would be appropriate for a breakfast cereal, and we wouldn't be surprised to discover she was eating breakfast). If Almond Eyes is listening to the radio, something must be being broadcast on it. Furthermore, the mention of the radio restricts to this century the time at which the reported event took place. Such is the world W evoked by (3.3.1). Of course, this need not be the way that the world spoken of in (3.3.1) turns out to be; but on the evidence we have, these are the kind of assumptions we make about it.

In the absence of indications to the contrary, we assume that the world spoken of is like the real world of our experience. W always seems to be understood at least partly in terms of that familiar, real world – even when W is a world of dreams or science fiction. Although we shall continue to use the term 'world spoken of', symbolized W, throughout the book, a more detailed analysis of context would need to identify a richer vocabulary of terms to properly describe what is spoken of. For instance, a work of fiction as a whole creates a world; individual utterances within the work may describe regions or localities within that world; furthermore, many a work of fiction is related to the real and familiar world by the places described in it, or some of the people named in it, and by reference to major real world events such as wars, and so forth: thus there are links between the world described in that work of fiction and the real world, suggesting that we should conceive of a universe containing the real world and also every world that can be spoken of (perhaps an infinite number). Incidentally, it is not only possible worlds that are spoken of: for instance there is no world possible in which there exists 'the largest prime number' and yet we can talk about the largest prime number in much the same way we can talk about the smallest prime number, cf.

(3.2.2) John insisted that the smallest prime number is 2.

(3.2.3) John insisted that the largest prime number is π.

What John insists upon in (3.2.2) is conventionally true (if not entirely uncontroversial); what John insists upon in (3.3.3) may be nonsense in point of fact, but the utterance is as grammatical and comprehensible as (3.3.2). Provided the co-operative principle is in operation it is quite possible to speak of things that could not "rationally" exist in any world, and to be understood.

If S is observing the co-operative principle he will try to ensure that H knows when he is reporting what he believes to be facts, when he is reporting opinions, and when he is fictionalizing. It is this co-operative act on S's part which aids H in distinguishing the kind of world spoken of. Suppose H is, for some reason or another, uncertain about the world spoken of – for instance, consider the world described through the following passage.

As Gregor Samsa awoke one morning from uneasy dreams he found himself transformed in his bed into a gigantic insect. He was lying on his hard, as it were armour-plated, back and when he lifted his head a little he could see his dome-like brown belly divided into stiff arched segments on top of which the bed-quilt could hardly keep in position and was about to slide off completely. His numerous legs, which were pitifully thin compared to the rest of his bulk, waved helplessly before his eyes.

What has happened to me? he thought. It was no dream. His room, a regular human bedroom, only rather too small, lay quiet between the four familiar walls. Above the table on which a collection of cloth samples was unpacked and spread out – Samsa was a commercial traveller – hung the picture which he had recently cut out of an illustrated magazine and put into a pretty gilt frame. It showed a lady, with a fur cap on and a fur stole, sitting upright and holding out to the spectator a huge fur muff into which the whole of her forearm had vanished.

We know enough about the nature of the real world to recognize that the world described here is imaginary: people do not turn into insects. Yet everything except the fact that Gregor Samsa has metamorphosed into an insect could be a description of something in the real world – a real world commercial traveller's bedroom in Prague in the first decade of the 20th century. In fact we have another important clue that W is fictional in this case: the passage comes, of course, from Franz Kafka's short story 'Metamorphosis', thus we know from the setting that it is fictional. The setting often gives a clue to the nature of the world spoken of. So does the textual environment, which we shall be discussing shortly.

W provides the framework for judgements of coherence in what is said. Within the framework of Kafka's 'Metamorphosis' we have to accept that Gregor Samsa has changed into an insect, and therefore he no longer has the body of a human being; we accept the kinds of effects this has on the short remainder of his own life, and on the lives of the people around him. Recognizing W is often crucial to our acceptance of utterances and language expressions of all kinds. For instance, the meaning of the word *morphology* is rather different in the following two passages because the worlds spoken of are different.

(3.3.4) These are all complex questions, and linguists studying morphology have not yet arrived at completely satisfactory answers to any of them. (Adrian Akmajian, Richard A. Demers, & Robert M. Harnish *Linguistics: An Introduction to Language and Communication* 1979:110)

(3.3.5) Instead of basing itself on the fancies of transcendentalist anatomists, therefore, modern morphology is based on the objective results of studies in comparative anatomy. (*Chamber's Encyclopaedia* Vol. 9, 1966:534).

In (3.2.4) W_4 is the world of linguistics, and in (3.2.5) W_5 is the world of biology: there is a common denominator of meaning in the two uses of *morphology* but in the world of linguistics it means "(study of) the forms and structures of words" and in the world of biology it means "(study of) the forms and structures of plants and animals". There will be many students of biology with no clear notion of the meaning of the word morphology in linguistics (W_4), and just as many students of linguistics who have no clear notion of the meaning of the word in biology (W_5). The importance of knowing which world is spoken of is generally recognized in the community: when someone asks you the meaning of an expression you will often ask for the 'context' so as to explain the meaning better; in asking for the 'context' you are really asking for the world spoken of – which is often constructed from the co-text.

Any utterance evokes a world, though it would be more accurately described as a locality in the world evoked by the text which contains U. The world spoken of, W, is usually comparable with the real world. Like the real world it has regions and localities and a geography that relates them; it has temporal sequence and events may occur at the same, or different, or overlapping periods of time. W will contain things that exist, i.e. have spatio-temporal locations within W, and there will be happenings and acts and events and imaginings, and so forth; and there will be things that do not exist in W and do not happen within W. W is generally expected to have some kind of recognizable coherence (unless, e.g. is a world of Monty Python or the like); thus things in it should be understandable within the terms of that world (e.g. in the world of *Star Trek* people 'beam' up and down between space ships and planets, though such behaviour is nonsensical in terms of the real world). It is the nature of W which determines judgements of coherence in what is said, and therefore the assessment of anomaly (e.g. a man turning into an insect), the identification of referring terms (who or what is being talked about), and the choice between ambiguous senses of expressions (as in the case of *morphology*, discussed above). The relationship between W and the real world is not of particular concern to the linguist; what he must concentrate upon is the meaning of U, and the meaning of U will often be determined in relation to W.

1.3.4   Textual environment

A text containing utterance U will identify what world is being spoken of, and hence what persons, places, objects, states, events, acts, and so forth are being spoken of in U. This is typically the case even when direct reference, including paralinguistic reference such as pointing, is being made to things in U's setting. The text in which U occurs, therefore, makes an important contribution to understanding the meaning of U.

Given that utterance U contains language expression E, which is an utterance constituent of any length between a morph and the whole utterance, the co-text of E consists of the language expressions that co-occur with it in the text containing E (not necessarily, notice, just within the utterance containing E). The co-text, or more likely some part of the co-text, will often make a significant contribution to the interpretation of E – and so, indirectly, to the interpretation of U. The several ways in which co-text can be interpretative are reviewed in the remainder of this section.

The emphasized expressions in (3.4.1-2) supply textual information on the relevant world in which to interpret the word 'morphology':

(3.4.1) the morphology of *the whale*

(3.4.2) the morphology of *the Athapaskan languages*

Co-textual interpreters of this kind are typically backed up by extensive evidence from the whole text – and perhaps from the setting as well, e.g. if (3.4.1) were taken from a book on comparative anatomy and (3.4.2) from a linguistics journal.

Co-textual interpretation may create more subtle meaning differences than those illustrated in (3.4.1-2). Consider the differing nonfigurative interpretations of 'lamb' in each of the sentences (3.4.3-13); the different interpretations are co-textually adduced to the core meaning "young sheep" which is the same for every occurrence of 'lamb'.

(3.4.3) The lamb gambolled in the field.

(3.4.4) The dead lamb was being eaten by crows and maggots.

(3.4.5) The lamb was stuffed and put into a museum.

(3.4.6) These bones are lamb, goat, and rabbit; but not human.

(3.4.7) Lamb is my favourite meat.

(3.4.8) The lamb was overcooked.

(3.4.9) My wife would prefer the lining to be lamb because it's warmer.

(3.4.10) We can't get the smell of lamb out of the car since we took the wretched animal to the vet in it.

(3.4.11) There was a painting of a lamb on the butcher's shop wall.

(3.4.12) The BBC archivist says he's got lamb on tape, but he can't do you the sound of a goat.

(3.4.13) The lamb is a delightful animal to keep as a pet.

The different interpretations arise from the co-operative obligation to interpret "young sheep" (the core meaning of *lamb*) compatibly with the rest of the utterance – i.e. with the rest of the world (W) as described in the utterance. We might characterize this as 'getting the pragmatic inferences right',[46] and we shall discuss what is involved in this process later in the book. However the importance of the different interpretations should be obvious: e.g. the lamb mentioned in (3.4.3) might subsequently end up on the butcher's slab and go from there to someone's dinner table; but such a thing cannot happen to the lamb painted on the butcher's wall – which is neither alive nor dead and therefore does not baa like a (live) lamb, nor does it smell like a lamb. Thus the co-textually adduced interpretations of the noun *lamb* in (3.4.3-13) evoke eleven different conceptions of the young sheep spoken of; and since each of these sentences is uttered "in isolation", we might reasonably say that we have in (3.4.3-13) eleven different, though relatable worlds W_3, W_4 . . ., W_{13}.

The interpretative power of co-text can be demonstrated from the fact that it can force an unlikely interpretation on an expression. Firstly, consider the following sentences, each taken in isolation:

(3.4.14) Jacqueline prefers leopard to silver fox.

(3.4.15) Nellie prefers lamb to rabbit.

Doubtless because leopard and silver fox are utilized by man for their pelts, (3.4.13) is usually understood to refer to the pelts of these animals – perhaps in the form of a coat; by contrast, although lambs-wool and rabbitskin are also used in making coats, the uncountable (mass) noun phrases *lamb* and *rabbit*[47] are customarily used to denote lamb meat and rabbit meat; thus (3.4.15) is usually interpreted as a sentence about Nellie's preference for one type of meat over another. But now consider

(3.4.16)
   a.   Max eats leopard all the time.
   b.   Max's favourite dish is leopard.

(3.4.17)
   a.   Ellie's coat is rabbit.
   b.   Ellie is wearing rabbit, that is to say, lapin.

In (3.4.16.a) the predicate 'eats' forces the interpretation of 'leopard' as something edible – and so, presumably, as meat. (3.4.16.b) is best understood to mean "the dished up food which Max most favours is leopard": however unlikely it may seem that someone or something (such as a dog called Max) would eat leopard meat, the co-text in (3.4.16) determines just such an interpretation.[48] The uncountable noun phrase *rabbit* is normally interpreted as denoting "rabbit meat" but in (3.4.17), since garments cannot be made of meat, we pragmatically infer that 'rabbit' must denote "rabbit skin". To take a quite different sort of example in which co-text forces an unexpected interpretation on an expression, consider the following adjacency pair of A's utterance and B's punning response.

(3.4.18)
  A: Time flies.
  B: I can't, they move too fast.

Assuming that at least the reasonableness condition is in operation, we are forced to recognize that B's pronoun 'they' is anaphoric to the putative noun phrase 'flies' in the preceding utterance, such that they putatively denote "insects of the family Muscidae". It is exactly this forced co-textual relation between 'they' and 'flies' which creates the pun, and which renders B's utterance sensical in context by interpreting A's gnomic statement as an imperative. Note that this interpretation is determined by pragmatic inference based on the reasonableness condition. The interpretation of pronouns and like phenomena is constrained by the rules of grammar, but it is often ultimately determined by pragmatic inference, as we shall see.

The co-textual correlation we have been discussing between 'they' and 'flies' in (3.4.18) is an anaphoric relation. Sometimes, pronouns are interpreted exophorically, which is to say by direct reference to the setting. This is usually the case with first and second person pronouns, which refer to S and H respectively;[49] and it will be the case where S points to someone in the setting and asks *Who is he?* or points to something and says *I'll take that one*, and so forth. The interpretation of anaphoric language expressions (in terms of objects, places, events, etc. in world W) is, however, a matter of co-textual correlation. In discussing anaphora we shall not distinguish between forwards anaphora as in (3.4.19) which has a full noun phrase antecedent and a succeeding anaphoric pronoun, and backwards anaphora as in (3.4.20) in which the pronoun precedes the full NP:

(3.4.19) When $\underset{(m)}{\text{Max}}$ came back, $\underset{(m)}{\text{he}}$ went straight to bed.

(3.4.20) When he $_{(h)}$ came back, Max $_{(h)}$ went straight to bed.

In these and the following examples relevant anaphoric relations are (oversimplistically) marked by subscript parentheses. The reason for ignoring the difference between forwards and backwards anaphora is that we shall not discuss the syntax of anaphora. However, it is necesary to mention zero anaphora, which is the co-textual correlation that holds between an expression and its ellipsis, cf.

(3.4.21) Tom $_{(t)}$ fell over and $_{(t)}$ broke the jug.

The zero anaphor is represented in the position it seems it would occupy if it were not elided: thus we understand from (3.4.21) that *Tom* broke the jug and hence place subscript (t) in normal subject position for the clause.[50]

Anaphors have the following general characteristics:

(i)   If not zero forms (i.e. elided expressions), anaphors are typically shorter than the full forms which govern them and often very considerably shorter;

(ii)   If not zero forms, anaphors are members of a smallish closed class of grammatical expressions;

(iii) if not zero forms, anaphors have very little semantic content (e.g. just number and gender); this gives them the potential to denote a very large number of phenomena in W and means that if S observes the co-operative maxims of quantity and manner (cf. §1.2.3.3) he will only use an anaphor when he is certain of H's ability to correctly infer from context what he is talking about;

(iv)   anaphors which are zero forms will also be used only when S is certain of H's ability to correctly infer from context what he is talking about.

These characteristics suggest that anaphors are used because they are generally more efficient as a communicative tool than the fuller expressions of their governing forms would be at the same location within the text. In fact, there are occasions when the governing expression simply cannot replace the anaphor, cf.

(3.4.22) The girl being kissed by him $_{((b))g)}$ hated the boy who was kissing her. $_{(g)b))}$ (($_b$

In (3.4.22) it is impossible to replace both pronouns simultaneously by their governing expressions, cf.

(3.4.22′) The girl being kissed by the boy who was kissing the girl being kissed by the boy who was kissing the girl being . . . etc.

It is generally more efficient to use anaphors than to repeat fuller forms, even when an anaphor is in fact longer than the governing form, cf. (3.4.23) where 'that man' is anaphoric to 'Ed'.

(3.4.23) $\underset{(e)}{\text{Ed}}$'s coming to tea tonight. Jesus, I hate $\underset{(\quad e\quad)}{\text{that man}}$.

The syntax of anaphoric relations has been much studied (see footnote 50) and we shall not discuss it here, notwithstanding the fact that a knowledge of the syntactic constraints on anaphora is a significant determinant in the interpretation of some anaphoric relations: e.g. in *John saw him* 'him' cannot be anaphoric to 'John'; in *Ed's picture of him* 'him' cannot be anaphoric to 'Ed'; in *Viv says she's OK* 'she' may or may not be an anaphor of 'Viv', depending on context; however in the idiomatic *Jim's off his rocker* 'his' has to be anaphoric to 'Jim'. All these judgements are based on our knowledge of the syntactic rules governing anaphoric relations. In addition, consider

(3.4.24) $\underset{(m)}{\text{Max}}$ came over and looked closely at $\underset{(e)}{\text{Ed}}$, and then $\underset{(m)}{\text{he}}$ hit $\underset{(e)}{\text{him}}$. So then $\underset{(e)}{\text{HE}}$ hit $\underset{(m)}{\text{HIM}}$.

(A syllable in capitals is stressed). The change in anaphoric relations between the unstressed and the stressed pronouns in (3.4.24) is a grammatical characteristic, although if S is assumed to be observing the co-operative maxim of quantity the acts described in the clauses 'and then he hit him. So then HE hit HIM' would have to be different, and so the reversive relation between the two clauses would be a pragmatic inference in any case.

Anaphoric relations can be subclassified according to the following criteria:

(i) the grammatical category and function of the anaphor and of its governing expression;
(ii) the form of the anaphor;
(iii) whether the governing expression and its anaphor are co-denoting (co-indexed here), i.e. denote the same object(s), place(s), event(s), etc. in a given world W (see §1.6.1); or whether they are like-denoting (not indexed here) and denote only similarly named objects, places, events, etc.

We shall consider only a sample of anaphoric relations, and not the full range.

(3.4.25) Madge$_f$ wants to go to Majorca$_m$ for their$_{(f \& h)}$ holidays, but her husband$_{(hf)h}$ won't go there$_m$.

The possessive pronoun 'their' is anaphoric to and co-denotes with 'Madge' and 'her husband' together; the possessive pronoun 'her' is anaphoric to and co-denotes 'Madge'; the locative pronoun 'there' is anaphoric to and co-denotational with 'Majorca'.

(3.4.26) I$_i$ can't believe it$_s$. They've given me$_i$ a rise$_s$.

This has a co-denotational anaphoric relation between 'I' and 'me' both of which would be exophorically related to S in the setting. The pronoun 'it' co-denotes with and is anaphoric to the whole sentence 'They've given me a rise'.

(3.4.27) His$_h$ name isn't really Rex$_r$, he$_h$ just calls himself$_h$ that$_r$.

Here 'his', 'he' and 'himself' are anaphors which co-denote the man bearing the name Rex; the demonstrative pronoun 'that' is anaphoric to and denotes the name 'Rex'.

(3.4.28)

A: What are you$_b$ doing?

B: $_{(b)}$ Trying to find the map.

In (3.4.28) the elided grammatical subject of B's utterance is understood to refer to B, as does A's to 'you'.

Floating and stranded quantifiers range over zero anaphors of things which occur in the co-text, e.g.

(3.4.29) Some boys$_b$ were sitting on the fence. All $_{(b)}$ were chewing gum.

Here 'all' ranges over the set described previously as 'some boys', i.e. it denotes every member of that set.[51]

There are anaphors that look like full noun phrases but are stricted to having a general term as the head noun, and they only seem to be used when S has either a very positive or very negative attitude to what is spoken of, cf. (3.4.23) and

(3.4.30) I never drink milk $(_m)$. Can't stand the stuff $(_m)$.

(3.4.31) Fluzy Suzie $(_f)$'s back in town. I'd love to see the girl $(_f)$ again.

(3.4.32) Ronnie was drunk $(_d)$ again last night. That sort of behaviour $(_d)$ will do her no good.

Something similar to anaphora occurs when an appositive descriptive expression is given as an alternative to some previously used descriptive; however, these expressions do not meet the normal criteria for anaphors, cf.

(3.4.33) Tom $(_t)$ bought me these flowers yesterday, the sweetie $(_t)$.

(3.4.34) The mechanic $(_m)$ ripped me off, the bastard $(_m)$.

Now compare

(3.4.36) Joan is after that house on the corner $((_h ( ) _h))$, and Edie wants the same one $(((_h ( )_h))$.

(3.4.37) Janie wants a new doll $( )$ for Christmas, and Ann wants the same thing $( )$.

In (3.4.36) 'the same one' is anaphoric to and co-denotational with 'that house on the corner and furthermore 'one' is anaphoric to and co-denotational with 'house'. In (3.4.37), although 'the same thing' is anaphoric to 'a new doll' it is only like-denoting, because 'thing' is not anaphoric to 'doll'. Had Joan and Edie wanted the same new doll, the anaphor would be 'the same one', as it is in (3.4.36). In (3.4.38), despite the fact that 'one' is co-denotational with 'bike', the NPs 'a bike' and 'another one' are only like-denoting.

(3.4.38) Mac bought Anna a bike $(((_b)))$ which she lost, and so he bought her another one $((((_b))))$.

The co-denoting vs. like-denoting contrast between 'the same one' in (3.4.36) and 'another one' in (3.4.38) results, of course, from the semantic difference between 'the same' and 'another'. Now consider:

(3.4.39) Last year in Trafalgar Square I saw (people jumping in the

fountains on new year's eve), and this year I saw (them) at it again.

(3.4.40) When a lizard loses (its tail), (it) will often grow again.

In (3.4.39) 'them' and 'people' are anaphorically related, but we infer
from our knowledge of the world (i.e. we pragmatically infer) that the
set of people jumping in the Trafalgar Square fountains on one new
year's eve is unlikely to be precisely the set of people doing the same
thing a year later. Turning to (3.4.40), it is obvious that the tail a lizard
loses cannot be the same tail that it subsequently grows.

Unlike whole clauses, anaphoric verbs and verb phrases are
necessarily zero-indexed, presumably because of the different participants involved; cf.

(3.4.41) Jo (wants to go to Spain and (so does) Fred.

(3.4.42) Caspar (took) three ((chocolates)) and Carol () two (( )).

Although the form (if any) and the grammatical function of the
anaphor is often a clue to whether or not it is co-denotational with its
governing expression, we see from (3.4.39-40) that pragmatic inference
is of overriding importance in determining the matter. And again,
although we have seen that knowledge of the syntactic rules governing
anaphoric relations is a significant element in the proper interpretation
of anaphors (including zero anaphors), knowledge of these rules is
insufficient to cope with all cases. The following, for instance, are
resolved by pragmatic inference:

(3.4.43) Ed lost the money to Max because he is a skilful player.

(3.4.44) Jo lost the money to Anna because she played badly.

In (3.4.43) we pragmatically infer that it must be the winner who is
described as a skilful player, and therefore that 'he' is anaphoric to
'Max'. In (3.4.44) we pragmatically infer the obverse, that the poor
player is the one that loses, and therefore 'she' must be anaphoric to
'Jo'. For another contrasted pair, consider

(3.4.45) His father punished George because he confessed to
    shoplifting.

(3.4.46) His father punished George because he disapproved of shoplifting.

In these tales of crime and punishment we infer that George has been punished for the crime of shoplifting; in (3.4.45) it is his confession to the crime that results in his punishment, hence we pragmatically infer that 'he' and the zero anaphor which is the understood subject of 'shoplifting' are both anaphoric to 'George'. In (3.4.46), knowing that it is generally the person who disapproves of a malefaction who instigates punishment on the malefactor, we pragmatically infer that 'he' is anaphoric to 'his [i.e. George's] father'; while the understood subject of 'shoplifting' is zero anaphoric to 'George' (as in the previous example). For a pair of final examples, compare

(3.4.47) I took my dog to the vet yesterday, and he bit him on the shoulder.

(3.4.48) I took my dog to the vet yesterday, and he injected him in the shoulder.

Although it is not impossible that a vet could bite a dog, this is so unusual that S would be violating the maxim of manner if he were to report such an event in the words of (3.4.47). In consequence we pragmatically infer from (3.4.48) that 'he' is anaphoric to 'the vet' and 'him' to 'my dog'.

The proper interpretation of anaphora is based in part on our knowledge of the syntax of anaphora, on the semantic content of the anaphoric expression, and on pragmatic inferences about the world spoken of – inferences which derive from the textual environment surrounding the anaphoric expression.

We can see from even the few examples considered here the importance of textual environment in constructing a reasonable world W from what S is saying.

1.3.5 Context – a summary

We use 'context' to refer to the setting of the utterance U, the world spoken of in U, and the textual environment of U. Setting is defined on the spatio-temporal location at which S issues the utterance U, and the spatio-temporal location at which H hears U. It is typically the setting to which the deictics in U will refer – in particular the first and second person pronouns; but the meaning of all deictics is defined in relation to setting (or imputed setting). Setting establishes the medium of utterance as spoken or written. It often conditions H's expectations concerning the variety of language he anticipates H will use, and may consequently help determine the meaningfulness of any manipulation of language variety by S. In face-to-face interaction paralinguistic accompaniments to speech such as gestures and facial expressions are a feature of setting: these often contribute to the meaning of the utterance, though it is not at present known how they can be accounted for within a theory of linguistic meaning.

The central notion of context is W, the world spoken of in U. It may be the everyday world familiar to H and to all of us, or some corner of that world unfamiliar to H and to us, or it may be a dream world, a fictional world, or a mix of fact and fiction. Languages permit us to describe "impossible" worlds and "impossible" entities such as *the perfect circle*, *a round square*, *the largest prime number* within an otherwise familiar world. In the absence of evidence to the contrary, we assume that W is the real world of our everyday experience; and, in any case, W is always understood at least partly in terms of the world of our experience – presumably it has to be!

The world spoken of in U provides a framework for the coherence and reasonableness of what is said. W is often revealed, or at least confirmed, by the textual environment of U, i.e. the text containing U will identify what persons, places, objects, states, events, acts, etc. are being spoken of in U. The particular meaning of U (or of an expression within U) is often determined by the particular world spoken of in U, and where this world is identified from U's co-text, the co-text will determine the meaning of U (or the expression within it). Co-text is of paramount importance in the interpretation of anaphoric expressions within U; however, we have seen that the proper interpretation of anaphora will often depend upon inferences derived from W, the world spoken of.

Within a theory of linguistic meaning W, the world spoken of, is the core component of context C. The most significant contribution of setting to the meaning of U is where it forms part of the world spoken of, as well as being the world spoken in. The contribution to utterance meaning of U's textual environment is most significant where it serves to identify the world spoken of; we can even regard the interpretation of anaphoric expressions as identifying entities within W.

1.4 The utterance, U

1.4.1 Defining the utterance

An utterance U issues from the mouth or pen of the speaker S at some particular time and place. Therefore, U has actual physical form – either phonetic or graphic – and it is spatio-temporally located. We define U as follows:

> An utterance U is a spatio-temporally located language datum that comes into existence when S uses a sentence Σ spoken with prosody Φ to communicate something to hearer H in context C.[52]

We may understand from this definition either that Σ (read 'sigma') is one of an infinite set of sentences of L to which any speaker of L has access; or alternatively, that in result of S's uttering U there is a sentence Σ in L. (The choice between these alternatives is like deciding whether the chicken or the egg came first.)

In §1.4.2 we discuss the relationship between the utterance U and the sentence Σ, and in §1.4.3 we briefly discuss the contribution to utterance meaning of the prosody Φ (read 'phi').

1.4.2 Utterances and sentences, and other etic and emic categories

We shall not use the term 'sentence' in exactly its everyday (every school day) sense. The sentence Σ is a syntactically structured string of morphemes of the language L, i.e. it is structured according to the rules of syntax for L. Σ is the abstract analytical category in a systematic description of the grammar of L which correlates with the pragmatic category U realized in the speech acts of L speakers.

An utterance U is the product of a speech act performed by a speaker to a hearer in a given context; it has physical form and exists at some location in space and time. The sentence, Σ, is none of these things: Σ is an abstract object, a theoretical construct postulated by the analytical linguist. U and Σ are members of complementary sets of corresponding categories: the pragmatic or ETIC categories which issue from the mouths and pens of speakers of a language L, and which have physical existence; and the abstract analytical or EMIC categories which are theoretical constructs in a systematic description of the grammar of L; cf. (4.2.1).

(4.2.1)   *Etic categories*   *Emic categories*
                utterance   sentence
                (etic) clause   (emic) clause
                (etic) phrase   (emic) phrase
                (etic) word   (emic) word
                lex   lexeme
                morph   morpheme
                phone   phoneme

Categories other than 'phone' and 'phoneme' are referred to in this book as 'language expressions'. For the most part, the lists in (4.2.1) rank the categories hierarchically, such that an utterance or sentence may consist of one or more clauses, a clause of one or more phrases, a phrase of one or more words, a word of a lex(eme) and perhaps one or more morph(eme)s as well,[53] a lex(eme) of one or more morph(eme)s.

Etic and emic categories are very different kinds of things. For instance, there may be a many-to-one relationship between them: the words *cats*, *dogs*. *horses*, *oxen*, *foci*, *crises*, *phenomena*, *stigmata*, *cherubim* contain respectly the morphs /s/, /z/, /əz/, /n/, /aɪ/, /iz/, /ə/, /atə/, /ɪm/, which are just some of the realizations of that abstract entity, the English morpheme "plural". The (emic) sentence "I'm cold" has occurred and will occur in innumerable (etic) utterances. There can be a one-to-many relationship between etic and emic categories, too; for instance a 'portmanteau morph'[54] may realize an amalgamation of morphemes, e.g. the English pronoun *mine* combines the three morphemes "first person + possessive + complement", the morph *-arum* in the Latin adjective *bonarum* combines "feminine + genitive + plural". But the really significant difference between etic and emic categories is that etic categories are physical entities used in actual utterances of L, the language being described, and the emic categories are terms used in the linguist's description of L. Thus in his Introduction to *The Logical Structure of Linguistic Theory* 1975, Noam Chomsky wrote of emic categories that 'they are not classes [of etic phenomena], sequences of classes [of etic phenomena], or anything of the sort, but simply abstract elements [. . .] in various abstract systems of representation' (pp. 29, 32). To put this another way: etic categories issue from the mouths and pens of speakers using the OBJECT LANGUAGE (the one being described), whereas emic categories are categories of the METALANGUAGE used by the linguist in describing and analyzing the object language.

There is no direct relationship between an etic category and the corresponding emic one, cf. Chomsky 1975:34. This is implicit in the remarks just quoted from Chomsky, and also in the variously many-to-one or one-to-many correspondences between etic and emic categories that were illustrated above. Jacob Bronowski in *The Origins of Knowledge and Imagination* 1978 described emic categories as being metaphorically related to etic ones. Albert Einstein in 'Physics and reality' 1973:294 says of emic and etic categories that their 'relation is not analogous to that of soup to beef but rather of check number and overcoat.' Within linguistics, emic categories are theoretical (metalanguage) constructs postulated by linguists using their intuitions about the nature of object language structure; these intuitions will only be verified if the emic categories form part of a coherent theory of language which is seen to model object language use correctly. The correspondences we have identified here between etic and emic categories are generally accepted within the discipline of linguistics, and to the best of our knowledge they are correct.

An awkward paradox arises when discussing emic categories. Unlike etic categories, emic categories are abstract and have no intrinsic form. Yet in order to talk about it, an emic category has to be represented by some physical form or other, e.g. to talk about the morpheme "plural" I have to spell out p-l-u-r-a-l on this page; thus we can only refer to an emic category by using an etic category! To add to the confusion, it is usual for linguists to do the kind of thing done in this book, which is to use English as a metalanguage for describing English as an object language. Where necessary we shall adopt the practice of representing emic (metalanguage) data by ". . ." and etic (object language) data by *italics*. But it is often convenient to represent emic data using the corresponding etic citation forms in italics; this will be done when the distinction between emic and etic data is not crucial; and it may be done when it is clear from the text that an emic category is being cited – e.g. 'the sentence *I'm cold*'.

Let's look at just one more consequence of the difference between the etic category U and the emic category Σ. The etic category U is uttered by S to H in context C. One property of the utterance is that H will assign it a value in relation to its context C, the type of value assigned depending on the kind of speech act which U manifests. An utterance in which S makes the statement *The prime minister is an old woman* will be assigned the value true or false, depending on the prime minister referred to; an utterance in which S asks the question *Where is my halberd?* may or may not be answerable in the context in which it is uttered; if S delivers a judgement such as *I hereby sentence you to death by garrotting* it will depend on the context whether or not the sentence has any standing in law. By definition, sentences are abstract objects independent of speaker, hearer and context, so Σ cannot be assigned a value. The Σ "The prime minister is an old woman" can be used in one utterance to make a true statement and another to make a false statement: it has no truth value as a sentence.[55]

We began this section by comparing the etic category U with the emic category Σ. And we conclude that the utterance U is a category in the object language corresponding to Σ in the metalanguage. This, however, ignores the inequity of the relationship, because U corresponds to Σ spoken with prosody Φ. The meaning of U is in large part determined by the meaning specified for Σ; but there is also a contribution from the prosody, to which we turn our attention next.

1.4.3   The prosody, Φ

In issuing a spoken utterance, S uses a sentence Σ spoken with prosody Φ. The prosody Φ comprehends stress, disjunctures, and intonation used in uttering U. In writing, prosody is somewhat grossly represented by punctuation, underlining, capitalization, italicization, etc. and for the purposes of discussion we shall generally count such devices under the heading of prosody. A syntactically structured string of morphemes (e.g. a phrase or sentence) uttered with different prosodies may mean something different with each prosodic change, as we shall see.

Prosodic stress is an emic category whose corresponding phonetic characteristics are a marked movement or sustention of pitch when uttering the stressed syllable, and this pitch obtrusion is often accompanied by greater amplitude (loudness) and greater duration in the syllable than is to be found in the adjoining syllables. Sometimes the stressed syllable has a different vowel quality from that which normally occurs in a comparable unstressed syllable; this can be illustrated from the contrast between the noun $\overset{1}{con}vict$ /'kɒnvɪkt/ and the verb $\overset{1}{con}vict$ /kən'vɪkt/. Hitherto we have indicated stressed syllables by writing them in capitals; but we shall from now on abandon that practice and indicate stress in phonemic transcriptions by '' before the stressed syllable, and in regular orthographic representations by a superscript '1' over the vowel in the stressed syllable (the reasons for this are given in §6.3). The function of prosodic stress is to stress something, i.e. to focus upon it, cf. §6.3; this is why a change of stress results in a change of meaning. Consider

(4.3.1) The purpose of hitchhiking is not to $\overset{1}{wa}lk$, but not to $\overset{1}{wa}lk$.

Here the scope of the negative in the two clauses changes with the stress change, hence the gloss: "It is not the purpose of hitchhiking to walk, but (it is the purpose of hitchhiking) to not walk."

In ordinary orthography, words are separated from one another by spaces, but in speech there is no comparable separation of words as a rule, so that /ə'tæk/ is the normal pronunciation for both *a tack* and *attack*, and both *I scream* and *ice cream* may be pronounced /aɪskri·m/, although the former is more likely to be pronounced /aɪ'skriim/ – either way, there is no pause between phonemes to correspond with the space between graphemes of the separate words. But of course there are pauses, i.e. disjunctures, in speech, and they do have meaningful effect. A disjuncture is produced by a momentary cessation of the articulatory mechanism – one that is not the accidental consequence of articulating a stop phone. By convention we assume that disjuncture immediately precedes the onset of utterance and acts as a boundary at the end of utterance. Disjunctures in speech always occur where punctuation marks like commas, colons, full stops, etc. appear in written English texts, but in many other places as well, cf. §6.4. We can demonstrate the use of disjuncture to disambiguate e.g. (4.3.2) from (4.3.3). Disjuncture is symbolized by the slash '/'.

(4.3.2) / Thanks for ringing, / John. /

(4.3.3) / Thanks for ringing John. /

In (4.3.2) S addresses his thanks to John, the hearer; in (4.3.3) S addresses his thanks to H who has rung John. Internal disjuncture can also be used to differentiate the following pairs of noun phrases.

(4.3.4)
a.   a bricklayer   b.   a brick / layer

(4.3.5)
a.   a highlight   b.   a high / light

(4.3.6)
a.   a blackbird   b.   a black / bird

The (a) examples consist of the sequence Article + Compound Noun, and compound nouns will not admit internal disjuncture. The (b) examples consist of the sequence Article + Modifier + Noun, and it is possible (though not necessary) for there to be a disjuncture between the modifier and the noun. There is, of course, a difference in meaning between these pairs, e.g. (4.3.4.a) means "a person who lays bricks" and (4.3.4.b) means "a stratum of bricks", (4.3.6.a) names a species of bird and (4.3.6.b) means "a bird which is black". There is typically a stress difference between the NPs in (a) and those in (b), cf. *a* $\overset{1}{blackbird}$ but a *black* $\overset{1}{bird}$; however it is not this stress difference, but the disjuncture, which is used to disambiguate these pairs, cf. Dwight Bolinger & Louis Gerstman 'Disjuncture as a cue to constructs' 1957, Philip Lieberman *Intonation, Perception, and Language* 1967:153. Consequently, the stress on the (b) examples can be shifted to the modifier, and the disjuncture is all that is left to differentiate (a) from (b), cf. *a* $\overset{1}{bricklayer}$ versus *a* $\overset{1}{brick}$ / *layer*.

The most important prosodic category is intonation. When speaking, an intonation contour is created by the variations in pitch which S makes by tightening or slackening the muscles that alter the length and thickness of his vocal cords as they vibrate when air is forced through them from the lungs. An intonation contour is co-extensive with a sense group (any sentence constituent will constitute a sense group) and it is always bounded by disjunctures – though in spontaneous speech they may not be adjacent disjunctures, cf. §6.5. The intonation contour is composed of two categories of phenomena: pitch levels or 'keys', and pitch movements or 'kinetic tones' within these keys. We identify three keys in English: high, mid, low.[56] A change in key may occur at the onset syllable following a disjuncture, or at a stressed syllable, or after a stressed syllable. We symbolize the key used by putting the mid key on the same line as the disjuncture symbol '/'; high key data will be located on the line above the disjuncture symbol, and low key data on the line below it. Compare

	the Robinsons.	[High key]
(4.3.7) / We gave it to our neighbours /	/	[Mid key]

(4.3.8) / We gave it to our neighbours /	/	[Mid key]
	the Robinsons.	[Low key]

The shift to high key for 'the Robinsons' in (4.3.7) shows that S regards it as important that 'it' was given to the Robinsons. In (4.3.8) S's downshift to low key for 'the Robinsons' indicates that he considers this information as parenthetical and relatively unimportant. Thus a key shift has meaningful implications, the details of which are discussed in §6.5.2.

The pitch movement we noted to be the main characteristics of stress provides the basis for the second component of intonation, the kinetic tones. These identify the direction of the pitch movement in a stressed syllable, and it is assumed that the resulting contour is maintained up to the next stressed syllable or disjuncture. There are five kinetic tones in English, the fall, symbolized by '`' over the stressed syllable, the rise '´', the rise-fall '^', the fall-rise '˅' and the level tone '¯'. We shall not examine here the full panoply of meanings associated with the various kinetic tones, they are discussed in §6.5.2, but we might compare the meaningful effects of the different tones on 'Stop it' in (4.3.9-13). (The bracketted descriptions are only illustrative and not definitive.)

(4.3.9) / Stòp it / you hòr   /   [Command]
                         rid little boy.

(4.3.10) / Stôp it /   /   [Advice]
                         that's mỳ advice.

                         I bēg you
(4.3.11) / Stóp it /   / I cān't tàke any more. /   [Plea]

                                   gīve me another
(4.3.12) / Stŏp it /   / And   kìss. /
                         you're tìckling me.
   [Playful]

(4.3.13) / Stŏp it / you knôw what'll happen if you dôn't.   [Warning]

There could be five utterances of the sentence *Stop it*, each one with a different kinetic tone and a different meaning.

Although we have identified three prosodic components – stress, disjuncture and intonation – it should be obvious that intonation is the most important prosodic category, because it comprehends the other two.

1.5 The meaning of U is composed from the meanings of its constituents

1.5.1 The compositionality of meaning

The meaning of S's utterance U delivered to H in context C is composed from (i) the (or a) meaning of the sentence Σ that S uses; (ii) the meaning contributed by the prosody Φ with which Σ is spoken; and (iii) the meaningful input to the interpretation of sentence Σ spoken with prosody Φ from the context C and from background information of various kinds. Each of these components of U's meaning is itself compositional. We saw in §1.4.3 that prosody consists of stress, disjunctural, and intonational components; and although I have no more to say at this point about the compositionality of contextual or background meaning, it will be exemplified in §1.6.3 and ch.8. Sentence meaning is compositional; in fact it manifests a compositional hierarchy such that the meaning of a sentence is composed from the meanings of its constituent clauses (and their connectives), the meaning of a clause is composed from the meanings of its constituent phrases, the meaning of a phrase is composed from the meanings of its constituent words, and those in turn from the meanings of their constituent lexemes and morphemes. Thus, the meaning of a sentence Σ is projected up through the hierarchy of syntactic levels from the meanings of the constituent lexemes and morphemes in Σ. In ch.5 we shall discuss ways in which this might be done in a theory of meaning. The meanings of the semantically primitive sentence constituents, lexemes and morphemes, cannot be computed from the meanings of their constituent parts like the meanings of other sentence constituents; instead they have to be listed in the theoretical dictionary, or LEXICON, and for that reason they will be referred to in this book as LEXICON ITEMS. We shall briefly describe the lexicon in §1.5.3, but before doing that it would be as well to clarify the relationship between the emic categories of word, lexeme, and morpheme.

1.5.2   Word, lexeme and morpheme

Consider

(5.2.1) give, gives, gave, giving, given.

In everyday parlance (5.2.1) lists five words, and concomitantly, five forms of the same word. To be more precise in our terminology we shall restrict the term 'word' to the first sense, i.e. (5.2.1) lists five words. However, we do distinguish between the etic word and the emic word. Etic words occur in utterances and consist of a lex and perhaps one or more morphs – which are of interest to a discussion of meaning for indicating their emic correspondents. The emic word occurs in the sentence Σ and is analyzable into a lexeme and one or more morphemes, which is of significant interest to us because these are primitives in the composition of sentence meaning. Like the phoneme and the morpheme, a lexeme is an abstract entity without intrinsic form; and in order to refer metalinguistically to a particular lexeme, we use the citation form of the word. The citation form is the form in which a dictionary entry for the word appears in standard (monolingual) dictionaries; and in English this is the unmarked lex, e.g. the bare infinitive of the verb, the singular form of nouns other than pluralia tantum nouns, etc. Thus, the lexeme exemplified in (5.2.1) is (in our metalanguage) "give"; the words *cat* and *cats* both manifest the lexeme "cat"; the pluralia tantum noun lexeme "scissors" has the form *scissors*.[57] The lexeme manifest in the words *I*, *me*, *my*, *mine* is usually called "1st person" rather than "I" in the metalanguage.

Note that the various words manifesting a lexeme are related by inflexional morphology: e.g.

word ≈ lexeme + morpheme [where '≈' is read "realizes" or
  "manifests"]
give ≈ "give" with no additional morpheme
gives ≈ "give + 3rd person singular subject agreement"
gave ≈ "give + past tense"
giving ≈ "give + present participle"
given ≈ "give + past participle"

And

disability ≈ "disability"
disabilities ≈ "disability + plural"

or the Latin noun *rūmor* "rumour"

rūmor ≈ "rumour + nominative singular"
rūmōris ≈ "rumour + genitive singular"
rūmōri ≈ "rumour + dative singular"
rūmōrem ≈ "rumour + accusative singular"
rūmōre ≈ "rumour + ablative singular"
rūmōres ≈ "rumour + nominative or accusative plural"
rūmōrum ≈ "rumour + genitive plural"
rūmōribus ≈ "rumour + dative or ablative plural"

And the Latin adjective *bonus* "good". e.g.

bonus ≈ "good + masculine nominative singular"
bonārum ≈ "good + feminine genitive plural"

Inflexions add secondary grammatical categories onto lexemes: e.g. tense, aspect, mood, voice, person/number agreement onto verb lexemes: number and case onto noun and pronoun lexemes; gender, number, case onto adjective lexemes, etc. Note that because the lexeme is an abstract entity it is quite legitimate to speak metalinguistically of the Latin adjective lexeme "good", which is manifest by the words *bonum* and *bonārum* among others; the same lexeme can, of course, be represented in any metalanguage, including Latin – where it is called "bonus, -a, -um" (based on the lexes for the masculine, feminine and neuter nominative singular forms, respectively).

It can be seen that the meaning of a word composed from the lexeme and inflexional morpheme transparently combines the meaning of the two; e.g. *cats* combines the meaning of "cat" and "plural" (though we shall need to consider in ch.5 just how these two bits of meaning actually do combine); *gave* combines the meaning of "give" with "in past time" (= "past tense"). Thus the meaning of a word analyzable into a lexeme stem and an inflexional morpheme can be computed from the meaning of these components. Words as such are therefore not found in the lexicon; what look like words in the lexicon are serving as vehicles for the representation of lexemes.

Words instantiating a given lexeme will differ from one another in their inflexional morphology, cf. (5.2.1). But to affix a derivational morpheme to any form of lexeme will create another, different, lexeme; e.g. the lexes (and words) *able, unable, ability, inability* all manifest separate lexemes, despite the fact that they are all formed on the root *able*.

Finally, it should be said that although the emic word typically contains a lexeme, there are certain lexemes whose citation forms consist of more than one etic word – at least if 'word' is to be understood in its everyday sense, cf. the phrasal verb *put up with* or the idiom *man-in-the-street*. There are various ways in which such data can be accommodated to what we have said about the relationship between words and lexemes, e.g. by allowing exceptions to it, or redefining 'word', but these need not detain us now.

1.5.3   The lexicon

We have said that the meaning of a sentence Σ is projected up through the hierarchy of syntactic levels from the meanings of the lexicon items within Σ. The lexicon items are the semantically primitive sentence constituents whose meanings have to be specified within the lexicon because they cannot be computed from their component parts. A lexicon item within Σ is matched with a lexicon entry by noting the form of the lexicon item and its syntactic category and distribution in Σ and finding an item with the same form and syntactic characteristics in the lexicon. Consequently lexicon entries include a phonological and graphological representation of the item; a representation of its syntactic category and syntactic distribution; and, of course, a representation of the meaning of that lexicon item. It can be seen that the lexicon required by a linquistic theory of meaning has a similar format to that of the everyday dictionary which stands on our bookshelves. Lexicon items are even arranged according to the sequence of phonemes or letters in their formal representation, cf. §4.12. However, the set of lexicon items in the theoretical lexicon is more comprehensive than the set of items in a standard dictionary.

The minimal set of lexicon items in a dictionary would be (i) all lexemes, and (ii) all inflexional morphemes. Many lexemes are, however, derived from lexemic or morphemic roots by affixing derivational morphemes; the meanings of these derivational components are known, permitting the meaning of the derived lexeme to be computed from them. E.g. the suffix *-ize* is causative and in a transitive clause such as in *A atomizes B* or *A legalizes B* it means "A causes or brings about that B has the property of being atoms" (in one clause) or "legal" (in the other). However, the meaning of derived lexemes cannot consistently be correctly computed from their derivational components, thus the meaning of *computerize* is not "*cause to be a computer", but "make suitable for feeding into a computer", and *womanize* does not mean "*cause to be a woman" but "chase or seek the company of women". Thus at least some derived lexemes must be entered into the lexicon; and for the sake of consistency it is nowadays generally agreed that all derived lexemes have to be entered in the lexicon along with root lexemes. Nonetheless, S and H not only know the meanings of lexemes and inflexional morphemes, as we have just seen they also know the meanings of derivational morphemes; and they know the meanings of stems, e.g. people know the meaning of the prefix *re-* and of the bound stem *-juvenate* in the lexeme *rejuvenate*, even though '-juvenate' "make young" does not exist in any other English lexeme. Derivational affixes and stems are used in the coining of new words whose meaning S will often intend H to compute from the meanings of the derivational components. Furthermore, one of the goals of a theory of meaning is to account for the semantic relationships between lexemes (and other expressions), and some of these relationships can be specified through derivational components such as derivational affixes and stems. Consequently, the lexicon must contain:

(i)   all inflexional morphemes
(ii)   all derivational morphemes
(iii)   all lexical stems
(iv)   all lexemes.

See ch.4 for further discussion.

1.5.4   Syntax and sentence meaning

Consider how the meaning of the English noun *undesirables* is structured in terms of its component morphemes.

(i)   To the root verb lexeme "desire" is attached.
(ii)   the "adjectivalizing [i.e. derivational] suffix -able", thus deriving the adjective lexeme "desirable".
(iii) The lexeme "desirable" is prefixed by the derivational "adjectival negative un-" morpheme to create the negative adjective lexeme "undesirable".
(iv)   Like some other adjectives[58] *undesirable* can be used as a noun, and this lexical class change is attributable to a zero-derivation morpheme[59] that has no corresponding morph, but which assigns the adjective the syntax and morphology of a noun. Thus the adjective lexeme "undesirable" becomes the noun lexeme "undesirable".
(v)   Finally, to this noun lexeme is suffixed the "plural" inflexion giving rise to the word *undesirables*.

We see from this analysis that the various lexemes and morphemes from which words are composed are not combined in random fashion, but are syntactically structured. The syntactic structure within the word *undesirables* is described above and also diagrammed in Figure 1.1.

The principles applicable to determining the meaning of words from the structured relations among their component lexemes and morphemes apply equally well to higher syntactic categories from phrase to clause to sentence. Just as we know that the sum of $2 + 3 + 7 + 9$ is the same as the sum of $9 + 3 + 7 + 2$, we also know that the meanings of sentences are not simply the sums of the meanings of the lexemes and morphemes within them: for instance, (5.4.1-3) each mean something different even though they share the same set of lexicon items – *the*, *the*, *-ed*, *-s*, *kill*, *hunter*, *crocodile*.

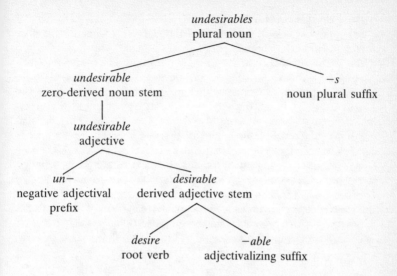

Figure 1.1 The syntactic structure of the word *undesirables*

(5.4.1) The hunters killed the crocodile.

(5.4.2) The hunter killed the crocodiles.

(5.4.3) The crocodile killed the hunters.

The way in which the constituent parts of Σ are combined crucially affects the meaning of Σ; so any account of Σ's meaning must include the contribution of its syntactic structure. This matter is taken up in chs 4 and 5.

1.6 Sentence meaning, denotation, and utterance meaning

1.6.1 Sense and denotation

It is important to recognize that sentence Σ has meaning independently of what S is using it to mean in a given utterance U. It is customary to speak of this as its SENSE, or SENSES if it has more than one sense. Take the Σ in

(6.1.1) The prime minister is an old woman.

This has the sense: "the chief minister within the national parliament is a woman of advanced years"; or, if the predicate is idiomatic "the chief minister within the national parliament is a man[60] who complains too much and is over-concerned with trivia." It is not only sentences which have sense, so does any emic expression; and, for instance, it is the sense or senses of lexicon items that are described in dictionaries. The sense of Σ is composed from the senses of its constituent lexicon items which supply the raw material from which S moulds his meaning; and the sense of Σ is the crucial part of the raw material from which H reasons out S's meaning in a particular utterance U.

When S utters U to H his utterance is context bound i.e. it is bound to a particular setting, a particular textual environment, and a particular world spoken of, W. Thus, in different utterances U_i and U_j, the same sentence Σ spoken with the same Φ can be used with different meanings – which we shall henceforth call different DENOTATIONS.[61] E.g. on one occasion S may use (6.1.1) to denote the same as (6.1.2):

(6.1.2) William Gladstone is a man who complains too much and is overconcerned with trivia.

And on another occasion he may use (6.1.1) to denote the same as (6.1.3):

(6.1.3) Golda Meir is a woman of advanced years.

By convention, we assume that all the constituents of S's utterance U denote in W, the world spoken of. There are two subcategories of denotation: referring and designating, which we shall just briefly describe here, leaving them to be discussed in greater detail in ch.7.

S REFERS to something[62] in W where he uses a noun phrase, clause, or utterance[63] to present the denotatum as existing (or at least, putatively existing) in W. Such NPs, clauses, and utterances are known as 'referring expressions'. E.g. S may use the NP *the prime minister* or the NP *William Gladstone* to refer to the 19th century British prime minister of that name; or he may use the NP *Mr Spock* to refer to the pointy-eared character in the fictional world of the television sci-fi series *Star Trek*; or the NP *a man Elizabeth Taylor was once married to* to refer to Mike Todd; or, S may utter *John F. Kennedy was assassinated in November 1963* and thereby refer to Kennedy's assassination. From H's point of view (which is the point of view we take for our theory of meaning), the use of such referring expressions implies (i.e conventionally implicates, cf. §3.9) that the denotatum exists in W. Note that a referring term denotes something that does (putatively) exist, according to S; something that only might exist is not denoted by a referring term, it is designated by a nonreferring term, cf. §7.11.3.

Not all NPs, clauses, and Us refer. We speak of S DESIGNATING in W with all the nonreferring expressions he uses; not only the nonreferring NPs and Us, but also articles, auxiliaries, adjectives, verbs, manner adverbs, and so forth – none of which are referring terms. Compare the following two utterances.

(6.1.4) Nobody's there.

(6.1.5) Is anyone there?

In both (6.1.4) and (6.1.5) 'there' will typically refer to a contextually identifiable place; but the sense of the NPs 'nobody' and 'anyone' makes it impossible for either to refer under normal conditions. Neither implies the existence of someone who can be described as 'nobody' or 'anyone'; therefore these two NPs can only designate. Although (6.1.5) implies the possible existence of someone 'there', it does not imply that they do exist, and therefore it is nonreferential. Because these NPs are nonreferential, you cannot seriously say *This is anyone* or *I'd like you to meet nobody: my uncle* in the way that you can say *This is the prime minister* or *I'd like you to meet sombody: my uncle*. With this in mind think about the source of humour in the following text.

'Who did you pass on the road?' the King went on, holding out his
    hand to the Messenger for some hay.
'Nobody,' said the Messenger.
'Quite right,' said the King: 'this young lady saw him too. So of course
    Nobody walks slower than you.'
'I do my best,' the Messenger said in a sullen tone. 'I'm sure nobody
    walks faster than I do!'
'He can't do that,' said the King, 'or else he'd have been here first.'
        (Lewis Carroll *Through the Looking Glass* 1965:182)

This is amusing because it plays on a misunderstanding so ridiculous that it would not arise in a normal conversational exchange: it is outlandish of the King to interpret the Messenger's nonreferring (= designating) NP 'nobody' as if it were referring to someone named Nobody.

We have looked at the NPs in (6.1.4-5) but not yet at the utterances themselves. In (6.1.4) the utterance refers to (the existence of) the fact that there is nobody 'there'. In (6.1.5), on the other hand, the utterance only designates – i.e. it is nonreferring: in making it, S is seeking to discover what the facts are, viz. he does not presuppose the existence of the fact that there is someone there, nor the existence of the fact that there is no-one there; consequently the expression he uses does not imply (i.e. does not conventionally implicate) the existence of either fact.

Except when he is being deliberately ambiguous, S will designate using only one particular sense of the nonreferring expression. For instance in an utterance of

(6.1.6) Golda Meir is an old woman,

we would say that S is using the predicate expression 'is an old woman' to designate of Golda Meir (to whom S refers) that she is a woman of advanced years. The nonreferring NPs of (6.1.4-5) each have only one sense, and that is necessarily the one designated by S in uttering them.

To sum up: Sense is an abstract property – the meaning of an emic expression; and we discuss this some more in the next section. Denotation is a property of an etic expression and, more importantly, it identifies what S is talking about in W, the world spoken of – whatever kind of world that may be, real or imaginary. We identified two subcategories of denotation: S refers to things that putatively exist in W, and designates everything else in W. For the time being, we can more or less ignore the distinction between reference and designation; but it is essential to distinguish between sense and denotation.

1.6.2 More about the notion of sense

On all occasions of use, the sense of the NP *the prime minister* will be the same, viz. "the chief minister within the national parliament". But this NP can be used to denote anyone who is a prime minister (or who can ironically or jokingly be called a prime minister, and so forth). Thus, the NP *the prime minister* can be used to denote (in fact, refer to) the same people as the NPs *Golda Meir*, *William Gladstone*, *William Pitt*, *Pierre Trudeau*, or *Bob Hawke*; but it can never have the same sense as any of these. No one would even think of confusing the senses of (6.2.1) and (6.2.2), yet it happens that they refer to (and therefore denote) the same person:[64]

(6.2.1) the man who invented parking meters

(6.2.2) the man who invented Yo-Yos.

Sense is a property of emic expressions, i.e. of abstract categories, and it is therefore an abstract property. Suppose you were asked, as a grammatical exercise, to translate the English NP *the prime minister* into another language; what is wanted is that you translate the sense as best you can, and it is unnecessary to have any particular individual in mind who satisfies the description 'the prime minister'; thus the translation into Polish might be *pierwszy minister*, into Hungarian *a miniszterelnök*, into Hebrew *rosh hamemshalah* – each of these bears the sense of the English NP *the prime minister*. The sense of a language expression E_o from object language L can only be given in terms of some other language expression E_m from the same, or from a different, language. That is why in the discussion above we have paraphrased the sense of the English NP *the prime minister* $(= E_o)$ as the metalanguage expression E_m "the chief minister within the national parliament" or we have translated it e.g. in terms of the Hebrew language expression "rosh hamemshalah" $(= E_m)$.

Sense is a property of the emic language expression. All language expressions except proper names have sense. The sense of an expression is commonly asked for in the question: *What is the meaning of 'E'?*, e.g.

(6.2.3) What is the meaning of 'trypanosoma'?

However, similar questioning of the meaning of proper names jars one's intuitions, because there is no satisfactory answer; cf.

(6.2.4) What is the meaning of 'Cedric'?

(6.2.5) What is the meaning of 'Colin'?

Both these questions are likely to receive the same answer:

(6.2.6) It's a boy's or a man's name.

(6.2.6) does not in fact answer the questions posed in (6.2.4-5): if it did, then one would have to accept that *Cedric* and *Colin* mean the same, which also jars one's intuitions – consider how odd it would be to agree that *It is a true fact about English that 'Cedric' means the same as 'Colin'*. (6.2.6) states what *Cedric* or *Colin* is, not what either of them means; i.e. it gives a classification, not a meaning; thus it is comparable with answering (6.2.3) with (6.2.7) instead of (6.2.8):

(6.2.7) It's a noun.

(6.2.8) A genus of parasite that causes sleeping sickness.

The reason for our difficulty with questions like (6.2.4-5) is that proper names like *Cedric* and *Colin* have no sense.[65] It may appear that there are vestiges of sense in such names, because – like the name *William Gladstone* – they could only be applied to males; something similar obtains with some other names, e.g. *Lake Victoria* could only be applied to a lake or *Mount Disappointment* to a hill or mountain. But consider what happens when we contrast a proper name such as *William Gladstone*, which either has no sense or only the putative sense "name for a male", with *the prime minister*, which has the sense "the chief minister within the national parliament". Anyone who satisfies the description 'the chief minister within the national parliament' can correctly be called 'the prime minister', and vice versa. But not everything which satisfies the description 'name for a male' will satisfy the description 'William Gladstone', or vice versa. Offering a full description for a certain 19th century British prime minister will not give the sense for the proper name William Gladstone, either, but only a description of one bearer of that name. Therefore we say that proper names do not have sense.

All language expressions other than proper names do have sense. Despite the fact that it is difficult to characterize the sense of many grammatical lexicon items such as the definite article *the*, the conjunction *and*, the present participle suffix *-ing*, the nominalizing suffix *-ness*, and so forth, their senses are given in the lexicon. In ch.2 we suggest a reason why the senses of such items are so difficult to express satisfactorily in the metalanguage.

1.6.3 The meaning of S's speech act

The principal aim for a theory of linguistic meaning is to explain the meaning of any utterance U uttered by speaker S to hearer H in context C – i.e. to account for the meaning of S's speech act. To achieve this, we have said in §1.2.1 that we shall model the steps neessary for H to determine what can reasonably be taken to be S's meaning in U. In rough outline, the steps necessary are the following.

(i)   Recognition of S's utterance act, i.e. that S makes an utterance U in language L to H in context C. The principal basis for this is brute perception.

(ii) Recognition that U consists of a sentence Σ spoken with prosody Φ in L, and of the sense or senses of this locution ΦΣ. This is based on the co-operative principle and H's knowledge of lexiconic, syntactic, and prosodic contributions to meaning.

(iii)   Recognition of S's denotational act – i.e. what S is using the
        locution $\Phi\Sigma$ to denote in W, the world spoken of – by recognizing
        what the referring expressions in $\Phi\Sigma$ refer to in W, and what the
        nonreferring expressions designate in W.

(iv)   Recognition of what S is doing in uttering U, i.e. the
        ILLOCUTIONARY POINT of his speech act: for instance, stating a
        fact or opinion, confirming or denying something, giving advice
        or permission, making a request, asking a question, issuing an
        order, making an offer or a promise, greeting, thanking,
        condoling, effecting a baptism, or declaring an umpire's decision.

The illocutionary point of S's speech act is sought through H's
presumptions about S's reason for uttering U in context C in the light
of various assumptions and presumptions of the co-operative principle,
knowledge of L and the use of L, facts about the context, and
background information of many kinds. This procedure is justified
because it is the aim of communication to bring about some effect in
people: more particularly, then, S's reason for speaking is that he
expects to affect H by bringing him to recognize the illocutionary point
of his speech act.

   In this chapter we have discussed the importance to utterance
meaning of the co-operative principle, of context, of lexicon items, of
syntax, of prosody, of sense, and of denotation but not the importance
of the knowledge of language use (pragmatics) or of background
information. Although their importance hardly needs demonstrating,
we might consider it in respect of interpreting the utterance in (6.3.1):

(6.3.1) I'm sure the cat likes you pulling its tail.

Let us assume this utterance is addressed to a child who is pulling the
cat's tail. Normally, then, S would be understood to be sarcastically
suggesting that H should stop pulling the cat's tail. Why is this so? Very
informally: it is part of our background knowledge that animals don't
like their tails pulled, and S must know this, therefore he is saying
something patently untrue, and presumably has some purpose in doing
so. It is part of our knowledge of language use (pragmatics) that people
say the opposite of what they mean in order to be sarcastic; it is quite
likely, therefore, that S is being sarcastic and really means "I'm sure
the cat does not like you pulling its tail"; in other words he is pointing
out that H is being unkind to the cat. In Anglo societies (among
others) being unkind to animals is frowned upon, it is generally thought
that people shouldn't do it. Therefore the illocutionary point of S's
speech act is to suggest to H that he should desist from pulling the cat's

tail. As speakers of English, S and H can both presume the other is privy to all kinds of background information: this mutual knowledge is often exploited by S in getting his meaning across, and it cannot be ignored in giving an account of linguistic meaning.

The steps through which we model H's reasoning of S's utterance meaning provide a loose framework for this book on linguistic meaning. The exception is step (i), because apart from §8.3.3 we have almost nothing more to say about utterance acts. Step (ii) provides us with three kinds of material: this arises from the fact that we view the sense or senses of the locution $\Phi\Sigma$ (sentence Σ spoken with prosody Φ) as compositionally derived from the senses of the constituent lexicon items in Σ, and the contribution from the prosody Φ. In ch.4 we deal with the senses of lexicon items and discuss what needs to go into the lexicon. In ch.5 we deal with theories of sentence meaning. And in ch.6 we discuss the prosodic contribution to meaning in English. Step (iii) raises the problem of matching the locution $\Phi\Sigma$ and its constituents to things in the world spoken of, W; some aspects of this problem are discussed in ch.7. Finally, step (iv) is dealt with at length in ch.8 on 'Speech acts'.

Chapter 2

What is meaning?

'Don't just stand there chattering to yourself like that,' Humpty
Dumpty said, looking at her for the first time, 'but tell me your name
and your business.'

'My *name* is Alice, but –'

'It's a stupid name enough!' Humpty Dumpty interrupted
impatiently. 'What does it mean?'

'Must a name mean something?' Alice asked doubtfully.

'Of course it must,' Humpty Dumpty said with a short laugh: my
name means the shape I am – a good handsome shape it is, too. With
a name like yours, you might be any shape, almost.'

(Lewis Carroll *Alice's Adventures in Wonderland* 1965:171)

2.1 Introduction

When we use a word to refer to an object, whether consciously or
unconsciously, we categorize that object together with others to
which we have applied and could apply the same term.
(Jeremy Anglin *Word, Object, and Conceptual Development* 1977:1)

In ch.2 we look for an answer to the question 'What is meaning?' by
considering various theories of meaning that have been proposed over
the centuries. We look at these theories with the particular aim of
extracting from them, if possible, a characterization of the property of
meaning that we can use within our own conception of a theory of
meaning. Anyone capable of reading this book knows (in some
fashion) what meaning is; and I have relied on this pretheoretical
knowledge in our discussion so far, and will continue to rely heavily
upon it while trying to specify, for the utilitarian purpose of
establishing a theory of linguistic meaning, just what this knowledge is
knowledge of. In §1.6 we distinguished three kinds of meaning: sense,

the property of meaning in abstract categories such as sentence, lexeme, morpheme; denotation, the use of sense in speaking of some particular world – i.e. the people, things, places, events, states, etc. within it; and utterance meaning, what hearer H rationally determines that speaker S intends his meaning to convey. In our discussion in §1.6 we said that a description of utterance meaning properly includes a description of denotation; and that a description of denotation properly includes a description of sense. This leads to the conclusion that sense is the common basis for determining other kinds of meaning; in other words our question 'What is meaning?' should be pared back to: 'What is sense?' In §1.6 it was said that the sense of an expression E_o of the object language L_o is translated into an expression E_m of some other language L_m which, for the purposes of establishing a theory of linguistic meaning, will be a metalanguage. This, of course, leaves open the question of what it is that is being translated. We have said that sense is an abstract property, but is there really no connexion whatsoever between this abstract property and what it is used to denote? In fact we find there is a connexion between a given sense of expression E and the salient characteristics of the prototypical denotatum for E.

2.2 Meaning as ostension

People all over the world teach meaning ostensively – i.e. by pointing to something in the setting and concomitantly uttering the name. The problem for H is to pick out which part of the setting is being indicated as the denotation of the language expression used; and so ostension works best when there is only one unknown, or when H has sufficient command of the language for the denotatum to be distinguished from a verbally specified field; thus, as Ludwig Wittgenstein put it: 'You must already be master of a language in order to understand ostensive definition' (*Philosophical Investigations* 1963:33). This implies that one must already know the meanings of at least some expressions in order to learn a new one ostensively; ergo, not all meanings can be learned ostensively. Furthermore, there are many expressions whose denotation cannot be indicated ostensively, e.g. *and*, *because*, *know*, *morpheme*, *the*, *the woman any son I should have might marry*, *all the riches of the Egyptian Pharaohs*.

Teaching or learning meaning ostensively is one thing, but can we make any sense of the hypothesis that meaning IS ostension? The proposition 'meaning is ostension' must be interpreted as (2.1),

(2.1) "The meaning of an expression E is its ostension (= the picking out) of a denotatum D in world W"

It should be immediately obvious in (2.1) the meaning of E cannot be understood as "the sense of E" if (2.1) is to be coherent; it must be interpreted "the denotation of E". Consequently (2.1) turns out to be the trivially true statement "the denotation of E is its ostension of a denotatum D in W". This tells us nothing about what sense is, nor even about S's using the sense of E in order to denote D in W; and so the hypothesis that meaning is ostension explains nothing about the nature of meaning.

2.3 Meaning as use

For a *large* class of cases – though not for all – in which we employ the word "meaning" it can be defined thus: the meaning of a word is its use in the language.
(Ludwig Wittgenstein *Philosophical Investigations* 1963:43)

The meaning of a word or combination of words is [. . .] determined by the set of rules which regulate their use.
(Moritz Schlick 'Meaning and verification' 1949:147)

There are two ways in which the meaning of a new word can be revealed by whomever coins it: in scientific or academic circles it may be formally defined; this is, however, an extremely rare procedure in ordinary language use where S commonly leaves H to figure out the meaning from context. Moreover, the meaning ascribed to a word by its use in particular contexts will take precedence over any formal definition of meaning which fails to be confirmed by usage. For example, in *An Outline of English Structure* 1951:53, George Trager & Henry Smith defined *morpheme* as the recurrent combinations of phonemes displaying regular patterns of distribution; but this meaning definition has given way to another, based on the way the word *morpheme* is actually used, i.e. to denote the smallest individually meaningful elements of sentences (cf. Charles Hockett *A Course in Modern Linguistics* 1958:123). Despite the fact that formal definitions of e.g. *word* and *sentence* have never been satisfactorily stated, English speakers know what these expressions mean by virtue of the way they are used. And finally, it should be obvious that the assignment of meaning by ordinary use is phylogenetically and ontogenetically prior to defined meaning: typically a child acquires the meanings of expressions from the way they are used by the people around him, and through other people's responses to his own use of them. On this evidence there seems little doubt that the meaning of a word is governed by its use.

It seems that use directly determines word meanings, but not the meanings of whole sentences. This is because there is, theoretically, an infinite number of sentences in any natural language L (cf. Noam Chomsky *Syntactic Structures* 1957:15) so that there will be sentences of L which have never been used by speakers of L, and whose meaning, therefore, cannot possibly have been directly determined by use. Certainly it is the case that individuals can both produce and understand meaningful sentences they have never before used nor heard used. It is impossible that the meanings of whole sentences should be directly determined by use and also unnecessary, if the meanings of their constituent lexicon items[1] (the number of which is finite) together with the (finite) set of rules for combining these into the meanings for sentences are determined by use. Thus, although no speaker could literally utter *I have just been decapitated* and its meaning could be said not to be directly determined by use, it is nevertheless indirectly determined by use (contra Jerry Fodor and Jerrold Katz *The Structure of Language* 1964:15) in the sense that the meanings of its constituent words and of the rules for combining these into the meaning of the whole sentence ARE determined by use.

In 'Literal meaning and logical theory' 1981:210 Jerrold Katz mistakenly says: 'the use theory is forced to predict that obscene words and their nonobscene medical synonyms – which have very different uses – are different in meaning.' But undoubtedly they are different in meaning! To generalize, the meanings of pairs of stylistically complementary words or phrases such as *faeces* and *shit*, *violin* and *fiddle*, *the woman who bore me* and *my mum* overlap, but they are significantly different in ways determined by the contexts (i.e. the worlds) in which they are used. On the same page Katz writes: 'Again, since almost every word has ironic as well as literal uses, the use theory is forced to predict that all ordinary words like "beautiful", "happy", "clever", etc. are ambiguous between their customary sense and the sense of their antonym'. This blandly assumes that people do not recognize and allow for different kinds of use: literal, figurative, ironic, playful,[2] pretentious, shocking, and so forth. We conclude that Katz's objections to the hypothesis that use determines meaning cannot be sustained.

To say that the meaning of a word (defined as above) is determined by its use, is not to say that the meaning of a word IS its use. As we noted earlier, the meaning of a word can be given by definition before the word is used – though it is usage which will determine whether that definition stands or falls. In any case, it is absurd to seriously hold that the meaning of a word is equivalent to its use just because the meaning is determined by its use. First consider an analogy: the value of a $1 bill is determined by its use as a legal tender (how much it buys); but it would be absurd to say either 'the value of a $1 bill is equivalent to its use as legal tender' or 'the value of a $1 bill is equivalent to what it will buy' rather than 'the value of a $1 bill is equivalent to 100¢'. Turning to a language example: suppose we determine from its use that one meaning of *grass* is "marijuana"; it would be absurd to say 'the meaning of *grass* is equivalent to its use denoting marijuana'; rather we leave out all reference to use and say directly 'the meaning of *grass* is "marijuana" ', where "marijuana" is a metalanguage expression. We therefore conclude that Wittgenstein was wrong when he said that 'the meaning of a word is its use in the language'.

2.4 Meaning as conditions on truth

> A statement is held to be literally meaningful if and only if it is either analytic or empirically verifiable.
> (Alfred J. Ayer *Language, Truth and Logic* 1946:9)

> To give truth conditions is a way of giving the meaning of a sentence.
> (Donald Davidson 'Truth and meaning' 1971:456)

The proposition that use determines meaning presupposes that any language expression E which occurs in utterance U will normally be used appropriately. It follows that a statement of the conditions under which E is used should yield a definition of E's meaning. There are two schools of language philosophy which have adopted this approach to the definition of meaning: verificationism and truth conditional semantics.

Verificationism was a product of an empirically orientated philosophical movement of the 1920s-40s called logical positivism which sought to put philosophy on a "scientific" basis by recourse to procedures for the empirical, observational, verification of statements.[3] Verificationists hold that the literal meaning of a statement is given by defining the method for observationally verifying the conditions under which the sentence expressing that statement is used. E.g. the meaning of a sentence *My brother is bald* is defined by a set of statements (Ayer

1946:11 calls them 'observation-statements') which express the means for observationally verifying that S has a brother and that S's brother is, at the time of utterance, bald. Ayer hints at practical difficulties with verificationism when he admits (Ayer 1946:12f) that sometimes the observation-statements defining the meaning of a sentence will be infinite in number. This is one of a number of flaws that render verificationism impossible to accept as a linguistic theory of meaning. Another is that verificationism treats only the meanings of declarative sentences which make statements; it would have to be extended to assign meanings to declarative sentences which do other things such as make promises, express thanks, pass verdicts, or execute legally binding acts. The theory would also need to be extended in order to define the meanings of imperative and interrogative sentences. A statement is only verifiable within the terms of the theory if it can be observed to be true in the world: this severely empiricist constraint creates difficulties with figurative expressions which necessarily fall outside the scope of the theory, so that meanings cannot be defined for them. Furthermore any statement unverifiable by observation such as *My toothbrush was dancing with Linda Ronstadt* or even *I think that I dreamt that my toothbrush was dancing with Linda Ronstadt* would be judged meaningless – which they are not, as readers can judge for themselves. Surely, the conditions under which a sentence is used can only be verified after we know (or think we know) the sense of the sentence. E.g. we can only recognize the means for observationally verifying the conditions which define the meaning of *My brother is bald* by virtue of the fact that we know its sense, and on this basis can proceed to match its sense with appropriate denotata in the world spoken of.

We conclude that, at best, verificationism offers one way of verifying the denotation of some sentences in language L provided their sense is known; but it has nothing to say about sense, and therefore nothing to say about the relationship between sense and denotation. Nor does verificationism offer any insights into the compositionality of meaning, viz. how the meanings of words are combined into meanings for sentences.

In 'Truth and meaning' 1971:456 Donald Davidson wrote: 'to give truth conditions is a way of giving the meaning of a sentence'. What Davidson suggests is that to know the meaning of a sentence such as, e.g. (2.4.1), is to know the conditions under which the assertion S makes with it would be true. These conditions are conventionally expressed as in (2.4.2), which is interpreted in (2.4.3):

(2.4.1) Gaius Julius Caesar did not die in his bed.

(2.4.2) *Gaius Julius Caesar did not die in his bed* is true if and only if Gaius Julius Caesar did not die in his bed.

(2.4.3) The object language sentence (2.4.1) [i.e. *Gaius Julius Caesar did not die in his bed*] is true if and only if [speaking metalingusitically now] it is true in the world spoken of that the person named Gaius Julius Caesar did not in fact die in bed.

As Davidson says in respect of another sentence (cf. 'Reply to Foster' 1976:37), (2.4.2) can be rephrased as (2.4.2'):

(2.4.2') *Gaius Julius Caesar did not die in his bed* means that "Gaius Julius Caesar did not die in his bed".

Because truth conditional semantics is founded on the giving of truth conditions instead of upon the means of observationally verifying the truth of the (statements made in the) sentence, it can be regarded as a refinement, a simplification, and an extension of one of the basic concepts underlying verificationism. Davidson has been optimistic about the extension of truth conditions to sentences other than those that make statements, cf. 'Radical interpretation' 1973:320; and truth conditional semantics does recognize the compositionality of sentence meaning. But even with these advantages over verificationism, truth conditional semantics is essentially a theory of denotation that has nothing to say about sense.

Truth is applicable to worlds. E.g. the truth of *My brother wasn't bald then* will be contingent on S having a brother, and on the time referred to as 'then' in whatever world is spoken of. A speaker in Boston, Massachusetts may say *It is 8 p.m. Wednesday 21 October here* but for the hearer on the phone to him in Melbourne, Australia it would be *10 a.m. Thursday 22 October*: so truth is contingent on place, too. So generalizing the formula introduced in (2.4.2) we get

(2.4.4) Σ as uttered in L_0 by S to H in C_i is true if and only if p is true in world W_i.

Where 'Σ' is the name of the sentence in the object language, and 'p' is the proposition that holds in the particular world spoken of, W_i. Obviously, p identifies the denotation of Σ, but how can the two be correlated? Take the following:

(2.4.5) *A miniszterelnök jobbkezes* (as uttered in Hungarian by S to H in C_i) is true if and only if Mrs Thatcher is right-handed.

Since Σ in (2.4.5) translates "the prime minister is right-handed", and since we might legitimately suppose that S is using the noun phrase 'a miniszterelnök' to refer to Mrs Thatcher in C_i, it would seem that (2.4.5) satisfied the formula in (2.4.4) and permits the Davidsonian paraphrase

(2.4.6) *A miniszterelnök jobbkezes* (as uttered in Hungarian by S to H in C_i) means that "Mrs Thatcher is right-handed".

Although the formula for the giving of truth conditions licenses this quite correct conclusion about the denotation of 'a miniszterelnök jobbkezes' it tells us nothing about the sense of that sentence. Indeed, this is the import of Davidson's predicate 'means that' (= "denotes that"): contrast the use of 'means that' in (2.4.2′) and (2.4.6) with 'means' (= "has the sense") in

(2.4.7) *A ministerelnök jobkazes* means "the prime minister is right-handed".

Thus, truth conditional semantics leaves the question 'What is sense?' unanswered; and since it has nothing to say about sense, truth conditional semantics leaves the relationship between sense and denotation a mystery.

2.5 Meaning as speaker's stimulus and hearer's response

The *meaning* of a linguistic form [is] the situation in which the speaker utters it and the response which it calls forth in the hearer.
(Leonard Bloomfield *Language* 1933:139)

With the growing status of "science" in the early 20th century, the human sciences, including linguistics, began trying to change their image of subjective speculativeness and assumed an objective empiricism thought to be characteristic of the natural sciences. The foremost advocate of the "scientific" or "mechanistic" approach to linguistics was Leonard Bloomfield; and his 'A set of postulates for the science of language' 1926 provided a charter for American structural linguistics, that survived until the Chomsky revolution 30 years later. Bloomfield proclaimed linguistics an empirical science, and maintained that objectivity in examining linguistic data can be safeguarded by the careful delimitation of the aims of enquiry, and a description of the procedures for analysis, followed by a statement of the results. There was also the requirement that all statements about language should be "vulnerable", i.e. open to verification or disproof. The lengths to which Bloomfield would go in defining his metalanguage for linguistic descriptions can be illustrated from 'A set of postulates' 1926 by Definition 5: 'That which is alike will be called SAME. That which is not the same is DIFFERENT'. In the early 1920s Bloomfield was converted to a belief in behaviourist psychology, and this strongly influenced his thinking about language processes. Behaviourism holds that language behaviour is a response (perhaps a mediated response) to some kind of observable (empirically verifiable) stimulus; so it is known as stimulus-response or *S-R* theory.[4] The theory holds that since behaviour is the result of learned responses to the environment, if we knew enough about the external stimuli on a person, and how he has learned to respond to previous stimuli, we could predict his language and behaviour in a given situation.

> Human conduct, including speech, [. . .] is part of cause and effect sequences exactly like those which we observe, say, in the study of physics or chemistry. [. . .] We could foretell a person's actions (for instance, whether a certain stimulus will lead him to speak, and, if so, the exact words he will utter), only if we knew the exact structure of his body at the moment, or what comes to the same thing, if we knew the exact structure of his organism at some early stage – say at birth or before – and then had a record of every change in that organism, including every stimulus that had ever affected the organism.
>
> (Bloomfield 1933:33)

It is against this background that we should understand Bloomfield's theory of meaning as speaker's stimulus and hearer's response; and his belief that such a theory provides observable, empirically verifiable criteria for the analysis of meaning.

Bloomfield 1933:139 defined meaning as follows: 'The *meaning* of a linguistic form [is] the situation in which the speaker utters it and the response which it calls forth in the hearer.' He went on to comment: 'the speaker's situation will usually present a simpler aspect than the hearer's response; therefore we usually discuss and define meanings in terms of a speaker's stimulus.' Earlier in the book Bloomfield identified the speaker's situation as providing the nonverbal stimulus S to speak, and the resulting utterance as his response r which provides the stimulus s for the hearer's observable nonverbal response R; i.e. Bloomfield postulates the following structure on speech acts:

Utterance of a language expression is seen both as a substitute for a nonverbal response R, and as a means of transferring the nonverbal stimulus on one person S to a nonverbal response in another person, H. This is illustrated by Bloomfield in the following story, into which his analytical structure is inserted.

(2.5.1) [S's situation: $S \rightarrow$] Jill is hungry. She sees an apple in a tree. [S's response to seeing the apple stimulates her to speak: r . . .] She makes a noise with her larynx, tongue, and lips. [This stimulates H to nonverbal response: $s \rightarrow R$] Jack vaults the fence, climbs the tree, takes the apple, brings it to Jill, and places it in her hand.

(Bloomfield 1933:22)

At first sight this might appear plausible, if a little rough-hewn; but on reflexion it is useless as a theory of meaning. What Bloomfield has given us is not a definition of meaning, but a statement that there are certain stimuli conditioning meaningful utterances. Since he suggests no method for itemizing these conditioning stimuli he has done no more than proclaim their existence – which is equivalent to making the general and uncontroversial claim that people are motivated to say what they do. Any attempt to itemize stimulus conditions would need to take into account many facts about S, e.g. his stored knowledge, psychological and physiological states, his sociological situation, the setting, the world spoken of. In addition there should be some way of assessing whether a stimulus is real or illusory. With all the external variables possible and the internal imponderables, stimulus conditions will not be adequately described or classifiable in the foreseeable future,[5] and so there is no theory of stimulus conditions to qualify them for use in Bloomfield's theory about meaning.

In (2.5.1) Bloomfield does not supply Jill's utterance, whose meaning the stimulus S identifies; but if his theory were correct any set of contextually appropriate utterances would be synonymous. However, when we start to list such utterances, we discover they need have few elements of meaning in common; cf.

(2.5.2)
    a. Look, there's an apple. I'm so hungry. Would you fetch it for me?
    b. I'm hungry.

c. I could just eat one of those apples!
d. You know I love apples, Jack.
e. I don't really like apples, but I'm so hungry. And I can't get one myself.
f. Hey honey, steal me an apple.
g. Bet you can't get me an apple with that wooden leg!
h. Ula ula ula ula. [Jill has a severe speech defect]

These sentences do not have the same meanings; indeed, (h) has no linguistic meaning at all and proves that Bloomfield's account of meaning is not constrained to language expressions. Since (a) through (h) do not have the same meaning, either Bloomfield's definition of meaning is at fault, or alternatively the sentences of (2.5.2) have different stimulus conditions (we could symbolize them S_a, S_b, . . ., S_h). Note that the only reason for drawing such a conclusion (momentarily leaving Bloomfield's hypothesis intact) is the recognition that there is a difference in meaning between each sentence of (2.5.2). If Bloomfield were correct, this recognition would be based on prior knowledge of the stimulus condition, i.e. S's 'situation' in each case. Obviously, this is untrue: we know the meanings of the sentences or utterances in (2.5.2) independently of knowing the stimulus conditions under which S utters them appropriately in a given context.

It should be obvious that a definition of meaning based on H's response would be no more successful than the one based on the S's stimulus. Perhaps the simplest demonstration is to suppose, say, that S commands *Shoot her!*, and consider some of H's possible responses: H might shoot S or himself, or throw his gun away, or burst into tears, or sing the national anthem, or do any number of things. There is no guarantee that H's response will correspond to what we know to be the meaning of the expressions used in the utterance. Indeed, the whole point of the kind of comedy illustrated by the story in (2.5.3) below plays on the difference between the meaning of an utterance, and the hearer's response to it; the comic effect would not exist if H's response constituted the meaning of the utterance.

(2.5.3)

Mrs. Rogers came into the kitchen. 'Good morning, Amelia Bedelia,' she said.

'Good morning', said Amelia Bedelia.

'I will have some cereal with my coffee this morning,' said Mrs. Rogers.

'All right,' said Amelia Bedelia.

Mrs Rogers went into the dining room. Amelia Bedelia got the

cereal. She put some in a cup, and she mixed Mrs. Rogers some
cereal with her coffee. She took it into the dining-room.

'Amelia Bedelia!' said Mrs. Rogers. 'What is this mess?'

'It's your cereal with coffee,' said Amelia Bedelia.

(Margaret Parish *Come Back, Amelia Bedelia* 1971:6-9)

Bloomfield was aware that the meaning of an expression should not
be defined on just one occasion of use, and recommended distinguishing those features common to all such situations; a recommendation
adopted in definitions of meaning by later structuralist grammarians.
E.g. 'The meaning of a linguistic form (a word, part of a word, or
combination of words) is the feature common to all situations in which
it is used' (Bernard Bloch & George L. Trager *Outline of Linguistic
Analysis* 1942:6). Note this has a Wittgensteinian flavour (cf. §2.2.3)
and, indeed, it may be treated as the reductio ad absurdum of the use
theory of meaning. The definition is not verifiable, because we can
never gain access to all situations in which an expression E is used. It
would only be possible to take a statistical sample of situations of use,
and this raises the question: How large a sample of situations in which
E is used does a speaker or hearer need to experience in order to know
the meaning of E? Before contemplating a method for answering this,
it is worth noting that the only means of access to any situations in
which E is used is E itself; and, furthermore, E is the only feature that
is indubitably common to all of the situations in which it is used.
Hence the Bloomfieldian definition of meaning spelled out by Bloch &
Trager is equivalent to the patent absurdity 'the meaning of E is E
itself'.

In conclusion, no matter how we try to come to grips with it,
Bloomfield's definition of meaning as S's stimulus and H's response is
unsatisfactory.[6]

2.6 Meanings as concepts: the ideational theory of meaning

Aristotle will not have been the first to remark that words are the
symbols of mental experiences (*On Interpretation* 16a, 3). John Locke
in his *An Essay Concerning Human Understanding* 1690 echoes
Aristotle, before going on to say that these mental experiences
constitute the meanings of words symbolizing them.

The use of Words, is to be sensible Marks of *Ideas*; and the *Ideas* they stand for, are their proper and immediate Signification.

¶2. [. . .] *Words in their primary or immediate Signification, stand for nothing, but the* Ideas *in the Mind of him that uses them*, [. . .]. When a Man speaks to another, it is, that he may be understood; and the end of Speech is, that those Sounds, as Marks, may make known his *Ideas* to the Hearer.

(Locke *Essay* III.ii.1-2. Emphasis here and in other quotations is from the original)

Thus, the ideational theory of meaning holds that meanings lie in the minds of S and H. 'Ideas' or 'internal Conceptions' (Essay III.i.2) are independent of words, but may be represented by words for the purposes of communication; and so they constitute word meanings. Language cannot be learned until a child has 'Ideas' or concepts of his own, and recognizes that they may correspond with the concepts others have, supposing '*their Words to be Marks of the* Ideas *in the Minds also of other Men, with whom they communicate*' (ibid. III.ii.4). Ideational meaning is private:

when he represents to himself other Men's *Ideas*, by some of his own, if he consent to give them the same Names, that other Men do, 'tis still to his own *Ideas*; to *Ideas that he has, and not to Ideas* that that he has not.

(Locke *Essay* III.ii.2)

Locke reckons that each individual has a slightly different concept corresponding to the word, and therefore a slightly different private meaning for it; which may well be true. However, he allows the common-sense presumption that people's concepts are alike, because their perceptions of the world we live in, and their abilities to reason, are broadly similar; so a considerable body of meaning is held in common. Language makes private concepts public; and if there is any difficulty over the meaning of a word, it can always be explained using 'several others, so that the meaning, or *Idea* it stands for, may be certainly known' (*Essay* III.iii.10).

Locke did not believe that all words represent concepts: 'Besides Words, which are names of *Ideas* in the Mind, there are a great many others that are made use of, to signify the *connexion* that the Mind gives to *Ideas, or Propositions, one with another*. [. . .] This it does several ways: as *Is*, and *Is not*, are the general marks of the Mind, affirming or denying' (*Essay* III.vii.1). He goes on to identify various sentence connectives or 'particles' that show 'restriction, distinction, opposition, emphasis, etc.' as well as connexion. Locke's reference to connectives here seems to have been moulded on Aristotle's category of 'σύνδεσμοι' [syndesmoi] which had roughly the same functions, cf. *Rhetoric* 1407a.[7] It is not clear what status these have in an ideational theory of meaning; but this uncertainty need not detain us, because there are more pressing problems with the ideational theory of meaning.

From the linguist's viewpoint it is not satisfactory to define meaning in terms of 'Ideas' or concepts, because it locates meaning in the psyche of the individual. Even if concepts could be made public so as to be postulated as meaning constituents for words, the linguist has an impossible problem trying to define them. For instance, suppose that the meaning of the lexeme "fishing" is defined in terms of the concept represented by the word *fishing*. What is this concept? Is it a boat full of men and nets on a stormy sea? A little girl netting a minnow? Hank Marvin playing a marlin? Caspar Milquetoast tying a fly? It could be any of these, or an infinite number of other scenarios. What they all have in common is "catching, or trying to catch, fish" – which is simply to give the sense of the word *fishing* by paraphrasing it. It may be objected that *fishing* corresponds to a complex concept; but everything said about *fishing* has its parallel when we consider the supposedly simpler concept represented by the word *human*. Is it male or female? Young or old? Dead or alive? Black, brown, yellow, or white? Trying to explain a concept other than by paraphrase involves all sorts of extraneous contextualization irrelevant to the statement of meaning. This is because we have been confusing the definition of concepts corresponding to lexemes with the images evoked by such lexemes. The only way that the concept represented by e.g. the word *human* has any relevance to linguistic analysis, is as the psychological correspondence to the language expression *human* and its synonyms. Whereas language expressions can be utilized in statements of meaning, their psychological correspondents cannot. Thus the ideational theory of meaning cannot function as a linguistic theory of meaning; and the hypothesis that meanings are concepts is of no use to us.

2.7 Meanings as abstract objects: a Platonist conception of meaning

The connexion H makes between a language expression and its denotation is an interesting epistemological matter and, obversely, so is the means S uses to choose the expression most appropriate to his intended denotatum. In *Letter VII*, Plato says that knowing and understanding e.g. the word *circle* and also what a circle is, is only partly gained through experience of circles: it only approximates to knowing the 'circle-itself' or what he calls the Form (ειδος) or Idea (ιδεα) of a circle. Platonic Forms, which exist for all objects, events, qualities, etc. are not sensible to mankind but exist in an immortal world separate from ours. Plato believed that a man may have access to the Forms through his immortal soul: 'The soul, then, being immortal, and having been born again many times, and having seen all things that exist, whether in this world or the world below, has knowledge of them all' (*Meno* § 81c). Thus, through his soul, a man may recollect the Forms of objects that he encounters, and so properly know those objects. Plato's theory of Forms offers a solution to the perennial puzzle posed by universals like *all circles*, or impossible objects like *a perfect circle*, or even the lexeme "circle" itself: how can we know the meanings of such expressions on the basis of having come across just a few instances of necessarily imperfect circles? Yet we do. If we are loath to accept Plato's metaphysical explanation, there are various updates on the machinery, but no one has offered a solution that is essentially different and at the same time satisfactory.

For the last decade, philosopher/semanticist Jerrold J. Katz has been moving towards Platonism, i.e. towards the view that language and its constituents, including meanings, are abstract objects that exist separately from S and H and from speech acts, cf. *Language and Other Abstract Objects* 1981. Katz's work is described in detail in ch. 5, and what concerns us here is just the notion of meanings as abstract objects. Katz is concerned only with meaning as 'sense' and not as 'denotation'; and in his semantic theory, he represents the sense of language expressions in terms of primitive semantic components that he calls 'semantic markers'. He then translates the sense of language expressions from the object language into his metalanguage 'semantic markerese' – which is quite similar to English. A semantic marker is intended to denote a class of equivalent concepts or ideas, and was first conceived in psychologistic terms as 'what is common to our individual ideas' (cf. 'Recent issues in semantic theory' 1967:129). However, in his book *Semantic Theory* 1972:38 Katz wrote that the concepts represented in semantic markers are not something that people have in mind on any one or any number of occasions: 'Concepts [. . .] are abstract entities. They do not belong to the conscious experience of anyone.' What Katz seems to intend here is that the content of semantic markers, i.e. the senses of language expressions, are abstract objects comparable with Platonic Forms.

In §1.4.2 we distinguished between pragmatic or etic categories such as utterance, lex, morph, phone, and abstract or emic categories such as sentence, lexeme, morpheme, phoneme. The abstract categories can be said to exist independently of S and H and the speech act. The notion of a language, such as English or Latin or Navajo is also an abstraction, an inductive generalization from spatio-temporally located phonetic or graphetic events. Saussure's notion of *langue*,[8] i.e. of a language as a social contract, presupposes that a language has existence independently of the individual S or H; and Chomsky's notion that a grammar of language L should model the ideal speaker-hearer's knowledge of L[9] presupposes L as the object of that knowledge, and hence that a language exists independently of S or H or a particular speech act. Thus there are many very important linguistic constructs other than meaning that are abstract objects existing independently of S and H and speech act. The question arises where it is these objects do exist. In *Language and Other Abstract Objects* 1981 Katz is at least as mysterious as Plato on that question, saying that they are atemporal and aspatial and exist outside the mind. However, he does not actually discuss whether and how these abstract objects exist independently of linguistic theory (which is where we find them). Plato believed that we apprehend the Forms through our immortal souls; according to Katz we apprehend abstract objects through intuition (cf. Katz 1981 ch.6) – the same way, he says, that we apprehend objects in mathematics and logic. Katz distinguishes the apprehension of (new) abstract objects through intuition from the apprehension of new information by introspection, perception or reasoning. The fact that abstract categories such as sentence, lexeme, morpheme and phoneme have always resisted necessary and sufficient definition in terms of etic categories (cf. Noam Chomsky Introduction to *The Logical Structure of Linguistic Theory* 1975:30-32) may be explained by the fact that their abstract nature puts them outside the bounds of brute perception, although they can be apprehended well enough by the intuition – and I would have thought through reasoning, too.

No matter how they are apprehended, senses are abstract objects – they are emic and their etic correspondents are denotations. Like other emic categories, sense by definition has no intrinsic form, so we represent sense by an expression in the metalanguage. This is all very well, it is in any case what we have done hitherto; however it does leave the general question 'What is meaning?' still to be answered in such a way as to reveal (if possible) the relationship between the sense of an expression and its denotation.

2.8   The naturalist hypothesis

> What's in a name? That which we call a rose
> By any other name would smell as sweet.
>> (William Shakespeare *Romeo and Juliet* II.ii.43)

One of the earliest and most persistent hypotheses about the nature of meaning is the naturalist hypothesis, which is that the form of a language expression, or, more precisely, a word,[10] somehow communicates the essential nature of whatever is denoted by it. Thus, the meaning of the word is the essence of the denotatum, as captured in the form of the word; i.e. the naturalist hypothesis presumes a natural connexion between the form and meaning of a word. To understand this point of view we shall first look at the way people conceive of the connexion between the form of a word and its denotatum.

Traditional semantics was almost exclusively concerned wth word-meaning, and the reason for this seems to have been the privileged status that words have as bearers of meaning. This privilege doubtless arises from the fact that words are mostly the names for objects, states, events, acts, actions, places, properties, quantities, and all the kinds of phenomena that human beings want to talk about. Words that don't name, e.g. conjunctions like *and*, *because*, *if*, the article *the*, etc. are relatively few in number. The fact that words typically name things, apparently leads to words being perceived as the semantic bricks used in building an utterance, i.e. as semantically homogeneous, but also as semantically and syntactically discrete: hence the physical independence given to individual words in our writing system, and, more significantly, Leonard Bloomfield's definition of the word as 'a minimum free form'.[11]

The psychological reality of the separate identity of individual words can be illustrated from two disparate sources. Firstly, Edward Sapir, one of the earliest investigators of North American Indian languages, observed the following:

> The native Indian, quite unaccustomed to the concept of the written word, has nevertheless no serious difficulty in dictating a text to a linguistic student word by word; he tends, of course, to run his words together as in actual speech, but if he is called to a halt and is made to understand what is desired, he can readily isolate the words as such, repeating them as units. He regularly refuses, on the other hand, to isolate the radical or grammatical element, on the ground that it 'makes no sense'.
>> (Edward Sapir *Language* 1921:33f)

It is interesting that Sapir attributes the ability to separate out the words of a language from both phrases and (bound) morphemes not only to the illiterate native speaker, but also to the investigating linguist – presupposing that words in any language have much the same characteristics. The second bit of evidence for the psychological reality of the separate identity of individual words is of quite a different and paradoxical kind, and can be found in studies of child language. When linguists speak of children using one, two, or three-word utterances as they progressively acquire language,[12], what they mean by 'word' is not necessarily the conventional orthographic word, but the smallest semantically homogeneous utterance constituent that is both semantically and syntactically discrete, e.g. in *allgone milk*, *allgone lettuce*, 'allgone' is reckoned as one word on these criteria.[13] The defining criteria for a word are known to the illiterate speaker, the literate speaker, and the sophisticated (psycho)linguist: knowing what a word is, is part of anyone's linguist competence. Stephen Ullmann relies on it when he writes: 'We can take [a] piece of connected speech and analyse it from the point of view of its content. *The smallest significant* unit isolated through this operation is the *word*' (*Words and Their Use* 1951:17, emphasis Ullmann's).

In modern linguistics it is common to find the morpheme defined as Ullmann has defined the word, e.g. Charles Hockett in *A Course in Modern Linguistics* 1958:123 says the morpheme is 'the smallest individually meaningful element in the utterances of a language.'[14] And of course Hockett is right from the linguist's viewpoint: Ullmann should have protected his definition by talking about the word as the smallest significant unit which is at the same time a free form.[15] However, it should be said in Ullmann's defense that he was not addressing linguists, but a lay public in whose minds the smallest significant language expression is – because of its semantic homogeneity and semantic and syntactic discreteness – the word.

Words can have a power that is denied to other language expressions. This is particularly true of proper names. In many societies people have had secret names, knowledge of which gives power over the name-bearer:[16] e.g. in Egyptian mythology, Isis gained power over the sun god Ra because she learned his name; and in the German folktale about the evil Rumpelstiltzkin, the discovery of his name destroyed the villain's power. In parts of ancient Greece the holy names of the gods were inscribed on tablets and sunk in the sea to avoid blasphemy. It was blasphemous to name the god of the Jews and his cohorts, thus his angel says to Manoah 'Why asketh thou after my name, seeing it is secret?' (*Judges* 13:18). The Jewish god's name was written without vowels *YHWH* but read out as 'adonai' meaning "lord" – a euphemism carried over into christianity. Euphemism is a standard means for combating the power of words. The ancient Greeks called the Furies 'the Graces' to avoid upsetting them. To avoid blasphemy the name of god is changed in such expletives as *'od's life, zounds, cripes, crust*, etc. *Disease* and *accident* were once euphemisms for sickness and misfortune respectively: *disease* was constructed from the prefix *dis-* (as in *disunited*) meaning "cease to be" and *ease* "comfortable"; accident derives from the Latin *accidens* "happening". Like other misfortunes, death is often spoken of euphemistically, e.g. *pass away* is used in place of *die*; and *undertaker* once meant "odd-job-man", and it was used euphemistically for the man who undertook to organize burial. Much of the language connected with human excretory functions and sexuality is subject to euphemism, cf. *go to the bathroom, go for a short walk, to proposition, sleep with*, etc. The *red and white meat* on a fowl were euphemisms in days when legs and breasts were not mentioned. The power of "four-letter words" like *piss* and *fuck* arises from the fact that their denotata are too controversial to mention in many circumstances, and the controversy extends to the words themselves. It is not unusual to hear someone say 'I hate that word' and sometimes 'I hate that phrase', but it is very rare to hear 'I hate that sentence'.

The power of words derives from the connexion between the words and the things they are used to denote. A word combines form with meaning: e.g. the sequence of phones [kʰ], [æ], [t] combines with the meaning "feline animal" into the word *cat*. People tend not to separate the form from the meaning of a word, and moreover they tend to associate the meaning of a word with its denotatum.

The father of modern linguistics, Ferdinand de Saussure, proclaimed as the first principle of linguistics that the correlation between the form of a language expression and its meaning is arbitrary, and conventional[17] – in the sense that everybody in a language community tacitly concurs in using a certain form with certain meanings, cf. *Course in General Linguistics* 1974:67. The notion is not a recent one, cf.

A word[18] signifies this or that by convention. No sound is by its nature a word, but only by becoming a symbol. Inarticulate noises such as are made by brute beasts may mean something: but no sounds of that kind are words. [. . .]
Every sentence has meaning, not as an instrument of nature, but – as we observed – by convention.

(Aristotle *On Interpretation* 16a, 30; 17a, 1)

This seems obvious enough: how does one explain that a canine animal is called *dog* in English, *chien* in French, *Hund* in German, *pies* in Polish, *ájá* in Yoruba, *kare* in Hausa, *mbwa* in Kiswahili, and so on and so forth, if there is supposedly a connexion between the meaning "canine animal" and the form of the word bearing that meaning?

Yet man seeks to explain many of the things that confront him in terms of causal relations.[19] If the form-meaning correlation in a word is arbitrary, any causal relationship between the form and meaning of a word is denied. It is understandable, therefore, that people have postulated a causal relationship between the two. Over the ages many scholars, as well as ordinary people, have believed that the original meaning of a word gave rise to its original form: hence the study of word-history was called 'etymology' meaning "the study of true form". Their belief embodies an hypothesis for the natural connexion between meaning and form, in which the form somehow communicates the essence of the denotatum in world W – often the real or natural world around us – and for this reason the hypothesis is known as the 'naturalist hypothesis'.

The naturalist hypothesis is worth considering since it is only by refuting it that we can be certain that word forms are correlated with their meanings on a purely arbitrary basis. I shall use as a vehicle for discussing naturalism Plato's *Cratylus*. Dating from around 385 BC this is the oldest extant European work on a linguistic topic. Plato's purpose was to question whether it is valid to study the natural world through discussion of the language denoting things in the world. Were the naturalist hypothesis correct, then a word would reveal the essence of its denotatum, so that the study of language would be as valid in the quest for knowledge about the natural world as a study of the world itself; on the other hand, if the conventionalist hypothesis is correct, then talking about the world cannot take the place of studying it directly through the physical sciences. So you see that Plato had a practical philosophical purpose in comparing the naturalist hypothesis with the conventionalist hypothesis for the correlation of the form and meaning of words.

The *Cratylus* is a Socratic dialogue. In the first part, Plato's mouthpiece Socrates (who does most of the talking) argues the naturalist hypothesis against the conventionalist Hermogenes (§§385-427). In the second part (§§428-440), Socrates refutes naturalism in discussion with Cratylus. I shall not stick rigidly to the text of the *Cratylus*, but take first of all the question of the origin of words and the diversity of languages; then examine the procedures for naturalist etymologies and the naturalist account of the supposed basis for the natural connexion between meaning and form; then finally consider the remnants of naturalism today, and its implications.

A problem for conventionalism is to explain how the original correlation between meaning and form – if they are arbitrary – became conventionalized. The naturalist explanation for the spread of words through the community is that people perceive the natural connexion between form and meaning. But who coined the original words? According to Socrates in the *Cratylus*, it was a wordsmith [νομοθέτης], a craftsman comparable with the blacksmith or the carpenter. It had to be a craftsman and not just anybody because 'a word is an instrument of teaching and for separating the natures of things signified, like the shuttle is an instrument for separating the threads in weaving'[20] (§388c). The wordsmith fashioned words from sounds in accordance with the natures of the things signified, just like the blacksmith forges tools from iron, or the carpenter shapes wood into a shuttle. If you are wondering how far back one has to go to find the original words, Socrates claimed that every language had its own wordsmith, and each wordsmith used different syllables and sounds to form the words, just as different pieces of iron are used by different blacksmiths to make the same kind of tool. This neatly accounts for the fact that different languages have different forms with the same meaning, as in our "dog" example above. But the notion of each language being invented by a wordsmith needs considerable revision in the light of present knowledge of the tangled web of relationships between languages.

Who were the wordsmiths? Under the naturalist hypothesis a wordsmith would have to understand the true essence of things in order to ply his craft. Since in Plato's view ordinary men are not capable of this (cf. his *Letter VII*, where Plato says that men have an idea what a thing is like, but cannot know its essential being, §342e), the wordsmith could be no ordinary man. Nor is he a god; because in *Cratylus* §439c Socrates shows that the wordsmiths are inconsistent and fallible; they cannot therefore be gods. So Plato leaves us no choice but to conclude that the wordsmith was a purely hypothetical construct, a "strawman" who couldn't have existed at all: therefore there has to be some other explanation for the origin of words.

We turn now to the etymological procedures used by naturalists. They sought a 'natural' connexion between meaning and form; but they did not go so far as pretending that a word duplicates its denotatum: obviously word and denotatum are completely distinct (cf. §432a-d). Nor was the word form thought to be a matter of sound-mimicry: otherwise words like *moo* and *cockadoodledoo* would 'name that which they imitate' (§423c). What a 'true' word-form must capture is the essence [οὐσίαν] of the denotatum. For instance, according to biblical legend the first man was named 'Adam' because he was created from the earth, which is called in Hebrew *adamah*. Although this demonstrates a 'natural' connexion between *Adam* and *adamah*, it leaves an important question unanswered: can the Hebrew form *adamah* be connected with the meaning "earth" in any natural way? This sort of question can be asked for each of Socrates' etymological analyses. They are extremely fanciful, with a cheerful disregard for the transposition of letters,[21] their omission, or insertion. Socrates' excuse (like that of the etymologists who followed him) was that 'the original names have been completely buried by those who wished to dress them up for they have added and substracted letters for the sake of euphony, and distorted the words in every way for ornamentation, or merely with the passing of time' (§414c). Let's take just two examples from *Cratylus*. According to Socrates the name of the god of Bacchanalia, *Dionysos*, derives from *didous ton oinon* meaning "giver of wine" (§406c); this would be very appropriate but it is a mystery how the three-word phrase was pared down in the one-word name. Greater imagination still is required to explain the collapse of *anathrōn ha opōpe* "looks up to see" into *anthrōpos* "man" (§399c). Such proposals are to be taken seriously, Socrates was not simply poking fun at naturalist etymologies: consider the etymologies constructed for two Latin words by Marcus Terentius Varro around 45BC.

> *Cervi* "stags" because they *gerunt* "carry" big horns derives from
> **gervi* "?carriers"; the word has changed G to C as has happened in
> so many words. [. . .] *Volpes* "fox" [is so-called] because it *volat*
> "flies" with its *pedes* "feet".
>
> (Varro *De Lingua Latina* V, 101)

Although Varro was a very learned man, both these etymologies are inaccurate in fact. In the first it is claimed that the verb *gerere* "carry" gave rise to the plural noun **gervi*, although in fact no such noun existed;[22] nor was there any systematic unvoicing of initial stops. The second example seductively claims that *volpes* is a blend of *volare* "fly" and *pes* "foot"; i.e. the fox is hypothetically described as "fleet-foot". Etymologies of this sort flourished in ancient and medieval times, and decreasingly through to the 19th century.

Where the etymologist could not come up with any other explanation, he could always claim that the word under analysis is of foreign origin, and its etymology could only be given in terms of its language of origin, cf. *Cratylus* §409d-e.[23] Thus, the naturalist gave his imagination free rein to etymologize without any kind of restraint. The method of analysis was:

(i) describe the denotatum of the word under analysis;
(ii) cast around for an appropriate phrase that bears some resemblance to the description, and which has a form bearing some resemblance to the word under analysis;
(iii) if this fails, the word must be of foreign origin and therefore unanalyzable.

Such fanciful procedures brought etymology into disrepute until more rigorous methods were adopted by 19th century philologists.

Most of the etymological investigation undertaken by Socrates in *Cratylus* is analyzing words (however fancifully) into a combination of semantic components that he called 'primary words' and which we might sometimes be inclined to think of as the precursors of morphemes, cf. the derivation of *Adam* from *adamah*, or of *volpes* from *vol*[*are*] + *pes*. The problem is to show a natural connexion between the forms of the primary words and their meanings. But all that naturalism can offer is that primary words are constructed on the basis of sound symbolism: viz. the whole edifice of the naturalist hypothesis rests on sound symbolism. Plato's degree of confidence in these foundations is indicated by Socrates' well-justified comment: 'I think my notions about the primary words are quite outrageous and ridiculous, though I have no objection to imparting them to you if you like, and I hope that if you can think of anything better you will tell me' (§426b). Sound symbolism is language specific and conventional, not natural. E.g. onomatopoeic words,[24] which supposedly mimic natural sounds, differ from language to language and obey the phonological conventions of the language in which they occur: cf. English *cockadoodledoo*, French *cocorico*, German *kikeriki*, Japanese *kokekokko*; and compare English *clang* with Tzeltal[25] *ĉan*, English *chip* with Tzeltal *ĉehp*, *screech* with *kiĉ*', and so forth. Languages have phonesthetic[26] networks which differ from language to language: e.g. the English words *flail*, *flame*, *flap*, *flare*, *flash*, *flay*, *flee*, *flick*, *fling*, *flit*, *flood*, *flop*, *flounce*, *flourish*, *flush*, *fly* have the common consonantal onset 'fl-' and all suggest sudden or violent movement; *bash*, *clash*, *crash*, *dash*, *flash*, *gash*, *lash*, *mash*, *slash*, *smash*, *thrash* have the common rhyme '-ash' and all involve violent impact. According to Socrates, naturalism is founded on something like phonesthesia; consider such postulates as the following: *r* represents motion (e.g. *rhein*, *rhoē* "flow", *tromos* "trembling", *trachys* "rugged"); *s* and other fricatives are pronounced with 'great expenditure of breath [. . . and] imitate what is windy' (e.g. *physōthes* "windy", *seiesthai* "to be shaken", *seismos* "shock", *zeon* "seething", *psychron* "shivering"); *l* has a liquid movement in which the tongue glides and expresses smoothness (e.g. *leia*, "level", *oliothanein* "glide, slip", *liparon*, "sleek", cf. §§426d-427b). But individual phonemes or letters are not consistently used in a particular sense. E.g. the word *smooth* has fricatives at either end, but it doesn't indicate something 'windy'; *lollop, laugh, hall,* and *toll* contain 'l' but no sense of 'smoothness' or 'slipperiness'; the 'r' in *rust, rot,* and *round* has nothing to do with motion; the 'fl' in *flint, flock* and *flower* brings no sense of sudden or violent movement to these words; nor do *ash, cash, sash* involve violent impact. Indeed, when arguing against naturalism in §§434e-435c of the *Cratylus*, Socrates himself cites counterexamples like these to force the conclusion that the form–meaning correlation in a word must be conventional and arbitrary – since it does not matter what the form of a word is, if its meaning is 'sanctioned by custom and convention'.

Nowadays, controversies over the earlier forms of words are generally left to experts trained in historical and comparative linguistics; but even today, there is a strong body of public opinion that the proper meaning of a word is the original meaning. This is revealed in school textbooks and frequent letters to newspaper editors asserting that the new meanings for words are 'misuses'. This is the view expressed in the following remarks about the English word *nice*.

> **nice** This word is very much overworked and misused. Its real meaning is *precise, exact,* and *delicately fine*; e.g.
> A nice difference in meaning.
> A nice ear for music.
> The word is now often used to mean *agreeable, delightful, pleasant,* etc. – because it is easier to say *nice* than to think of a more suitable word.
> (Walter Wright *A First English Companion* 1978:91)

It would be interesting to know why Wright believes it is 'easier' to think of *nice* than of some other word, and whether 'easier' implies greater communicative efficiency – but these wonderings are strictly beside the point. Regrettably, Wright's remarks about *nice* demonstrate a woeful ignorance. Today, the 'real meaning' of *nice* includes "agreeable", "delightful", "pleasant" just as much as (and arguably more than) it includes "precise", "exact", and "delicately fine" which were its 17th and 18th century meanings and are a shade archaic today.

English *nice* derives from Latin *nescius* "ignorant", and we can trace a path through its earlier senses to its present meaning:

> 14th & 15th centuries: "stupid", foolish", "foppish › 17th & 18th
> centuries: "fastidious", "precise" › 18th & 19th centuries:
> "balanced", "agreeable" › 20th century: "pleasant", "pleasing".

To speak of one or more of the earlier meanings being the 'real' meaning of *nice* is absurd. It suggests that the current meaning is in some way degenerate. The degeneracy of contemporary language is, in fact, a recurrent theme in the naturalist tradition, because the naturalist hypothesis leads to a belief that the original word bore the proper form and proper meaning, therefore any subsequent change is a degeneration from the perfectly natural original form (that should be halted or preferably reversed). However, it is fair to ask the naturalist for evidence that the original language (or the original form of his language) was a better instrument of communication than the language of today, or, indeed, of another time in recorded history. The answer is, of course, that there is none.

With Plato's help, we have seen that the naturalist hypothesis will not stand scrutiny: the forms of words do not capture the essence of their denotata; in fact there is no natural connexion between the form of a word and its meaning. Instead we embrace the view that the form–meaning correlation is arbitrary, but it is also conventional – in the sense that everybody within a language community tacitly agrees to use certain forms with certain meanings. In consequence: 'There is nothing to stop things which are at present called *round* being called *straight*, and vice versa; and their stability would be in no way impaired if everyone made this transposition' (Plato *Letter VII* §343b).

However, our conclusion that the forms of words have no natural connexion with their denotata gives us no reason to assume that the senses of words are likewise arbitrary with respect to the denotata: in §2.9 we shall see that they are not.

2.9   Sense and the perceived characteristics of the denotatum

2.9.1   The relationship between the form of an expression, its sense, and its denotatum

Just as all men have not the same writing, so all men have not the

same speech sounds; but the mental experiences, which these
directly symbolize, are the same for all; as also are those things of
which our experiences are images.

(Aristotle *On Interpretation* 16a, 3)

This is Aristotle's way of saying that a language expression combines
form and sense, and is used to pick out a denotatum from W, the world
spoken of: e.g. the word *cat* combines the sequence of letters $c+a+t$
with the sense "feline animal" and is used to denote a cat. Others have
written of a 'semiotic triangle'[27] in which the relationship between form
and denotatum is mediated through sense; this is represented linearly
in (9.2.1):

(9.2.1) form $\leftrightarrow$ sense $\leftrightarrow$ denotatum

But proper names have no sense to mediate between form and
denotatum, cf. §1.6.2, so (9.2.1) cannot apply to them. Furthermore,
(9.2.1) suggests parity in the relationships between form and sense on
the one hand, and sense and denotatum on the other, although there is
none: the relation of form to sense is arbitrary and conventional,
whereas the relation of sense to denotatum is nonarbitrary – as we shall
see in §2.9. The relationship between form and denotatum is in reality
much more complicated than (9.2.1) or the 'semiotic triangle' suggests.
A better description of what is involved was made by certain scholastic
grammarians at the beginning of the 14th century,[28] and the
relationships they wrote of are presented schematically in Figure 2.1.
In Figure 2.1 the original Latin terms are given with a free translation,
and divisions are indicated between psychological, semantic, and
pragmatic areas of interest (divisions which owe nothing to the
medieval grammarians, of course). Figure 2.1 clearly shows that both
the form and the sense of a word are completely distinct from the
denotatum, and the only way to relate the word with its denotatum is
through some mental act. Details of this mental act lie outside the
scope of linguistic semantics; so we shall not be describing how, e.g.,
the denotatum of the word *cat* is recognized by H.[29] But we do assume,
of course, that if H knows the sense of the word *cat* he has the ability
to recognize what is denoted when S uses the word. In §2.9 we shall
show the reason why knowing the sense of an expression is a basis for
recognizing its denotation.

Saying that the sense of *cat* is "feline animal" or the sense of *open* is
"not shut" suggests that what we call the sense of an expression
describes what is common to typical denotata of that expression.[30] This
is not to say that the sense of an expression describes the denotatum

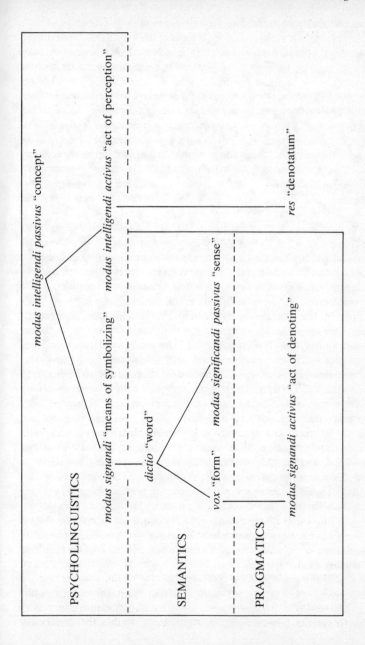

Figure 2.1 Relationships between form, sense and denotatum, based on the work of two early 14th century grammarians

(using the predicate 'describes' in its normal sense); rather we should say that, in giving the sense of an expression E, we usually refer to the characteristic properties common to the genus of things which E may properly be used to denote – or, to put it another way, characteristic properties of a prototypical denotatum; in consequence, to label an intended denotatum D with the expression E has the effect of ascribing certain properties to D as a function of E's sense. For example, if someone paints a design in blue and black and entitles it 'Cat' we look for the familiar characteristics of a feline animal upon the canvas. What we find will depend how abstract the design is – which is of no importance to the present discussion. The point of interest is what we look for in the painting on the basis of knowing the sense of the expression *cat*, and what we look for is certain properties in the intended denotatum.

Not all denotata can be apprehended through the senses (i.e. perceived) like a denotatum for *cat* can: for instance, the denotatum of an abstract entity such as a *phoneme* cannot be. Abstract entities are figments of the mind, they are concepts and never percepts. Conceptual prototypes for abstract entities exist in the mind along with the conceptual prototypes for concrete entities which have been constructed from data apprehended by the senses of sight, hearing, touch, etc. It is the characteristic properties of prototypes both for abstract and for concrete entities which are referred to in spelling out the senses of the language expressions denoting those entities. Consequently, it is the difficulty in finding properties characteristic of the denotata of words like *of* and *the* and bound morphemes like *-ness* which accounts for the problems we have in ascribing sense to them. We cannot do much but speculate on the correspondence between the sense of a language expression labelling an abstract entity and the characteristic properties of its abstract denotatum; but for a language expression labelling a concrete phenomenon, we can show that its sense does correspond to the perceived characteristics of its proto-typical denotatum. We shall consider evidence from children's acquisition of their first language, from experiments in which people are asked to name rather similar objects so that the criteria for using different names can be distinguished, from experiments in which the denotational scope of a word is studied, from the distribution of colour terms over the spectrum, from the use of noun classifiers in many languages, and from number marking in English. The discussion of noun classifiers and number marking is introduced to show that it is not only the sense of lexemes which is based upon the perceived characteristics of denotata, but also the sense of grammatical forms.

2.9.2 The overgeneralizations of very young children

It is characteristic of the language of very young children (between approximately one and two-and-a-half years old) to overgeneralize the sense of words, and so to use them with too wide a denotational scope. These extensions typically derive from perceived similarities in the denotata,[31] e.g. *doggie* might be used to denote a range of four-legged creatures such as dogs, cats, cows, and horses. As Eve Clark points out in 'What's in a word? On the child's acquisition of semantics in his first language' 1973:74 this is not because the child is unable to perceive the difference between the animals, but because he is not yet aware of the particular set of characteristics proper to the denotatum of *doggie*. Among many other examples, Clark 1973 lists the following overextensions by a variety of children: *bird* was used to denote sparrows, cows, dogs, cats, any animal moving (p. 79); *mool* [= *moon*] was used to denote the moon, cakes, round marks on a window, writing, round shapes in books, tooling on leather book covers, round postmarks, the letter *o* (p. 80); *bow-wow* was used to denote a dog, a fur piece with glass eyes, cuff links, pearl buttons, a bath thermometer (p. 80); *fly* was used to denote a fly, specks of dirt, dust, small insects generally, his toes, crumbs of bread, a toad (p. 81). For the most part, the perceptual connexion between the things denoted by the same word is an obvious one, such that for these examples, 'bird' has the sense "moving animal"; 'mool/moon' has the sense "round object"; 'bow-wow' seems to have the sense "bright, reflective and round" – presumably inspired by the dog's eyes; and 'fly' has the sense "small, disparaged object" (or something of the sort).[32] Children also undergeneralize the denotational scope of words; e.g. a child may recognize the denotata of *ketchup* and *lollipop* but not know they fall within the scope of *food*; or he may know the meaning of *ant*, *butterfly* and *starfish*, but not recognize that these fall within the denotational scope of *animal*, cf. Jeremy Anglin *Word, Object, and Conceptual Development* 1977:157. When the child has finally recognized just the appropriate perceived characteristics of the typical denotatum of a word as used by the rest of his language community, he will have grasped the conventional sense of the word, cf. Anglin 1977:230.

2.9.3 Perceiving

We have been speaking of the 'perceived characteristics' of a denotatum without, so far, explaining what we mean by an act of perception. Perception is a mental act or reflex using knowledge as a filtering device to categorize cues that typically come from phenomena (objects, states, events, acts, etc.) in the real world we live in; cues which have been mediated, therefore, through the senses of sight, touch, hearing, taste, and smell. In addition there are proprioceptions such as the sense of balance, the sense of danger, and bodily sensations like pain. Categorization is a matter of matching sense data with conceptual prototypes, cf. Michael Posner *Cognition* 1973. Data supplied to the senses by a phenomenon are not necessarily given the same categorization on different occasions or in different environments: e.g. a piece of ribbon beside a piece of string is saliently broad and flat; but beside a handkerchief it is saliently long and thin. Conversely, the same categorization can be made for different sets of data; for example a sprig of flowers and a kind of perfume can both be categorized as jasmine. It is this independence of phenomena from the perception of them, and yet their inaccessibility except through perception, that has troubled philosophers trying to determine the true nature of phenomena – certainly since the time of Descartes and Locke, and perhaps since the time of the Ancients, cf. Henry H. Price *Perception* 1932:19. We are not concerned with this philosophical problem, only with people's perceptions of phenomena and the consequences this has for the linguistic labelling of them, and with the correlation between the perceived characteristics of the phenomena and the senses (meanings) of those labelling expressions.

There are three significant aspects of categorizing sense data.[33] Perhaps the most important is the recognition or recurrence of pattern[34] in the sense data, giving them some structural organization. A very simple exemplification of this is the naming of astral constellations on a visual pattern, cf. the Great Bear, the Plough, the Southern Cross. When very young children overgeneralize a word like *doggie* to all four-legged animals, it is because they have recognized a distinctive configurational pattern; and although their categorization is not quite conventional, it is obviously being made on the basis of structural organization of sense data.

The recognition of some structural organization automatically sets up expectancies as to the nature of the phenomena being perceived: these expectancies constitute the second significant aspect of categorizing sense data. The expectancies result from a convergence of the sense data with some prototype concept or category stored in the memory, such that what is perceived is taken to be an instance of that category. Thus expectancies are based on past experience[35] and may override sense data in the process of perception, cf. K. Duncker 'The influence of past experience upon perceptual properties' 1939. Efficiency in perception is the reason for people jumping to conclusions on the basis of a partial recognition; most of the time, of course, their conclusions are correct, cf. Anglin 1977:156. During the course of an experiment on the recognition of incongruous playing cards – red spades, black hearts, etc. Jerome S. Bruner & Leo Postman ('On the perception of incongruity' 1949:212) report that 96% of the subjects made 'a "perceptual denial" of the incongruous elements in the stimulus pattern. Faced with a red six of spades, for example, a subject may report with considerable assurance, "the six of spades" or "the six of hearts" depending on whether he is color or form bound.[. . .] In both instances the perceptual resultant conforms with past expectations about the "normal" nature of playing cards.' In other words, the divergence of the sense data from the prototype concept or category is simply ignored; this kind of misperception is partly a result of the "couldn't believe my eyes" syndrome, and it is usually resolved by a longer look.

The third significant aspect of categorizing sense data is the availability of linguistic coding, backed by the knowledge of how to use it appropriately. The average English speaker faced with the set of symbols in (9.3.1) can identify it, describe it in conventional terms, and remember it without difficulty; but faced with the set in (9.3.2) he is in difficulty because there are no familiar names for the sense data.

(9.3.1) 2 3 6 8

(9.3.2) ٢ ٣ ٦ ٨

This is not to say that the average English speaker cannot perceive the Arabic numerals, but that his perception is qualitatively different from that of someone familiar with the sense data from these symbols, and with their conventional interpretations. It is generally the case that where the sense data are familiar there is a handy language expression to denote them; and the more familiar the phenomenon, the shorter and more convenient that expression will normally be, cf. Roger Brown & Eric Lenneberg 'Studies in linguistic relativity' 1959. So that, although a language label is not the sine qua non of categorization, there can be no doubt of its importance in the perceptual process.

All three aspects of categorizing sense data rely on a constancy in the relationship between phenomena and the properties perceived of them.

Wherever possible, the perceived properties of phenomena which are relevant to defining the sense (meaning) of language expression will be perceivable by more than one of the senses (sight, touch, hearing,

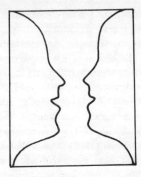

Figure 2.2   An ambiguous figure

etc.) alone. This is because the evidence of only one sense is unreliable, as the Ames distorted room proves (cf. Richard L. Gregory *Eye and Brain: the Psychology of Seeing* 1966, Magdalen D. Vernon *The Psychology of Perception* 1971); and, much more simply so does the ambiguous diagram in Figure 2.2, which may be seen as either two faces opposed to profile or as a candlestick. This ambiguity is the result of our only having visual data with which to perceive the phenomenon (tactile data will tell us only that Fig. 2.2 is on paper). Immediately, one perceives a problem with two dimensional representation: visual data is not necessarily adequate to decide the true configuration of the phenomenon represented; it is only adequate where the observer's knowledge of the conventions of perspective can be called on.[36] In Fig. 2.2 the conventions of perspective are entirely missing and the ambiguity of the picture cannot be resolved. If instead of a picture we had to deal with a similarly visually ambiguous three dimensional model, the ambiguity would disappear at a touch. Just after birth, a child's accretion of knowledge through perception is largely restricted to the processing of visual data; but as the child gets older, there is increasing exploratory handling of solid figures in the search for their intrinsic defining properties, cf. Eleanor Gibson *Principles of Perceptual Learning and Development* 1969:361. Under ordinary circumstances the tactile verification of visual cues about configuration is necessary for only an initial few instances. E.g. the visual data from the spherical configuration of a ball will be confirmed on a few occasions by handling it; and thereafter the sight of a ball can, if necessary, be correlated with the expectation of the tactile sensation of its sphericity and other visually perceived properties. Thus we learn the ability to predict the intrinsic properties of a phenomenon that has only been seen, by induction from our past experience of the same or similar phenomena. With unfamiliar objects there is a proven tendency for the contours to be visually scanned in emulation of tactile exploration (cf. Gibson 1969:55). In this way knowledge stimulated by the data from a single sense (commonly sight) is typically transformed, though not consciously, into projections about the nature, function, and behaviour of the perceived phenomenon in relation to its environment; this is such a normal experience that when it is thwarted unexpectedly we complain of being deluded. The general expectations aroused by uni-sensory cues are what was described earlier as the filtering of sense data through knowledge, and they lead from the sensory cues to a projection of the intrinsic defining properties of the phenomenon perceived from the prototype stored in memory; thus perception results from the identification of sense data via a conceptual prototype. But not all denotata are perceived directly through one or more of the senses of sight, touch, hearing, taste, smell, or proprioception: we also perceive things in the mind's eye as the result of some cognitive process like thinking, or imagining. These indirect perceptions – which would more properly be called conceptions – also arise from filtering data (some of it, at least, originating as sense data) through knowledge; and they also lead to projection of the intrinsic defining properties of the abstract entity conceived in the mind. However, we elected in §2.9.1 to leave expressions denoting abstract entities out of our discussion; so we shall sum up this section by saying that the defining properties projected from the prototype of a concrete phenomenon are the 'perceived characteristics of the denotatum' which, we claim, are referred to in giving the sense (meaning) of a language expression labelling that (perceivable) phenomenon. However, we shall refine this notion slightly in §2.9.10 in result of the discussion that follows.

2.9.4 What makes a cup a cup (rather than a mug)?

William Labov's 'Denotational structure' 1978 reports various kinds of labelling tasks involving the application of such labels as *cup*, *mug*, *bowl*, *glass*, *goblet*, and *vase* to line drawings of containers of different shapes and configurations; some of the pictures used are reproduced in Figure 2.3. Some subjects were asked to label a picture without any particular context being mentioned, or where it was to be imagined that someone was drinking coffee out of the container, or the container was full of mashed potatoes, or had soup in it, or the container was on a shelf with cut flowers in it. In some experiments containers were said

Figure 2.3 Pictures of containers used in some of the experiments reported in Labov 1978

to be made of a particular material such as china, glass, or aluminium. Sometimes subjects freely chose a label, and sometimes they were given a label and asked whether or not it could denote a particular container appropriately. These experiments leave no doubt that the decision to use one word rather than another in labelling a particular object is a matter of correlating the sense of the word chosen with the perceived characteristics of the object denoted by it. In the experiments reported by Labov, the decision is made on the following bases: (a) the shape and configuration of the container – proportion of height to width, whether or not the container is tapered, whether or not it has a handle; (b) the material from which the container is made; (c) the purpose to which the container is put; (d) where the container is located (cf. also Anglin 1977:252). Predictably, since we are discussing perceptually similar objects whose labels are correspondingly similar in sense, there were containers which attracted different labels, e.g. objects 7 and 10 in Fig. 2.3 could be called either *cup* or *mug* in a neutral context. On the other hand, objects 4 or 5 in Fig. 2.3 have characteristics close to those of the prototypical cup, and objects 8 or 11 are close to a prototypical mug. The prototypical object is an abstraction, a concept, with all the perceived characteristics of the typical denotatum to which we refer in spelling out the sense of the denoting expression. What this implies, of course, is that some denotata are closer to the conceptual prototype than others; i.e. some denotata correlate more closely with the sense of the denoting expression than other denotata. We turn to this matter next.

2.9.5 Prototypical denotata and fuzzy sets

In 'Category norms for verbal items in 56 categories' 1969 William Battig & William Montague report the following experiment given to 270 students from the University of Maryland and 172 from the University of Illinois: the subjects were given 56 category headings such as Colour, Vegetable, Fruit, Toy, Disease, Bird, Vehicle, for each of which they had to list as many examples as they could within 30 seconds. The resulting lists were then correlated according to the relative orders and frequencies of items listed. E.g. the first ten ranked under Vegetable are (1) carrot, (2) pea, (3) corn, (4) bean, (5) potato, (6) tomato [which was also ranked (15) under Fruit], (7) lettuce, (8) spinach, (9) asparagus, (10) broccoli. Such rankings will vary for sociolinguistically distinct populations of English speakers, cf. W.P. Brown 'A cross-national comparison of English-language category norms' 1978. For Battig & Montague's population *carrot* is the prototypical vegetable, *broccoli* is the tenth best instance of a vegetable, and so forth. *Garlic*, *leek*, and *black-eyed peas* were each listed by only one person, and must therefore be counted among the worst possible examples of a vegetable; but surely leeks would be rated higher in Wales, and black-eyed peas rated higher below the Mason-Dixon line. Nonetheless, Battig & Montague's findings tended to be confirmed by an experiment carried out by Eleanor Rosch on 113 summer school students at Berkeley. She selected six items ranked at intervals between the top and bottom of some of Battig & Montague categories and asked her subjects to rank them on a 7-point scale ranging between 'a good example' of the category, and a 'very poor' one, cf. 'The internal structure of perceptual and semantic categories' 1973. In general Rosch found the rankings correlate with those reported in Battig & Montague 1969; e.g. the kinds of Vegetable were ranked in the order carrot, asparagus, celery, onion, parsley, pickle in both reports. A warning note on the validity of such experiments is sounded by a discrepancy in the ranking of *cold* as a Disease in the two experiments: in Rosch 1973 it is ranked lowest among diseases, much lower than in Battig & Montague 1969. This discrepancy could have been caused by: (a) the number of people suffering from colds at the time of the experiment (for someone with a cold it would be a salient disease); and or (b) it could be that among Rosch's list of diseases – cancer, measles, malaria, muscular dystrophy, rheumatism, cold – *cold* is the mildest. Both experiments offer only crude measures of the relative saliency of terms within a conceptual field, and therefore of relative proximity to the category prototype. They can only confidently be held valid for the populations tested, and should not be projected for all English speakers.

In 'Hedges: a study in meaning criteria and the logic of fuzzy concepts' 1972, George Lakoff interprets such rankings in terms of membership within fuzzy sets. A fuzzy set is a class of objects with a continuum of grades of membership (cf. Lotfi Zadeh 'Fuzzy sets' 1965:338, also Zadeh, 1971, 1972). If we treat a category like Vegetable as a fuzzy set, then its members will manifest different degrees of membership in accordance with their ranking on, say, the Battig & Montague table. The grades of membership are assigned a quotient between zero and one. For instance, a sparrow is absolutely not a member of the category Vegetable, so we assign it a value 0. A carrot seems to be the best instance of a vegetable, so it should be assigned a value 1.[37] Using Battig & Montague's figures, and giving *carrot* a value of 1, asparagus as a value 0.43, celery 0.3, onion 0.14, parsley 0.04, and pickle only 0.006.[38] We can use these computations to compare the extent to which a *tomato* belongs to two different categories: in the fuzzy set Vegetable it has a value 0.68, and in the fuzzy set Fruit it has the value 0.14 – which shows just how much more of a vegetable than a fruit the tomato is in folk taxonomy. The reason for this is probably that a tomato is normally used like a vegetable, in salads and savory dishes, rather than for desserts like other fruits are.

2.9.6 The sense and denotation of basic colour terms

For some very convincing evidence that sense is determined by the perceived characteristics of the denotatum we turn to the semantic field of colour terms. The sense of colour terms can be compared against the perceptual field of colour, which is definable in terms of physical phenomena such as Munsell Color Chips, or by wavelength, degree of reflectance, etc. The standard work in this area is Brent Berlin & Paul Kay *Basic Color Terms: Their Universality and Evolution* 1969, which has recently been supplemented and corrected in significant respects by Paul Kay & Chad McDaniel 'The linguistic significance of the meanings of basic color terms' 1978. After postulating criteria for identifying basic colour terms (which will be given below), Berlin & Kay established for each of 20 languages what their basic colour terms are; then, using a patterned array of Munsell Color Chips,[39] they asked native-speakers to identify the best instance or 'focus' of each basic colour term in their language, and also to plot where its outer boundaries fall. The results of this investigation led them to postulate the following implicational universals for the evolution of colour terms. According to Berlin & Kay there are languages to exemplify every stage, and any increase in the number of basic colour terms among a few speakers will instantiate the next stage up in the hierarchy.

There is no language with just one colour term.

Stage I: All languages contain terms for white and black.
Stage II: A three term language also has a term for red.
Stage III: A four term language adds either a term for yellow or one for green (but not both).
Stage IV: A five term language has terms for both yellow and green.
Stage V: A six term language also has a term for blue.
Stage VI: A seven term language adds brown.
Stage VIII: If a language has eight or more terms then it has a term

for purple, pink, orange, grey, or some combination of these.

This thesis was checked against reports of colour vocabulary in a further 78 languages and examples of each stage are given, with discussion, in Berlin & Kay 1969. Let's consider their findings more closely.

We begin with the four criteria which Berlin & Kay 1969 postulate for a basic colour term: (i) consistency and relative simplicity of form; (ii) all basic terms should be of equivalent semantic status; (iii) they should be widely applicable; and (iv) be psychologically salient. We shall discuss 'these four criteria in turn. (i) A basic colour term is 'monolexemic', i.e. it consists of only one non-compound lexeme (cf. basic *blue* versus non-basic *lemon-coloured* or the *colour of rust*). There is a tendency for it to be monomorphemic or to consist of a colour-designating stem with inflexional, but not derivational, affixes (cf. basic *mw-eupe, ny-eupe, ch-eupe, vy-eupe*, etc., 'class prefix-white' in Kiswahili, but non-basic English *blu-ish*). Typically, basic colour terms in a language will have a consistent morphological structure, e.g. English basic colour terms are all monomorphic; those in the Amerindian language Nez Perce are mostly reduplicated, cf. *xayxayx* "black", *ʔilp'ilp* "red", *magsmags* "yellow", *ku·skú·s* "blue" (Berlin & Kay 1969:89). (ii) Basic colour terms all have equivalent semantic status in that no basic colour term is semantically included within another, e.g. *blue* and *red* are basic but *crimson* and *scarlet* (which are kinds of red) are not. (iii) A basic colour term should not be applicable to only a narrow class of objects, e.g. non-basic *auburn* is used only of hair, whereas basic *brown* can be applied to anything. (iv) A basic colour term should occur near the beginning of a list of colours elicited without cues; e.g. the eleven basic colour terms of English are listed as 1 - 10 and 12 in Battig & Montague 1969:10. Psychological saliency of this kind should be stable across idiolects and occasions of use. In addition to these positive criteria for basic terms, Berlin & Kay offer such caveats as that recent foreign loans are suspect, and so are terms for substances that instantiate the colour e.g. *gold, chocolate*, or *ash*.

These criteria for basic colour terms should generalize to the analysis of basic terms in other semantic fields.

To what extent do people agree on a best instance for a category? The field of colour is testing because adjacent colour categories appear to merge into each other, e.g. blue into green into yellow. In *Basic Color Terms* Berlin and Kay make a number of claims about the foci and boundaries of colour categories that have since been revised. On p.13 they state that the foci of basic colour terms in a particular language are remarkably consistent between speakers, and for the same speaker on different occasions. To conflict with this, their discussion of the Mayan language Tzeltal reveals that 31 out of 40 speakers located the focus of *yaš* as green, the other nine as blue (p.32).[40] Berlin & Berlin in 'Aguaruna color categories' 1975 and Kay in 'Synchronic variability and diachronic change in basic color terms' 1975 explain that such cases of multiple focus for a colour category indicate the transition between one stage of development and the next – in the case of Tzeltal from Stage IV to Stage V. This may be so, but what prompts the change? An answer is offered in Kay & Chad McDaniel's 'The linguistic significance of the meanings of basic color terms' 1978, which will be discussed below. Kay & McDaniel also argue that the boundaries of colour categories are as well-defined as their foci, contradicting Berlin & Kay 1969:13.

Berlin & Kay 1969:10 claim that *"the foci of basic color terms are similar in all languages* [emphasis theirs]." In her review of the book, Nancy Hickerson 1971 points out that this could be an effect of the fact that Berlin & Kay's subjects all lived in the San Francisco Bay area, all knew and used English, and therefore were influenced by a common colour system. In justification for her objection, she cites Lenneberg & Roberts' report in 'The language of experience' 1956 that monolingual Zuñi Amerindians have different colour categories and foci from bilinguals – whose colour system more closely approximates to English. Since then, Berlin & Berlin 1975:81 have shown comparable influence from Spanish on the colour system of the Aguaruna Jívaro. Why should language contact effect changes of this kind? Shortly, we shall consider a possible answer from Kay & McDaniel 1978.

A revision of the doctrine that the denotation of a basic colour term has a single focus (Berlin & Kay 1969:10) became necessary after Eleanor Heider ('Probabilities, sampling and ethnographic method: the case of Dani colour names' 1972) discovered that *mola* in the language of the Dugum Dani from Irian Jaya supposedly meaning "white" has a focus in or near English focal red. Berlin & Berlin 1975:84 suggest that *mola* really means something more like "warm-light", a composite category dominated by red. Red remains the dominant focus of the "warm" category when the achromatic white splits off in the transition to a Stage II language.

The venerable idea that correct naming is strongly influenced by our perception of the thing named is reinforced by the findings of Kay & McDaniel in 'The linguistic significance of the meanings of basic color terms' 1978. Kay & McDaniel show that a human being has a direct neurophysiological response to just four hues in the colour spectrum: RED, YELLOW, GREEN, and BLUE.[41] Unique hue points, corresponding to these four primary colours (as I shall call them), can be associated with wave-lengths, which are identical to the wavelengths of the perceived foci of the same colours, as chosen by English speakers. Kay & McDaniel deduce from this that neural response categories form the basis for colour perception and hence for the semantic categories of red, yellow, green and blue (p.626). They generalize on these findings to state that 'the semantics of basic color terms in all languages directly reflect the existence of these pan-human neural response categories' (p.621). Given that Berlin & Kay 1969 found the foci of these colours were consistently identified in langues that differentiated the four primary colours, the generalization is justified. Kay & McDaniel argue that the boundaries of colour categories are not variable, as Berlin & Kay 1969:13 thought them, but are determined by the foci of the adjacent primary colour categories: thus the boundaries for GREEN are focal BLUE on one side and focal YELLOW on the other; YELLOW is bounded by focal GREEN on one side and focal RED on the other (p.625). Summing up: primary colour categories each have an objectively defined focus, and have boundaries set by adjacent objectively defined foci. Kay & McDaniel 1978 postulate the area between the two boundary foci as a fuzzy set, with the hue point, or focus, having the value 1; and points towards the outer boundaries approaching 0.

It may seem illegal to regard a colour category like green as constituting a set of any kind (cf. Francis Pelletier *Mass Terms: Some Philosophical Problems* 1979) but the inventor of the fuzzy set theory, Lotfi Zadeh explicitly suggests that terms like *green*, *blue*, *yellow* and *red* may be regarded as the names of fuzzy subsets of elements in a universe of discourse which are of the colour named, cf. 'Quantitative fuzzy semantics' 1971:165 ex.6 and §3.5.1 footnote 17. It is clear that Kay & McDaniel are referring to points within a colour continuum, and that these constitute the membership of the fuzzy set which is the colour category. Alternatively, we could look at the matter this way: each colour category is defined by the set of colour percepts assigned some positive degree of membership within it; and, as one moves from the focus of the category out towards its boundaries, there is a decline from 1 towards zero. Treating colour categories as fuzzy sets provides a much sharper measure of category membership than was available in earlier discussions of colour terms, which admit only the three relations: at focus, not at focus but within the boundary, outside the boundary. We can now say that, e.g. a yellow-green light with a wavelength of 520nm can be accurately measured as 0.67 GREEN and 0.33 YELLOW (and 0 RED and 0 BLUE).[42]

In addition to the chromatic colour categories, there are the achromatic BLACK and WHITE with shades of the secondary grey in between. Kay & McDaniel claim that 'the existence, at some neural level of response, of categories corresponding to the sensations of black and white is supported [. . .] by a wide range of psychophysical evidence' (p.626). They argue that the focus of the semantic categories of black and white in a Stage V language (in which all six primary colours are differentiated) corresponds to the focus as objectively determined by the degree of reflectance: the fuzzy set BLACK has a value 1 at zero reflectance, and WHITE has the value 1 at 100% reflectance. Between the two are shades of grey. Location of a point within a colour category should take account of possible dilution of hue by achromatics (black, grey, white); but Kay & McDaniel do not write this into their computation of set membership. However, they demonstrate the effect in the colour sphere reproduced here as Figure 2.4.

Black and white complete the set of primary colours. The six primary colours RED, YELLOW, GREEN, BLUE, WHITE and BLACK occur in languages from Stage V onwards. In earlier stages, some or all colour categories are composites of more than one primary colour. The most common composite category, because it is the last to be lost in the transition from Stage IV to Stage V, is green-blue or "grue". Kay & McDaniel show (p.630) that the foci of both GREEN and BLUE have a value of 1 in this fuzzy set (no value is necessarily restricted to just one member in fuzzy set theory), whereas the intermediate colour – a blue-green – only has the value 0.5; this means it is less salient than either focal GREEN or focal BLUE and accounts for the behaviour of speakers who choose one of these rather than blue-green, as the focus for grue.

Up to Stage V basic lexica develop by decomposition of composite categories into the six primary colours. Thereafter, they begin to develop secondary categories by the addition of terms that refer to regions of colour space where the fundamental neural response categories overlap. Whereas composite categories are unions of the fuzzy sets of primary colours, the secondary colours are formed from their intersections.[43] Strictly speaking the highest value of any intersection should be 0.5, but this contradicts experimental evidence, such as that good examples of orange are assigned to the category orange with as much confidence as good examples of RED are assigned to RED. Moreover, good examples of orange are not so confidently assigned to either RED or YELLOW. Thus, empirically, orange is

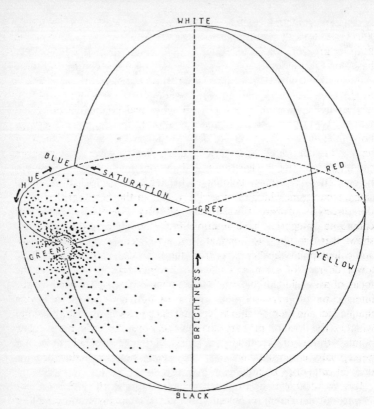

Figure 2.4   Colour sphere with 3 sections of green cut away. Green is the hemisphere whose boundary is defined by the horizontal axis blue-yellow and the vertical axis white-black. The density of stippling shows the degree of membership in green: it is thickest close to focal green, which has the fuzzy set membership value of 1. (From Kay & McDaniel 1978:628)

perceived to be as good a colour as RED or YELLOW (whether or not the neural response is a composite of the two). For this reason Kay & McDaniel compute the focus of orange as twice the intersection of RED and YELLOW (cf. p.632ff.) and take its boundaries to lie in focal RED and YELLOW.

So Kay & McDaniel have described three kinds of colour terms: (i) Primary colour terms BLACK, WHITE, RED, YELLOW, GREEN, BLUE. (ii) A set of composite colour categories consisting of the fuzzy union of two or more primaries: BLACK ∪ GREEN ∪ BLUE = "dark-cool"; WHITE ∪ RED ∪ YELLOW = "light-warm"; RED ∪ YELLOW = "warm"; GREEN ∪ BLUE = grue or "cool". And finally (iii) the set of secondary colours based on fuzzy intersection: BLACK ∩ YELLOW = brown; RED ∩ BLUE = purple; RED ∩ WHITE = pink; RED ∩ YELLOW = orange; WHITE ∩ BLACK = grey; but in addition one could add WHITE ∩ YELLOW = off-white, ?beige, ?cream; WHITE ∩ GREEN = teal green or eau de nil; WHITE ∩ BLUE = Russian *goluboy*; BLACK ∩ RED = maroon or bordeaux; BLACK ∩ GREEN = dark bottle green; BLACK ∩ BLUE = navy (Russian *siniy*); GREEN ∩ BLUE = aquamarine or turquoise; GREEN ∩ YELLOW = chartreuse. I shall comment on these additions below. The six primary colours each have a physiologically defined single focus from which membership values in the fuzzy set decline in the direction of zero towards the category boundaries. The four composite categories have multiple foci (though empirical evidence shows that one tends to dominate, for an as yet unexplained reason), and colour points further away from the focus do not necessarily have lower degrees of set membership – although zero is reached at the focus of an excluded colour. The secondary colours produced by the intersection of fuzzy sets are similar to primary colours in having unique foci and membership values that decline away from the foci; but whereas the foci of primary colours are physiologically unique hue points, those of secondary colours are not; instead they are perceptually equidistant between two unique hue points deciding the derived category's boundaries.

Kay & McDaniel now reinterpret the Berlin & Kay *Basic Color Terms* 1969 statement on colour universals and the evolution of colour terms, in the light of the hypothesis presented in their paper and taking account of new data. This is summarized in Figure 2.5. The figure embodies a reinterpretation of the evolutionary sequence in which the development of the colour system is seen not as the successive encoding of foci, but as the successive differentiation of previously existing basic colour categories. The dotted arrow is meant to indicate that grey (i.e. BLACK ∩ WHITE) may occur as early as Stage IIIa. The reason this secondary colour may occur much earlier than the others may be due to the fact that achromatic colours have a different kind of neurophysiological response from chromatic hues, cf. Kay & McDaniel 1978:626f. Stage I can be characterized as the binary opposition "light-warm" versus "dark-cool". At Stage II the light-warm composite begins to be differentiated, a process that may continue until its component primary colours are teased out in Stage IIIb; or alternatively, in Stage IIIa both achromatic primaries are extrapolated, leaving chromatic

118   *What is meaning?*

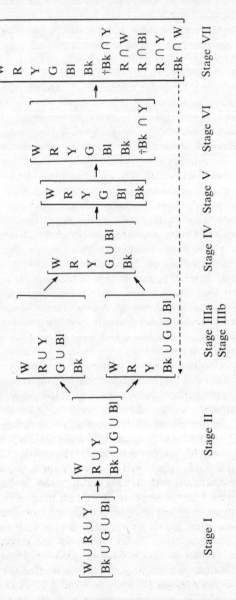

Key

W = white   Bk = black   R = red
Y = yellow   G = green   Bl = blue

Figure 2.5   The evolution of basic colour terms, cf. Kay & McDaniel 1978:639

† It is suggested on p.119 that this should perhaps be the intersection of Bk ∩ R

composites. Either way, languages at Stage IV are left with the last composite, grue. Stage V languages have basic terms for all primary colours. Stage VI which adds just brown to the basic colour term system is slightly suspect. The first doubt can be expressed through the question 'Why brown rather than any other secondary colour?' This is especially pertinent because the developmental step between Stage VI and VII is unique: the remaining secondary colours 'are added quickly to the lexicon' (Berlin & Kay 1969:20), so why the hiatus between Stage VI and Stage VII? It is at least possible that Berlin & Kay originally, and Kay & McDaniel subsequently, are wrong to postulate a separate Stage VI. In Berlin & Kay 1969 it is exemplified by only 5 languages, fewer languages than any other stage. Furthermore, the word for brown in one of the Stage VI languages, Javanese, is *tjokolat* which violates both caveats against misclassifying basic colour terms because it is a loan (from Mexican Nahuatl via Dutch) and also the name for a substance that instantiates the colour. Then, Cantonese, for example, has some other secondary colours but not brown among its basic colour terms. None of this disproves the existence of Stage VI, but it does render it suspect. Another point of interest is that a survey of the colour chart mappings in Appendix I of *Basic Color Terms* suggests that there is as much justification for calling brown the intersection of BLACK and RED as there is to describe it as BLACK ∩ YELLOW. Should that suggestion be correct, then except for achromatic grey – which is exceptional in other ways as we have seen – all the secondary colours named in Fig. 2.5 as basic colour terms at Stage VII, would be intersections with RED, thus imposing a homogeneity on their development. If basic colour systems go on adding secondary colours in future we might speculate that new ones will intersect with BLUE, given the differentiation between Russian *goluboy* "light blue" and *siniy* "dark blue". In this regard it is interesting that in Battig & Montague 1969:10, the table of colour terms lists accepted English basic terms from 1 through 10, then continues '(11) violet, (12) grey, (13) turquoise, (14) gold, (15) indigo' – three of these five are shades of blue (i.e. intersections with BLUE), and a fourth is the basic colour term grey. What I wish to draw attention to is the possibility that some sort of developmental process might be discovered for secondary colours as basic colour terms, based on intersection with a particular primary.

It seems that languages do not divide up the perceptual field of colour in an entirely arbitrary fashion, otherwise there would be a much wider variation in colour systems than we find exists. The work initiated by Berlin & Kay's *Basic Color Terms* 1969 and revised by Kay & McDaniel in 'The linguistic significance of the meanings of basic color terms' 1978 has shown that in all language communities when the senses (meanings) of basic colour terms are compared against their denotata, they are found to be governed by the perceived characteristics of those denotata; and these perceptions are themselves governed by neurophysiological response categories shared by all normal human beings; in the case of colour, then, the senses (meanings) of basic colour terms are, by and large, the effect of our biological makeup; and own wonders how many other semantic fields are similarly controlled. Nonetheless, speech communities show several stages of differentiation in colour terminology; but as Fig. 2.5 demonstrates, these different stages are not arbitrary. There is an increasing differentiation, first of primary colours from composites; and subsequently of intersections of primaries into secondary colours. Because this increasing differentiation is roughly correlated with technological development, according to Berlin & Kay 1969:16, it seems probable that the development of colour names goes hand in hand with a communicative requirement for greater differentation. Eleanor Rosch has shown, in 'On the internal structure of perceptual and semantic categories' 1973:112ff, people with a Stage I language can quickly learn to differentiate between secondary colours – which don't naturally appear until after Stage V; thus it is not differentiation in perception that develops, but the motivation to name the differentiations using basic terms.[44]

We see that, beyond the shadow of a doubt, the senses of basic colour terms are determined by the perceived characteristis of their denotata. These perceptions are affected by the context of a particular act of perception. Consider the fact that when S says *This shirt is green* he is implying, among other things, that the shirt is not blue (cf. §3.5.1), despite the fact that GREEN and BLUE intersect such that there are colour points with membership of both of them. A little reflexion reveals that under normal circumstances the use of the label *green* means "closer to the focal GREEN than to any other basic colour"; thus, e.g., a colour point that is 0.8 GREEN and 0.2 BLUE could reasonably be called *green*, and it could only be called *blue* under such unusual circumstances as identifying peripheral examples of BLUE. A colour point with a membership value of 0.5 GREEN and 0.5 BLUE could reasonably be called either *green* or *blue*, but in such cases it is usual – and necessary if S wants to be precise – to choose an alternative colour term such as *turquoise*, *aquamarine*, or *half-way between blue and green*. And, of course, the same strategy could be employed in the case of the colour point which is 0.8 GREEN and 0.2 BLUE: it could be called *a slightly bluey green*. It is surely clear that S's intention in such utterances is to use the sense of the expression to indicate the perceived characteristics of the denotatum.

2.9.7 The semantics of noun classifiers

In discussing the correspondence between the senses of basic colour terms and the perceived characteristics of their denotata, we stressed the significance of neurophysiological response categories affecting the human perception of colour and the corresponding senses (meanings) of colour terms. The panhuman characteristics of colour naming are not the only linguistic evidence we have that human beings the world over perceive their physical environment in similar ways and encode some of these perceptions in their language. For instance, there are remarkable similarities between classifiers for nouns in many unrelated and geographically separated languages from Africa, the Americas, Asia, Australia, and Oceania. In several syntactically distinct types of classifier systems (cf. Keith Allan 'Classifiers' 1977) certain morphemes or words are used to denote a perceived or imputed characteristic of the denotatum of an associated noun, thereby classifying the noun (or, more accurately, the phenomenon it denotes) according to one or more of seven categories of classification: material make up, shape, consistency, size, location, arrangement, or quanta. These seven categories (and their many subcategories)[45] range over all the predictable bases for classification except colour. The reasons for colour being excluded are: (a) it is perceivable only by the one sense of sight, whereas all the other categories of classification are perceivable by more than one sense alone;[46] (b) colour varies with the ambient lighting, and so is unstable; (c) colour alone, without application to a particular substance or shape, cannot portray an entity.

Consider some examples of classifiers. The Sino-Tibetan language Thai (Thailand) has a large number of classifiers that occur in expressions of quantity, cf. (9.7.1), in deictic expressions like (9.7.2), and anaphoric expressions like (9.7.3). (Classifers are emphasized).

(9.7.1)

a.	bùrì·	sɔ̌·ŋ	*muan*	
	cigarette	two	stick	"two cigarettes"
b.	bùrì·	sɔ̌·ŋ	*sɔ·ŋ*	
	cigarette	two	pack	"two packs of cigarettes"
c.	bùrì·	sɔ̌·ŋ	*lŏ·*	
	cigarette	two	dozen	"two dozen cigarettes"
d.	mǎ· sì·		*tua*	
	dog	four	body	"four dogs"

(9.7.2)

a.	mă·	*tua*	nán	
	dog		body	that	"that dog"
b.		*tua*	nán	
		body	that	"that" [animal, coat, trousers, table]

(9.7.3)

sì·	*tua*	
four	body	"four (of them)" [animals, coats, trousers, tables]

Bantu noun class prefixes are classifiers in our sense, cf. the Kikuyu (Kenya) series with the noun stem *-ti*:

> *mu*-ti "tree", *gi*-ti "wooden artifact, seat", *ma*-ti "woody mass, undergrowth".

And the Luganda (Uganda) series:

> *mu*-ganda "Ganda person", *ba*-ganda "Ganda people", *ki*-ganda "Ganda culture", *lu*-ganda "Ganda language", *bu*-ganda "Ganda country".

The distribution of Bantu classifiers can be illustrated by the Kiswahili (East Africa) sentence (9.7.4) where *vi*- is the plural inanimate object/artifact classifier:

(9.7.4)

vi-su   *vi*-dogo *vi*-wili hi-*vi*   amba-*vy*-o nili-*vi*-nunua
knives small   two   these which   I+bought-them

ni   *vi*-kali sana
are sharp   very

"These two small knives which I bought are very sharp."

The Athapaskan language Navajo (southwest U.S.A.) has about a dozen predicate classifiers, including the following trio:

(9.7.5)

a.	béésò	sì-ʔą́
	money	lie-perfect+of round object
	"A coin is lying (there)"	
b.	béésò	si-*nìl*
	money	lie-perfect+of collection
	"Some small change is lying (there)"	

c. béésò   sì-*łtsòòz*
    money   lie-perfect+of flat flexible object
    "A bill/note is lying (there)"

The fact that noun classifiers in unrelated and geographically separated languages should be used to make similar classifications of phenomena is not surprising if one takes the view that human perceptions are generally similar and that they stimulate a cognitive classification of the world which is reflected in the senses (meanings) of language expressions – whether these expressions are "content words" like nouns, adjectives, and verbs or "grammatical morphemes" like classifiers, number markers (see §2.9.8), and the like. This view is at variance with a strong interpretation of Benjamin Lee Whorf's claim that 'users of markedly different grammars are pointed by their grammars toward different types of observations and different evaluations of externally similar acts of observation, and hence are not equivalent as observers but must arrive at somewhat different views of the world' (*Language, Thought, and Reality* 1965:221). The evidence from classifier languages and colour terminology confutes a strong interpretation of Whorf's hypothesis – that perception is wholly constrained by language. However, a weak interpretation of the Whorfian hypothesis is tenable: viz. that a language directs its speakers towards certain aspects of perceived phenomena – but, because perception is independent of language, other aspects of the phenomena perceived can be commented upon, if desired, by circumlocution, or by the novel use of a language expression. Generally speaking, George K. Zipf's principle of least effort seems to hold: i.e. there is a tendency for the length of a language expression to be correlated with its significance within the everyday life of the speech community (hence, there will often be a correlation with the frequency of occurrence, cf. *Human Behavior and the Principle of Least Effort* 1948); e.g. *automobile* becomes *car*, *television* becomes *tv*, *long playing records* become *lps*, French *cinématograph* becomes *cinéma* then simply *ciné*.[47] In Eskimo there are the simple nouns

(9.7.6) aput, qana, piqsirpoq, qimuqsuq

denoting what we would have to express through more complex nominals in English (cf. Franz Boas *Handbook of American Indian Languages* 1911:25f):

(9.7.7) snow on the ground, falling snow, drifting snow, snow drift

The difference in the complexity of expression in the two languages is usually explained in terms of the hypothesis that the Eskimo environment makes it significant for Eskimos to distinguish various kinds of snow by simple nouns, whereas the environment in which the English language developed presents little need for such nouns. There is, as we see from (9.7.7) no limitation on the capacity of the English language to denote what the Eskimo nouns denote. The point to be taken (and we shall come back to it in §2.9.8) is that phenomena are linguistically categorized according to those of their characteristics that are perceived to be significant in a given context or set of contexts (cf. Eleanor Rosch et al. 'Basic objects in natural categories' 1976); in consequence the same phenomenon can be denoted by one language expression in one context, and by another (perhaps more complex) expression in another. With respect to the use of noun classifiers, for instance, a speaker may use an unusual classification to get some particular point across to H – the unusual classification will rank on a scale between dead metaphor and innovation: e.g. tall people can be classified by the "long" classifier in some Bantu languages, in Japanese, and in the Mayan language Yucatec (Mexico); Paul Friedrich ('Shape in grammar' 1970:36) cites the innovative classification of a Volkswagen Beetle as a round object in Tarascan (Mexico), where cars are normally classified as long objects – reasonably if you consider the salient shape of American cars over the last fifty years. Admittedly, the use of classifiers is highly syntacticized in almost all languages, so it is not so freely governed by S's perceptions as the foregoing remarks might suggest. Nevertheless, there can be no doubt that the basis for classification, and hence for the original sense of classifiers, is the characteristic perceived to be salient in the phenomenon they classify. Confirmation for this has recently become available from the work of Jack Gandour and others on the use of classifiers by young speakers of Thai. Typically, where they use the wrong classifier, it is because they seize on some unconventional characteristic perceived in the classified phenomenon, e.g. a cigarette should be classified by *muan*, cf. (9.7.1), but children may use *thên* the classifier for saliently one-dimensional rigid objects, or *lɔ̂d* the classifier for tubular objects. There are many instances of such perception-based misclassifications.

2.9.8   Number registration in English and the perceived characteristics of noun phrase denotata

A three-month shooting trip up the White Nile can offer a very good mixed bag, including, with luck, Elephant, Buffalo, Lion, and two animals not found elsewhere: Nile or Saddle-back (Mrs Gray's) Lechwe and White-eared Kob.

(H.C. Maydon *Big Game Shooting in Africa* 1951:168)

English NPs are either countable or uncountable, and in the paradigm cases that which is countable is denumerable by denumerators *a(n)*, *each*, *every*, *either*, *one*, *two*, (and all natural numbers), *several*, *many*, *both*, *(a) few*. Uncountable NPs are nondenumerable. Countability often has perceptual correlations: the (concrete) denotatum of a countable NP is ordinarily perceived in terms of one or more discrete entities. What is uncountable is typically, though not necessarily (cf. Keith Allan 'Nouns and countability' 1980), perceived as an undifferentiated unity. It is just this distinction that gives (9.8.1) its bite:

(9.8.1) It is because I like lambs that I don't like lamb.

In this section we shall discuss ways in which number registration in English can be exploited by S to indicate his perception of the NP's denotatum. We shall find that significantly discrete phenomena are labelled with countable NPs; nondiscrete phenomena such as liquids which have, so far as the ordinary speaker is concerned, no natural units, are labelled with uncountable NPs except where the liquid is contained in some conventional artificial unit. Phenomena whose natural units are only significant en masse, e.g. salt and sugar, are denoted through uncountable NPs. So countability in English nicely distinguishes between what are normally perceived to be significant individuals and what are normally perceived to be either insignificant or nondiscrete phenomena. We also find that a number of phenomena (a plurality) can be denoted either as a number of individuals – which is the normal state of affairs – or as a set, whose members are not perceived to be significant as individuals. All these perceptions of the denotata are indicated through exploitation of number registration (in English).

Typically, the grammatical number of an English NP is indicated by the presence or absence of a plural inflexion on the head noun, e.g. the emphasized morph in

cat*s*; somebody's ox*en*; sugar m*i*ce; their fo*ci*; the fella*h*in; etc.

There are other indications, too; e.g. in the sentence

(9.8.2) Those sheep are losing their wool

we know that 'sheep' is plural, although the morphology of the NP head shows nothing, because 'those', 'are', and 'their' are all in plural concord with it. Such concordant indications of number are subsumed to three kinds of number registration exemplified by those three words. (i) There is NP-internal number registration between the head and demonstratives *this*, *these*, *that*, *those*, indefinite articles *a(n)*, *some*, and quantifiers, e.g. *each*, *one*, *two*, *several*. There are also two kinds of NP-external number registration: (ii) subject-verb registration, between the finite verb and the head of its subject NP; (iii) pronominal registration, between a pronoun co-denotational with it, and the NP which governs the anaphor (cf. 'their' in (9.8.2)). But of these three kinds of number registration, only NP-internal concord invariably reflects the number of the NP head. Thus, in any dialect of English which contrasts *dog* with *dogs* and *this* with *these*, the following possibilities exist:

(9.8.3)

$$\text{NP} \, [\{ {a \atop this} \} \quad \text{chair}]$$

$$\text{NP} \, [\{ {four \atop these} \} \quad \text{chairs}]$$

$$*\text{NP} \, [\{ {a \atop this} \} \quad \text{chairs}]$$

$$*\text{NP} \, [\{ {four \atop these} \} \quad \text{chair}]$$

The superficial concords and discords of (9.8.3) reflect correlative semantic concords and anomalies, and it is these which account for the given judgements of grammaticality.

Although NP-external number registration is usually concordant, it can be discordant. An example from British, Canadian, and Australian (but mostly, not U.S.) dialects is the subject-verb number discord that may occur where the subject NP head is a singular collective noun such as *admiralty*, *aristocracy*, *army*, *assembly*, *association*, *audience*, *board*, *class*, *clergy*, *committee*, *crowd*, *flock*, *government*, *herd*, etc.

(9.8.4)
a.   The herd $\{ {is \atop are} \}$ getting restless, and they are beginning to move away.

b.   The clergy $\{ {is \atop are} \}$ striking for higher stipends; which I think is disgraceful of them.

c. The government { $^{\text{is}}_{\text{are}}$ } once again asking for more time,

so that they can get the economy straight.

d. My collection { $^{\text{is}}_{\text{are}}$ } fetching good prices; much better than

expected.

To explain this state of affairs we postulate two categories of denotation for singular collective nouns:

(9.8.5) NPs headed by singular collective nouns may manifest one of two categories of denotation: with singular NP-external number concord they make MONADIC denotation, i.e. denote the collection as a whole or as a unity; and with plural NP-external number registration they make POLYADIC denotation, i.e. denote the members of the collection.

With NPs that denote institutions e.g. *the BBC*, *the company I work for*, *the library*, *the local authority*, *the university*, the institution itself – as building, location, or as an entity – is denoted monadically; whereas the people associated with the institution can be polyadically denoted; cf.

(9.8.6)

a. The university { $^{\text{is}}_{*\text{are}}$ } architecturally interesting.

b. The university { $^{\text{pays}}_{\text{pay}}$ } us in the third week of the month.

(9.8.7)

a. The library { $^{\text{is}}_{*\text{are}}$ } located in the new civic center.

b. The library { $^{\text{charges}}_{\text{charge}}$ } a heavy fine on overdue books.

(9.8.8)

a. Oxford { $^{\text{is}}_{*\text{are}}$ } the most beautiful place.

b. Oxford { $^{\text{is}}_{\text{are}}$ } going to win the boat-race.

Internally plural proper names like *The United States* or *the Himalayas* can also be used to denote monadically or polyadically. The name of a country will, because it denotes a single entity, normally have singular NP-external number registration; with plural external number registration the NP denotes the government or people of the country, or perhaps the federation of separate states. Geophysical features like mountains, lakes, or continents may either be viewed as a place, in which case the plural proper name referring to them will have singular external number registration; or they may be seen as a number of entities, in which case the NP will have plural external concord.

Where the subject NP is determined by *a(n)* or *one*, both of which have the sense "one" and so predispose the NP to the unity of monadic denotation, discord with the verb is unlikely, cf.

(9.8.9)

    a.   A committee {$\substack{\text{was} \\ \text{?were}}$} asked to investigate the problem.

    b.   One herd {$\substack{\text{was} \\ \text{?were}}$} seen near the waterhole.

Some predicates also require monadic denotation from their singular collective subject NPs, e.g.

(9.8.10)

    a.   The committee {$\substack{\text{is} \\ *\text{are}}$} composed of notable scholars.

    b.   The committee {$\substack{\text{consists} \\ *\text{consist}}$} of both men and women.

    c.   The committee {$\substack{\text{contains} \\ *\text{contain}}$} many men of distinction.

The reason for distinguishing the two categories of denotation, as we saw in (9.8.5), is that certain kinds of phenomena may be perceived either in terms of the set as a whole and monadically denoted, or they may be perceived as a plurality of members in the set and polyadically denoted through plural NP-external number registration. We could look upon the two alternatives as focusing on different aspects of sets. Denumerated plural NPs which normally have plural external number concord may, with predicates like *all*, *too many*, *too few*, *enough*, *sufficient*, and singular NP-external number registration (discord), be used to focus on the quantity of whatever S is talking about rather than upon the entities quantified. Consider

(9.8.11) Three lions is too many to let roam free in a TV studio; suppose they attack someone?

(9.8.12) Two men isn't going to be enough to lift a fifty-foot girder, is it mate?

(9.8.13) Five men have volunteered, which isn't many; but I think it will be enough.

In (9.8.11-12) the focus shifts from the quantity to the entities themselves and vice versa in (9.8.13). Thus, interpreting (9.8.11) for instance: the worry is that a lion, or more than one lion, might attack someone (it being a matter of common knowledge that any lion is potentially dangerous); so if three is too many, four or five would certainly be too many – although one might be acceptable. The sense data provided by three lions can give rise to a perceptual focus on the (one) quantity which is therefore perceived as a singular and labelled as such through singular NP-external number registration; or, more commonly, the three lions will be perceived as a number of individual entities and labelled as such through plural NP-external number registration. I leave it open whether focusing on quantity makes the denumerator NP head instead of the noun, but it is certainly the case that when there is no denumerator, and therefore no quantity to focus upon, an internally plural NP cannot be used with singular external number registration, cf.

(9.8.14)
 a.   *Those lions is too many to let roam free indoors.
 b.   *The men here isn't enough to lift a fifty-foot girder.
 c.   *These men, which isn't many, have volunteered to guard the Pope next time he goes to Sofia.

Number registration is also used to mark focus within classifier constructions. English has seven kinds of classifier constructions defined on the kind of classifier they contain:

unit counters:	*a piece* of equipment
fractionals:	*three quarters* of the cake
number sets:	*many hundreds* of people
collectives:	*two clumps* of grass
varietals:	*two species* of wheat
measures:	*two pounds* of cabbage
arrangements:	*two rows* of beans

All seven kinds of classifiers can be found in other languages.[48] A plural denumerated unit counter, fractional, varietal, measure, or arrangement classifier with a singular classified NP may have either singular NP-external number registration and focus upon the quantity of whatever the classified NP denotes; or there may be plural external number registration with focus upon the plurality in the classifier. These plural denumerated classifier constructions are, therefore, comparable with the plural denumerated NPs exemplified in (9.8.11-13)

(9.8.15) Four pieces of cake $\{^{is}_{are}\}$ enough for anyone but a glutton.

(9.8.16) Three quarters of the cake $\{^{was}_{were}\}$ put on Ed's plate.

(9.8.17) Two pounds of flour $\{^{was}_{were}\}$ what I needed.

In (9.8.16), for instance, we interpret the singular external number registration as focusing on the quantity of cake: so it could well be that a single piece of cake amounting to three quarters of the whole cake was put on Ed's plate (it doesn't have to be a single piece of cake, but it does have to amount to three quarters of the whole cake). With plural external number registration there is a focus on 'quarters'; consequently the interpretation is that the cake had been cut into (separated) quarters, and three of these were put on Ed's plate. Plural number registration would be inappropriate if there were a single piece of cake (amounting to three quarters of the whole) put on Ed's plate. There is sometimes a prosodic distinction made between the differently interpreted classifier constructions. For instance compare

(9.8.17′)
  a.   / Two pounds / of flour / was what I needed. /
  b.   / Two / pounds of flour / were what I needed. /

A singular fractional, collective, measure, or arrangement classifier with a plural classified NP may have either singular NP-external number registration and so focus upon the classifier, or plural external number registration and focus upon the classified NP, cf.

(9.8.18)
  a.   A half of the diamonds was not enough for Sid.
  b.   A half of the tomatoes were bad.

(9.8.19) The heap of logs $\{^{is}_{are}\}$ piled against the wall.

(9.8.20) A row of trees $\{^{stand}_{stands}\}$ on the ridge.

Collectives are the only internally singular NPs that may have plural as well as singular NP-external number registration. Where a unique entity is denoted it can occasionally be perceived as the sum of its parts; however, this is not indicated by number registration but by co-occurrence constraints exercised by the verbal predicate. Verbs like *assemble, glue together, scatter* require that whatever is assembled, gathered, glued together or scattered be a set of entities, i.e. their object NP in an active clause or subject NP in a passive clause, is typically either plural or else a singular collective:

(9.8.21)

a. He gathered the $\{{}^{crowd}_{chairs}\}$ together.

b. Parliament was assembled at the Queen's behest.

c. The herd was scattered all over the plain.

d. Jemima scattered Cyril's ashes over the cliff.

But on occasion we find singular non-collective NPs predicated by these verbs, and then the NP denotes the component parts of the whole entity, cf.

(9.8.22) He gathered *the chair* together.

(9.8.23) *The machine gun* was assembled in the plane.

(9.8.24) After the accident *his body* was scattered all over the road.

(9.8.25) Bernie glued *the plate* together.

In (9.8.22) 'the chair' is interpreted "the bits of the chair"; in (9.8.23) 'the machine gun' is interpreted "the parts of the machine gun"; and similarly for the emphasized NPs in (9.8.24-25). These interpretations are projected onto the singular NPs from their textual environment – more precisely, in consequence of the verbal predicates ranging over them.

Towards the beginning of this section we said that NP-internal number registration between the NP head and demonstratives *this*, *these*, *that*, *those*, indefinite articles *a(n)*, *some*, and quantifiers such as *each*, *one*, *two*, *several*, *much* is invariably concordant; and we showed in (9.8.3) that discord in NP-internal number registration is semantically anomalous, e.g. $*_{NP}$[one chairs], $*_{NP}$[four chair]. There are, however, apparent counter-examples to this postulate, cf.

> On the way back to camp we sighted two giraffe on the other side of the river, which were coming down to the water's edge to drink.
>
> (A. Arkell-Hardwick *An Ivory Trader in North Kenya* 1903:285)

Consider also:

(9.8.26)

a. At Tsavo we filmed *several rhino* as they came down to the river.

b. *These three elephant* my uncle shot were good tuskers, such as you never see today.

    c.   *These cucumber* are doing well; it's a good year for them.

    d.   *Four silver birch* stand sentinel over the driveway entrance.

The emphasized NPs in (9.8.26) are not semantically anomalous even though they have plural determiners and the head nouns are not morphologically marked as plurals; they are in fact interpreted as plural NPs denoting more than one animal, plant, or tree. Many grammarians have described the unmarked plural head nouns of such NPs as 'collectives',[49] yet in important respects they are different from collectives like, say, *cattle* or *herd*. These nouns can be used to denote individuals, cf. *a giraffe*; but **a cattle* is impossible, and *a herd* is collective. Furthermore, such nouns typically have marked as well as unmarked plural forms, and these are noncollectives, cf. *giraffes*, *rhinos*, *elephants*, *cucumbers*, *birches*. Thus, nouns like those which head the emphasized NPs in (9.8.26) we shall call COLLECTIVIZED,[50] and this term is extended to the NPs they head and to their denotata – which I shall refer to as collectivized animals, trees, plants, etc. Despite the fact that collectivized nouns can often be replaced by regular plural forms of the same nouns without anomaly, and often without any significant change in meaning, we shall see that the use of collectivized nouns rather than the corresponding plural forms does reflect a different perception of the denotata.

    The mark of collectivizing is the lack of number registration on the NP head; in all other respects the NP has plural internal and external number registration: thus even without the quantifiers and pronouns the subject NP of (9.8.27) is collectivized, that of (9.8.28) refers to an individual:

(9.8.27) The (three) elephant are downwind of us (, are they?)

(9.8.28) The (one) elephant is downwind of us (, is it?)

To start explaining collectivizing, therefore, we should look to the properties associated with the form of the noun which, in English, is morphologically unmarked for number: for convenience we shall symbolize this $N_\emptyset$. $N_\emptyset$ is the form used for the head noun in uncountable NPs and in singular countable NPs: it is the form characteristically used of denotata perceived as a unity – or, conversely, it is the form characteristically used of denotata which are NOT perceived to be significant as a number of individuals. Although the choice between these converse descriptions is somewhat equivocal, the second, negative one is to be preferred because $N_\emptyset$ is negatively defined as the (morphologically) 'unmarked' form by contrast with the plural form. We therefore postulate the following principle of $N_\emptyset$ usage:

(9.8.29) $N_\emptyset$ (the form of the noun morphologically unmarked for
number) is used to denote a phenomenon or set of phenomena
whose composition is perceived (either conventionally or in some
particular context C_i) to not divide into a number of significant units.

This principle is self-evident with respect to single discrete objects such
as a single cup, but less obviously true for certain mass nouns such as
coffee, wheat, sugar, sand. In uncountable NPs such nouns denote
phenomena which are separable into readily perceived natural units
such as coffee beans; grains, ears, spikelets or stalks of wheat; granules
of sugar or grains of sand. However *coffee*, *wheat*, *sugar* and *sand*
cannot be used as if they are collective nouns to denote these natural
units polyadically, cf.

(9.8.30)

a.   The wheat $\{^{is}_{*are}\}$ growing well, $\{^{isn't\ it?}_{*aren't\ they?}\}$

b.   The spilt sugar $\{^{was}_{*were}\}$ being carted away by ants.

Given Zipf's principle of least effort (cf. the discussion of (9.7.6-7) in
§2.9.7), we can explain this constraint on the grounds that the natural
units which compose these substances are conventionally perceived to
be too insignificant as individuals to merit a simple noun as the
common term of denotation; instead, when we do want to talk about
them, they are labelled by a compound noun or classifier construction,
e.g. *coffee bean* or *grain of sand*. Liquids are not ordinarily perceived
to be composed of natural units and therefore they are typically
denoted by $N_\emptyset$ in an uncountable NP. The exception is where
contextually identifiable artificial units exist, such as are denoted in

(9.8.31) Could I have three $\{^{milks}_{beers}\}$ please?

'Milks' means "containers (bottles, cartons, cans) of milk"; 'beers'
means "containers (bottles, cans, glasses) of beer". Nouns like *coffee*,
tea and *sugar* are also used to head countable NPs that denote
contextually identifiable units, cf.

(9.8.32) Give me two $\{^{sugars}_{coffees}\}$ please.

Here 'sugars' is typically interpreted "lumps, cubes, spoonsful of
sugar"; 'coffee' is open to such interpretations as "spoonsful of coffee,
cups of coffee" and even "kinds of coffee [Kenyan Mocca, New Guinea
Gold]". This unitizing into significant artificial units contrasts with the

comparative insignificance, of the natural units from which the substances are composed.

Certain so-called mass nouns such as *wine*, *wheat*, and *coffee* typically occur in uncountable NPs, cf.

(9.8.33)
   a. All wine is acidic.
   b. All wheat is highly nutritious.
   c. Coffee is grown at a lower altitude than tea.

But the same nouns head countable NPs when they are used to denote a variety, kind or species, cf.[51]

(9.8.34)
   a. We have about fifty wines on our list, sir.
   b. Up in Nyeri you need a wheat that likes a high altitude.
   c. The Arabian and "robusta" coffees provide most of the world's trade in coffee.

The plural form of nouns denoting fishes, e.g. *salmons*, *trouts*, is used, particularly by ichthyologists and other cognoscenti, to denote a number of species rather than a number of individuals – for which the collectivizing $N_\emptyset$ is used. Cf.

> *The cat-fishes*, of which there are about fifty distinct forms arranged in four families, constitute the largest group, with probably the greatest number of individuals per species. In some parts of the country where nets are little used and fishing is mainly done with traps and long lines, at least three-quarters of the annual catch is of *cat-fish*.
>
> (J.B. Welman *Preliminary Survey of the Freshwater Fishes of Nigeria* 1948:8 [emphasis added])

It is plain from this quotation that 'cat-fishes' refers to different species of cat-fish, whereas 'cat-fish' denotes individuals (from one or more species) caught by fishermen. If $N_\emptyset$ is used for collectivizing, then according to the principle of $N_\emptyset$ usage stated in (9.8.29) the composition of the collectivized phenomena is perceived to not divide into significant units. How do we accommodate this principle to the use of the $N_\emptyset$ to denote a plurality of fish, and more strikingly, how can we make sense of it in relation to the collectivizing of such large animals as elephants and rhinos? To answer this question we need to investigate conditions on the collectivizing animals.

Not all animals can be collectivized and one can suggest the following scenario in order to explain the scope of collectivizing: the evidence is that collectivizing was originally limited to animals hunted with weapons, then extended to game reared or preserved for hunting, thence to contexts of game conservation and hunting with a camera or a spotter's notebook. Because hunting for food phylogenetically antedates hunting for sport, we would expect collectivizing to have applied first to animals hunted for food and then, by analogy, to those hunted for sport – perhaps with special constraints placed upon the collectivizing of non-food animals. This would explain why exotic animals such as elephants, lions, and rhinos and certain birds such as blackbirds are only optionally collectivized and then only in hunting or conservation contexts. It also explains why vermin such as rats and dingos are not collectivized even though they are hunted. The motivation for using $N_\emptyset$ in the collectivizing of hunted animals was presumably that the hunter was not primarily interested in the animals as individuals; originally what was significant to him was the animal's flesh for food, and later the horns, skins, tusks, feathers, etc. for trophies. Although domestic animals are not collectivized, $N_\emptyset$ is used in the collectives *cattle* and *swine* and for the plural of *sheep* – all of which denote animals reared for food. By contrast, pets like dogs and cats, and beasts of burden like horses, mules and donkeys are not collectivized, and $N_\emptyset$ is only used to denote a single individual animal. The significance of the animals as a source of food rather than as individuals was the original motivation for collectivizing, i.e. for using $N_\emptyset$.

$N_\emptyset$ is also used to denote meat when the consumer eats flesh from an animal at a sitting, cf. (9.8.35) – though it then heads an uncountable NP whereas the collectivized noun heads a plural (countable) NP. Where the whole of one or more food objects is eaten at a sitting, they are apparently significant as individual units and labelled using a countable NP, cf. (9.8.36).

$$(9.8.35) \quad \text{We are having} \left\{ \begin{array}{l} \text{lamb} \\ \text{rabbit} \\ \text{chicken} \\ \text{goat} \end{array} \right\} \text{for dinner.}$$

$$(9.8.36) \quad \text{We are having} \left\{ \begin{array}{l} \text{pilchards} \\ \text{ham sandwiches} \\ \text{oysters} \end{array} \right\} \text{for lunch}$$

The principle of $N_\emptyset$ usage stated in (9.8.29) is that $N_\emptyset$ is used to denote a phenomenon or set of phenomena whose composition is perceived to not divide into a number of significant units. The foregoing discussion confirms that this principle is generally correct. We have not discussed the collectivizing of tree or plant nouns but it is evident from such sentences as (9.8.37) that this is also governed by the principle of N$_\emptyset$ usage:

(9.8.37)
    a.   Meg bought three beetroot for a dollar.
    b.   These oak and beech must have been here for a couple of
        hundred years.

Cf. also (9.8.26.c-d). The principle of N$_\emptyset$ usage postulates a perceptual basis for the sense of the form; and the point of introducing it in §2.9 has been to show that it is not only the sense of lexemes which is based upon the perceived characteristics of denotata, but also the sense of grammatical forms such as those which register number in English noun phrases.[52]

2.9.9   The Aristotelian tradition in grammatical analysis

In ch. 4 of *Categories* Aristotle divided up the world of our experience into ten 'categories', each of which he associated with a grammatical class: Substance is represented by nouns; Quantity by quantifiers and quantifying adjectives like *large* and *small*; Quality by other adjectives; Relation by, among other things, comparatives and superlatives; Place and Time by adverbials; Posture or position by imperfects like *be lying*, *be sitting*; State or Condition by perfect participles like *shod*, *armed*; Action by finite active verbs; and Affection by the passive voice. In making these correlations between the perceived world and grammatical classes, Aristotle assumed that the sense of a grammatical class reflects the perceived characteristics of the denotata of that class.

    In direct line of intellectual descent from Aristotle were the medieval monks of the 13th-14th centuries known as the scholastic grammarians. They developed the analysis of Latin by the 6th century Byzantine grammarian Priscianus, reinterpreting it in terms of the meanings of grammatical classes, relations, and functions, which they believed to reflect the nature of the world we perceive. E.g. they perceived the world to be divided between Parminedean permanence represented by the class meaning of nouns, and Heraclitean flux represented by that of verbs. Syntactic rules they described in terms of the 'modes of signifying' of the resulting constructions such as modifier and head, or topic and comment. Being Christian monks, the scholastic grammarians thought that God created a logically organized world; and because they believed that the sense of grammatical classes is determined by the nature of the world we live in, they thought this must necessarily be logical, too – hence the study of grammar fused with the study of logic and philosophy. Moreover, since the scholastics believed with Aristotle that our perceptions of the world are common to all men and women, and since it is these perceptions which determine the sense of grammatical classes, relations, and functions, these must also be universal. Thus in the 13th century, Roger Bacon wrote in *Lingua Graecae*: 'He that understands grammar in one language understands it in another, as far as are concerned the essential properties of grammar. The fact that he cannot speek or comprehend another language is due to the diversity of words and their different forms, but these are the accidental properties of grammar.' What Bacon calls 'the essential properties of grammar' came to be known in the 17th and 18th centuries as 'general grammar',[53] and in 1960s as 'deep structure' or the 'universal base'.[54] The main difference between the general grammarians of the 17th-18th centuries and the scholastic grammarians 400 years before was that instead of taking the sense of grammatical classes and constructions to reflect the structure of world we perceive, the general grammarians believed them to reflect the structure of the mind that perceives the world – and for this reason they are often called rationalist grammarians. The philosophical dispute between realists and rationalists need not concern us as linguists; we simply assume that the senses of grammatical classes, grammatical relations, and grammatical functions reflect the perceived characteristics of their typical denotata.

2.9.10 Summary of the evidence that sense reflects the perceived characteristics of the concrete denotatum

It has been our purpose in §2.9 to examine evidence of several kinds that the sense of a language expression reflects the characteristics perceived in its denotatum and represented in the conceptual prototype for the denotatum. We take perception to be a mental act or reflex in which sensory cues filtered through knowledge set up expectations from which are projected the intrinsic defining properties of the (abstract) prototype of the phenomenon perceived. It is these characteristic properties of the prototype which are referred to in giving the sense of the language expression used to label (i.e. denote) the phenomenon. The characteristics of a phenomenon perceived in some particular context will approximate to the prototype, the degree of approximation being measurable in terms of a fuzzy set with membership quotients ranging in value from 1 for identity with the prototype, to close to 0 for a marginal member of the set, and 0 for a non-member. We saw that the characteristics of prototypes can be confirmed experimentally.

To summarize the other important points made in §2.9. (a) We saw that a child's overgeneralizing or undergeneralizing the meaning of a word is due to his not having yet recognized the appropriate perceived characteristics in a prototype; consequently he is ignorant of the conventional sense of the word. (b) There is evidence from systems of noun classification that a wide range of phenomena are perceived in very similar ways by people from quite different linguistic and cultural groups in different parts of the world. (c) People from different language communities can always encode much the same set of perceptions in expressions of their different languages, but the degree of simplicity in encoding (i.e. the degree of complexity in the language expression labelling the phenomenon perceived) tends to be correlated with the degree of significance accorded to the denotatum – either in a particular context, or generally – with the principle of least effort ensuring a positive correlation between the simpler expression and the more significant denotatum. Thus the extent to which a perceptual or conceptual field is differentiated through the senses of individual morphemes and lexemes is a function of the extent to which it is communicatively desirable to differentiate it. E.g. from the time of Aristotle (cf. *Poetics* 1456b, 22) to the late 19th century the term *letter* was used for both the grapheme and the phoneme it typically symbolizes; it was only when emphasis on the priority of speech over writing led to the development of phonetics, that it became necessary to differentiate phonological from graphological symbols. Communicative requirements can lead to less differentiation, too: Australian butchers once used to distinguish three kinds of sheep-meat: lamb, hogget, and mutton. Nowadays *hogget* "one year old sheep" has been dropped in favour of *lamb* – which supposedly has greater appeal because it is thought to be tenderer.[55] (d) We saw that the sense of an expression, whether it is a lexeme or a larger "content" expression, or a grammatical form like number registration, or a grammatical class, relation, or function, will reflect the salient characteristics perceived in or conceived of the denotatum.

2.10 What meaning is, and the linking of sense and denotation

We are now in a position to say what meaning is, and also to say how sense and denotation are linked. The sense of a language expression E_o is an abstract object which we (as linguists) represent in terms of a language expression E_m describing the characteristics of a prototype denotatum. The language expressions E_o and E_m are generally thought to correspond to a concept (perhaps a quite complex concept) in the mind of the language user: thus the sense of E_o does correspond to a concept. But the sense of E_o is not a concept because sense is an abstract object and a concept is a psychological object.

Because the sense of E_o is expressed in terms of, i.e. corresponds to, the characteristics of the prototype denotatum, there is a natural link between sense and denotation. A phenomenon is perceived directly through one or more of the senses of sight, sound, touch, hearing, taste, smell, proprioception, or alternatively in the mind's eye from a creative cognitive act (i.e. it is conceptual); it is denoted via recognition of salient characteristics of the phenomenon that approximate to the prototype described by the sense (meaning) of some language expression. Thus denotation is the use of the sense of an expression to label a phenomenon whose salient characteristics in a given context approximate to those of a prototype denotatum for that expression.

Chapter 3

Meaningful properties and meaning relations

'Our religion is based on a belief in God the creator and the worship of our ancestors.' This is what a minister told teachers the other day. 'Our dead parents are living; it is they who protect us and intercede for us.'

(V.S. Naipaul 'A new king for the Congo' 1980:189)

3.1 Introduction

Having established in ch.2 what meaning is, we shall now discuss the meaningful properties an expression can have, and the meaning relations that hold between two or more expressions. In §3.2 we look at the properties of meaningfulness, anomaly, (in)determinability, and contradiction. In §3.3 we examine classifications for expressions with more than one meaning, discussing the properties of ambiguity and polysemy, and the relation of homonymy. In §3.4 we turn to the values placed on various kinds of utterances, such as the truth value of a statement, the genuineness of a promise, the appropriacy of an apology, the authority of a verdict. In §3.5 we discuss semantic predicates as meaning components. We begin by interpreting relationships of inclusion between categories e.g. 'Colour contains Blue' such that the expression labelling the included category (*blue*) has a semantic component represented by the expression labelling the including category, i.e. *blue* has the semantic component COLOUR. We then describe the history and development of the componential analysis of vocabulary before arguing that a semantic component such as COLOUR is no more than a permissible semantic predicate on *blue*, viz. their semantic relation can be properly expressed in terms of the proposition *Blue is a colour*. In §3.6 we describe synonymy, the relation of semantic identity between propositions. More particularly, after defining synonymy as symmetric semantic implication between propositions, we discuss synonymy between clauses containing symmetric predicates and those with converse predicates, and finally crossvarietal synonymies. In §3.7 we look at asymmetric semantic implication and the relation of hyponymy; and at antonymy and hyponymy in §3.8. In §3.9 we turn to semantic implication, conversational implicature and conventional implicature. Tautology is the topic of §3.10. Semantic overlap and semantic difference between propositions is discussed in §3.11, with most attention being given to psychologist Charles Osgood's semantic differential – a device for measuring connotative meaning. Finally in §3.12 we look at the meaning relations which result from changes in meaning over the course of time.

3.2 The property of being meaningful or not

3.2.1 E is meaningful

Any expression E of language L is meaningful, i.e. it has meaning and is sensical, provided it is neither anomalous, indeterminable, nor contradictory.

3.2.2 Anomaly

(29)   *I ate three phonemes for breakfast.
           (James D. McCawley 'Concerning the base component of
                                transformational grammar' 1968:265)

The following sentences have been said to be ANOMALOUS:[1]

(2.2.1) That electron is green.

(2.2.2) I ate three phonemes for breakfast.

(2.2.3) My hair is bleeding.

(2.2.4) That unicorn's left horn is black.

(2.2.5) The drum was made by the prune.

These sentences have been said to be anomalous because they or their constituents are thought to be incapable of denoting in any world spoken of. For instance, electrons are theoretical constructs that cannot absorb or reflect light and therefore cannot be predicated as green, even metaphorically. Phonemes are abstract objects, one cannot eat abstract objects, therefore (2.2.2) is nonsense – or more precisely, it is anomalous. Hair has no blood vessels, so it can't bleed; hence (2.2.3) must be anomalous. Since by definition unicorns only have one horn and (2.2.4) implies that the unicorn spoken of has more than one, it must be anomalous. And finally, prunes do not make drums.

These sentences are judged anomalous because they do not fit the familiar everyday world. According to some people they do not denote in any world. However, I should like to throw some doubt on that claim, a doubt that is significant for the definition of anomaly. Anomaly has to be defined, I believe, in relation to the particular world, W, that is being spoken of. Sentences (2.2.1-5) look anomalous at first sight because they are decontextualized and one judges them in relation to the familiar everyday world. Consider some worlds in which such sentences could be uttered meaningfully, i.e. nonanomalously. Let's start with (2.2.1). Suppose an explanatory model of an atom were constructed in which an electron was represented by a green flash: then it would be quite legitimate to say in reference to the model, *That electron is green*, without there being any anomaly. Now take (2.2.2). Consider a world in which breakfast cereal is made in the shape of letters, rather like those in alphabet soup; and further suppose that this breakfast cereal were fed to participants in a Linguistics Society conference, provoking some witty linguist to say *I ate three phonemes for breakfast*, thereby referring to the fact that he had eaten a 'p', a 't', and a 'k' shape. Such a remark would be just as reasonable as John L. Austin saying *France is hexagonal*,[2] which has never been rejected as anomalous. No-one who has ever heard children talking about their paintings should find (2.2.3) necessarily anomalous; and a two-horned unicorn, such as is implied by (2.2.4) is only slightly more peculiar than a three-legged quadruped or a two-headed dog. Finally, it is at least conceivable that a wrinkled, old, black drum-maker might be nicknamed 'the prune' – which would render (2.2.5) sensical (although its punctuation might need rectifying).

In all these cases, what we have done is to find contexts in which the sentences can make sense. Note that it is not the sequence of lexemes nor the expression as such which is judged anomalous, but what it evokes – its would-be denotation. When we find a world in which the expression can reasonably denote, it ceases to be anomalous. This is not to say that any sequence of lexical items can be made nonanomalous: anomaly is a misfit between an expression and the world spoken of. We have already admitted that sentences like (2.2.1-5) are anomalous if applied to the familiar everyday world without qualification; and, certainly, some sequences of lexical items seem likely to be anomalous under any conditions. Thus although *But me no buts* is sensical, the following would seem to be anomalous in any imaginable context.

(2.2.6)
  a. The in anded some thes.
  b. This blue and on speak conferenced uply.
  c. Peter thated nine an equipment.

3.2.3 Indeterminability

It does not matter much whether we say of the assertion "The King of France is bald" that it is false or pointless or what not, as long as we understand *how* it goes wrong.

(John Searle *Speech Acts* 1969:158f)

An anomalous expression makes the utterance in which it occurs INDETERMINABLE if it is impossible to figure out from context what the expression means. Any indeterminable expression is anomalous.[3] For example, none of (2.2.6) is determinable, nor is (2.3.1): we cannot fathom out what it means.

(2.3.1) The verb is in the indicative tense.

We can see by comparing (2.2.6) and (2.3.1) that there are degrees of determinability corresponding with the number of anomalous constituents: in (2.3.1) it is only the expression 'indicative tense' which is anomalous. An utterance of (2.3.1) will be completely indeterminable if we cannot decide from context whether S means "indicative mood" or "present", "past", or "future tense". Many anomalies resulting from slips of the tongue and the like, result in utterances which, although superficially indeterminable, are, on reflexion, determinable from context. E.g. when the usher says *Let me sew you to your sheet* or someone utters *Ronald Reagan's p'lice pan for the Mid-East* or *Women have had to fart very hide for their rights*, we can figure out from context what S intended to say provided he was abiding by the co-operative principle. Consider the following anomalous text which is nonetheless determinable.

(2.3.2)
  Wants pawn term dare worsted ladle gull hoe lift wetter murder inner ladle cordage honor itch offer lodge dock florist. Disc ladle gull

orphan worry ladle cluck wetter putty ladle rat hut, end fur disc
raisin pimple caulder Ladle Rat Rotten Hut. Wan moaning Rat
Rotten Hut's murder colder inset: 'Ladle Rat Rotten Hut, heresy
ladle basking winsome burden barter and shirker cockles. Tick disc
ladle basking tudor cordage offer groin murder honor udder site
offer florist. Shaker lake, dun stopper laundry wrote, end yonder nor
sorghum stenches dun stopper torque wet strainers.'

'Hoe-cake, murder', resplendent Ladle Rat Rotten Hut, end tickle
ladle basking an stuttered oft. Honor wrote tudor cordage offer groin
murder, Ladle Rat Rotten Hut mitten anomalous woof.

. . . Etc.[4]

Quoted in (2.3.2) is the beginning of the story of Little Red Riding
Hood. Given the communicative presumption, the reasonableness
condition, and other tenets of the co-operative principle, we can assign
meaning to what at first sight looks like a randomly sequenced list of
English words. The passage is rendered determinable because of the
punctuation in the piece, and the phonetic similarity between the
sequence of words in the passage and sensical sequences of words
which develop the story of little Red Riding Hood. Although all the
words in (2.3.2) are individually meaningful, the sentences they
compose (taking a sentence to lie between full stops) are anomalous.
Yet we can translate these anomalous sentences into meaningful
equivalents by exploiting our knowledge of English, the context of each
expression within a sentence, and our background knowledge. Thus the
determinability of an expression, or even a whole text, is its property of
making sense, i.e. successfully denoting, within the world spoken of
(once this world can be identified).

This brings us to another aspect of determinability. Consider the
following set of sentences.

(2.3.3)
    a.   The present king of France is bald.
    b.   The present king of France is not bald.
    c.   Is the present king of France bald (or not)?
    d.   Where is the present king of France living?
    e.   Kill the present king of France!
    f.   I order you to assassinate the present king of France.
    g.   I promise to assassinate the present king of France.
    h.   Thank you for offering to assassinate the present king of France.
    i.   I hereby sentence to death the present king of France.

Supposing all these to be uttered in 1980, they would normally be indeterminable because there is no-one in the familiar everyday world who can properly be called 'the present king of France'. Similarly, if one is out on a hunting expedition and someone says

(2.3.4) Tomorrow let's see if we can bag a lion and a unicorn.

the utterance will be indeterminable in the familiar everyday world, because there are no such animals as unicorns except in mythology.

3.2.4 Contradiction

> I went to the pictures tomorrow;
> I took a front seat at the back.
> I fell from the pit to the gallery,
> And broke a front bone in my back.
> A lady she gave me some choc'late;
> I ate it, and gave it her back.
> I phoned for a taxi and walked it.
> And that's why I never came back.
>   (Anonymous)

An indeterminable expression may be CONTRADICTORY. For example, consider (2.4.1):

(2.4.1) According to the U.S. President Ronald Reagan himself, he is at the moment both 70 and 72.

In the familiar everyday world U.S. President Ronald Reagan inhabited when he erred in giving his age, it is anomalous to claim to be both 70 and 72 at the same time because only one of these is possible. This renders (2.4.1) indeterminable. Furthermore, it is contradictory since to predicate someone as 70 is to implicitly deny that they are any other age, including 72 (and vice versa). Thus a contradiction arises when we have to accept the logic of being unable to predicate both P and *not-P* simultaneously of some argument A. Take two other examples:

(2.4.2) X is a round square.

(2.4.3) My brother is an only child.

If X is round it has no angles; if X is square it has four angles: X cannot simultaneously have no angles and four angles, therefore (2.4.2) is contradictory. If B is S's brother then S is B's sibling, therefore the person labelled 'my brother' necessarily has a sibling (namely, the speaker). It follows that (2.4.3) is a contradiction because the person labelled 'my brother' cannot both have a sibling and be an only child.

Contradiction is the property of one expression. Two expressions which contradict each other are known as CONTRADICTORIES; thus *X is round* and *X is a square* are contradictories; so are *B has a brother* and *B is an only child*, or *R is 70* and *R is 72*.

We remarked in §1.2.2 that because S is normally assumed to be reasonable in what he says and expected to act in accordance with the co-operative principle, any apparently contradictory utterance will normally be intended and interpreted as non-contradictory and determinable. Cf.

(2.4.4) The film is both good and not good.

We assume that when S utters such a sentence as (2.4.4) he is not deliberately contradicting himself, but indicating that in some respects the film is good in his opinion and in other respects it is not. Ordinarily he will be expected to explain what he means by such a statement; e.g. that the photography was good but the story-line poor.

3.3   Expressions with more than one meaning

Kissinger should be bloody well hung.
He is, my dear, he is. (Signed) Mrs. Kissinger.

(Graffito on graffito)

3.3.1   Ambiguity, polysemy, and homonymy

We take it a priori that every expression has at least one meaning; many, of course, have more than one, i.e. they are AMBIGUOUS. Given that a theory of linguistic meaning aims to explain the meaning of any and every expression in the language, we take this to comprehend explaining the conditions under which an expression is ambiguous, and also the conditions under which the several meanings of a putatively ambiguous expression are distinguished from one another. Accidentally ambiguous utterances are comparatively rare: speakers take care to avoid them because they violate the co-operative maxim of manner. However, S may be purposely ambiguous – as Shakespeare was for a comic purpose in the passage quoted in §1.2.3.3 from *Henry IV, 2*, or as I shall be with some of the examples given below. Normally it is context which disambiguates a potentially ambiguous expression; but syntactic distribution will e.g. distinguish the noun *work* from the verb *work* (cf. *the works* vs. *he works*), or the auxiliary verb *can* "be able to" from the main verb *can* "put in cans" (cf. *He can can the fish he catches*). And occasionally form can be used to disambiguate an expression in one medium (say, the written) by recasting it in another (the spoken) – thus the orthographic noun *lead* could be pronounced either /liid/, for walking the dog, or /lɛd/, the metal; or the phonologically ambiguous noun /tɛɪl/ could be rendered either *tale* or *tail* in the written medium.[5]

In traditional semantics it has been usual to distinguish two kinds of ambiguity: POLYSEMY and HOMONYMY.

Polysemy is the property of an expression with more than one
   meaning.
Homonymy is the relation between two or more expressions which
   have the same form but different meanings.

There are many instances of a polysemous word whose meaning has in time split apart to become the property of two homonymous words; but no one has yet succeeded in defining the point of separation between the polysemous word and the homonymous pair derived from it. Nonetheless, within this section we shall endeavour to precisely clarify the difference between polysemy and homonymy.

3.3.2 Polysemy

Polysemy is, by tradition, the property of an emic expression with more than one meaning. In traditional lexicography a polysemic word is entered once in the dictionary with its multiple meanings, whereas unrelated homonyms are each entered separately. For instance, we find the following entry for the polysemic noun *bachelor* in *The Macquarie Dictionary* 1980, and something very similar in other reputable dictionaries.

> **bachelor** /'bætʃələ/ *n*. **1**. an unmarried man of any age. **2**. a person who has taken the first or lowest degree at a university: *Bachelor of Arts*. **3**. a young feudal knight who followed the banner of another. **4**. a young male fur seal kept from the breeding grounds by older males.

The assumption made here by the lexicographers is that the emic word *bachelor* is four ways ambiguous; and they have used the criteria of semantic and morphological relatedness to determine that *bachelor* is four ways polysemous rather than a set of two, three, or four homonyms. Sense **1** "an unmarried man" is the predominant sense of *bachelor*, and senses **2** and **3** are historically related to it (in ways we need not go into); sense **4** is obviously an extension from sense **1**, i.e. from "human males who have no mate" to "fur seal males that have no mate." But are these kinds of semantic relatedness appropriate criteria for deciding that there is only one, polysemous, noun lexeme *bachelor* rather than a number of homonyms?

If we take it that the predominant meaning of *bachelor* is sense **1** "an unmarried man", i.e. "a man who has no mate", then sense **4** has presumably derived through metaphorical extension of the word to fur seals that have no mate (indeed, one occasionally finds the word used of other male animals which have not found a mate, cf. Richard Dawkins *The Selfish Gene* 1976:154). It is conceivable that these two senses given for *bachelor* should rather be regarded as contextually distinguished interpretations of the same sense. This suggestion brings to mind the eleven interpretations of the word *lamb* exemplified in §1.3.4 exx. (3.4.3-13) all of which were based on the common core sense "young sheep" – for convenience they are repeated in (3.2.1) below.

(3.2.1)
  a. The lamb gambolled in the field.
  b. The dead lamb was being eaten by crows and maggots.
  c. The lamb was stuffed and put into a museum.
  d. These bones are lamb, goat, and rabbit, but not human.
  e. Lamb is my favourite meat.
  f. My wife would prefer the lining to be lamb, because it's warmer.
  g. We can't get the smell of lamb out of the car since we took the wretched animal to the vet in it.
  h. There was a painting of a lamb on the butcher's shop wall.
  i. The BBC archivist says he's got lamb on tape, but he can't do you the sound of a goat.
  j. The lamb is a delightful animal to keep as a pet.

In §1.3.4 it was argued that each interpretation is contextually distinguishable from the others; and because further interpretations of *lamb* might turn out to be possible in some as yet unrecognized contexts, it is presumptuous to place an upper bound on the total number of interpretations conceivable for any lexeme, cf. Philip N. Johnson-Laird 'Mental models of meaning' 1981:123. Consequently, it is uncertain that we could ever list all possible interpretations for every lexeme in the theoretical dictionary.[6] With our *lamb* examples we said in §1.3.4 that the meanings must be accounted for by inferring from context some reasonable and relevant interpretation based on the core sense "young sheep". Obviously this procedure can be generalized to the interpretation of all expressions: that is, we can impose a convention on the linguistic theory of meaning that every emic expression has a unique sense (what we have referred to as 'the core meaning') and this unique sense is the basis for contextually dependent interpretations of the expression. The emic expression will then be polysemous to the extent of the interpretations made of it in all the contexts in which it occurs – an upper bound which we have already said will be impossible to exactly predict.

Returning to the senses given for *bachelor* in *The Macquarie Dictionary*, we proposed that senses **1** and **4** be redefined as contextually determinable interpretations of the same sense, "male without a mate". However, it seems a trifle forced to paraphrase "a man who has never married", which is the dominant sense of *bachelor*, as "a male human without a mate." Here we are faced with a common lexicographical dilemma: to choose a polysemic entry, "male, typically human or occasionally a fur seal, that has no mate", or alternatively, two homonymous but closely related entries "man who has never married" and "a male fur seal, and occasionally other kind of male animal, that is without a mate during the breeding season." We shall opt for the latter. Turning to senses **3** and **4**, "a person who has taken the first or lowest degree at a university" and "a young feudal knight who followed the banner of another", both are historically related to the predominant sense, "an unmarried man", which is why the lexicographer included them under this same polysemic entry. The etymological relationship is not in question, yet so far as the present day lay speaker of English is concerned such a relationship is semantically irrelevant because it is impossible to contextually interpret either sense **2** or sense **3** from sense **1**. Given the convention proposed above that each lexeme have a unique sense (which is interpretable in a variety of ways according to context) then we shall require *bachelor* to have four separate entries in the dictionary that forms part of our theory of meaning,[7] i.e. we have the four homonyms

bachelor$_m$ "man who has never married"[8]
bachelor$_a$ "male seal, or occasionally other kind of male animal, that has no mate during the breeding season"
bachelor$_e$ "a person who has taken the first or lowest degree at a university".

bachelor$_k$ "a young feudal knight who followed the banner of another, or, nowadays, a simple knight not belonging to a special order".

This brings us to the discussion of homonymy.

3.3.3 Homonymy

'Mine is a long and sad tale!' said the Mouse, turning to Alice, and sighing.
   'It *is* a long tail, certainly,' said Alice, looking down with wonder at the Mouse's tail; 'but why do you call it sad?'
               (Lewis Carroll *Alice's Adventures in Wonderland* 1965:39)

Homonymy is a relation holding between two or more etic expressions that have the same form but a different meaning. Complete homonyms have the same pronunciation and the same spelling: classic examples are the nouns *bank*$_s$ "institution for the custody of money" and *bank*$_b$ "raised body of earth". (3.3.1) is ambiguous partly because of their homonymy:

(3.3.1) A bird flew into the bank.

An actual utterance of this clause is unlikely in fact to be ambiguous because of the context in which it occurs; thus the ambiguity discernible in (3.3.1) disappears as a consequence of the textual environments provided in (3.3.2-4), each of which imposes a distinct interpretation on the clause.

(3.3.2) While I was cashing a cheque yesterday, a bird flew into the bank and perched on the safety screen between the teller and me.

(3.3.3) While I was cashing a cheque yesterday, a bird flew into the bank, pushed me aside and pointed a gun at the teller in front of me.

(3.3.4) Harry was busy tieing a fly when a bird flew into the bank not ten feet from where he stood. He hadn't realized there are kingfishers nesting along there.

Assuming in all these that the world spoken of is the real world, or is patterned on the real world, then the pragmatic inferences which associate cheque cashing, safety screens, and hold ups with *bank*$_s$ make this the only feasible interpretation of 'bank' in (3.3.2-3). Pragmatic inferences from the nesting habits of kingfishers and the fact that Harry was tieing a fly (presumably with a view to fishing) suggest that 'bank' in (3.3.4) must be a river bank, i.e. a "raised body of earth". Pragmatic inferences about avian behaviour, such as perching and nesting (plus the reference to kingfishers in (3.3.4)), contrast with inferences concerning such non-avian behaviour as gun-toting and thrusting people aside in a hold up, and they lead to the different interpretation of 'bird' in (3.3.3) from that in (3.3.2) or (3.3.4).

Homonymy is not a relationship limited to words. The constituent lex and morph in *wants* are ambiguous between the noun lexeme "want + plural" morpheme on the one hand, and the verb lexeme "want + 3rd person singular subject agreement" morpheme on the other. Cf. the textual disambiguation in (3.3.5-6).

(3.3.5) His wants are few.

(3.3.6) He wants for nothing.

Note that despite the similarity in meaning between the noun *want* and the verb *want* they are of different lexical classes and therefore count as different lexemes – i.e. as meaningfully distinct expressions. Moving up to a higher level expression, the sentence in (3.3.7) is ambiguous:

(3.3.7) Jimmy says he hates boring students.

Once again, context will normally clarify whether it is Jimmy or the students who is/are boring. Note the importance in this example of syntactic relations in resolving the ambiguity: cf. " he hates boring (*j*) (*j*) students" versus "he hates students who are boring". The homonymy is between the noun phrase *boring students* consisting of participial attributive plus its head noun, and the embedded participial clause *boring students* consisting of a nonfinite verb and its object; it is the context of the particular utterance U which will determine for H which of these is intended.

Homonymy can be subdivided into HOMOPHONY, same pronunciation but different meaning, and HOMOGRAPHY, same spelling but different meaning. The homonymous expressions we have discussed so far have been both homophonous and homographous; however, *tale* and *tail*, for instance are homophonous /teɪl/ and not homographous; and in my speech /pɔɔ/ is ambiguous between the adjective *poor*, the verb *pour*, the verbs and nouns *pore* and *paw* – all of which are homophones. Sometimes the written forms of pairs of zero derived lexemes and their source words are homographous but not homophonous, cf. noun–verb pairs like *use* /juːs/, /juuz/, *convict* /ˈkɒnvɪkt/,

/kn'vɪkt/ in addition, there are words like *lead* ambiguous between the noun /lɛd/ and the unrelated verb /liid/. The noun phrase *the Bolivian silver tray* is homographously ambiguous, but the meanings are – or can be – differentiated prosodically from one another, cf.

(3.3.8)   / the Bolivian silver / tray /   "the tray for Bolivian silver"

(3.3.9)   / the Bolivian silver tray /   "the tray made of Bolivian silver"

(3.3.10) / the Bolivia / silver tray /   "the silver tray from Bolivia"

Homonyms may arise from a change in pronunciation and or spelling. E.g. homophones *sea* and *see* were once /sææ/ and /see/ respectively before the time of the great English vowel shift. *Sound* meaning "channel of water" is from Old English and Old Norse *sund*; meaning "healthy, secure" it is from Germanic *gesund*; meaning "noise" it is from Old English and Old French *son*.[9] Homonyms also arise from zero derivation, cf. the verbs *helicopter* and *waitress* from the homonymous nouns; nouns like *catch* and *work* from the homonymous verbs; and nouns like *black*, *oral*, or *newly-wed* from the homonymous adjectives. Ellipsis gives rise to ambiguities like (3.3.7), *Jimmy hates boring students*, where ambiguity is unavoidable without a complete change in phraseology. There is avoidable ellipsis of the end-rhymes in rhyming slang[10] which often results in a homonym, cf. *china* "crockery" and *china* "mate" from *china plate*; or *whistle* "(instrument for producing) a sharp sound caused by air passing over a gap", and *whistle* "suit" from *whistle and flute*. Finally, homonyms arise through euphemisms, e.g. *bull* is ambiguous between "male, typically bovine, animal" and "rubbish, nonsense" – the latter being a euphemistic elliptical form of the metaphorical pejorative *bullshit*; other examples of euphemistic homonyms are *ass* "arse", *crust* "Christ", *sugar* "shit [expletive]".

Homonyms also arise across different dialects or varieties of a language. E.g. the following words have, or may have, different meanings in British as against American English: *biscuit*, *braces*, *corn*, *cot*, *fender*, *hood*, *knock up*, *pavement*, *robin*, *rubber*, *suspenders*, *vest*.[11] In the jargon of, e.g. the drug subculture, words like *connection*, *brown sugar*, *coke*, *fuzz*, *grass*, *head*, *high*, *hit*, *horse*, *joint*, *junk*, *roach*, *score*, *shit*, *smack*, *snow*, *tea* are homonymous with standard English words.

Homonyms are usually kept distinct in actual utterance by the constraints of the context in which they are used. Very often they are grammatically distinct from one another: e.g. the noun *waitress* and the homonymous zero derived verb *waitress* are distinguished by being in different lexical classes, and hence by their morphosyntactic potential[12] and grammatical function. The ambiguity of the noun *bull*, mentioned above, is not usually at issue because in the sense "male, typically bovine, animal" it heads a countable noun phrase, cf. *a bull*, [*three*] *bulls*; in the sense "rubbish, nonsense" it heads an uncountable noun phrase, cf. *that's a load of bull*. The common noun *mayday* "vessel in distress" (from French *m'aidez*) contrasts with the proper name *May Day*. Of course, denotation is the ultimate distinguisher because the sense of an expression reflects the salient characteristics perceived in the denotatum; thus describing a male human as *a queen* means something quite different from describing a female as *a queen*.

Where a word has a taboo homonym with which it could be confused because it is syntactically as well as formally similar, it will often be dropped from the language. Since the 1960s the adjective *gay* has been less and less used in the sense "bright, full of fun" because it also has the meaning "homosexual". British English still uses *cock* to mean "rooster" but this use of the word has died out in American English and is very rare in Australian English because of the taboo homonym meaning "penis". The Biblical *coney* meaning "rabbit" dropped out of English in the 19th century because of the taboo homonym meaning "cunt".[13]

As we mentioned previously, there is no sharp definition between polysemy and homonymy. For instance, the adjective *gay* was metaphorically, and euphemistically, extended to homosexual males because of the belief that they dressed more gaily (i.e. more brightly) than straight males; this was a polysemous extension. However, one's intuitions today are that *gay* meaning "homosexual" has split away from *gay* in its earlier sense of "bright, full of fun" and cannot be contextually determined from it, so that the two adjectives form a pair of etymologically related homonyms. Supporting evidence for this analysis comes from the existence of the noun *gay* which uniquely means "a homosexual", and which is lexically distinct from the original adjective *gay*. Through association with this noun, the adjective *gay* meaning "homosexual" must also be presumed lexically distinct from the original adjective meaning "bright, full of fun". Notice that we have introduced an additional criterion for distinguishing homonymy from polysemy. Homonyms exist when two or more interpretations of an etic expression cannot be derived (by reference to context) from a common source – i.e. from a lexeme having a unique sense. Where there is doubt, appeal can be made to the following discovery procedure if it should apply:

Given an expression E₁ which is formally identical with and semantically related to an expression E₂ of the same lexical or morphological class, but which cannot readily be derived from the sense of E₂, and given also that E₁ is semantically and morphologically related to another expression E₃ that is lexically distinct from E₁, then E₁ and E₂ are homonyms.

The case of *gay* is not uncommon: an extension in the meaning of a word is often what leads to the establishment of a homonym. Not many people today think of *flour* and *flower* as having anything other than a homophonous relationship, yet flour "meal made by finely grinding up seed from a cereal plant" has its origin in the ellipsis of *flower of the meal* "the finest or choicest part of the meal" (this sense of *flower*, cf. *flower of the country's manhood*, is related to *flower* "blossom" because the latter is the choicest part of the plant). The spelling difference which contributes to our certainty that *flour* and *flower* are homonyms, did not always differentiate them; e.g. in Samuel Johnson's *Dictionary* of 1755 both lexemes are spelled *flower*.

Formally identical expressions which are lexically distinct are homonyms. What makes them lexically distinct is their morphosyntactic potential and syntactic distribution, but most significantly their semantic difference. For instance, in languages like French with nominal gender, a difference in gender between formally identical nouns may correlate with a difference in meaning, i.e. it may serve to mark the homonymy of pairs like *un manche* [masculine] "a handle", *une manche* [feminine] "a sleeve" or *le mémoire* [masc.] "the memo, report" *la mémoire* [fem.] "the memory"; yet the difference in gender may simply mark the contextually different interpretations of a single lexeme, e.g. "élève = "pupil" as in *un élève* "a male pupil", *une élève* "a female pupil". In such languages as French a difference in the gender of identical nominal forms is no guarantee of homonymy between them. There is something rather similar in English, where we have seen that for *bull* to head a countable noun phrase normally indicates the lexeme "male, typically bovine, animal", whereas the formally identical noun heading an uncountable noun phrase will almost certainly be the homonymous lexeme "rubbish, nonsense". Yet the single lexeme "lamb" = "young sheep" is used in both uncountable and countable NPs. In all these cases the semantic content is the deciding factor, not the syntactic environment of the expression.

With this in mind consider the following correlations between 'gave' and 'donated' in (3.3.11) and (3.3.12).[14]

(3.3.11)
  a. Tom gave $10 to the Salvation Army.
  b. Tom donated $10 to the Salvation Army.

(3.3.12)
  a. Max gave $10 to Ed.
  b. ?*Max donated $10 to Ed.

The facts presented in (3.3.11-12) do not warrant us postulating two homonymous verbs $give_1$ and $give_2$ on the basis of the semantic difference revealed in the use of *donate*: it is not relevant to the meaning of *give* whether the recipient is an institution (or fund) or alternatively one or more individuals. Such a difference is no more relevant to specifying the sense of the lexeme "give" than it would be relevant to distinguish two senses of *drop* because of the different effects of the actions described in (3.3.13-14):

(3.3.13) Max accidentally dropped his spectacles into the furnace.

(3.3.14) Max accidentally dropped his spectacles into the pool.

3.3.4 Definitions for polysemy and homonymy

Ambiguities in expression are usually resolved from context, but we have seen that syntactic distribution, morphosyntactic potential, and sometimes an alternative medium of expression will disambiguate. The traditional distinction between the property of polysemy in an emic expression and the relation of homonymy between etic expressions was of interest to lexicographers because they were concerned to identify the criteria for what should count as a separate dictionary entry. We have proposed as a convention for the theoretical dictionary that every entry should have a unique sense which is open to a variety of interpretations in different contexts: this will define polysemy. Homonymy is then the relation that holds between formally identical etic expressions which correspond with separate lexeme or morpheme entries in the dictionary. The ambiguity of higher level expressions than words will be decided on the basis of their lexemic composition, including zero anaphors as lexemes.

3.4   Values

3.4.1   Introduction

Early in life one is schooled to distinguish true statements from false ones. Take for example

(4.1.1) The Earth is roughly spherical.

(4.1.2) The Earth is a perfect cube

We recognize that the statement in (4.1.1) is true and the one in (4.1.2) is false: i.e. it is true that the Earth is roughly spherical and false that the Earth is a perfect cube. Thus we say that a statement has a truth value. To make a statement is to perform one kind of speech act; utterances used to perform other kinds of speech acts (cf. §1.6.3 and ch.8) will have different kinds of values. E.g. utterances of (4.1.3-6) cannot be used to make statements and therefore they will not have truth values.

(4.1.3) What's your name?

(4.1.4) Was it a good film?

(4.1.5) Eat your spinach!

(4.1.6) Thank you for the chocolates.

We cannot reasonably say that any utterance of these is either true or false under any circumstances. The following examples (4.1.3'-6') are anomalous because the complement sentences within them cannot be associated with truth values:

(4.1.3') *It is either true or it is false that what's your name?

(4.1.4') *It is either true or it is false that was it a good film?

(4.1.5') *It is either true or it is false that eat your spinach!

(4.1.6') *It is either true or it is false that thank you for the chocolates.

What sort of values do (4.1.3-6) have? Before answering such a question we should clarify what we mean by the value of an utterance in a particular kind of speech act.

The term 'value' is used to mean the value that H places on a particular utterance U in relation to its context C. Utterances can be classified for the purposes of value assignment according to the kind of speech act in which they are used. The following kinds of speech acts (cf. §8.5) have the different sets of values indicated:

statements have truth values
predictions have probable-truth values
commissives (i.e. promises and offers) have genuineness values
directives (imperatives, interrogatives, and requests) have compliance
    values
acknowledgments (e.g. greetings, thanks, condolences) have
    appropriacy values
authoritatives (permissives and advisories) and declaratory acts have
    authority values

A statement is a purported fact about W, the world spoken of. Its truth
value is based on whether or not H judges it to really express a fact
about W. A prediction is similarly based on its probable truth in
relation to W. The value H places on a commissive, such as a promise,
is determined by his judgement of its genuineness, i.e. whether or not
it is apparent that S genuinely intends to carry out his promise in W.
Utterances of (4.1.3-5) have compliance values – judgements on
whether the request or command can be complied with, whether a
question can be answered. An acknowledgment such as (4.1.6) is
judged on the basis of its appropriacy – e.g. whether or not thanks is
warranted in the context in which (4.1.6) is uttered. A declaratory act
such as a legal judgement is assigned a value based on the authority
with which it is uttered, i.e. whether it is such as to make the
judgement legally binding. It is notable that negative values – false
statements, highly improbable or impossible predictions, nongenuine
commissives, impossible requests or commands, unwarranted acknowledgments, unauthoritative permissives etc. – threaten H's negative
face (cf. §1.2.3.3) and are therefore unco-operative. By contrast,
positive values tend to maintain H's face.

For value to be assigned, an utterance U must be determinable.
Indeterminability generally reduces value assignments to comparative
insignificance. Certainly indeterminable utterances cannot be assigned
positive values, and they tend to be assigned negative values in
conversational interaction. However, indeterminable statements, predictions, or commissives appear to have indeterminable values;
whereas other indeterminable utterance types have to be assigned
negative values.

3.4.2   The notion of truth in language

The philosopher's notion of truth is not necessarily ideal for a linguist because the philosopher is typically interested in what is true, thanks to God or Nature, in this world (and only occasionally in some other worlds); whereas the linguist must concern himself with truth values as they are relevant to language and language use – and hence with truth as it is perceived by language users whatever the world they may be speaking of. The relevance of truth within a theory of linguistic meaning can be simply demonstrated from a comparison of (4.2.1-2).

(4.2.1) My son Ed stepped over the log OK, but his sister, who's only five, couldn't.

(4.2.2) My son Ed stepped over the Empire State Building OK, but his sister who's only five, couldn't.

If the world spoken of is the familiar everyday world, then (4.2.2) is anomalous unless 'the Empire State Building' refers to a smallish model; we know this because it cannot be true that a human being is able to step over the real Empire State Building. Without the notion that (4.2.2) has a truth value, i.e. that it could not be true in the familiar everyday world, we should be unable to recognize and describe the anomaly within it.

Although logicians have generally clung to the bivalent notion of truth, i.e. to the notion that a statement is either true or it is false, for natural language truth has to be considered a fuzzy notion with absolute truth having a value 1 and falsity having a value $0.$[15] This correlates precisely with the notion that denotational categories are fuzzy sets (cf. §2.9.5). For instance, a yellow-green colour with a wavelength of 520 nm can be said to be green with a truth value of 0.67 and yellow with a truth value of 0.33; it is utterly false (with a truth value of 0) that the colour is either red or blue. The notion of fuzzy truth in language is only acceptable if we believe that truth is a convention – like language itself; and just as language conventions change over time so do conventions concerning truth. For instance it was thought in the 13th century that (4.2.3) was true and (4.2.4) false; nowadays, of course, these judgements are reversed.

(4.2.3) The Earth is roughly flat.

(4.2.4) The Earth is roughly spherical.

Before there was recognition of the Earth's gravitational force it would have been absurd to believe that the Earth could be spherical because everyday experience with spherical objects shows that things fall off them, not towards them; thus it stood to reason that the Earth must be flat, and (4.2.3) was therefore held to be true while (4.2.4) was held to be false. It is as wrong to insist that (4.2.3) was false for the 13th century writer, as it would be to insist that it is true today.[16]

This raises the question of folk-taxonomies, the language users' classifications of the world about them, which may not correspond with the classifications of a natural scientist. For instance many people classify spiders as insects and whales as fishes, although this is zoologically inept. If an ordinary person describes a spider as an insect we don't accuse them of making a false statement, though we might say they are mistaken; nevertheless, I think we have to allow that the category of insects includes spiders as peripheral members. Folk taxonomies generally differ from systematic biological and other "scientific" taxonomies in a number of ways. Harold C. Conklin notes the following.

[Folk taxonomies] usually relate only to locally relevant or directly observable phenomena. They are defined by criteria which may differ greatly from culture to culture. The number and positions of levels of contrasts may change from one sector of a folk system to another. There are no formal rules for nomenclatural recognition or rejection of taxa [. . .] though new groupings may be added productively with considerable ease. In respect to any particular local biota, there is no reason to expect the folk taxa to match those of systematic biology – either in number or in range. The Hunanóo classify their local plant world, at the lowest (terminal) level of contrast, into more than 1800 mutually exclusive folk taxa, while botanists divide the same flora – in terms of species – into less than 1300 scientific taxa.
   [. . .] Unlike scientific taxa, folk segregates may belong simultaneously to several distinct hierarchic structures. The same segregates may be classed as terminal categories in a taxonomy based on form and appearance and also as terminal or nonterminal categories in another taxonomy based on cultural treatment (e.g. morphologically distinguished kinds of floral segregates vs. functional categories of plants as food cultigens, medicines, ornamentals, etc.).
                 (Conklin 'Lexicographical treatment of folk taxonomies'
                                                                    1967:129)

For additional discussion cf. Stephen Tyler (ed.) *Cognitive Anthropology* 1969:28-90, 165-89; Brent Berlin, Dennis E. Breedlove, & Peter

H. Raven *Principles of Tzeltal Plant Classification* 1974. Taxonomies of natural phenomena will differ from one community to another because the way we analyze the world around us does differ from culture to culture and between subcultures (such as lay folk and the scientific community). A particular taxonomy becomes conventional within its particular context of use presumably because it is thought to be the best available by the majority of people who use it (cf. David Lewis *Conventions* 1969). Thus, to claim that any one of the possible taxonomies is the "true" one is simply a mistake: folk taxonomies are as valid for the folk for whom they are conventional as scientific taxonomies are valid among scientists. There may be reasons for preferring one taxonomy over another in a given context, but they will be based on the perception of its consistency, coherence, and efficiency within the context. In a different context these advantages may not be perceived to obtain.

The relevance of context in determining what counts as true was first pointed out by John L. Austin when he said that for the casual traveller it may be true enough to say that *Oxford is sixty miles from London*. This would be too imprecise for the cartographer, who requires something akin to the absolute truth when measuring distances between places. But note that this absolute truth is hard if not impossible to come by: it would be possible to measure the distance between some fixed point in London and some fixed point in Oxford, but there would be no guarantee that – even were the measuring device accurate – movements in the Earth's crust would not make fractional and insignificant differences to that measurement over a period of time. This makes the notion of absolute truth in statements of measurement a somewhat dubious one. Certainly linguists have to work with a fuzzy conception of truth, and one that is determined by the conventions applicable to the context in which a particular statement is made.

Consider the truth values of the indeterminable contradictory statements in (4.2.5) and (4.2.6), on the assumption that they are uttered in 1980 purportedly about the familiar everyday world.

(4.2.5) The present King of France is bald.

(4.2.6) The present King of France is not bald.

Both statement making sentences are indeterminable because there was no King of France in 1980. Furthermore, the truth values of the statements are indeterminable, and the reasons for saying this are as follows. (4.2.5) and (4.2.6) are contradictories, therefore it should be the case that if either one is true the other is false, cf.

(4.2.7)
    a.   Margaret Thatcher is bald.   [False]
    b.   Margaret Thatcher is not bald. [True]

(4.2.8)
    a.   Kojak is bald.   [True]
    b.   Kojak is not bald.   [False]

However, we can only reasonably say that neither of (4.2.5-6) is true; so presumably neither can be false either! Hence the truth value of an indeterminable statement is indeterminable too. We seem to have derived the following three-term system for truth values: true, not-true (indeterminable), and false.

3.4.3 Predictions and probable-truth values

Predictions like those in (4.3.1-3) do not have straightforward fuzzy truth values such as statements of purported fact do. Statements of purported fact are either absolutely true (to a value 1), relatively true (to a value of <1 and >0), or absolutely false (to a value 0). Predictions are judged on their probability of becoming true when the content of the utterance is matched against what is known of the world spoken of, W.

(4.3.1) If it is hot in Adelaide today, it will be hot in Melbourne in a couple of days' time.

(4.3.2) Prince's Ears will win the cup on Saturday.

(4.3.3) Doris will be home by now.

Anyone who knows something about the weather patterns in southern Australia knows that (4.3.1) is about 0.65 probable. The probability of (4.3.2) turning out true may be judged on the reputation of S as a tipster, on what H knows of Prince's Ears' form, and the going on cup day. The probability of (4.3.3) turning out to be accurate will depend on such things as the length of Doris's journey, the traffic density, how long Doris is known to have taken to make similar journeys in the past, etc.
    Determinable predictions have truth values ranging between probably-true and probably-false. But indeterminable predictions such as *The present King of France will (not) fly to America tomorrow* have the value not-possibly-true.

3.4.4 The genuineness of a commissive

A commissive is an utterance in which S makes a promise or offer and thereby commits himself to some future act. If S were to say

(4.4.1) I hereby promise to give every orphan in Africa, India and South America $1 million each

and he is deemed to be talking about the familiar everyday world, then his promise could not be judged genuine because no individual, institution or even nation would have enough money to go round. However, if someone utters (4.4.2) there is a good possibility that his commissive speech act is genuine.

(4.4.2) OK, I'll take you to a movie tomorrow.

The judgement of its genuineness will depend on what is known of S's sincerity, and his plans for the next day, and whether or not there will be a movie screened then; nevertheless a commissive is more often than not genuine, because speakers normally observe the co-operative principle.

An indeterminable promise, such as *I promise to assassinate the present King of France on December 24, 1980*, is neither genuine nor insincere.

3.4.5 Compliance values

The value placed on utterances of such sentences as (4.5.1-4) depends upon the reasonableness of asking H to comply with them.

(4.5.1) What's the capital of Burma?

(4.5.2) Is a phoneme acoustically definable?

(4.5.3) Can you pass the salt?

(4.5.4) Eat your spinach!

It would be unreasonable to ask the average two year old the question in (4.5.1) or to ask the question in (4.5.2) of anyone who had no training or self-education in linguistics, because in both cases the question could not be expected to be answered by the person addressed. Like all other values, compliance values are often context bound. Of course, some questions are unanswerable in any context, e.g. *Which came first, the chicken or the egg?* and some commands could never be complied with, e.g. *Discover which came first, the chicken or the egg!* But this makes no difference to the general constraint that compliance values are context bound. Note that the compliance value is not judged on the success of the speech act in getting H to comply, but on the reasonableness of asking or telling him to comply; in consequence an indeterminable imperative such as *Shoot the present King of France on December 24, 1980* cannot be complied with.

3.4.6 The appropriacy value of an acknowledgment

The value placed on a greeting, an apology, expression of condolence, congratulation or thanks is judged on whether the acknowledgment is warranted or not under the circumstances. E.g. the expression of condolence in (4.6.1)

(4.6.1) I'm deeply sorry that your wife has died

is only appropriate if H's wife has died. If H has no wife, (4.6.1) is indeterminable but still inappropriate. Similarly for other acknowledgments.

3.4.7 Authority values

There are many kinds of utterances whose value is determined by the authority with which they are delivered, e.g. those which give permission, advise or warn, cast legal verdicts, veto, declare umpires' decisions, effect baptism, marriage, appointments, sackings, or legal sentencing. Consider

(4.7.1) Yes, you can go out and play with Tommy.

(4.7.2) I warn you not to press that red button [or else we've all had it].

(4.7.3) Guilty.

(4.7.4) The ball was out!

(4.7.5) You're fired!

For utterances of these sentences to be effective, they must be made by someone with the appropriate authority vested in them. E.g. H's mother might give permission for him to go and play with Tommy because she is recognized to have the authority to do so. A warning such as in (4.7.2) can only be appropriately given by someone in the know. When the jury foreman utters (4.7.3) the defendant is found guilty and the remark has legal status because of the authority vested in the jury. And so forth for the other examples. When such an utterance is indeterminable S loses his authority by virtue of being unreasonable.

3.4.8   Values – a summary

All determinable utterances have a value of one kind or another; the particular kind of value ascribed to an utterance is decided by the kind of speech act which it is used to perform. Values are context bound, though sometimes the form of the utterance is such that one particular value will be assigned no matter what the context of utterance. Only six kinds of value have been identified here (though further study might show the need for either more or fewer), they are as follows: statements have fuzzy truth values; predictions have values between being probably true and probably false; commissives have genuineness values; imperatives, interrogatives, and requests have compliance values; acknowledgments have appropriacy values; and declaratory acts, permissives, and advisories have authority values.

3.5   Semantic predicates as meaning components

3.5.1   Introduction

In terms of ch.2 categories such as Bird, Disease, Fruit, Vegetable, Red, Blue, Action, State, Event, or Quality – each of which correspond to the denotation of a language expression identical with the category name – are fuzzy sets, some of whose members will be closer to the prototype for the category than others will. Members of such fuzzy sets can be regarded as proper subsets that are themselves fuzzy sets. Thus the categories are relateable to one another in ways familiar from set theory: e.g. the category of Colour contains the categories Red and Blue i.e. Colour $\supset$ Red & Blue; the category Orange is the intersection set of the categories Red and Yellow i.e. Orange = (Red $\cap$ Yellow); the category Tomato is a member of the intersection set of Fruit and Vegetable i.e. (Fruit $\cap$ Vegetable) $\supset$ Tomato.[17] These set relations mirror semantic relations between the expressions labelling the categories – semantic relations which will be discussed in §§3.5-3.7.

It has not been customary within semantics to relate the meanings of category names in quite the way described here; instead they have been related via the notion of shared semantic components. Yet suppose we take expression E_c (e.g. *carrot*) which has the semantic component K_v (e.g. VEGETABLE): this is descriptively equivalent to saying that the category labelled E_c (Carrot) is a member of the category labelled by K_v (Vegetable). In §3.3 we examine the notion of semantic components and relate them to the notion of categories.

By way of introducing semantic components, consider the componential table in (5.1.1) showing semantic components ADULT, YOUNG, MALE, FEMALE, BOVINE, EQUINE, OVINE distributed among nine expressions (lexemes) in such a way that the meaning of each expression can be defined in terms of its semantic components so as to contrast with the meaning of all the other expressions in the componential table (cf. Louis Hjelmslev *Prolegomena to a Theory of Language* 1961:70f, John Lyons *Introduction to Theoretical Linguistics* 1968:472, Adrienne Lehrer *Semantic Fields and Lexical Structure* 1974:46).

(5.1.1)

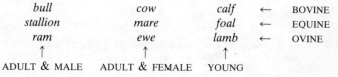

bull	*cow*	*calf*	←	BOVINE
stallion	*mare*	*foal*	←	EQUINE
ram	*ewe*	*lamb*	←	OVINE
↑	↑	↑		
ADULT & MALE	ADULT & FEMALE	YOUNG		

Extrapolating from the table we can define the meaning of each lexeme, e.g. *bull* is ADULT & MALE & BOVINE; *stallion* is ADULT & MALE & EQUINE; *ewe* is ADULT & FEMALE & OVINE; *foal* is YOUNG & EQUINE.

Because of the importance of componential analysis in recent semantic theories we shall look through its history for the rationale behind it, before seeking to establish what a semantic component is in §3.5.3.

3.5.2 Componential analysis

Within modern linguistics, the componential analysis of meaning was adapted from distinctive feature analysis in morphosyntax which in turn had its roots in the methodology of Prague school phonology. In *Principles of Phonology* 1969:86 Nikolai Trubetzkoy analyzed Sanskrit stop phonemes into the four-member bundles in (5.2.1).

(5.2.1)

```
p ———— ph    t ———— th    k ———— kh
|          |    |          |    |          |
b ———— bh    d ———— dh    g ———— gh
```

The bundles at each place of articulation – bilabial, dental, velar – are correlated with the distribution of components of aspiration and sonority, so that each stop within a bundle can be differentiated by a conjunction (symbolized '&') of oppositions (symbolized 'v'), viz.

(ASPIRATED v UNASPIRATED) & (VOICED v VOICELESS)

Thus:

/bh/	is BILABIAL & ASPIRATED & VOICED
/p/	is BILABIAL & UNASPIRATED & VOICELESS
/gh/	is VELAR & ASPIRATED & VOICED

From these descriptions we can see at a glance e.g. what components /bh/ and /gh/ have in common, and in what they differ. A complete articulatory description of the whole series is possible using just seven features and the two connectives '&' and 'v'.[18]

The same sort of componential analysis was used in Roman Jakobson's 'Beitrag zur allgemeinen Kasuslehre' 1936 to describe case forms in terms of a minimal set of components that together describe the complete case system of a language. For example, the noun paradigms in Latin are traditionally set out as in (5.2.2)

(5.2.2) a. First declension: *femina, -ae* Fem. "woman"

Singular	Nominative	-a	fēmina	"(the, a) woman (subject)"
	Genitive	-ae	fēminae	"of (the, a) woman, (the, a) woman's"
	Dative	-ae	fēminae	"to/for (the, a) woman"
	Accusative	-am	fēminam	"(the, a) woman (object)"
	Ablative	-ā	fēminā	"from/with/in/by (the, a) woman"
Plural	Nominative	-ae	fēminae	"(the) women (subject)"
	Genitive	-ārum	fēminārum	"of (the) women, (the women's)"
	Dative	-īs	fēminīs	"to/for (the) women"
	Accusative	-ās	fēminās	"(the) women (object)"
	Ablative	-īs	fēminīs	"from/with/in/by (the) women"

b. Third declension: *rūmor, -ōris* Masc. "rumor"; *nox, noctis, -ium* Fem. "night"; *sīdus, -eris* Neut. "star"

	Sing.	Pl.	Sing.	Pl.	Sing.	Pl.
Nom.	rūmor	rūmōrēs	nox	noctēs	sīdus	sīdera
Gen.	rūmōris	rūmōrum	noctis	noctium	sīderis	sīderum
Dat.	rūmōri	rūmōribus	noctī	noctibus	sīderi	sīderibus
Acc.	rūmōrem	rūmōrēs	noctem	noctēs/īs	sīdus	sīdera
Abl.	rūmōre	rūmōribus	nocte	noctibus	sīdere	sīderibus

(5.2.2) illustrates only a handful of noun paradigms, others can be found in any Latin grammar. It can be deduced from the examples in (5.2.2) that every suffix realizes four covert categories: Case, Gender, Number, and Declension. The forms of the suffixes can be predicted from the particular combination of contrastive components from each of the four categories, as in (5.2.3).

(5.2.3)

Case:	NOMINATIVE v GENITIVE v DATIVE v ACCUSATIVE v ABLATIVE
Gender:	MASCULINE v FEMINE v NEUTER
Number:	SINGULAR v PLURAL
Declension:	1 v 2 v 3 v 4 v 5

(5.2.3) describes the set of all possible components for the Latin case system. Each noun suffix can be specified individually in terms of one component from each category of Case, Gender, Number, and Declension, cf.

(5.2.4)

ACCUSATIVE & FEMININE & SINGULAR & 1 → -*am* (e.g. *fēminam*)
GENITIVE & NEUTER & PLURAL & 3 → -*um* (e.g. *sīderum*)
ABLATIVE & MASCULINE & SINGULAR & 2 → -*ō* (e.g. *puerō*)

The (inflexional) noun suffixes of Latin are what Charles Hockett (in 'Problems of morphemic analysis' 1947) called 'portmanteau morphs' because they comprise a bundle of components, none of which has independent morphological realization. This is typical of the components revealed by componential analysis.

In his 'Componential analysis of a Hebrew paradigm' 1948,[19] Zellig Harris analyzed the Hebrew verb paradigm in much the same way that we have just analyzed the Latin noun paradigm. Although Harris might have said he was analyzing morphosyntax, the components he identified for the categories of Tense, Person, and Gender are arguably semantic, and the paper presents a bridge between componential analysis in morphosyntax and componential analysis in semantics. In a slightly later paper 'A system for the description of semantic elements' 1951:7, Eugene Nida contrasted Greek λύσονται "they will loose themselves" and λύω "I loose", cf.

λύ- :	LOOSE	λύ- :	LOOSE
-σ- :	FUTURE TENSE	-ω :	PRESENT TENSE & (INDICATIVE V
-o- :	INDICATIVE MOOD		SUBJUNCTIVE MOOD) &
-ν- :	PLURAL NUMBER		SINGULAR NUMBER & 1st PERSON
-τ- :	3rd PERSON		& ACTIVE VOICE
-αι- :	MIDDLE VOICE		

Nida referred to the components of the portmanteau morph '-ω' as 'semes' meaning semantic components.[20]

It is a smallish step from the componential analysis of closed morphosyntactic systems like noun and verb affixes to the componential analysis of closed lexical systems like kinship systems. Anthropologists had for many years been comparing widely differing kinship systems in culturally distinct societies by interpreting them in terms of universal constituents that we might reasonably equate with semantic components. E.g. Alfred Kroeber in 'Classificatory systems of relationships' 1909 postulated the following components: generation; relative age within a generation; consanguineal vs. affinal; lineal vs. collateral; sex of ego,[21] kinsman, and linking kinsman; condition – living, or deceased – of kinsman. Two of the earliest articles in componential analysis of meaning appeared consecutively in *Language* 32, 1956, both were analyses of kin terms: they are Floyd Lounsbury's 'A semantic analysis of the Pawnee Kinship usage' and Ward Goodenough's 'Componential analysis and the study of meaning' (an analysis of the meanings of Trukese kin terms). Lounsbury's paper begins with a comparison of the following sets of English and Spanish kin terms, noting that there is in Spanish a regular superficial marking for the sex of kin that has no compeer in English.

(5.2.5)

MALE			FEMALE
uncle	tio	tia	aunt
son	hijo	hija	daughter
grandfather	abuelo	abuela	grandmother
brother	hermano	hermana	sister

Despite the fact that there are no gender morphs in the English words to correspond to Spanish *-o* and *-a*, gender is a significant component in the meaning of the English terms. For instance, it is anomalous to call one's uncle an aunt, or one's sister a brother just because the covert gender of the kin terms must be compatible with the sex of the person denoted. Thus, when the terms *aunt* and *uncle* are extended to close friends of ego's parents, they are assigned on the basis of the sex of the denotatum. Children early become aware of the covert gender in English kin terms, cf. Lamb's 1965:37 quote of a 6 year old saying, 'Mommy, what are girl nephews called?' And although gender is not morphologically marked in English, it does have grammatical consequences: the personal pronoun anaphoric to *uncle* is *he/him*, the one for *aunt* is *she/her*. And whereas the sentence *My aunt is pregnant* is grammatical, **My uncle is pregnant* is anomalous.

Today it is no longer necessary to justify the study of semantic components using arguments about their syntactic effects; but in the 1950s semantics was still regarded by many linguists as metaphyiscal and unfit for the kind of scientific enquiry into observable language structures that they believed linguistics should undertake. The early writers on componential analysis in morphosyntax and kinship systems were responsible for changing contemporary linguistic opinion on the status of semantic analysis, by showing that it can be carried out using approved methods of structural analysis, such as those used to filter out the phonetic components of the Sanskrit stop phonemes in (5.2.1). Just as we can compare and contrast /bh/, /p/, and /gh/ so we can compare and contrast *father*, *uncle* and *aunt*. These three kin terms all have in common that they are FIRST ASCENDING GENERATION; *father* and *uncle* additionally have in common that both are MALE whereas *aunt* is FEMALE; *aunt* and *uncle* are both COLLATERAL, whereas *father* is LINEAL. Thus via the semantic components we have identified, we can show the meaning relationships between *father*, *uncle*, and *aunt*.

Having briefly reviewed the origins of componential analysis in semantics, we shall take stock of the assumptions implicit in an analysis of this kind. (a) Componential analysis seeks to analyze the sense of an expression E into a set of semantic components; each semantic component corresponds to a category of which the category labelled by E is a subset. (b) Every expression E in language L should be analyzable into one or more semantic components. (c) There is no one-to-one correlation between morphs and semantic components. (d) Expressions that share semantic components are semantically related. (e) Being components of sense, semantic components reflect the characteristics of prototypical denotata. (f) There is a hierarchy of semantic components (because there is a hierarchy of categories, cf. §3.5.1); e.g. FELINE, which is a semantic component of *cat*, entails the semantic component ANIMAL which is also, therefore, a component of *cat*. Because semantic components reflect the characteristics of prototypical denotata, the hierarchy of components corresponds to perceived hierarchies among denotata. This suggests a thesaurus-like structure for semantic components.

The two assumptions (b), that every expression E in language L should be analyzable into semantic components, and (f), that these components will be structured into hierarchies which correspond to perceived hierarchies among denotata, lead to the consequence that all perceived hierarchies which can be encoded in language will correspond to semantic components. Thus the universal set of semantic components for L can be discovered by listing for L all perceived hierarchies that exist among the denotata of language expressions in L. As we remarked above, such a list would be rather like a thesaurus. There have been a number of attempts to carry out such a task, the most successful of them being Bishop John Wilkin's *An Essay Toward a Real Character and a Philosophical Language* 1668. Wilkins was contemporary with the general grammarians briefly discussed in §2.9.9. Like them he accepted the Aristotelean tradition that although natural languages may differ from one another superficially, there is inter-translateability because all men's perceptions are essentially similar, and it is these experiences which a natural language encodes. It was Wilkin's purpose to construct a universal or 'philosophical' language by categorizing all of human experience[22] and labelling each category by a symbol (vocabulary item) in his 'philosophical language'. Each category could be regarded in our terminology as a semantic component, which Wilkins labels by a symbol in his 'philosophical language'. Wilkins described what he was doing in the following words:

> The second part shall contein [sic] that which is the great foundation of the thing here designed, namely a regular *enumeration* and *description* of all things and notions, to which marks or names ought to be assigned according to their respective natures, which may be styled the *Scientifical* Part, comprehending *Universal* Philosophy. It being the proper end and design of the several branches of Philosophy to reduce all things and notions unto such a frame, as may express their natural order, dependence, and relations.
>
> (Wilkins 1668:1)

Wilkins invented a symbol (vocabulary item) for each 'thing and notion' in such a way as to represent its place in the natural order and its relation to other 'things and notions'. These symbols constitute the 'real character' of his title, and the forms for writing the vocabulary of his 'philosophical language'. Other parts of the *Essay* describe a pronunciation system for the language; and, of course, there is a syntax for it, too. The final part of the book consists of a dictionary which translates English words 'according to the various equivocal senses of them' into the 'philosophical language'. The result is a componential analysis; *father*, for instance, is defined as "oeconomical relation (= the first and most natural kind of association of men into Families) of the consanguinous type, of the species direct ascending, of the division male". Through the various components named in this meaning definition, *father* can be semantically related to other words whose meanings contain the same components. Since Wilkin's time no one has attempted anything so comprehensive.[23] There was Jost Trier's unsatisfactory analysis of categories of Knowledge and Understanding in German[24] and more recently some reasonably satisfactory componential analyses of HAVE-related verbs in Edward H. Bendix *Componential Analysis of General Vocabulary* 1966, dimensional adjectives in Manfred Bierwisch 'Some semantic universals of German adjectivals' 1967, kinship terms in Stephen A. Tyler *Cognitive Anthropology* 1969, cooking verbs and sounds in Adrienne Lehrer *Semantic Fields and Lexical Structure* 1974.

3.5.3 Semantic components as semantic predicates

Semantic components are usually presented in much the same way as they have been presented in the discussion above: e.g. *bull* is said to have the semantic components ADULT & MALE & BOVINE (cf. the table in (5.1.1) above and Lyons 1968:472). On the assumption that the semantic components reflect the salient characteristics of prototypical denotata, the justification for postulating these components is a set of inferences along the following lines:

(5.3.1) For any entity B that is properly called a *bull*, it is the case that B is adult & B is male & B is bovine.

The phraseology here reveals that so-called semantic components are not strictly speaking the components of expressions in the object language, but components of the metalanguage used in making a semantic analysis of the expression. In (5.3.1) we see that the lexemes "bull", "adult", "male" and "bovine" are used to label properties of some real or imagined object B. We can deduce from (5.3.1) that any object which has the property of being a bull also has the properties of being male, adult, and bovine. Following Rudolph Carnap (*Meaning and Necessity* 1956:222-29) we might refer to these inferences as 'meaning postulates' but since they are metalanguage predicates we shall call them semantic predicates instead.[25]

The equivalence between semantic components and semantic predicates is enshrined in a tradition stretching back to Aristotle (*Categories* 1b, 13) and is recognized for instance by Manfred Bierwisch 'Semantics' 1970:169. One place predicates like *being a bull*, *being male*, *being adult*, *being bovine* assign a property to a sole 'argument' which is typically expressed by a nominal such as 'B' in (5.3.1). Thus in (5.3.2) the subject NPs are assigned various properties by the emphasized one place predicates:

(5.3.2)
  a. Max *died*.
  b. Tom *is dead*.
  c. B *is bovine*.

The particular property assigned to the argument ('Max', 'Tom', or 'B' respectively in (5.3.2)) is named by the semantic content of the predicate. Semantic predicates with more than one argument name a particular kind of relationship between the arguments, which is determined by the semantic content of the predicate and takes into account the syntactic structure of the construction. E.g. in (5.3.3) there is a relationship of killing between Ed and Jo, and it is Ed who does the killing:

(5.3.3) Ed killed Jo.

We shall examine methods of analyzing the meanings of such sentences later on, the point to be taken here is that the predicate *kill* names a particular kind of relationship between its arguments – 'Ed' and 'Jo' in (5.3.3). Because predicates are a functional category that assign properties to sole arguments[26] and relations between arguments, they are not in one-to-one correspondence with any particular lexical class or grammatical category; verbs, adjectives, complement noun phrases, quantifiers, prepositions and adverbs all function as semantic predicates, though we shall not discuss here the manner of their doing so.

Let's return from this brief discussion of what a predicate is to our semantic analysis of *bull* given in (5.3.1). We said there that any object which can properly be called a bull, i.e. which is predicable as a bull because it has the property of being a bull, any such object also has the properties of being male, adult, and bovine. Furthermore, because bovines are animals, a bull has the property of being animal entailed in its being bovine. Put another way, the category Bull is a member of the subset Bovine of the set Animal, and also a member of the sets Male and Adult. According to (5.3.1) Bull is the intersection of these sets. In point of fact, though, (5.3.1) is incorrect because two of the inferred propositions are false.

Firstly, *bull* is not restricted in application to bovines, it is also properly used of male elephants, male whales, male seals, male alligators, etc. The initial plausibility of (5.3.1) is due to the fact that it describes the prototypical bull. The world of the English speaker is such that *bull* is much more likely to denote a bovine than any other species of animal – thus, the fuzzy set Bull has elephants, rhinos, seals, etc. only as peripheral members with a value closer to 0 than to 1. These peripheral uses of *bull* are surely examples of 'meaning extension' from bovines to certain other kinds of large animals; consequently they require that the context make it abundantly clear that a bovine is NOT being denoted; this is often achieved by spelling it out in a construction such as *bull elephant* or *bull whale* which is of greater complexity than the simple noun *bull* used of bovines.

Secondly, it is quite incorrect to say that *bull* is only predicable of adult animals since a new-born male calf is properly called a bull. Nonetheless, it is true that the sex of an animal is hardly significant until it is capable of reproduction – and even for very young human beings the pronoun form can be *it* rather than *he* or *she*; thus a sex differentiating term, like *bull*, is generally used of adult animals. When used of young animals the context must generally make the denotation clear e.g. by using the phrase *bull calf* rather than the noun *bull* on its own.

Although *bull* will more often denote an adult than a young animal, this is not a significant characteristic of the expression *bull* itself, but – as we have already noted – a property of any expression which sex differentiates animals. Thus it is not part of a general semantic characterization of *bull* that it typically denotes adults, instead it is part of the characterization of complementary sets of male and female animals. Prototypical bulls are also ungulates and mammals and quadrupeds, but these properties follow from the fact that bulls are bovine and are not significant properties in the semantic analysis of the expression *bull*; thus, a bull alligator is not a mammal, and a bull whale is not an ungulate. In consequence, though it is the norm that bulls are quadrupeds, a three-legged bull still counts as a bull, and the abnormality does not render the creature 'not a bull' only an 'abnormal bull'. By contrast, a so-called "bull" that is not male does not count as a bull at all!

We should therefore rephrase (5.3.1) as follows, this time using truth conditions left implicit earlier.

(5.3.4) If it is true for any entity B that B is an animal and B is properly called a *bull*, then it is necessarily true that B is male, and true to a value close to 1 that B is bovine.

The actual value assigned to the property of being bovine would need to be computed experimentally by methods such as those discussed in ch.2, but I would guess it to exceeed 0.9.

We now have a basis for the examination of semantic relations between language expressions.

3.6   Synonymy, or semantic identity between propositions

3.6.1   Synonymy as symmetrical semantic implication between propositions

There is a relation of synonymy between *A is a man who has never married* and *A is a bachelor$_m$*; we can see this if we compare the semantic descriptions given in (6.1.1) and (6.1.2)

(6.1.1) For any entity A of which it can properly be said that A is a man who has never married, then it is necessarily true that A is a man and necessarily true that A has never married.

We could further analyze the semantics of the predicates 'is a man' and 'has never married', but for present purposes this is unnecessary, as well be obvious when (6.1.1) is compared with (6.2.2)

(6.1.2) For any entity A of which it can properly be said that A is a bachelor$_m$, then it is necessarily true that A is a man and it is necessary true that A has never married.

The semantic identity of (6.1.1) and (6.1.2) is obvious from inspection; but we can spell it out using the double-headed arrow '$\longleftrightarrow$' to symbolize the mutual or symmetric implication relation. Synonymy is a special case of semantic implication, namely, symmetrical implication. Symmetrical implication occurs where (a) E_1 semantically implies E_2, i.e. $E_1 \rightarrow E_2$, and concomitantly (b) E_2 semantically implies E_1, i.e. $E_1 \leftarrow E_2$: hence there is the mutual or symmetric implication relation $E_1 \longleftrightarrow E_2$ (or, equivalently, $E_2 \longleftrightarrow E_1$). We see this spelled out in (6.1.3).

(6.1.3)

	INFERENCE	BASIS
a.	A is a man who has never married $\longleftrightarrow$ (A is a man) & (A has never married)	(6.1.1)
b.	A is a bachelor$_m$ $\longleftrightarrow$ (A is a man) & (A has never married)	(6.1.2)
c.	A is a bachelor$_m$ $\longleftrightarrow$ A is a man who has never married	a & b

With a one place predicate like *bachelor*$_m$ or *man who has never married* we can apparently draw a further inference by simply cancelling the words 'A is a' from (6.1.3.c) giving

d. bachelor $_m$ $\longleftrightarrow$ man who has never married.

However we see that, when the predicate has two or more arguments, this kind of cancellation is illegitimate; and so for consistency's sake it ought to be illegitimate for one place predicates too. Consider the meaning of *A kills B at time T*:

(6.1.4)
- a. A kills B at T $\longleftrightarrow$ A bring it about that B die at T
- b. *(kill $\longleftrightarrow$ bring it about that die)
- c. kill $\longleftrightarrow$ bring about a death

(6.1.4.b) is an illegitimate inference from (6.1.4.a); but (c), which reinterprets the proposition 'that B die' in terms of an unspecific nominal, is acceptable at first sight, but not on reflexion. Note the implication in (c) that the subject of 'kill' and the subject of 'bring' are identical: without such an implication there is no indication in (c) of who does the killing and who gets killed – although this is spelled out in (a); furthermore, there is no indication in (c) of whose death is brought about by the killing – although this is also spelled out in (a). We therefore conclude that the cancellation of arguments in statements of synonymy is strictly speaking illegitimate for two place predicates; and for the sake of consistency, we shall assume it is also illegitimate in the case of one place predicates. Thus, synonymy is a relation holding between propositions.

The negation of one of a pair of synonyms is equivalent to negating the other member of the pair; cf.

(6.1.5) If it is not the case that A is a man who has never married, then it cannot be the case that A is a bachelor$_m$. Conversely, if it is not the case that A is a bachelor$_m$, then it cannot be the case that A has never married (i.e. he must have married at some time).

Using '~' as a symbol of negation, we can restate (6.1.5) in terms of (6.1.6):

(6.1.6) ~(A is a bachelor$_m$) $\longleftrightarrow$ ~(A is a man who has never married).

Synonymy is a sense relation, and the term is not applicable to sameness of reference. Take Frege's classic examples[27] wherein the ancient Greeks referred to the planet Venus seen in the western sky during the evening as *the evening star*, and seen in the morning in the eastern sky it was referred to as *the morning star*. Although the expressions *V is the morning star* and *V is the evening star* may refer to the same thing, namely the planet Venus, these propositions are not synonymous because it is not the case that ANY object which can properly be called 'the morning star' can also properly be called 'the evening star'. The reasons are obvious from a comparison of (6.1.7) with (6.1.8)

(6.1.7) Any star seen in the morning sky can properly be called a morning star, and one particular such object can in certain contexts be called 'the morning star'.

(6.1.8) Any star seen in the evening can properly be called an evening star, and one particular such object can in certain contexts be called 'the evening star'.

Other cases of sameness of reference between two propositions can be dealt with in a similar way. Thus synonymy is a sense relation only.

Now consider another conundrum. It is (according to books on philosophy) contingently true that creatures with hearts all have kidneys; thus, (6.1.9) is true.

(6.1.9) For any entity O which can properly be said to have a heart, it can be properly said that O has a kidney.

Does this render *O has a heart* synonymous with *O has a kidney*? Well, of course, it does not. It is clear that since *have* is a two place predicate these sentences could only be synonymous if *X is a heart* and *X is a kidney* were synonymous – which is not the case, cf.

(6.1.10) It is not the case for any X that if X can properly be called a heart, then X can properly be called a kidney.

Synonymy is defined as a symmetrical semantic implication between propositions, say Q_1 and Q_2, where $(Q_1 \rightarrow Q_2)$ & $(Q_1 \leftarrow Q_2)$ such that $Q_1 \longleftrightarrow Q_2$. Consequently the negation of either proposition necessarily implies the negation of (i.e. cancels) the other, viz. given $Q_1 \longleftrightarrow Q_2$, then $\sim Q_1 \longleftrightarrow \sim Q_2$. Now consider some types of synonymous relation.

3.6.2 Synonymy between clauses containing symmetric predicates

The pair of clauses *the dog chased the man* and *the man chased the dog* are not synonymous because the roles of the arguments 'the dog' and 'the man' are different in the two clauses: in the first the dog is doing the chasing and the man is being chased, and vice versa in the second. However, there are in English a number of symmetric predicates where a change in the order of NP arguments has no effect on meaning; thus the following pairs are synonymous.

(6.2.1) A is married to B $\longleftrightarrow$ B is married to A

(6.2.2) Boston is near New York $\longleftrightarrow$ New York is near Boston

(6.2.3) The nuts are mixed in with the raisins $\longleftrightarrow$ The raisins are mixed in with the nuts.

(6.2.4) Max left with Sue $\longleftrightarrow$ Sue left with Max

It does not matter which way round their NP arguments are distributed, these pairs of clauses are synonymous. The choice of subject NP is a matter of information structure, cf. §7.7.

Like other synonyms, negation of one of a pair of clauses with symmetric predicates effectively negates the other, cf.

(6.2.5) $\sim$(Max is married to Ann) $\longleftrightarrow$ $\sim$(Ann is married to Max)

I.e. if it is not the case that Max is married to Ann then it is not the case that Ann is married to Max. We can contrast this with the negating of an asymmetric predicate such as *chase*, cf. *It is not the case that the dog chased the man* is quite compatible with *The man chased the dog*.

3.6.3 Converse predicates

Like clauses with symmetric predicates, clauses with converse predicates are synonymous. Like symmetric predicates their NP arguments switch; but unlike symmetric predicates, the predicate itself is also changed. Consider the following synonymous pairs:

(6.3.1) A is B's husband $\longleftrightarrow$ B is A's wife

(6.3.2) F is taller than G $\longleftrightarrow$ G is shorter than F

(6.3.3) A buys B from C at T $\longleftrightarrow$ C sells B to A at T

Like other synonymous pairs, negation of one implies negation of the other:

(6.3.4) ~(A is B's husband) $\longleftrightarrow$ ~(B is A's wife)

I.e. if it is not the case that A is B's husband, then it is not the case that B is A's wife.

We can analyze (6.3.1) as follows:

	INFERENCE	BASIS
a.	A is B's husband $\longleftrightarrow$ (A is a man) & (A is married to B)	lexicon entry
b.	(A is a man) & (A is married to B) $\longleftrightarrow$ B is a woman	knowledge of the world
c.	A is married to B $\longleftrightarrow$ B is married to A	symmetric clause
d.	(B is married to A) & (B is a woman) $\longleftrightarrow$ B is A's wife	c, b, lexic. entry
e.	A is B's husband $\longleftrightarrow$ B is A's wife	a & d

3.6.4 Cross-varietal synonymies

Therefore you clown, abandon – which is in the vulgar 'leave' – the society – which in the boorish is 'company' – of this female – which in the common is 'woman'. Which together is: abandon the society of this female, or, clown, thou perishest! Or, to thy better understanding, diest! O, to wit, I kill thee! Make thee away! Translate thy life into death!

(William Shakespeare *As You Like It* v.i.52)

There are many expressions in English which mean more or less the same but which are used in different dialects, varieties, or styles of the language. Compare such sets of expressions as

(6.4.1)
  a. Girl, lass, bird, chick, broad.
  b. Brotherly, fraternal. Lying, mendacious.
  c. [American] fender, [British] bumper.
  d. Fiddle, violin.
  e. Tempo, time. Presto, fast.

f. Taraxacum densleonis, dandelion. Canis lupus, wolf. Patella, kneecap.

g. Go to the loo, go to the bathroom, go for a short walk, spend a penny, take a leak, urinate.

Semantic relations of this kind can be dealt with in terms of a formula like the following:

(6.4.2) For any entity D which is properly called Taraxacum densleonis in contexts $C_{i...m}$, D is properly called a dandelion in contexts $C_{j...n}$.

The contexts in which a particular expression is used will be peculiar to the class of expressions of which it is a member; thus the scientific name for a plant will be used in the same kinds of contexts as any other scientific name for a plant. These contexts should be identified by a set of pragmatic rules for the language – which lie beyond the scope of a theory of linguistic meaning.

Like other kinds of synonyms, cross-varietal synonymy is preserved under negation (i.e. to negate one synonym is to imply negation of the other), cf.

(6.4.3) For any object J of which it is properly said in contexts $C_{i...m}$ that J is not a wolf, it is not the case that J can be called Canis lupus in contexts $C_{j...n}$.

However, it is possible to negate one of a pair of cross-varietal synonyms and assert another, because the first was used in the wrong context: cf.

(6.4.4) Yehudi Menuhin didn't play the fiddle¹ in Beethoven's Opus 61 in D Major, he played the violin¹, for chrissake. ['¹' marks contrastive stress.]

3.7 Asymmetric semantic implication and the relation of hyponymy

Asymmetric semantic implication occurs where the sense of one proposition, say Q_1, semantically implies the sense of another, Q_2, but the sense of Q_2 does not imply that of Q_1. Thus we have the relation $Q_1 \rightarrow Q_2$ and $\sim(Q_1 \leftarrow Q_2)$. In such an asymmetrical relation, Q_1 is said to be the hyponym of the implied proposition Q_2. For instance, we saw in (6.1.3.b) that

A is a bachelor$_m$ $\longleftrightarrow$ (A is a man) & (A has never married)

It follows that

(7.1) A is a bachelor$_m$ $\rightarrow$ A is a man.

The relation is asymmetric because although for any A, *A is a bachelor*$_m$ necessarily implies *A is a man*, there is no sense of *A is a man* for which it is necessarily true that *A is a bachelor*$_m$. Therefore we say that the proposition *A is a bachelor*$_m$ is a hyponym of *A is a man*.

The asymmetric implication relation holds between propositions, like the synonymy relation. Consider

(7.2) A kills B at time T $\rightarrow$ B die at T

which can be read: if it is true that A kills B at time T, then it is true that B dies at time T. We cannot legitimately cancel the arguments from (7.2) to infer (7.3):

(7.3) *(kill $\rightarrow$ die)

(7.3) is illegitimate because it falsely suggests that the subject of 'kill' is also the subject of 'die', and therefore that *(A kill B $\rightarrow$ A die).[28]

It is notable that the asymmetric semantic implication relation between propositions is the exact inverse of the corresponding category inclusion relation between their respective predicates. I.e. the category named by the predicate in the implied proposition properly includes the category named by the predicate in its hyponym. It is this fact which justifies the asymmetric implication relation between the propositions: e.g. it is because the category Man properly includes the category Bachelor$_m$ that *A is a bachelor*$_m$ $\rightarrow$ *A is a man*. Or, because the category Flower properly includes the categories Pansy & Peonie & Dandelion & Daisy & Rose (& every other kind of flower), *F is a flower* has for its hyponyms the propositions *F is a pansy*, *F is a peonie*, *F is a dandelion*, etc. In consequence:

(7.4) For any F of which it can properly be said that F is a flower, then F could be a pansy, or F could be a peonie, or F could be a dandelion, or F could be a daisy, or F could be a rose, or F could be any kind of flower.

From (7.4) we may conclude

(7.5) F is a pansy $\rightarrow$ F is a flower

(7.6) F is a peonie or F is a dandelion or F is a daisy $\rightarrow$ F is a flower

(7.7)   F is a kind of flower $\longleftrightarrow$ F is a flower.

The reasons for this synonymy in (7.7) are too obvious to elaborate.
  Negating the implied proposition in an asymmetric semantic implication relation implies negation of all its hyponyms. E.g.

(7.8) $\sim$(F is a flower) $\rightarrow$ $\sim$(F is a pansy) & $\sim$(F is a peonie) . . .

However, negating the hyponym has rather disorientating consequences:

(7.9) For any entity D of which it is properly said that D is not a daisy,
      then it is possible that D may be a flower of some other kind, or that
      D may be anything else at all, or even nothing at all.

Because S normally observes the co-operative principle, such propositions as *D is not a daisy* are normally not so disorientating in ordinary
conversational interaction as (7.9) might suggest – but we shall take up
this matter in the next section.

3.8   Antonymy and hyponymy

Antonymy is a relation holding between a proposition and its negation:
e.g. the antonym of *A is married* is *A is not married*. The relation of
antonymy is relevant to a discussion of hyponymy because a set of
hyponymyous propositions which all imply the same proposition form
an antonymous set – an antonymous set of co-hyponyms. The reason
for this is that the predicates in the hyponymous propositions each
label a distinct subset of the category labelled by the predicate of the
implied proposition. For instance, Pansy, Peonie, Dandelion, Daisy,
etc. are each distinct (non-overlapping) subsets of the category Flower;
thus the proposition *D is a daisy* has for its co-hyponymous antonyms a
conjunction of propositions such as *D is not a pansy & D is not a
peonie & D is not a dandelion & D is not a rose*. Thus,

(8.1) For any object D of which it can be properly said that D is a
      daisy, then it is not the case that D is a pansy, nor that D is a peonie,
      nor that D is a dandelion, nor that D is any other kind of flower than
      a daisy.

To sum up so far: the co-hyponyms of a proposition Q are in an
antonymous relation with one other such that for any hyponym G,
where $G \subset F$ and F is an antonymous set of hyponyms consisting of
$G \cup G'$, then $G \rightarrow \sim G'$.
  For an example of the relevance of these notions, consider the

difference in meaning between (8.2) and (8.3).

(8.2) B is a blackbird.

(8.3) A is a black bird.

(8.2) implies that B is no other kind of bird than a blackbird, viz. B is not a robin, nor an eagle, nor a vulture, nor a gull, nor a thrush, and so forth. (8.3) implies two propositions:

A is a black bird $\longleftrightarrow$ (A is black) & (A is a bird).

Thus (8.3) implies both that A is no other colour than black (viz. A is not red, nor white, nor green, nor blue, etc.); and also that A is no other creature than a bird (viz. A is not an insect, nor a fish, nor an elephant, nor a man, etc. cf. Rosch et al. 1976). So we see that the meaning relations of (8.2) and (8.3) are considerably different in consequence of different antonymous sets of co-hyponyms to which they belong.

In §3.7 we saw that negation of an implied proposition implies negation of all its hyponyms, but that negation of a hyponym has rather disorientating consequences, cf. ex. (7.9). We also said that in ordinary conversation the consequences are rarely so bleak because it is mutually expected between S and H that S observes the co-operative principle. Suppose S says

(8.4) My pen is not red.

(8.4) does not tell us what colour S's pen is; nonetheless, the fact that the pen has been predicated as being not red, i.e. not of one particular colour, implies that S is talking about the colour of his pen (and so the message is that S's pen is some other colour than red). This inference is not a semantic implication, but a conversational implicature based on the assumption that S is observing the co-operative principle. We take up this difference between semantic implication and conversational implicature in §3.9 below. To sum up: negating one of an antonymous set of co-hyponyms conversationally implicates a disjunction of co-hyponyms (with respect to (8.4) that the pen is white or black or green or yellow or purple, etc.); but there is no single proposition that can be inferred for certain, other than the one uttered – since every proposition implies itself.

Certain relative predicates such as *tall* and *short*, *hot* and *cold*, *happy* and *sad* form antonymous pairs which identify opposite ends of a scale. Such predicates are described as relative because, e.g. *A is tall* means "A is taller than the norm for the average A within a given context", or

Z is cold means "Z is colder than such things as Z typically are within a given context". Within propositions, these antonymous pairs of relative predicates bear the following kinds of semantic relationship to one another. We take the example of *hot* and *cold*.

(8.5) For any Y of which it can properly be said that Y is hot, then it is not the case that Y is cold.

(8.6) For any Z of which it can properly be said that Z is not cold, then it is the case that Z is hot to some extent – i.e. hotter than 'cold'.

For instance, if S says

(8.7) This beer isn't cold

it does not necessarily imply that the beer is hot, but only that the beer is hot (or warm) to some extent. In fact, if the beer were truly hot, S would be expected to say so, because under these circumstances (8.7) would violate the co-operative maxim of quality by being misleading. The general rule, then, for antonymous pairs of relative predicates P_{rel} and R_{rel} predicated on object A;

(8.8)

$$
\begin{array}{ll}
\text{A is } P_{rel} & \rightarrow \quad \sim(\text{A is } R_{rel}) \\
\text{A is } R_{rel} & \rightarrow \quad \sim(\text{A is } P_{rel}) \\
\sim(\text{A is } P_{rel}) & \rightarrow \quad \text{A is } R_{rel} \text{ to some extent} \\
\sim(\text{A is } R_{rel}) & \rightarrow \quad \text{A is } P_{rel} \text{ to some extent}
\end{array}
$$

3.9 Semantic implication, conversational implicature, and conventional implicature

The semantic relations of synonymy and hyponymy are defined on semantic implication, which is a sense relation. We have already argued in §3.6.1 that synonymy is a sense relation; and since synonymy is the relation of symmetric semantic implication between propositions, we shall assume that the asymmetric semantic implication relation of hyponymy is also a sense relation. A CONVERSATIONAL IMPLICATURE is not a sense relation but a pragmatic inference arising from S's use of a particular language expression in a particular context under conventional co-operative conditions.

To contrast semantic implication with conversational implicature, first consider the asymmetric semantic implications of (9.1) spelled out in (9.2).

(9.1) That red car you told me about has been sold.

(9.2)
    a.   That red car you told me about . . . → That car you told me about is red.
    b.   That car you told me about is red → That car you told me about is not blue.

(9.2.b) follows from the fact that for any X, *X is red* and *X is blue* are antonymous co-hyponyms, cf. §3.8. Now consider an utterance of (9.3).

(9.3) That red car you told me about is blue.

Semantically, the sentence used in (9.3) contains a contradiction, cf. §3.2.4:

(9.4)
    a.   That red car you told me about is blue ⟷ (That car you told me about is red) & (That car you told me about is blue)
    b.   That car you told me about is red → That car you told me about is not blue
    c.   That car you told me about is blue → That car you told me about is not red
    d.   That car you told me about is red and not red, and it is blue and not blue.

(9.4.d) is obviously contradictory, and it spells out the effects of the semantic implications in (9.3). However, in a typical utterance of (9.3) the co-operative principle leaves it mutually expected between S and H that S would not be so unreasonable as to contradict himself in so blatant a fashion, and so (9.3) is understood to conversationally implicate that the car S had been informed was red has turned out to be blue in fact.

Consider another example of a conversational implicature.

(9.5)
    A: What happened to that steak I left thawing on the window sill?
    B: The dog was looking very pleased with himself when I came in.

On the assumption that the co-operative principle is being observed and therefore that B's utterance is a relevant response to A's question in (9.5) we may infer that B is suggesting the dog ate the steak. This suggestion is a conversational implicature of B's remark; and it is clearly not a semantic implication, because the sentence (proposition)

The dog was looking very pleased with himself does not per se imply that *The dog ate the steak*. The conversational implicature and its recognition are based upon the assumption that the co-operative principle is in force, and there is a certain amount of relevant mutual background knowledge. Matching the dog's looking pleased with himself with the missing steak we rely on such inferences as the following: *M is steak* → *M is meat* (semantic implication); dogs are known to enjoy eating meat (background knowledge); furthermore, allowing for a little anthropomorphic licence on the speaker's part, because stolen delights are sweeter than legitimate ones (background knowledge) if the dog stole some meat he might be thought to be pleased with himself. Hence, we conclude that in (9.5) B is conversationally implicating that the reason for the dog looking pleased with himself is that he stole the steak – which indirectly answers A's question.

Does (9.6) semantically implicate (9.7) or is the latter a conversational implicature?

(9.6) Granny has boiled the potatoes for 20 minutes.

(9.7) The potatoes are cooked.

We noted in §3.7 that negating the semantically implied proposition also cancels its hyponym (e.g. if *D is not a flower*, then *D is not a daisy, nor a pansy*, etc.); however, the negating of (9.7) will not ordinarily cancel (9.6), cf.

(9.8) The potatoes aren't cooked, even though Granny has boiled them for 20 minutes.

In (9.8) the implicated proposition is denied while the implicating proposition is asserted; compare this with the parallel but nonsensical **This isn't a flower, even though it is a peonie*. Thus, unlike semantic implications, conversational implicatures can be negated without cancelling (i.e. negating) the proposition which implicates them.

The notion of a conversational implicature was first described by H. Paul Grice in 'Logic and conversation' 1975.[29] In the same place Grice briefly introduced a notion of conventional implicatures, giving for his only examples inferences derived from the use of nonlogical conjunctions such as *but* and *therefore*. Compare (9.9) with (9.10)

(9.9) Ann got pregnant and Ed was pleased.

(9.10) Ann got pregnant but Ed was pleased.

The different implications arising from the use of the different conjunctions in these two examples derive from their semantic content; in particular, *but* conventionally implicates (according to Grice) a proposition involving some sort of contrast, unexpectedness, or the like. This is presumably a direct effect of the meaning (i.e. sense) of *but*, and intuitively, therefore, a sort of semantic implication. However, the semantic implications we have discussed hitherto have held between propositions and, more particularly, have been identifiable with predicates within those propositions. The conventional implicatures will not fit this mould (but cf. ch.5 *n*32, and §§5.4, 7.3), and yet like semantic implications they cannot be cancelled without creating a contradiction. Take for example (9.11) in which the conventional implicature of *but* is spelled out:

(9.11) Ann got pregnant but, unexpectedly, Ed was pleased.

Contrast this with the absurdity of (9.12) in which the conventional implicature of *but* is cancelled:

(9.12) *Ann got pregnant but, not unexpectedly, Ed was pleased.

If 'but' in (9.12) is replaced by *and* the result is, of course, acceptable:

(9.13) Ann got pregnant and, not unexpectedly, Ed was pleased.

It is notable that our expectations of S observing the co-operative principle are so strong that we are inclined to interpret (9.12) as if it were (9.13).

   Conventional implicature extends to other non-predicate elements of sentences. For instance, compare the conventional implicatures of the articles emphasized in (9.14) and (9.15)

(9.14) On entering the room Kathy went straight to *the* window.

(9.15) On entering the room Kathy went straight to *a* window.

If there has been no prior mention of the window in question, (9.14) conventionally implicates that the room has only one window, whereas (9.15) conventionally implicates there is more than one.[30] These are conventional implications because they derive directly from the senses of the respective articles – without, of course, being the senses of the articles. To cancel the conventional implicature leads to absurdity:

(9.16) On entering the room Kathy went straight to the window;
   $\left\{ \begin{array}{l} \text{there was only the one.} \\ \text{*there were three of them.} \end{array} \right\}$

Conventional implicature is also characteristic of noun phrase arguments. Take the subject NP in (9.17).

(9.17) The present King of France is bald.

The NP 'the present King of France' conventionally implicates that there is (i.e. exists) something which can properly be called *the present King of France*. This particular kind of implicature has been called a presupposition, originally by Gottlob Frege in 'On sense and reference' 1892/1966 but widely within linguistics since the mid 1960s; this is a speaker-oriented view of the phenomenon instead of the hearer's viewpoint adopted in this book. Like all conventional implicatures, that of a definite non-generic NP like the one in (9.17) derives from the meaning of the expression; and if the implicature is cancelled as in (9.18), the result is an absurdity.

(9.18) *The present King of France (who doesn't exist) is bald.

Semantic implications are a special kind of conventional implicature, namely conventional implicatures that hold of propositions, and, more particularly, result from logical predicates within propositions. Other kinds of conventional implicatures hold of other sentence constituents. We therefore find implications which combine semantic implication and conventional implicature, e.g.

(9.19) Sid killed Bert at time T → Someone died at T

A semantic implication of the lefthand proposition in (9.19) is given in (9.20).

(9.20) Sid killed Bert at T → Bert died at T

Cf. ex. (7.2) above. A conventional implicature of the NP 'Bert' in (9.19-20) is

(9.21) Bert → There is someone called Bert

From (9.20) and (9.21) we can deduce (9.22):

(9.22) Bert died at T ⟷ There is someone called Bert died at T

This, therefore, has the semantic implication shown in (9.23):

(9.23) There is someone called Bert died at T → Someone died at T

This justifies the proposition to the right of the arrow in (9.19). Because semantic implication is just a special kind of conventional implicature, rather than saying the proposition to the right of the arrow in (9.19) combines semantic implication and conventional implicature, we might as well simplify matters and just say that it is a conventional implicature!

In a sentence such as (9.24) there is a superficial contradiction:

(9.24) John is a bachelor$_m$, so who did he marry?

The contradiction arises because the first conjunct has the conventional implicature shown in (9.25).

(9.25) John is a bachelor $_m$ → John has never married anyone

(We may interpret *John has never married anyone* as "There has never been someone whom John has married.") The second adjunct in (9.24) has the conventional implicature shown in (9.26):

(9.26) who did John marry? → John $\{ \begin{matrix} \text{has married} \\ \text{did marry} \end{matrix} \}$ someone.

Combining the implicatures of the conjuncts in (9.24) we get the contradiction

(9.27) *John has never married anyone and he has married someone.

Thus the conventional implicatures of (9.24) lead to a contradiction; but the conversational implicature of (9.24) is rather different. The utterance can be used to conversationally implicate that although S has been informed that John married someone, he has some reason for asserting to the contrary that John is a bachelor$_m$, and in order to resolve the conflict between these propositions he wants to be informed of the identity of the supposed wife (because if there is one he must have been mistaken about John's being a bachelor).

3.10 Tautology

A tautology arises when a criterial part (usually the whole) of the meaning of a predicate is conventionally or conversationally implicated by one of its arguments. Provided it is determinable, a tautologous statement is one that is necessarily true in virtue of its meaning, and for this reason it is said to be ANALYTICALLY TRUE. Compare (10.1) with (10.2)

(10.1) This girl is my daughter.

(10.2) My daughter is a girl.

(10.1) is not a tautology and it would not necessarily be true if uttered. It is not a tautology because the meaning of the subject NP, which we can represent as *This G is a female human being* does not semantically imply the predicate 'is my daughter', viz.

(10.3) *(this G is a female human being → G is my child & G is a female human being)

To deny that G is my daughter is not to deny that G is a girl, which would have to be the case were (10.1) tautologous – because negating the implied proposition cancels the hyponym.

(10.2) is tautologous and, provided that the subject NP 'my daughter' successfuly refers (i.e. that S has a daughter), an utterance of (10.2) will be analytically true. S takes an entity, call it (her) D, which he labels 'my daughter'; we can represent this by *D is my daughter*. S then predicates D 'is a girl' which we can represent as *D is a girl*. Now consider the semantic implications of these two representations.

(10.4) D is my daughter ⟷ (D is my child) & (D is a female human being)

(10.5) D is a girl ⟷ D is a female human being

We see that the righthand side of (10.4) includes the righthand side of (10.5) and since (10.4-5) express relations of synonymy this amounts to saying that the lefthand of (10.4) semantically implies the lefthand side of (10.5):

(10.6) D is my daughter → (D is a female human being ⟷ D is a girl)

Thus in (10.2), the subject NP semantically implies the whole of the meaning of the predicate, and (10.2) is tautologous and analytically true.

Anyone who understands the meaning of *daughter* understands that a person labelled someone's daughter must be a girl. This makes (10.2) a pernicious tautology because it is impossible to imagine a context in which the sentence could be uttered without violating the co-operative maxim of manner and still be intended to communicate some information. Although *girl* can be used of a woman any age, it can also be used to contrast with *woman*; however it would be unco-operative of S to utter (10.2) with the intention of meaning either "My daughter is just a girl" or "My daughter is not yet a woman": if this is what he means, this is what he should say.

Another pernicious tautology is exemplified in

(10.7) Abdul sold the camel for money.

The meaning of *sell* as contrasted with the meanings of *barter*, *exchange* or *trade*, for instance, semantically implies "exchange FOR MONEY": thus a criterial part of the meaning of the predicate in (10.7) is implied by its argument 'for money', creating a tautology. There is no way that speaker S could co-operatively utter (10.7) to convey a message that could not be communicated by the sentence *Abdul sold the camel*. If S wished to focus on the exchange of money he would have to spell out the meaning of *sell* by saying something like (10.8) which has primary stress on 'money':

(10.8) Abdul exchanged the camel for mōney.

   Pernicious tautologies can arise across conjunctions. Compare the following two sentences (which show, incidentally, that natural language conjunction is not symmetric like logical conjunction: logical conjunction requires that the sequence "E_1 & E_2" mean the same as "E_2 & E_1").

(10.9)   My neighbour is a woman, and she is pregnant.
(10.10) My neighbour is pregnant, and she is a woman.

(10.9) is not tautologous because having said that his neighbour is a woman, S can reasonably add the information that his woman-neighbour is pregnant – the predicate *be pregnant* is not semantically implied in *be a woman*. (10.10) is tautologous – or perhaps one should call this kind of thing quasi-tautology because it is different from the tautologies discussed hitherto – for the following reason. S takes an entity N and labels it 'my neighbour', conversationally implicating that N is a human being; he then predicates of N that N is pregnant. Now, only females can become pregnant, so S conversationally implicates that N is a female human being. In the conjoined clause the argument 'she' is anaphoric for the female human being N, labelled 'my neighbour'; the predicate on this argument, 'is a woman', has the sense "be a female human being": thus the sense of the predicate is conversationally implicated within the meaning of the argument, and the second conjunct is quasi-tautologous. It is difficult to see that the whole of (10.10) could be used to communicate anything different from either (10.9) or the first conjunction alone of (10.10); thus, as it stands, it violates the co-operative maxims of manner and quantity.

   Not all tautologies are pernicious. We noted in §1.2.2 ex. (2.2.10) that it is possible to say things like

(10.11) The prime minister īs the prime minister, after all.

We also give definitions using tautologous sentences:

(10.12) A bachelor is a man who has never married.

And the following are acceptable tautologies if the conjunctions are either included in the utterance or else understood.

(10.13) Max is Ellie's husband and she is (therefore) his wife.

(10.14) John ran into Ed, who (also) ran into him.

(10.15) The football match was nearly over. The final whistle blew and it was over.

In (10.15) the redundancy of the final conjunct 'it was over' is outweighed by the stylistic effect of emphasizing the significance of that final whistle.

Tautologies are not restricted to statements, they also occur in other propositional types, e.g.

(10.16) Is your pregnant neighbour a woman?

(10.17) Sell the carpet for money, I tell you!

In consequence, the property of analyticity holds for the values of speech acts other than statements – provided that the meaning of the predicate is WHOLLY implicated by the meaning of one of its arguments. E.g. the following have analytic compliance values:

(10.18) Eat the food you are eating!

(10.19) Are you who you are?

(10.20) Was it Monday, the day before last Tuesday?

(10.21) Can you please pass me the salt that you are passing me?

Note that, as with many other tautologies, one can imagine contexts in which (10.18-21) could reasonably be used, i.e. with reasonable conversational implicatures.

3.11 Semantic overlap and semantic difference between propositional constituents

3.11.1 Introduction

Two propositions may overlap semantically by having semantically related constituents, e.g. the propositions in (11.1.1) and (11.1.2) have semantically identical predicates.

(11.1.1) John is a bachelor$_m$.

(11.1.2) Ed is a bachelor$_m$.

The degree of semantic overlap between propositions is variable and may turn out to be measurable in terms of a comparative weighting between semantic similarity and semantic dissimilarity between the propositions. For example, one's intuitions are that there is a greater degree of semantic overlap between (11.1.1) and (11.1.2) than either has with (11.1.3), and more with (11.1.3) than either has with (11.1.4), and more with (11.1.4) than either has with (11.1.5).

(11.1.3) Marcia is a spinster.

(11.1.4) Robin is a woman.

(11.1.5) This is a woodscrew.

Consider the relevant semantic implications of (11.1.1) spelled out in (11.1.6).

(11.1.6)
   a. John is a bachelor$_m$ $\longleftrightarrow$ (John is a man) & (John has never married)
   b. John is a man $\rightarrow$ John is a human being
   c. John is a human being $\rightarrow$ John is a living organism
   d. John is a living organism $\rightarrow$ John is a physical object.

There is a greater semantic distance between *John is a bachelor*$_m$ and *John is a physical object* than there is between *John is a bachelor* and *John is a human being*: this semantic distance correlates with the number of levels of implication between the two propositions. If we take it that in (11.1.6) each predicate labels a category to which John belongs, there are six such categories in (11.1.6) ranged in a taxonomy. The category Bachelor$_m$ is the intersection of the categories Those-Who-Have-Never-Married and Man (= male human being); these two categories are both included within the category Human Being, which is included within Living Organism, which is included within Physical Object. The notion of semantic distance between two expressions seems intuitively, to correlate with the number of category boundaries that lie between the two categories they label; e.g. there are more category boundaries between Bachelor$_m$ and Physical Object than there are between Bachelor$_m$ and Human Being, and hence a greater semantic distance between *(being a) bachelor*$_m$ and *(being a) physical object* than between *(being a) bachelor*$_m$ and *(being a) human being*.

The degree of semantic overlap between (11.1.1) and (11.1.3) may be judged from a comparison of (11.1.7) with (11.1.8).

(11.1.7)
  a. John is a bachelor$_m$ $\longleftrightarrow$ (John is a man) & (John has never married)
  b. John is a bachelor$_m$ $\rightarrow$ John has never married.

(11.1.8)

  a. Marcia is a spinster $\longleftrightarrow$ (Marcia is a woman) & (Marcia has never married)
  b. Marcia is a spinster $\rightarrow$ Marcia has never married.

Propositions with the predicates *be a bachelor*$_m$ and *be a spinster* semantically imply a proposition with the same predicate *has never married*; they differ in their arguments, of course, and in the fact that the former implies a proposition with the predicate *be a man* and the latter a proposition with the predicate *be a woman*.

The degree of semantic overlap between (11.1.1) and (11.1.4) may be judged from a comparison of (11.1.9) with (11.1.10).

(11.1.9)
  a. John is a bachelor$_m$ $\longleftrightarrow$ (John is a man) & (John has never married)
  b. John is a bachelor$_m$ $\rightarrow$ John is a man
  c. John is a man $\longleftrightarrow$ (John is male) & (John is adult) & (John is a human being)
  d. John is a man $\rightarrow$ (John is adult) & (John is a human being)

(11.1.10)
  a. Robin is a woman $\longleftrightarrow$ (Robin is female) & (Robin is adult) & (Robin is a human being)
  b   Robin is a woman $\rightarrow$ (Robin is adult) & (Robin is a human being)

Propositions with the predicates *be a bachelor*$_m$ and *be a woman* semantically imply a conjunction of propositions with the predicates *be adult* & *be a human being*, but not at the same level of implication. Their semantic difference, apart from the different arguments, is that the former implies propositions with the predicates *has never married* & *be male*, whereas the latter implies a proposition with the predicate *be female*.

The degree of semantic overlap between *John is a bachelor*$_m$ and

This is a woodscrew (= ex. (11.1.5)), could be elaborated in a similar way to the examples above; their semantic difference is very considerable, because the closest category that bachelors and wood-screws have in common is Physical Object.

3.11.2   Osgood's semantic differential: a measurement of connotative meaning

It was observed in §3.11.1 that the semantic difference between two expressions seems to correlate with the number of category boundaries that lie between the two categories labelled by the expressions; but we did not attempt to sketch a metric for measuring semantic distance. In this section we review a technique for measuring semantic distance which has been described by the psychologist Charles Osgood. The simplest account of Osgood's 'semantic differential' technique is given in §7.2.2 of Charles E. Osgood & Thomas A. Sebeok *Psycholinguistics* 1954; a more extensive one in Osgood 'The nature and measurement of meaning' 1952; and the fullest in Charles E. Osgood, George J. Suci, & Percy H. Tannenbaum *The Measurement of Meaning* 1957. Uriel Weinrich's review of the latter book, 'Travels through semantic space' 1958, offers an excellent critique of Osgood's work from a linguist's view-point. However, Osgood's semantic differential is a method for the measurement of connotative meaning and not of sense or the denotative meaning we have discussed hitherto in this book; so what is connotation? As ordinarily understood, the connotation of an expression E is the set of implicatures deriving from the conventional use of E within a certain dialect, variety, or style of the language – implicatures which can result from prejudices about the people who use such dialects, varieties, or styles. Thus, cross-varietal synonyms (cf.§3.6.4) have different connotations; e.g. each of the nouns *steed, nag, gee-gee*, and *horse* denotes an equine animal, but the lexemes have different connotations. *Steed* connotes a noble animal ridden on festive occasions, or ridden to war in olden days; it has an archaic ring. *Nag* is pejorative. *Gee-gee* smacks of either racing slang or baby-talk. Whereas, *horse* connotes nothing in particular, being the unmarked lexeme among the four. It was the taboo connotations of words like *ass, coney*, and *cock* which led them to be dropped as animal names – in some or all English dialects – in favour of *donkey, rabbit*, and *rooster*, none of which has a homonym with obscene connotations. When we examine Osgood's semantic differential, we shall see that his experimental technique reveals people's subjective connotations of expressions, and these will be valid for the population he surveyed (mostly north American college students) without necessarily holding true for the language as a whole. Because the connotation of E presupposes the denotation of E, Osgood's semantic differential presumably comprehends denotative semantic distance; but it is important to bear in mind when reviewing it that the semantic differential is primarily a measure of connotative meaning.

Osgood has said[31] that he envisioned the psychological representation of meaning in terms of 'concept-studded semantic space', a sort of mental thesaurus, and that he sought to map the location of (certain) concepts in relation to other concepts within that 'space'. Osgood, Suci & Tannenbaum 1957:330 saw their research leading to the

> construction of a 'functional dictionary of connotative meanings' – a quantized Thesaurus – in which the writer [?] would find nouns, adjectives, verbs, and adverbs (all lexical items) listed according to their locations in the semantic space, as determined from the judgements of representative samples of the population.

To quantize the mental thesaurus, subjects were presented with up to 76 pairs of antonymous adjectives separated by a seven point scale, e.g.

```
HAPPY ____ : ____ : ____ : ____ : ____ : ____ : ___  SAD
HARD  ____ : ____ : ____ : ____ : ____ : ____ : ___  SOFT
SLOW  ____ : ____ : ____ : ____ : ____ : ____ : ___  FAST
```

The subject was then asked to rate a concept, i.e. a noun or noun phrase, by locating its most suitable position on the scale. In the experiment using 76 scales (cf. Osgood, Suci & Tannenbaum 1957:53-61) the 20 expressions judged were

foreigner, my mother, me, Adlai Stevenson:	'person concepts'
knife, boulder, snow, engine:	'physical objects'
modern art, sin, time, leadership:	'abstract concepts'
debate, birth, dawn, symphony:	'event concepts'
hospital, America, United States, family life:	'institutions'

(ibid. p.49). It is clear from the inclusion of three proper names and the two indexical expressions *my mother* and *me*, that subjective connotation and not sense or denotation is to be assessed. A semantic profile is built up by rating each expression on a large number of scales. By comparing the semantic profiles of a number of expressions, the expressions can be ranked in semantic space.

The kind of analysis that results is given in Tables 3.1 and 3.2 and in Figure 3.1; these refer to a different experiment from the one described above, and the expressions used in it can be read off Table 3.1. This time the semantic profiles were built up from 50 scales, whose results are conflated into just nine by using 'factor analysis': it was found that judgements on a set of scales like e.g. GOOD-BAD, FAIR-UNFAIR, CLEAN-DIRTY, KIND-CRUEL, NOBLE-BESTIAL, etc. are highly correlated, and so could be conflated into a single 'evaluative factor'. The justification for factor analysis is 'to make possible the selection of a minimum number of specific scales which taken together, will give the maximum coverage of semantic space' (Osgood & Sebeok 1965:178). In other words, factor analysis is a method of sampling for the purpose of making the results of the experiment simpler to interpret. The differential scales in Table 3.1 have been reduced to three factors: I = 'evaluative', II = 'potency', and III = 'oriented activity'. To compensate for the unreliability of sampling each factor by just one scale, three are used.

Table 3.1 Responses from one subject

		quicksand	*white rose buds*	*death*	*hero*	*methodology*	*fate*	*virility*	*gentleness*	*success*	*sleep*	
		A	B	C	D	E	F	G	H	I	J	
I	good	−3	3	−3	3	3	−1	3	2	3	1	bad
	beautiful	−3	3	−3	2	1	−1	2	3	2	2	ugly
	fresh	−2	3	−3	3	3	−2	3	1	3	2	stale
II	strong	3	−3	2	3	1	1	3	−3	3	−2	weak
	large	3	−3	1	3	−2	0	3	0	3	1	small
	loud	−1	−3	0	1	−1	−2	3	−3	2	−3	soft
III	active	−3	−3	−3	3	1	−3	3	−3	3	−3	passive
	tense	−2	−3	−2	−1	2	−1	2	−3	0	−3	relaxed
	hot	−3	−1	−3	3	1	−2	3	1	3	−1	cold

Columns A through J represent "concepts", whose scores on the scales described in the rows are computed with higher positive numbers indicating closer proximity to the left pole (e.g. *good*), and higher negative ones to the right pole (e.g. *bad*). Cf. Osgood & Sebeok 1965:179, Osgood, Suci & Tannenbaum 1957:88.

Table 3.2 The matrix showing the semantic differences between all the connotative meanings of expressions A through J in Table 3.1. Cf. Osgood & Sebeok 1965:180

	A	B	C	D	E	F	G	H	I	J
A										
B	13.34									
C	2.65	12.77								
D	12.77	12.04	13.27							
E	12.41	8.31	12.12	7.14						
F	4.90	9.38	4.12	11.53	9.17					
G	13.78	13.64	14.11	3.61	7.35	12.57				
H	11.66	4.24	11.36	10.15	8.60	8.00	12.33			
I	13.08	12.61	13.49	1.41	7.14	11.87	2.24	11.18		
J	9.27	5.10	9.43	9.85	8.25	6.32	11.75	3.46	10.54	
	A	B	C	D	E	F	G	H	I	J

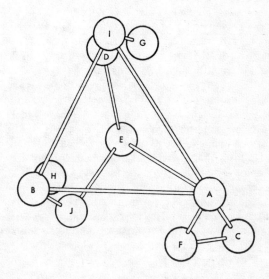

Figure 3.1 Three dimensional model constructed from the distance measurements in Table 3.2. G = *virility*, I = *success*; D = *hero*; E = *methodology*; J = *sleep*; B = *white rose buds*; H = *gentleness*; A = *quicksand*; F = *fate*; C = *death*. Cf. Osgood, Suci & Tannenbaum 1957:95

The semantic differences (= distances) between the various expressions A through J in Table 3.1 have been computed using the formula

$$D = \sqrt{\Sigma d^2}$$

where 'D' is the quotient of semantic difference; 'd' is the difference between the locations of two expressions on the same scale, and since 'd' may have a minus value, it is squared to make it a real number; 'Σ' is the sum of the squared differences for all scales. Table 3.2 gives the distances of every connotative meaning from every other connotative meaning according to this formula. Because the distances on Table 3.2 are given in equivalent units relative to the same dimensions, it is possible to plot the positions of the respective connotative meanings of the expressions A through J in the same dimensionality as the number of factors, which in the present case is three. Hence we can plot A through J in semantic space, as shown in Figure 3.1. Pictorial representation in more dimensions would be difficult to interpret; but there is no reason why a D-matrix like that of Table 3.2 should not be laid out based on a very much larger set of dimensions.

Osgood et al. predicted that the combination of two expressions (two 'concepts') should, when measured using the semantic differential technique, give a quotient midway between their individual quotients: in other words, the connotative meaning of a construction should be predictable from the meanings of its parts (cf. Osgood, Suci & Tannenbaum 1967:275ff). However, this prediction was not consistently verified – at least, not with adjective-noun concatenations, which were the only ones tested. It was found that the more widely divergent the adjective and noun in their individual quotients, the less predictable was their combination. Also there was consistent deviation towards the connotation of the adjective except where the noun was a comparatively emotive one like *prostitute* or *thug*: Osgood et al. found a tendency for any derogatory or unfavourable connotation to dominate the whole construction and so thrust the connoting constituent into semantic prominence.[32] However, postulating tendencies to semantic prominence on a small sample of adjective-noun combinations is suspect; and in any case, the degree of semantic prominence could not be predictively quantified.

The semantic differential is intended to identify similarity and difference in meaning; and, if we contemplate Figure 3.1, it broadly matches our intuitions about the semantic interrelations of the expressions appearing on it. But the semantic differential has only limited value in determining semantic relations and properties: for instance, it is difficult to see how it could bring about conventional or conversational implicatures, or contradictions; and it is even uncertain whether synonymy and antonymy could be established. These limitations result from the fact that the semantic differential measures connotative meaning, whereas these are the properties and relations of either senses or denotative meaning.

The clustering in Figure 3.1, showing semantic similarities and difference, is not the most important output of the semantic differential as an analytical technique. It seems likely that any form of cluster analysis (cf. Samuel Fillenbaum & Amnon Rapoport *Structures in the Subjective Lexicon* 1971:28ff) could have produced much the same result; perhaps, even, simply asking subjects to locate the ten expressions within a square on the basis of similarity and dissimilarity in meaning. What makes the semantic differential unique is the authors' claim that it quantizes semantic differences; and to evaluate this unique characteristic we need to question its accuracy as an instrument of measurement. The whole enterprise is based on the placement of an expression on a seven-point scale between two antonymous adjectives, so the following questions are appropriate:

(i)   What is the justification for using adjectives rather than, say, nouns or verbs on the scales measuring semantic differentials?
(ii) Why should the scales be bounded by antonyms?
(iii) Why should the scales between antonymous adjectives have seven places rather than any other number?
(iv) What governs the choice of the scales actually used in experiments?
(v)   What is the contribution of factor analysis to the measurement of semantic distance?
(vi) When a small number of scales is used in an experiment, why do some scales occur that are not found among larger scale experiments?
(vii) Is the choice of antonyms likely to affect the computation of semantic differentials?

We shall take each of these questions in turn.

(i) The semantic profile of an expression E describes E's connotation; thus the scale on which E is judged is, necessarily, descriptive. In English, as in many other languages, it is the function of adjectives (or, more generally, adjectivals) to describe: it is therefore appropriate that the scales be adjectival rather than, say, nominal or verbal. This decision might appear to be influenced by the fact that the only expressions analyzed by Osgood's semantic differential are nominals. But a moment's reflexion reveals that when we start thinking about the connotations of e.g. the verb *to run*, we immediately nominalize it and start predicating adjectival descriptions on *running* – for instance, *running is active, motional, energy-consuming*, etc. This is particularly likely when we are looking for short, one-word descriptions – cf. *running is motional* rather than *running involves movement*. It is therefore, both justifiable and economical to use adjectives to build-up connotative profiles of expressions, even though more complex syntactic constructions could have been used.

(ii) Having decided that adjectives should be used in making semantic descriptions, it is easy to see why descriptions are framed by antonymous pairs of them. Take the descriptor GOOD, for instance. An expression like *success* might be rated extremely close to GOOD; whereas another, e.g. *quicksand* might be rated as far from GOOD as possible – in other words, extremely close to the antonym for GOOD, namely BAD. Conversely, *success* will be located as far from BAD as possible. Any expression rated on a scale outward from an adjective will be located between it and its antonym. Thus the rationale for scales bounded by antonymous adjectives is simply that any scale outward from an adjective is necessarily bounded at its furthest limit by the antonym of that adjective.

(iii) There is no objection to using a scale between antonymous adjectives as a means of describing connotation, but the length of the scale is critical when it comes to measurements based on the location of an expression at a certain point along that scale (measurements symbolized 'd' in the formula for calculating semantic distance). The seven-point scale is described in all of Osgood's reports of the semantic differential technique; but the choice of seven places is not based on its biological or psychological validity for human beings in general.[33] The choice of seven alternatives, rather than, say, five or nine, was decided by trial and error, on the basis that seven was the optimum number to use in experiments with college students. The optimum number in similar tests with other groups is reported by Osgood, Suci & Tannenbaum 1957:85 to be fewer: three for American Legion members; and five for grade-school children. It is obvious that the choice of seven places on the scale between antonymous adjectives is based on experimental expedience rather than any hypothesis about the structure of the mind or mental processes. The measurement of semantic differentials on, say, a five-point scale would differ from those based on a seven-point scale, although the clustering tendencies and relative differences would remain comparable. The arbitrariness of the metric is nonetheless worth emphasizing, because the unique attribute of Osgood's semantic differential is the quantitative analysis of semantic differences in the mental thesaurus. This analysis is acceptable only if we recognize that the quotients are in themselves meaningless: they need to be interpreted relatively to one another.

(iv) Of the original 289 pairs of antonymous adjectives drawn from *Roget's Thesaurus*, experiments were conducted with a maximum of 76 and as few as nine (cf. Osgood, Suci & Tannenbaum 1957:48 & 276). Ideally a semantic profile would be constructed from a check of all possible scales lest sampling bias the results; but since adjectives form an open class this is an unrealizable goal. Nor, for practical reasons, could the semantic differential comprehend all adjectives attested up to, say, the year 1950. Nevertheless, 289 pairs is not a particularly large sample; although it seems to have been reasonably comprehensive in range, without any obvious lacunae. The original set of 289 was reduced to 76 by having about twenty people sort them into representative sets. As an example of their accomplishment, the antonymous pair PROGRESSIVE-REGRESSIVE is to represent all the following: *increasing-decreasing, approaching-receding, progressive-degenerate, restoring-relapsing, attracting-repelling, pursuing-avoiding* (Osgood, Suci & Tannenbaum 1957:55). It is immediately apparent that there are many things which may be judged regressive which would not also be called decreasing, receding, degenerate, relapsing, repelling or avoiding: all these may mean something roughly similar, but they certainly do not mean the same, nor even something very similar. Thus a semantic profile constructed on 76 scales might be quite considerably different in detail from one constructed on 289 scales; and the detail matters, because the semantic differential technique claims to quantize semantic differences using detailed figures, as we see from Table 3.2.

(v) The sampling of scales called into question in (iv) was made largely for administrative convenience, without there being any concomitant hypothesis about semantic organization in the human mind. However, 'factor analysis' was said to establish just eight factors relevant to the analysis of vocabulary, and presumably this does imply a claim about organization in the mind. The technique has been described above, in relation to Table 3.1. It is a legitimate statistical procedure used to analyze the complex correlations between all the scores for the 76 scales of one experiment, and the 50 scales of another. E.g. the factor that completely determines the placement of expressions on the GOOD-BAD scale, i.e. the 'evaluative' factor, affects their placement on other scales: viz. it has a 37% influence on the OPTIMISTIC-PESSIMISTIC scale, a 20% one on the COLOURFUL-COLOURLESS scale, a 16% one on the STABLE-CHANGEABLE scale, 9%

on the OBJECTIVE-SUBJECTIVE scale; but none at all on many others, e.g. FAST-SLOW or ORNATE-PLAIN. We have already seen (on Table 3.1) examples of scales manifesting three factors: I – 'evaluative', II – 'potency', and III – 'oriented activity'. The other five factors are: IV – 'stability' (e.g. STABLE-CHANGEABLE, RATIONAL-INTUITIVE, ORTHO- DOX-HERETICAL), V – 'tautness' (e.g. ANGULAR-ROUNDED, STRAIGHT- CURVED, SHARP-BLUNT); VI – 'novelty' (e.g. NEW-OLD, USUAL- UNUSUAL, YOUTHFUL-MATURE); VII – 'receptivity' (e.g. SAVOURY- TASTELESS, INTERESTING-BORING, PUNGENT-BLAND); VIII 'aggressive- ness' AGGRESSIVE-DEFENSIVE (only). There are also 15 scales not assigned to any of the eight factors; cf. Osgood, Suci & Tannenbaum 1957:53-61. The different factors are not all equally effective, e.g. factor I ('evaluative') is said to be twice as weighty as factor II, 3.5 times as weighty as III, five times as weighty as IV, and seven times as weighty as factors V through VIII. Weinrich in 'Travels through semantic space' 1958/1980 has been severely critical of factor analysis, showing for instance, that the eight factors exhaust, on average, only about 32% of the 76 scales (1980:22); and claiming that the factors identified 'have little classificatory power when applied to the universe of "concepts" (1980:24). Thus factor analysis must further distort the quantizing of semantic differentials.

(vi) The set of 50 scales published in Osgood, Suci & Tannenbaum 1957:37 is not a proper subset of the set of 76 scales on pp.53-61; where the former includes YELLOW-BLUE, RED-GREEN, BLACK-WHITE, the latter lists COLOURFUL-COLOURLESS instead. One of the reasons for this discrepancy is that some scales were thought to be irrelevant to the semantic profiles of certain expressions: cf. 'particular scales [. . .] must be carefully selected by the experimenter to suit his purposes' (Osgood, Suci & Tannenbaum 1957:80). Such selectiveness must prejudice the measurement of semantic differentials.

(vii) The last doubt to express about the accuracy of Osgood's instrument of measurement devolves on the choice of antonyms. Although the choice of an antonym for a particular adjective is often dictated either by convention or by morphology (e.g. *optimistic* is conventionally opposed to *pessimistic*, *sociable* is morphologically opposed to *unsociable*), there are times when more than one antonym could be chosen; and the one actually picked could have a different scaling effect from its alternative. E.g. KIND was paired with CRUEL; but it could have been paired with UNKIND. This might have affected measures of semantic distance, because for instance *spider* might be judged more cruel than unkind, and *schoolmarm* more unkind than cruel. Other instances of alternative antonymies are HEALTHY paired with SICK rather than UNHEALTHY; RATIONAL with INTUITIVE rather than with IRRATIONAL; and STRAIGHT with CURVED rather than with CROOKED. The choice of antonyms in such cases must surely have affected the semantic profiles of expressions judged on those particular scales, and therefore the choice of antonyms will have affected the quantizing of semantic distances.

One is forced to conclude that the semantic differential technique described in detail in Osgood, Suci & Tannenbaum's *The Measurement of Meaning* 1957, though interesting, does not reliably measure semantic differential – i.e. the distances between the connotations of expressions; still less does it succeed in quantizing the mental thesaurus so as to pinpoint the location of concepts in semantic space.

3.12 Meaning change

3.12.1 Introduction

> But mice and rats and such small deer
> Have been Tom's food for seven year.
> (William Shakespeare *King Lear* III.iv.144)

You can see from a comparison of present day English with the early modern English of Shakespeare or the Middle English of Chaucer or the Old English of Beowulf that time wreaks changes on the syntax, semantics and phonology of a language. The quotation from *King Lear* at the head of this section serves to demonstrate that the meaning of *deer* has changed since the first decade of the 17th century by narrowing its denotational scope from "animal" to "member of the family Cervidae". It is only lexemes, and very occasionally morphemes, which change in meaning – i.e. lexicon items. Meaning changes in larger expressions are the consequence of meaning change in lexicon items. Like other aspects of language change, meaning change is neither completely regular nor completely unsystematic, and we identify the following types: meaning change as a consequence of a change in the nature or conception of the phenomenon denoted by a lexicon item; change resulting from either an extension or a narrowing in the denotational scope of a lexicon item – or the one followed by the other; meaning change that results from a connotation; and finally, meaning transfer – where a label shifts from one phenomenon to another closely related phenomenon.[34]

3.12.2   Meaning change as a consequence of a change in the nature or conception of the phenomenon denoted by a lexicon item

The constantly changing environment in which we live can cause concomitant changes in the meanings of and meaning relations between lexicon items. The most drastic effects are the invention or discovery of a new phenomenon that requires labelling; or, alternatively, the obsolescence of an item when the phenomenon it denotes becomes outmoded and disappears from the scene. An example of a lexeme whose meaning has changed with the nature of the phenomenon it denotes is *window*,[35] which derives via *windore* from old Norse *vindauga* literally "windeye". "Windeye" transparently describes the hole in the wall that let in light and air, and which – before the days of glass windows – was closed with a shutter; it was the latter which led to the word being reinterpreted as the transparently descriptive *windore* or *wind-door*. *Windore* is a transference of meaning (cf. §3.12.6) from the hole to its cover. Nowadays a window must be glassed in order to be properly called a window instead of a hole in the wall, and this constraint has changed the meaning of *window*. More recently, a change in meaning has occurred with *atom*. The word is built on Greek roots meaning "indivisible", which the atom was thought to be; but with the discovery that the atom is divisible and can be split, the lexeme's meaning has changed.

A change in the nature of the phenomenon denoted by a lexicon item need not affect the meaning of the item. For instance, we call *bread* that white polystyrene-like substance sold in supermarkets, despite the fact that it can bear little physical or gustatory resemblance to what was called bread three hundred years ago. The change in the nature of bread has not caused any concomitant change in the meaning of the lexeme *bread* – unless it might be said that its denotational scope has simply expanded to include these novelties. For another example, the verb *book [a seat]* has always meant "reserve [a seat]", but it used to be transparently obvious why the zero-derived *book* was used since one's name was entered into a book when making the reservation (as it still is when booking a table in restaurants). Despite the fact that, nowadays, one often books without having one's name entered into a book (but gets a ticket instead), the meaning of the verb *book* hasn't really changed although its meaning relations have, insofar as the implications of booking are different in the manner described.

There is often a diachronic loss in transparency of a lexeme's meaning: for instance the meaning of old Norse *vindauga* "windeye" was transparent, as that of *skyscraper or housewife* is today; but *window* is not transparent. The relational status of the man of the household, his wife, and servant were once transparently indicated by the terms *hlæfdiʒe* "loaf-kneader" for the mistress, *hlafweard › hlaford* "loaf-warden" for the master, and *hlafæta* "loaf-eater [masculine]" for the servant. The latter has died out altogether; and *hlæfdiʒe* ('diʒe' is connected with modern *dough*) has become *lady*; her husband, the loaf-warden, became *lord*. The meaning of *lord* and *lady* shifted in unison after the Norman Conquest, but the formerly transparent relationship expressed through the form and gender of *hlaford* and *hlæfdiʒe* respectively has by now been completely lost. This loss in transparency is in part a function of phonological change; but sometimes a change in the nature of the phenomenon denoted can be the sole cause of a loss in transparency. E.g. for hundreds of years education and learning in Europe were conducted in Latin, and the quill pen used in writing was called by its late Latin name *penna*, an extension of the original meaning, "feather". English *pen* derives from *penna* and to the educated man its meaning would once have been relatively transparent; but with the demise of both a Latin education and the quill pen, the meaning of *pen* is no longer obviously descriptive.

Such diachronic loss in the transparency of a descriptive term is very common, but even a radical change in the nature of the phenomenon denoted by a lexicon item need not result in meaning change provided the most significant characteristics of the prototypical denotatum remain the same: consider how weapons have changed over the centuries, yet *weapon* means the same now as it did in middle English because it is significant as an instrument for killing or wounding, no matter how it effects this. Thus it is only when some critical aspect of the phenomenon denoted by a lexicon item changes, that the meaning of the lexeme will change concomitantly.

3.12.3 Extension in the denotational scope of a lexeme

Most semantic change is the effect of extending the scope of a lexeme's denotation to a phenomenon literally or metaphorically similar to a former denotatum. E.g. the English noun *cook* derives from the late Latin masculine noun *cocus* and was applied only to men up until the 16th century, when it was extended to women too. In 20th century American English the lexeme *guy* has been extended from males to females, and can be heard used of inanimate objects, too. *Uncle* derives directly from French *oncle* which comes from Latin *avunculus* "mother's brother"; the French and English words have extended their denotation to a male sibling of either of ego's parents. As a further extension *uncle* is used as a courtesy title for ego's parents' close male friends, too. The meaning of *ship* has been extended to accommodate *steam-ship*, *air-ship*, *space-ship* and *star-ship*, thus expanding from "vehicle for sea travel" to "vehicle for sea, air, or space (but not land) travel". There is a comparable extension in the meaning of Hausa *jirgi*, originally "boat", now used in compounds denoting airplanes, trains, and trucks – all manufactured vehicles.

The extension of meaning can lead to the splitting of a lexeme into two homonyms. We explained in §3.3.3 how the original relational noun *flower (of)* split to give the homonyms *flower* meaning "bloom" and *flour* meaning "finely ground seed of a cereal plant". The extension in Latin of *pupilla* "little girl, doll, ward" to the eye's pupil – metaphorically the "child of the eye" – led to the splitting of *pupilla* into the two homonyms English has borrowed: *pupil* "school student", and *pupil* "opening in the iris of the eye". *Crane* was originally the name of a long-shanked, long-necked bird; its use was figuratively extended to a lifting device whose shape was reminiscent of the bird's shape. In the light of the definitions of polysemy and homonymy given in §3.3 we have to say that *crane* has split into two homonyms because these different meanings need to be separately specified in the dictionary and cannot be contextually determined from a common base sense.[36] A fuel *tank*$_c$ and an army *tank*$_g$ are homonyms. During World War I when the army tank was being developed, secrecy prevented it being called anything suggesting an engine of war, and *tank* was presumably decided upon because the metal-box-like structure of the vehicle was reminiscent of the metal-box-like structure of the contemporary water or fuel tank: in other words *tank*$_g$ was conceived as a figurative extension of *tank*$_c$ which led directly to the establishment of a homonym. Finally, *pigeonholes* were literally that – stacked rows of roosting boxes for homing pigeons. The phrase was figuratively extended to stacked rows of boxes for mail and suchlike, whence it has become a compound lexeme[37] homonymous with the literal phrase. The verb *pigeonhole* meaning "classify" is a zero-derivation from the compound noun, and a further step away from the literal and original phrase.

Another kind of extension and splitting is the extension of proper names to a wider set of denotata (cf. §4.7.6) e.g. the use of trade names such as *Biro*, *Hoover* or *Kleenex* for all makes of ball-point pens, vacuum-cleaners, and paper tissues – at least for a time; or the creation of the verbs *boycott* and *lynch* from the surnames of Captains

Boycott and Lynch respectively. An earlier example is the coining of *dunce*. This is based on the name of John Duns Scotus (1265-1308) whose works on philosophy, theology, and logic were highly influential during the late middle ages, but fell under the attack from renaissance scholars in the 15th and 16th centuries; Duns's work was defended by 'dunses', whose arguments fell to the proponents of the new learning: so a *duns* or *dunce* was regarded as someone who rejects learning, and the label was extended to anyone who rejects learning.

3.12.4 Narrowing in the denotational scope of a lexeme

The meaning of *nice* has changed over the centuries by an extension in its denotational scope followed by a narrowing, so that its meaning progresses through the following (somewhat idealized) steps: "stupid or foolish › foolish or foppish › foppish or fastidious › fastidious or precise › precise or balanced › balanced or agreeable › agreeable or pleasant". Narrowing in the denotational scope of a lexeme, say *b*, is often the result of an encroachment on its domain by the extension in the scope of another lexeme *c*, which eventually completely usurps that part of *b*'s meaning. E.g. *meat* once meant "food" (as opposed to drink), but within the last hundred years its meaning has narrowed down to "animal flesh" (as opposed to fish) because the lexeme *food* has usurped much of its former denotational scope. Presumably the dominance of the lexeme *food* is due to its connexion with the verb *feed*.

Meaning shifts often involve a number of lexemes jostling one another for semantic space; Figure 3.2 shows a more complicated picture of changing meaning and meaning relations than we have considered so far. Until the 16th century the lexeme *girl* denoted a child of either sex. As early as the 11th century *child*, which had originally meant "baby", began to be used in its present day sense and so was in direct competition with *girl*. In the 14th century *baby* took over from *child* the meaning "baby", leaving both *girl* and *child* denoting children of either sex, beyond babyhood. Also in the 14th century *boy* took over from *knave* the denotation of a male child, probably because *knave* had already begun to be used in its present day sense. This left no particular term for female child, and allowed the possibility that either *girl* or *child* could narrow its meaning to fill the gap: *girl* did so in the 16th century.

Euphemistic uses of lexemes for various kinds of taboo topics have led to their being narrowed in meaning to the taboo topic alone. This

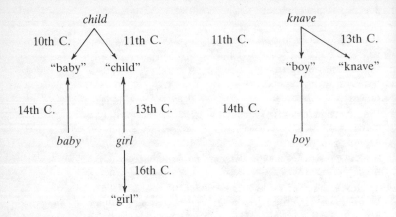

Figure 3.2   The effect of pressure in the system on the narrowing of the meaning of *girl*

compares with what happens when a lexeme as a taboo homonym, cf. §3.3.3: a word having a taboo homonym with which it could be confused will often be dropped from the language, leaving the field to the taboo word alone, cf. *cock*, *coney* and *gay* (which is on its way out as an adjective meaning "bright or full of fun"). The lexeme *accident* once meant "that which happens or a chance event" after the Latin *accidens*; because an unfortunate event is said to happen by accident, the noun has been contaminated by misfortune and narrowed to denote only an unfortunate chance event (except in the phrase *happy* or *lucky accident*). Similarly with *disease*: originally compounded from *dis-* and *ease* it denoted any disquieting, discomforting or incommodious event, including illness; contaminated by its association with illness, *disease* has narrowed down to its present meaning. Mental defectives are by definition defective human beings and were, among other things, euphemistically called 'christians'; more particularly, they were known in Swiss French as *crétins* (dialect for *chrétiens*) whence English *cretin* is derived. An *undertaker* once transparently denoted an agent who undertook to do things, a contractor; since the late 17th century the lexeme has been used as a euphemism for a funeral director, and in consequence has narrowed to that meaning alone. We could reasonably say that in all cases we have just been discussing the meaning change is a consequence of taboo connotations.

3.12.5 Meaning change as the result of a connotation

If a lexeme comes to have taboo or unfavourable connotations, these will tend to take precedence over any other aspect of its meaning, and the lexeme will be treated accordingly. We have already discussed what happens with taboo words, so we turn to some examples of downgrading because of the unfavourable connotations of a lexeme. E.g. French *fille* originally meant "girl" but came to be used as a euphemism for a prostitute, and nowadays tends to have unfavourable connotations; in consequence *girl* is translated *jeune fille*. The English words *churlish*, *rude* and *villain* have also been downgraded because of their unfavourable connotations. *Churlish* first meant "rustic or common", *rude* "uneducated or uncultured", and *villain* "low-born or base-minded rustic". The connotations of uncultured and vulgar rusticity have led all three to become pejorative terms.

On a different plane altogether, there are certain lexicon items in French that once had a positive sense but, because they commonly occur within negative contexts, have come to take on a negative value. Consider the following in which the Latin sources show the original positive sense against the contemporary French negatives.

	Latin		French negatives	
passus	"step"	*ne. . .pas*	"not"
punctum	"point"	*ne. . .point*	"not at all"
persona	"person"	*ne. . .personne*	"nobody"
rem	"thing"	*ne. . .rien*	"nothing"
aliquem unum	"another one"	*ne. . .aucun*	"not any"
jam magis	"already more"	*ne. . .jamais*	"never"

Because of their association with the negative, the words *pas*, *point*, *personne*, *rien*, *aucun*, *jamais* can all be used on their own with the negative senses given them above.[38]

3.12.6 Meaning transfer – the shift of a label from one phenomenon to another contextually associated one

Meaning quite often changes as the result of the denotation of a lexicon item being transferred from one phenomenon to another contextually associated phenomenon. The classic example of meaning transfer is the lexeme *bead* which originally meant "prayer". In the middle ages when the Pater Noster and the Ave Maria were said repeatedly, a check was kept on the number of prayers said by counting them off against little balls strung on a rosary: hence, *counting* or *telling one's beads* meant "counting one's prayers". But since it was the little pierced balls that were actually being checked off in the counting, the label *bead* transferred to them, and stayed with them. The lexeme *tank* was borrowed into English from Gujerati *tankh* meaning "pond or cistern"; this was originally the meaning in English, but *tank* got transferred to the container for holding and storing water, and subsequently it has been extended to any large, manufactured container for holding and storing liquid. Other examples of transfer are the word *electricity* formed on the Greek word for amber, the reason being that rubbing amber creates static electricity. The lexeme *zipper* was transferred from the proper name for a type of boot – whose slide fastener was the unique characteristic of the boot – to the slide fastener. A *mail of letters* was originally a "bag of letters", but *mail* has transferred to the carriage of letters, and the letters themselves. *Underground* and *subway* in the senses of transport systems of a particular kind are transferred uses of these lexemes. Finally, *brothel* is a sort of transferred term. Originally it meant "worthless person or whore" and so was used in the phrase *brothel house* which gradually replaced the older *bordel house* meaning "whore house". Eventually, by a process of ellipsis, *brothel* alone came to mean "whore house" and ceased to mean "whore"; thus its meaning was transferred.

3.12.7   Meaning change – a summary

In §3.12 we have been considering meaning relations across time in the vocabulary of a language. We have seen that meaning change often comes about through an extension in the denotative scope of a lexicon item (usually a lexeme) on either a literal or a metaphorical basis; or, alternatively, through a narrowing in denotative scope either because of expansion in the scope of other lexicon items, or as a means of avoiding taboo topics and other unfavourable interpretations or misinterpretations. We also saw that meaning shifts may result from such contextual factors as the textual environment of a lexicon item or the transfer of a lexicon item from one phenomenon to another contextually associated one.

Although it is important to recognize that meaning, like other aspects of language, does change (in fact it probably changes more rapidly than syntax or phonology), the process of change is only peripheral to a linguistic theory of meaning, and we shall leave the matter here.

3.13 Meaningful properties and meaning relations – a summary

It has been our purpose in ch.3 to identify the kinds of meaningful properties to be found in language expressions and the kinds of meaning relations which hold between language expressions. In the course of the chapter we have established the following.

Any expression E of language L is MEANINGFUL provided E is neither anomalous, indeterminable, nor contradictory.

An expression E of L is ANOMALOUS if it is incapable of denoting in W, the world spoken of.

An utterance U in L made in context C is INDETERMINABLE if it is impossible to figure out from C what U means.

A CONTRADICTION arises when a pair of antonyms is predicated of the same argument simultaneously, e.g. where it is said that *A is P and simultaneously A is not-P*

ANTONYMY is a relation holding between a proposition and its negation, viz. between Q and ~Q.

Two expressions which contradict one another are known as CONTRADICTORIES.

EVERY EXPRESSION E IN L HAS AT LEAST ONE MEANING; any expression with more than one meaning is AMBIGUOUS.

Every emic expression E entered in the theoretical dictionary of L has a unique sense which is open to a variety of interpretations when E is used in different contexts: these different interpretations manifest the POLYSEMY of E.

HOMONYMY is the relation that holds between formally identical etic expressions which correspond with separate lexical entries – i.e. with lexeme or morpheme entries in the theoretical dictionary.

For any determinable utterance U there is a VALUE that hearer H places on U in relation to its context C. The type of value assigned depends on the kind of speech act which U manifests (cf. ch.8). Statements have fuzzy truth values; predictions have values between being probably true and probably false; commissives have genuineness values; directives have compliance values; acknowledgments have appropriacy values; and authoritatives and declaratory acts have authority values.

An expression E is said to have the SEMANTIC COMPONENT K if the category labelled by E is a member (subset) of the category labelled by K.

Every expression E of L is analyzable into one or more semantic components; but there is no one-to-one correlation between the constituent morphs of E and its semantic components.

Semantic components reflect the salient characteristics of prototypical denotata.

There is a hierarchy (taxonomy) of semantic components in L.

A semantic component of E is equivalent to a SEMANTIC PREDICATE which takes E for its argument.

SYNONYMY is defined as symmetrical semantic implication between propositions, viz. where $(Q_1 \rightarrow Q_2)$ & $(Q_1 \leftarrow Q_2)$ such that $Q_1 \longleftrightarrow Q_2$. Consequently, the negation of either proposition necessarily implies negation of (i.e. cancels) the other, viz. given $Q_1 \longleftrightarrow Q_2$, then $\sim Q_1 \longleftrightarrow \sim Q_2$.

A relation of CROSS-VARIETAL SYNONYMY exists when Q_1 in contexts $C_{i...m} \longleftrightarrow Q_2$ in contexts $C_{j...n}$.

ASYMMETRIC SEMANTIC IMPLICATION occurs where the sense of one proposition, Q_1, asymmetrically implies another, Q_2, such that Q_2 does not also imply Q_1: viz. $(Q_1 \rightarrow Q_2)$ & $\sim(Q_1 \leftarrow Q_2)$. Under these circumstances, Q_1 is a HYPONYM of Q_2. The negation of Q_2 necessarily implies negation of Q_1 but the converse does not hold.

The co-hyponyms of a proposition Q are in an antonymous relation with one another such that for any hyponym G, where $G \subset F$ and F is an antonymous set of hyponyms consisting of $G \cup G'$, then $G \rightarrow \sim G'$.

For an antonymous pair of relative predicates P_{rel} and R_{rel} predicated on argument A: A is $P_{rel} \rightarrow \sim(A$ is $R_{rel})$, A is $R_{rel} \rightarrow \sim(A$ is $P_{rel})$, $\sim(A$ is $P_{rel}) \rightarrow A$ is R_{rel} to some extent, $\sim(A$ is $R_{rel}) \rightarrow A$ is P_{rel} to some extent.

A SEMANTIC IMPLICATION is a special kind of CONVENTIONAL IMPLICATURE, namely, a conventional implicature that holds between propositions. Other kinds of conventional implicature are implications holding of other sentence constituents. If a conventional implicature or a semantic implication is cancelled (negated) the implicating expression is also necessarily cancelled (negated).

A CONVERSATIONAL IMPLICATURE of S's utterance U made in context C under conventional co-operative conditions is a pragmatic inference determined from U considered in the light of C and relevant background information. A conversational implicature can be cancelled (negated) without cancelling the utterance which implicates it.

A TAUTOLOGY arises when a criterial part of (usually the whole of) the meaning of the predicate is conventionally or conversationally implicated by one of its arguments.

The value of a speech act is ANALYTIC if the value necessarily holds in
virtue of the fact that the meaning of the predicate in the proposition
uttered is wholly implicated by one of its arguments.

Two propositions OVERLAP semantically if they have semantically
related constituents.

The SEMANTIC DISTANCE between two expressions seems, intuitively,
to correlate with the number of category boundaries that lie between
the two categories they label.

The CONNOTATION of E in L is the set of implicatures deriving from the
use of E within a certain dialect, variety, or style of L – implicatures
which can result from prejudices about the people who use such
dialects, varieties, or styles in L.

DIACHRONIC MEANING RELATIONS are only peripheral to the theory of
meaning being discussed in this book, and therefore we merely note
that the meaning of a lexeme (or, occasionally, a morpheme) may
change over time through extension or narrowing in its denotative
scope, or the one followed by the other, or because of unfavourable
connotations, or under contextual influence of one kind or another.

Chapter 4

Lexicon semantics

> Words are not coined in order to extract the meaning of their elements and compile a new meaning from them. The new meaning is there *first*, and the coiner is looking for the best way to express it without going to too much trouble. If parts can be found whose meanings suggest the one in mind, so much the better, but that is not essential.
>
> (Dwight Bolinger *Aspects of Language* 1975:109)

4.1 Introduction

We have said in §1.5.1 that utterance meaning consists in part of sentence meaning, and that sentence meaning is compositional in the following manner: the meaning of a sentence is composed from the meanings of its constituent clauses and their connectives, the meaning of a clause is composed from the meanings of its constituent phrases, the meaning of a phrase is composed from the meanings of its constituent words, and those in turn from the meanings of their constituent lexemes and morphemes. Thus, ultimately, the meaning of a sentence is projected up through the hierarchy of syntactic levels from the meanings of the constituent lexemes and morphemes in the sentence. We consider the projection problem in ch.5, and it is our purpose in this chapter to examine the semantics of the constituent lexemes and morphemes in a sentence. The meanings of these lexemes and morphemes cannot be computed from the meanings of their constituent parts like the meanings of other sentence constituents, instead they have to be listed in the theoretical dictionary; for that reason we shall refer to them as LEXICON ITEMS, and it is to be understood that 'lexicon' refers to the theoretical dictionary.

There is no doubt that all root (non-derived) lexemes and all inflexional morphemes will be lexicon items, but it is by no means clear at this stage whether derived lexemes and derivational morphemes should also be counted lexicon items. Nor is it clear exactly what constitutes a lexeme: e.g. the idiom *kick the bucket* might be thought to consist of just one lexeme – such that an idiom is by definition a lexeme – or, alternatively, it might be said to consist of three lexemes corresponding to the three words in the idiom. And when S coins a word, what sorts of constraints does he observe in order to be certain that H will correctly interpret what he says? In order to throw light on these and other aspects of lexicon semantics we shall discuss lexeme formation – or as it is conveniently called 'word formation' – in some detail, to establish how the meaning of the word is to be specified in our theory of meaning. Note that we are not interested in word formation rules,[1] but in the possibility of predicting the meaning of words on the basis of their morphological form, e.g. by using the meaning of the word's lexeme and morpheme constituents to predict its meaning.

4.2   The meanings of words that consist of a lexeme and inflexional morphemes

In §1.5.2 we showed that the meanings of words consisting of a lexeme and inflexional morphemes transparently combine the meanings of these emic constituents, e.g.

> *cats* ≈ "cat + plural", *cat* ≈ "cat", *gave* ≈ "give + past tense", *gives* ≈ "give + 3rd person singular + nonpast tense", [Latin] *bonarum* ≈ "good + feminine + plural + genitive case", *sheep* ≈ ("sheep") v ("sheep + plural").

We see that there is no one-to-one correlation between the etic morphs and the emic morphemes. There are portmanteau morphs like the '-arum' suffix on *bonarum* or the '-s' suffix on *gives* which realize a number of morphemes with no individual morphological form; and there are zero morphs like the plural morpheme in (plural) *sheep*. We recognize the effect of the morphemes in a portmanteau or zero morph from context and by means of contrastive analysis. For instance, the etic form *sheep* is known to be polysemous between the lex *sheep* and the combination '*sheep* + zero plural morph', and on any occasion of use, the etic word *sheep* will be assigned one or the other interpretation (by H) on the basis of whichever best fits the context. Consider

(2.1) Those sheep are losing their wool.

(2.2) That sheep is losing its wool.

In (2.1-2) the NP-internal and NP-external number registration indicate that in (2.1) 'sheep' ≈ "sheep + plural", and in (2.2) 'sheep' ≈ "sheep" (singular). As often as not the textual environment will disambiguate an etic form in an obvious way; but sometimes in a less obvious way. Take the following interchange:

(2.3)
    A: What is your favourite animal?
    B: Sheep.

Here 'sheep' ≈ "sheep + plural" even though A's question is couched in the singular; we can show this on the basis of contrastive analysis, cf.

(2.4)
    A: What is your favourite animal?
    B: $\{{}^{Cats.}_{*Cat.}\}$ / $\{{}^{Pigs.}_{*Pig.}\}$ / $\{{}^{Koala\ bears.}_{*Koala\ bear.}\}$

If someone points to a field full of sheep and says *Sheep!* it will be interpreted from the world spoken of as "sheep + plural"; had they uttered *Sheep!* when pointing to a lone animal, the utterance would be interpreted "sheep" (singular).

The meanings of inflexional morphemes are primitive in the sense that they cannot be determined compositionally and so must be specified in the lexicon; thus inflexional morphemes are lexicon items. The meanings of certain lexemes, such as "sheep" would seem to be primitive in just the same way and they too must be lexicon items. But are all lexemes lexicon items? We shall answer that question in §4.3

4.3   Are derived lexemes lexicon items?

4.3.1   Lexical derivation

In §4.3 we shall examine whether the meaning of a derived lexeme can be predicted from a combination of the meanings of the lexical root and the derivational morphemes; if it can be predicted, then the set of lexicon items will comprise the set of morphological roots in the language, the set of derivational morphemes, the set of inflexional morphemes, and the set of root lexemes. If the meaning of a derived lexeme cannot be predicted from a combination of the meanings of the root and the derivational morphemes, we shall have to ask whether or not derivational morphemes should be counted lexicon items. For the sake of simplicity and clarity in exposition, lexemes and morphemes are italicized in the following discussion instead of appearing in double quotes.[2]

In English there are four kinds of lexical derivation involving derivational morphemes, they are:

(i) Zero derivation. With zero derivation, a zero affix (i.e. a morpheme that has no corresponding morph), attaches to an existing lexeme, causing it to shift its lexical class, thus to become a different lexeme.[3] The derived lexeme adopts the syntactic distribution, syntactic function, and the inflexional morphology of the new lexical class. E.g. the noun *waitress* can be changed into the verb *waitress* as in *She's been waitressing at the Hilton for the past year*.

(ii) Prefixing an existing lexeme. E.g. *unable* derives by prefixing *un-* to *able*. In English all prefixes are derivational morphemes and none are inflexional morphemes; this is not the case for all languages, even one so close to English as Welsh, for instance.

(iii) Suffixing an existing lexeme. E.g. *ability* derives by suffixing the nominalizing suffix *-ity* to *able*. In English, suffixes may be either inflexional or derivational morphemes, and – as we shall see – it can be hard to tell the difference at times.

(iv) Combinations of bound morphemes. E.g. *abbess* consists of *abb-* + *ess*, *ornithology* of *ornith-* + *-ology*.

Other languages may infix derivational morphemes, but English doesn't.

4.3.2 Zero derivation

A simple and popular way of deriving a new lexeme from an existing one is to use it as if it were a member of some other lexical class. This is achieved by assigning it the syntactic distribution and function of some other part of speech, and the regular inflexional morphology appropriate to its new lexical class. In English the source lexeme is most commonly a noun or a verb, and least likely to be an adverb or one of the other minor classes like article, pronoun, or preposition. Most zero derived lexemes are nouns and verbs, which take inflexions, but there are instances of adjectives and adverbs, which don't. There are no standard examples of zero derived articles or pronouns, etc.; though it is thought that locative prepositions are historically zero derived from adverbs.

The majority of zero derived lexemes are nouns used as verbs and verbs used as nouns. According to Hans Marchand *The Categories and Types of Present-Day English Word Formation* 1969:373 'deverbal substantives [nouns derived from verb lexemes] are much less numerous than denominal verbs.' However, he admits that it is often unclear which came first. Of the following lists of words that belong to both lexical classes (i.e. are both noun and verb lexemes) those listed under (n) started as nouns, and those under (v) as verbs.

(n)   age, balloon, bath, campaign, carpet, cash, doctor, experience, gas, honeymoon, lamb, moon, parody, race, sandwich, scape-goat, scheme, shop, snow, star, trumpet, waitress, whale, wolf.

(v)   catch, come-back, cough, drop out, eats, go-between, haunt, kill, lift, lounge, move, offer, reject, reprieve, resolve, shudder, smile, sneak.

There seem to be no constraints on the kind of noun or verb represented in either the source lexeme or the derived lexeme. And whichever direction the derivation takes, there is a huge variety of relationships between the meaning of the noun and the meaning of the verb. These relations have been classified, e.g. by Marchand 1969 or Valerie Adams *An Introduction to Modern English Word Formation* 1973 among others, but their classifications are neither watertight, nor do they reveal any clear constraints on zero derivations between nouns and verbs. In short, there is no consistent semantic pattern to the derivations, other than the inescapable one that the derived lexeme adopts a different lexical class meaning from the source lexeme – derived verbs have implications consistent with their being doing or becoming words, derived nouns have implications consistent with their being naming words. E.g. the verb and the noun *cough* are closely connected semantically; the noun and the verb *wolf* are more distantly connected; and the noun and the verb *doctor* are poles apart semantically. There is no apparent explanation for the noun *eats* being pluralia tantum[4] when *drink* is not. The meaning of zero derived lexemes is a cocktail made from the meaning of the source lexeme, the lexical class meaning of the derived lexeme, and commonsensical inference from context. It is the latter that leads us to recognize that the verb *age* is active in (3.2.1) and inchoative in (3.2.2):

(3.2.1)   We age this wine in oak.

(3.2.2) She had aged perceptibly since I saw her last.

It is arguable that deverbal nouns ending in *-ing*, e.g. *drinking*, *sitting*, *swimming*, *thinking*, are zero derived from the present participle form of the corresponding verb. (The alternative is, of course, that *-ing* is a nominalizing suffix on the verb lexeme.) Most of these derived nouns occur in uncountable noun phrases, but others adopt the plural inflexion from time to time, cf. *three sittings, lots of goings and comings*.

A few zero derived deadjectival verbs (i.e. verbs derived from adjectives) like *savage* and *shy* have the sense "act in a . . . manner". Most deadjectival verbs take on a causative sense, cf.

(3.2.3) Automobiles, totalled by shells, lay belly-up like helpless insects.

'Totalled' means "caused to become total write-offs". Similarly the verbs *blind, clear, dirty, idle, slim, sour, tame* all have the sense "cause to become . . .", where '. . .' is the sense of the source adjective. Thus the meanings of deadjectival verbs are mostly predictable.

Zero derived deadjectival nouns fall into three basic types. (i) Colour adjectives like *black, brown, red* which change lexical class to name colours. (ii) A miscellany: *oral* and *post-natal* signify kinds of examinations; *daily, weekly, monthly* signify kinds of newspapers/magazines; *musical* a kind of film or stage show; but the largest number signify some kind of human being, cf. *black, hopeful, newly-wed, regular, savage, undesirable*. (iii) There is a set of adjectives which function as the head constituent of a definite generic noun phrase signifying a class of human beings; however, they have a fixed morphological form so it is uncertain whether or not they are zero derived nouns. They fall into two kinds: (a) nationalities, e.g. *the Dutch, the English, the French, the Welsh* – each with a final palato-alveolar segment [ʃ] or [tʃ]; (b) *the poor, the unemployed, the workshy*, etc. which is a very productive set. Although types (i) and (iii) zero derived deadjectival nouns are readily recognizable, as such, and their meaning is thereafter quite predictable, the type (ii) nouns depend on context for their interpretation.

Nouns and verbs are occasionally created from other parts of speech, e.g.

(3.2.4) Though I Thee[verb] Thee[pronoun] and Thou[verb] Thee,[pronoun] I am no Quaker. (*OED*)

(3.2.5) But[conj.] I pray you, but[verb] me no buts[noun].

(3.2.6) The boss, who has a down[noun] on me, downed [verb] his drink, put his glass down[adverb] and went down[prep.] the stairs.

(3.2.7) He has used an[art.] an[noun] where there should be a the[noun].

In all of these, the meaning of the source lexeme together with the class meaning of the derived lexeme, is called upon to give meaning to the derived lexeme; so that their meaning is pretty well predictable. E.g. what could the verb *thee* mean but "call someone 'thee' ", given that the source pronoun *thee* is appellative?

Some adjectives zero derive from adverbs, e.g. *daily*, *down*, *faraway*, *far out*, *monthly*, *up*, *way out*, *well off* (note that many derive from a pair of adverbs). It is arguable that deverbal adjectives mostly zero derive from the past participle of verbs, cf. *broken*, *burnt*, *metalled*. In attributive position these adjectives describe the state or condition of the grammatical object or intransitive subject of the corresponding paraphrase with the source verb, cf. a *known criminal*, a *wanted man*, a *grown giraffe*, a *well-acted play*.[5] As complements of *be*, such adjectives are at first difficult to distinguish from the past participles of the verb. Historically the past participle may be either stative or nonstative,[6] thus (3.2.8) is ambiguous:

(3.2.8) The window was broken.

The stative interpretation is "the window was already broken" and the nonstative interpretation is "the window got broken". Only the participial inflexion permits a nonstative interpretation, the derived adjective is invariable stative. Whether one should classify all stative past participles forms, i.e. *-(e)d/n* suffixed verb forms, as zero derived adjectives is a point worthy of consideration. An interesting case on which the decision could turn is the contrast between a doublet like the past participle *opened* and the corresponding adjective *open*. *Opened* is invariably nonstative, the adjective *open* is invariably stative, cf.

(3.2.9)   The window is opened.

(3.2.10) The window is open.

Where there are doublets like *opened* and *open*, the past participle is always nonstative, the adjective stative. It therefore seems reasonable to classify all stative *-(e)d/n* complements as zero derived adjectives, and all nonstative ones as verbs with the past participle inflexion.

Perhaps because nouns regularly function as both attributives and complements, they do not convert to adjectives. Compare the noun *stone* with the adjective *stoney*: an intensifier like *incredibly* can modify the adjective but not the noun, cf.

(3.2.11)
   a.   a stoney path
   b.   an incredibly stoney path

(3.2.12)
   a.   a stone path
   b.   *an incredibly stone path

And, of course, the adjective may take a comparative or superlative inflexion, but the noun cannot:

(3.2.13) stoney, stonier, stoniest

(3.2.14) stone, stoner ≠ "more stone", *stonest

Adverbs are not generally derived by zero affixation, but some manner adverbs have the same form as corresponding adjectives, cf.

(3.2.15) Max drove hard and fast at first, and then dead slow.

There is no change in meaning between adjective and adverb, only a change in scope from noun to verb.

Many locative adverbs double as prepositions, and historically the prepositions derive from adverbs. The process now seems to be over, and there are certain words such as *down*, *over*, *up* which function as both prepositions or adverbs; for syntactic reasons it may be desirable to postulate a pair of homonymous lexemes, but there will be no semantic difference between them.

Lexemes occasionally zero derive from bound morphemes. E.g. the nouns *isms*, *pros* and *cons*, and perhaps also *morph* and *phone* (in linguistics). The adjectives *emic* and *etic* which we have been using in this book are lexemes zero derived from bound morphemes.

Let's end this exemplification of zero derivation with a text which parodies the language used by former U.S. Secretary of State Alexander Haig, who was notorious for his zero derivations. Despite the originality of many of the lexemes in this piece, the reader should be able to follow the text quite easily by using his or her knowledge of the meaning of the source lexemes, implications of the lexical class meaning of the derived lexeme, and inference from context.

(3.2.16) *Alexander the Haigiographer*
   General Alexander Haig has contexted the Polish watchpot
somewhat nuancely. How, though, if the situation decontrols can he

stoppage it mountingly conflagrating? Haig, in Congressional
hearings before his confirmatory, paradoxed his auditioners by
abnormalling his responds so that verbs were nouned, nouns verbed
and adjectives adverbised. He techniqued a new way to vocabulary
his thoughts so as to informationally uncertain anybody listening
about what he had actually implicationed. At first it seemed that the
General was impenetrabling what at basic was clear. This, it was
suppositioned, was a new linguistic harbingered by NATO during the
time he bellwethered it. But close observers have alternatived that
idea. What Haig is doing they concept, is to decouple the Russians
from everything they are moded to. An example was to obstacle
Soviet ambassador Dobrynin from personalising the private elevator
at Foggy Bottom. Now he has to communal like everybody else.
Experts in the Kremlin thought they could recognition the word-
forms of American diplomacy. Now they have to afreshyly language
themselves up before they know what the Americans are subtling.
They are like chess grandmasters suddenly told to knight their
bishops and rook their pawns. If that is how General Haig wants to
nervous breakdown the Russian leadership he may be shrewding his
way to the biggest diplomatic invent since Clausewitz. Unless, that
is, he schizophrenes his allies first.

(London *Guardian* 3 February 1981)

Our lengthy discussion of zero derivation has revealed the characteristic features of derivational morphology. The most important one
for our purposes is the variability in the correlation between the
meaning of the source lexeme and that of the derived lexeme.
Sometimes the meaning of the derived lexeme is readily predictable
from the meaning of the source lexeme taken together with the class
meaning of the derived lexeme; yet on other occasions the meaning is
distant, and even quite distinct from that of the source lexeme. The
only general principle would seem to be that the rarer a zero derived
lexeme is, the more likely is its meaning to be predictable; but
currently there is no documentary evidence to back this impression.
The inconsistency in the predictability of the semantics of morphologically derived lexemes is matched by an irregularity in the application
of zero derivation to a set of lexemes. E.g. we cannot safely say that
any noun will zero derive a verb, or vice versa. Some regularities do
exist, e.g. colour adjectives regularly give rise to colour nouns; but
although we have the deadjectival noun *oral*, for instance, we do not
standardly have a parallel deadjectival noun *written*, cf.

(3.2.17) I have an oral this morning, and a *written this afternoon.

(3.2.18) I have an oral this morning, and a written test this afternoon.

Both the semantic inconsistency, and the irregular application of zero derivation, are typical of derivational morphology in general,[7] and recur in the other three kinds of lexical derivation involving derivational morphemes; so we shall deal with them quite briefly.

4.3.3 Lexemes derived by prefixing and suffixing derivational morphemes

In *Categories and Types of Present-Day English Word Formation* 1969, Hans Marchand lists nearly 80 prefixes and more than 80 suffixes that can, in contemporary English, attach to an existing lexeme or – in many cases – to a bound morpheme, so as to derive a new lexeme (e.g. *disagree, dissuade; ex-boxer, exhibit; incredible, inert; subway, sublimi-nate; believable, credible; advantageous, spurious; baker, vintner; lioness, abbess*). The meaning of the derived lexeme is sometimes predictable from the meanings of its derivational constituents, but often it is not. Consider some cases.

The words *co-occur* and *co-operate* have the same prefix *co-* meaning "together with". The contribution to the meaning of *co-occur* of both the prefix and the stem is transparent in the meaning of the derived lexeme: "occur together (with)". By contrast, the meaning of *co-operate* has shifted from the transparent "operate together (with)" to "be helpful".

The contribution of both stem and suffix to the meaning of, e.g. *atomize* or *legalize*, is transparent; but the meaning of *-ize*, "cause to become", is slightly buried in *revolutionize* "bring about a revolution", more deeply buried in *computerize* "make suitable for feeding into a computer", and lost altogether in *womanize* "chase women".

The meanings of, e.g. *readable* or *admissible*, are more or less predictable from the meanings of their respective stems and the suffix *-able/-ible*. The same cannot be said of *possible*, since the stem *poss-* has no meaning outside of *possible* and *impossible* – and none within them, either.[8] *Invincible* can be analyzed into the negative prefix 'in-', the stem '-vince' and the suffix '-ible'; assuming that *-vince* from Latin *vincere* means "conquer", the meaning of the derived lexeme *invincible* is predictable from its constituent morphemes: "unconquerable". But the stem *-vince* as it occurs in, e.g. *convince* or *evince* does not mean "conquer"; so how confident should we be in assigning this meaning to the stem of *invincible*?

The meanings of most words suffixed *-ology* "the study of " are predictable (to those who know the meaning of the stem), cf. *anthropology* "the study of man", *ornithology* "the study of birds", *psychology* "the study of the mind", *phonology* "the study of sound". But of course, the latter is inexact: *phonology* is not just the study of sound, but rather the study of sound systems of human languages; so the meaning of the whole is not completely predictable from the meaning of the parts even here. The prefix *tele-* from ancient Greek τηλε meaning "from afar" occurs in many English words, including the familiar *telephone* (stem from the Greek word meaning "sound") and *television*. The meanings of *telephone* and *television* are not truly predictable from the meanings of their component morphemes, cf. "sound from afar", "vision (? picture) from afar", although it is easy to see the connexion between the meaning of each constituent and the meaning of the whole lexeme.

Seeking to predict the meaning of a derived lexeme from the meanings of its derivational components, we will often be led astray. Derived lexemes are quite inconsistent with one another in the degree to which the meaning of the whole lexeme can be derived from the meaning of its constituents. For lexicon semantics, the only reasonable solution to the problem is to consistently assign meaning to every lexeme as a whole, irrespective of the meaning of its constituent morphemes. Thus derived lexemes will be treated quite differently from inflected words: the morphological boundary between stem and inflexion coincides with the boundaries of semantic components, and the meaning of the inflected word will be computed from the meanings of the lexeme and the inflexional morphemes within it. The derived lexeme, once constructed, attains independence from its derivational origins by being recognized as a word in its own right, viz. as a semantically homogeneous free form, that is both semantically and syntactically discrete; thereafter, its meaning may change with use, and eventually even obscure its origins.

To assign meaning to every lexeme in the language is a necessary condition on a theory of meaning, but not a sufficient condition. S and H not only know the meanings of lexemes, but also the meanings of derivational morphemes, both affixes (including the zero affix) and stems; moreover, speakers coin new words using derivational morphemes. The meanings of newly coined derived lexemes must normally be determined from the meanings of their derivational components and the context of use[9] – until the lexeme has entered the regular lexicon of the language. This is one reason why the lexicon is required to assign meanings to derivational morphemes, as well as to lexemes. There is another: one of the goals of a theory of meaning is to account for semantic relationships between words; and, obviously, derivational morphemes semantically relate many, if not all, of the lexemes in which they are found. Take for example the words in (3.3.1).

(3.3.1) abduce, adduce, conduce, deduce, educe, induce, produce, reduce, seduce, traduce, transduce.

The bound stem *-duce* in these words comes from Latin *ducere* "lead", and the meaning of each one of them is connected with the notion of leading. It is probably incorrect to posit that the stem necessarily means "lead" in all the words listed, but an account of linguistic meaning should certainly show that a semantic relationship exists between them.

4.3.4 Lexicon items

The set of lexicon items so far identified comprises the following:

  (i)   all inflexional morphemes;
 (ii)   all derivational morphemes;
(iii)   all lexical stems (including roots);
 (iv)   all lexemes (as wholes).

Although there is no question of determining the meaning of the derived lexemes which appear in the lexicon from the meanings of their derivational components, the meanings of words consisting of a lexeme and inflexional morphemes will be computed from the meanings of these constituents.

4.4 Compounds

Compounds are lexemes composed from two or more free forms, e.g. *blackbird*, *son-in-law*, *air-condition*, etc. Like other derived lexemes, their meaning is only occasionally predictable from the meanings of their components. Sometimes history obscures an earlier transparency, e.g. the Old English compounds *hlafweard* "loaf-warden" (i.e. "man of the house") and *hlæfdiʒe* "loaf-kneader" ("woman") have reduced to the opaque noncompounds *lord* and *lady* respectively. The compound *crayfish* is an anglicization of Old French *crevice* – it never was semantically transparent. Attempts to classify the kinds of relationship that exist between the component words of a compound (e.g. Hans

Marchand *The Categories and Types of Present-Day English Word Formation* 1969, Valerie Adams *An Introduction to Modern English Word Formation* 1973, Judith Levi *The Syntax and Semantics of Complex Nominals* 1978) serve to demonstrate their boundless variety. Consider the following sample of compound nouns

> *chimney sweep* "one who sweeps chimneys", *play-goer* "one who goes to plays", *heavy-smoker* "one who smokes heavily", *looker-on* "one who looks on", *stay-at-home* "one who stays at home", *night owl* [fig.] "one who stays up late at night, like an owl", *left-wing* [fig.] "people holding socialist views", *skyscraper* [fig.] "a building so tall it seems to scrape the sky", *hand-me-down* "something handed down", *girl friend* "a friend who is a girl", *bakehouse* "a place where baking is done", *bus-stop* "a place where the bus stops", *oil refinery* "a place where oil is refined", *drive-in* "a place one drives into for service", *air pump* "a pump supplying compressed air", *airgun* "a gun using compressed air" (extended to "guns using a spring"), *fighter-bomber* "a plane that is both a fighter and a bomber", *blackbird* "a species of bird that is characteristically black", *eating-apple* "an apple for eating", *teaching profession* "the profession of teachers", *cockfight* "fight between roosters", *small talk* "talk about insignificant matters", *hairdo* "the outcome of having one's hair done", *Parkinson's Disease* "a disease discovered by P", *Kinsey Report* "the report written by K", *Valentine's Day* "day commemorating St. Valentine", *cheapskate* "someone who does things on the cheap, ungenerously", *River Thames*.

Long as this list is, it does not exhaust the different types of noun compounds. In addition, there are compound verbs, e.g. *aircondition*, *mass-produce*, *two-time*; compound adjectives, e.g. *cut and dried*, *easy-going*, *uncalled for*; and compound adverbs, e.g. *down-under*, *far-off*.

Traditional studies of compounding set up taxonomies based on the meanings of the compound's constituent words and their syntactic or functional relationship with one another. Marchand 1969 and Adams 1973, for example, propose many different derivations for compounds without offering any explanation why there should be so many complicated ways to achieve the same – comparatively simple – result, i.e. a compound lexeme. Even so, they do not pretend to have shown that the meaning of a given compound lexeme can necessarily be predicted from the meaning of its component words. Other scholars, such as Levi 1978, have drawn on the mechanisms of transformational grammar to derive compounds from sentential paraphrases. Levi reduces the set of relationship between the components of a compound noun to 16 basic patterns, sometimes at the expense of forcing a dubious interpretation on a particular compound. Furthermore, she guarantees only to have reduced the options on the possible meanings of a given compound, and expressly discounts the 'semantic information idiosyncratically accruing to a particular surface form' – i.e. its proper meaning (p. 19). On both traditional and transformationalist accounts of compounding, there are compounds which can be assigned alternative derivations among the proposed analyses, without any effect whatsoever on the interpretation of the compound. This lack of semantic discrimination between the analyses proposed, throws doubt on claims that they represent a compound's meaning. To sum up, both traditional and transformationalist rules for compounding are unsatisfactory because: (i) they are too powerful – in that they predict compounds which are unlikely to occur, and some of which may be impossible; and (ii) they are too weak because they fail to generate all possible compounds. This paradoxical inadequacy is a consequence of the mistaken assumption that bounded sets of conditions for and constraints on compounding can be deduced from the analysis of sentential paraphrases of conventional compounds.

Thanks to Pamela Downing's 'On the creation and use of English compound nouns' 1977, we need not despair of bringing order and reason to the semantics of compounds. Although Downing's paper discusses only compound nouns, her findings should, mutatis mutandis, be generally applicable to compounds. The main difference between her work and the studies discussed earlier, is that she concentrates her attention on novel compounds, i.e. compounds that are not conventional or 'lexicalized' (her term). This is interesting because like any newly coined lexeme, the novel compound relies for its interpretability on the meaning of its components and the context of use. The most impressive parts of Downing's paper[10] are reports of experiments in which (i) subjects were asked to provide interpretations for novel compounds in the absence of any context; and (ii) subjects were asked to evaluate the appropriateness of various interpretations proposed for a number of compounds, both novel and conventional. The results may be summarized as follows.

(a) There was no difference shown in the complexity or ingenuity of the interpretations offered for conventional compounds like *bullet hole* and novel ones like *pea-princess*. Interpretations given for *bullet hole* were not restricted to the typical sense of the compound "hole made by a bullet", but included such things as "a hole in which to hide bullets", "part of a bullet-forming apparatus" (Downing 1977:820). These show that when asked to interpret a compound (or any other expression) out of context, people[11] put their imagination to work.

(b) Three kinds of novel compounds of varying degrees of implausibility were offered for interpretation: (i) compounds like *butler-maid*, *fork-spoon*, *circle-square* in which the compound words are, prima facie, mutually exclusive; (ii) compounds like *head-hat*, *time-hour*, *hog-pork* in which the head component typically implies the modifier, making it redundant; (iii) compounds like *bird-door* and *night-Democrat* which are implausible, because, e.g., people aren't Democrat by night and Republican by day. All three kinds of compounds were judged possible if the subject could think of something for the compound to denote: e.g. a piece of cutlery that is a fork at one end and a spoon at the other could be called a 'fork-spoon'; 'When soy-pork is a common dish, hog-pork will described the genuine article' (Downing 1977: 833); a door for birds to pass through could just as well be called a 'bird-door' as a door for cats is called a *cat-door*.

(c) A *cousin-chair* could be a "chair for a cousin"; but everyone rejected the suggestion that it could be "a chair reserved for non-cousins" (Downing 1977:824). A negative relationship must normally be morphologically signalled.

(d) The experiments described above, together with another in which subjects were asked to create names for drawings of entities with no conventionalized names, generally showed that the relationship between the component meanings of a compound is regarded as permanent unless there is good reason to regard it as fortuitous. E.g. a *cow-tree* was described as 'a tree under which cows LIKE to stand or TEND to gather' (Downing 1977:834 [emphasis in original]).

Downing 1977 identifies a small set of conditions and constraints on noun compounds, and there is every reason to think that they will generalize to other classes of compound, too. Under the co-operative principle, S must ensure that H can understand him, and therefore H must be able to reconstruct the meaning of a novel compound, or a novel use of a conventional compound, from the meaning of its component words and the context in which it is used. One of the interpretative strategies H will use is pattern-matching with existing compounds; but because of the boundless variety of relationships that exist between the constituents in compounds, the consequences of pattern recognition will have to be checked in the light of the compound's constituent meanings, and the context in which the compound is used. The tendency for there to be a permanent relationship between the meanings of the compound's constituents will constrain the class of probable interpretations. On the other hand, an apparently anomalous spontaneous compound like *apple-juice seat* will be recognized as perfectly reasonable when its intended denotation is recognizable from context: Downing 1977:818 reports that someone was asked to 'Sit in the apple-juice seat' – identifiable from context as the (only) seat before which there sat a glass of apple-juice. The existence of such unusual compounds leads Downing to suppose that the number of possible compounding relationships is unbounded, and that the class of such relationships may vary from one context to another. She concludes:

> The data examined here reflect tendencies for compounds to be based on permanent, non-predictable relationships of varying semantic types, depending on the nature of the entity being denoted. Since compounds often serve as ad-hoc names for entities or categories deemed nameworthy, these tendencies indicate more about the process of categorization than they do about derivational constraints on the compounding process. The more nameworthy the entity or category defined by the compound, the wider the temporal and spatial range of speech situations within which the compound will be useful and interpretable. It is in this sense that the speaker is constrained in his creation and usage of compound nouns.
> (Downing 'On the creation and use of English compound nouns' 1977:841)

We conclude that conventional compounds will be entered in the lexicon, and have the status of lexemes; in consequence they will be assigned meanings as wholes. Novel compounds, like any newly-coined derived lexemes, will not be entered in the lexicon as wholes, and so their meanings will need to be determined from the meanings of their constituent words (or rather the lexemes which those words manifest) and the context. In fact, they will be subject to the same interpretative process as inflected words, phrases, and larger structures.

Since novel compounds are subject to the same interpretation procedures as phrases, there is no need for us to distinguish them from phrases (though we can). But conventional compounds are another matter: they should be listed in the lexicon and assigned meanings like other lexemes. Because lexicographers have recognized no clear dividing line between compounds and phrases, they have been very inconsistent in their treatment of conventional compounds, cf. Levi 1978:229ff. Nevertheless, some discriminatory guidelines can be established. The conventional compound has the grammatical charac-teristics of a lexeme and word rather than those of a phrase, viz. the compound falls into a particular lexical class, with the distribution and functions typical of that lexical class; and it is semantically homogeneous, and both semantically and syntactically discrete. For instance, the compound *blackbird* has the distribution, function and morphology typical of a noun; the compound *air-condition* is in every way a verb. Morphological and syntactic processes, together with their semantic effects, show compounds to be word-like (and therefore lexeme-like) islands.

(a) Like words, compounds are prosodic islands; i.e. compounds normally admit no internal juncture, and this property is shared by words but not phrases. E.g. the word *understandably* will not admit internal disjuncture (indicated below by a slash '/'):

> understandably, *under/standably, *understand/ably,
> *understandabl/y.

Phrases do admit internal disjuncture, even though the disjuncture may not appear in every utterance:

> a black / bird   "a bird which is black"
> a metal / container   "a container made of metal"
> the man / in the street   "the man who is in the street"

Compounds do not admit internal disjuncture, so the insertion of disjuncture turns the compound into a homologous phrase, cf.

> a $\overset{1}{\text{blackbird}}$ "a species of bird"
> a $\overset{1}{\text{black}}$ / bird   "a bird which is $\overset{1}{\text{black}}$"
> a $\overset{1}{\text{metal}}$ container   "a container for metal"
> a $\overset{1}{\text{metal}}$ / container   "a container made of $\overset{1}{\text{metal}}$"
> the man in the street   "the ordinary person"
> the man / in the street   "the man who is in the street"

Many compounds are normally stressed on their first constituent word whereas the homologous phrase is normally stressed elsewhere. But not all compounds are front-stressed, cf. *$\overset{1}{\text{headmaster}}$* or *string $\overset{1}{\text{quartet}}$*; and phrases can be front stressed (as we see above) in order to emphasize the stressed word. The criterial prosodic characteristic for words and compounds is not their stress pattern, but the fact that they will not admit internal disjuncture, whereas phrases will. Given that disjuncture marks the boundaries of sense-groups, the inadmissibility of disjuncture within words and compounds is evidence of their semantic homogeneity (semantic islandhood) in contrast to phrases.

(b) A compound word, like any other word, consists of either a single lexeme, or a lexeme and inflexional morphemes; thus its inflexional possibilities are those applicable to any word of its lexical class. E.g. the only inflexional morphology applicable to noun compounds is noun morphology, which in English means the possible attachment of a plural suffix. Where appropriate, this will attach to the head noun constituent of the compound if there is one, otherwise it will be suffixed to the end of the compound, cf. *blackbirds*, *housewives*, *courts martial*, *lookers-on*, *sons-in-law*, *drive-ins*, *stay-at-homes*. When the final constituent of a noun compound is a noun other than the head constituent, the suffix is sometimes attached there, cf. *son-in-laws*. Because of their lexemic status, there is no other kind of morphological variation within compounds, e.g. no kind of agreement, so that one says *my hand-me-down*, *your hand-me-down*, *his hand-me-down* not **your hand-you-down*, **his hand-him-down* etc., and *she is a stay-at-home* not **she is a stays-at-home*.

(c) It is generally possible to expand a phrase by placing additional words between the words composing the phrase, e.g. *a new house* › *a new brick house*. It is characteristic of words, (and therefore of lexemes), that other words (or lexemes) cannot be placed within their boundaries, cf. *fantastic* › **faneversotastic*, *kangaroo* › **kangahoppingroo*.[12] Likewise with compounds; e.g. the compound *man-in-the-street* cannot be expanded into *man who is in the street* like the homologous phrase can; and *blackmetalbird* might be "bird made of black metal" or "metal bird which is black" – both of which are phrase paraphrases – but it cannot be **"metal blackbird"*. The exception to this constraint on both words and compounds is that both allow expletives within their boundaries, cf. *absobloominlutely*,[13] *fanfuckingtastic*,[14] *kangabloodyroo* and *man-in-the-bloody-street*, *blackfuckingbird*, etc. The reason for the interruptibility constraint on both words and compounds is that both are semantic and syntactic islands.

(d) With respect to certain semantic-syntactic processes, words and compounds are islands whereas phrases are not. (4.1) and (4.2) have the same structure and differ only in predicate nouns 'bird' and 'blackbird', respectively.

(4.1) There is a bird over there.

(4.2) There is a blackbird over there.

The structure of (4.3) is different:

(4.3) There is a black bird over there.

We can isolate the adjective 'black' from the phrase in (4.3) but not the constituent 'black-' from the compound in (4.2); thus (4.4) necessarily follows from (4.3), but not from (4.2):

(4.4) There is a bird over there which is black.

In fact there are some species of blackbirds with brown females, thus we can reasonably say

(4.6) There is a brown blackbird over there,

or

(4.6) There is a blackbird over there which is brown.

But we cannot say either of (4.7) because they are contradictory.

(4.7)
    a.   *There is a brown black bird over there.
    b.   *There is a black bird over there which is brown.

The sentences in (4.7) are contradictory because a bird which is predominantly black cannot at the same time be predominantly brown. Thus parts of compounds cannot be isolated for grammatical purposes in the same way that parts of phrases can be.

Another instance would be that constituents of a phrase such as *black bird* can be clefted out, but the constituents of compounds cannot, cf.

(4.8) It was black, that bird Ed saw.

(4.9) It was a bird, that black thing Ed saw.

Both of these mean "Ed saw a black bird", not "Ed saw a blackbird". The semantic homogeneity of the compound, and its semantic-syntactic islandhood, do not allow for its constituents to be separated in this way.

(e) Finally, compounds, unlike phrases, are subject to morphological processes. We have already seen that they may take inflexions appropriate to their lexical class. They may also be subject to derivational processes in which the whole compound falls within the scope of a derivational affix, whereas the same affix attached to a homologous phrase ranges over only the word to which it is affixed. E.g in (4.10) the suffix '-like' ranges over 'bird', but in (4.11) the same suffix ranges over 'blackbird':

(4.10) It's a black birdlike creature.

(4.11) It's a blackbirdlike species.

Notice the illegitimacy of

(4.12) *It's a black birdlike species.

Even in folk-taxonomy, blackbirds are reckoned a species of bird but birds do not constitute a species (they are a class, *aves*). In (4.10) whatever is being referred to by 'it' is one of the class of creatures like a bird (note the scope of '-like'); in (4.11) whatever is being referred to by 'it' is of a species like a blackbird (again, note the scope of '-like'). The scope of the suffix *-like* is the stem word, whether compound or not. The scope of a prefix may, similarly, be the whole compound; it cannot be a phrase. A *non-blackbird* is something that is not a blackbird (it might be almost anything, depending on context cf. §§3.7-8); but a *non-black bird*, is a bird that isn't black. The scope of the prefix *non-* is the stem word, be it compound or non-compound.

What we have seen in the preceding paragraphs is that criteria can be established that will discriminate between compounds and phrases. Tests based on these criteria can be developed and used to determine which language expressions are compound words whose constituent lexemes should be included in the lexicon as compound lexemes.

4.5 Phrasal verbs

By phrasal verbs I mean such verbs as *cut down on*, *cut up*, *egg on*, *give in*, *look after*, *make do with*, *put up with*, *type up*, *wake up to*, etc. These have been called, more appropriately, 'compound verbs' by E. Kruisinga *A Handbook of Present Day English* 1932 §§2204-2211, and they are very much like compounds except for the fact that many of them can be 'discontinuous', i.e. object noun phrases can be placed between the verb and the particle constituents, and sometimes must be: cf. *cut the tree down*, *type him that letter up*, *play the communists off against the fascists*, *do Edgar out of his inheritance*, *do out Edgar of his inheritance*. Phrasal verbs are lexemes, and the means of discriminating them from homologous polylexemic expressions have been described by e.g. Dwight Bolinger *The Phrasal Verb in English* 1971. I shall just briefly summarize the relevant characteristics they share with conventional compounds and other lexemes.

When the parts of a phrasal verb are contiguous they admit no disjuncture between them, but disjuncture is admissible before a preposition that does not form part of a phrasal verb. Cf.

(5.1) We cut it up / up in the field.

(5.2) He was looked after / after a time.

(5.3) They egged him on / on Saturday.

Consider the meaning of

(5.4) Look / up the tree!

Here we have the verb lexeme "look" and the prepositional phrase 'up the tree', which directs H where to look; in the written language there would often be a comma between 'look' and 'up'. (5.4) might be continued as in

(5.5) Look / up the tree! / Can you see the frogmouth?

Now consider the following:

(5.6) ?? Look / up the tree / in *Native Trees of Australia*.

These sentences, with disjuncture between 'look' and 'up', cannot be interpreted "find out the name of the tree by looking in *Native Trees of Australia*". A similar sentence without disjuncture between 'look' and 'up' does have that meaning though, because 'look up' can then be interpreted as the phrasal verb *look up* with the meaning "find out by looking"; cf.

(5.7) Look up the tree / in *Native Trees of Australia*.

The inadmissibility of disjuncture between contiguous parts of the phrasal verb is a characteristic shared with the compound lexeme. However, discontinuous instances of phrasal verbs need not comply with the disjuncture constraint, cf.

(5.8) He cut the tree, / which had fallen across the road, /up into firewood.

It is notable that the discontinuity seen in some phrasal verbs is restricted to the placing of object noun phrases between the verb constituent and the particle constituent, cf. (5.8) and

(5.9) Max cut Marge the tomatoes all up.

Neither the passive *by*-phrase, nor most adverbials, can interrupt phrasal constituents:

(5.10)
   a.   *The onions were chopped by Max up.

   b.   *Max chopped quickly the onions up.
   c.   *Ed made the story on impulse up.
   d.   *Max chopped last night up the onions.

However, manner adverbs in *-ly* are often heard to occur between the object NP and the particle in speech, although the result is unstylish, cf.

(5.11)
   a.   Max chopped the body carefully up into little pieces.
   b.   Ed looked the property cursorily over.
   c.   They took the body quickly away.
   d.   June played the men skilfully off against one another.

So the discontinuity which sets some phrasal verbs apart from other lexemes is severely constrained. And, despite the occasional discontinuity, the constituents of phrasal verbs cannot be separated from one another by such grammatical processes as clefting and co-ordinate deletion – the latter creating a zero anaphor, cf. §1.3.4. Compare the effect of clefting on the phrasal verbs *give up* and *chop up*, with its effect on the verb and adverb sequence *climb up*.

(5.12) It was up that Ed climbed. ["Ed climbed up."]

(5.13) It was up the mountain that Ed climbed. ["Ed climbed up the mountain."]

(5.14) *It was up that Tom gave. ["Tom gave up."]

(5.15) *It was up the onions that Tom chopped. ["Tom chopped up the onions."]

The semantic homogeneity of phrasal verbs, and their semantic-syntactic discreteness, blocks the clefting of the particle because the latter makes no sense in isolation from the rest of the phrasal verb, cf. (5.14-15). For the same reason, co-ordinate deletion cannot apply to either constituent of a phrasal verb on its own, although it can apply to the whole phrasal verb – as we shall see. First, though, consider

(5.16) Then the mouse ran up the pipe, not down it.

Here, 'up the pipe' and 'down it' are prepositional phrases; the verb lexeme "run" is deleted from the second clause – which is left to be interpreted from its co-ordination with an antecedent clause. Contrast (5.16) with

(5.17) *Ed cut the tree up, not it down.

This cannot be used to mean "Ed cut the tree up, he didn't cut it down"; because there is only partial identity between the phrasal verbs *cut up* and *cut down*, and each phrasal verb is a semantic-syntactic island. Of course, a whole phrasal verb can be deleted under the usual co-ordinate identity condition, because it is recoverable as a zero anaphor, cf.

(5.18) Ed cut up the fence, not the tree.

(5.19) Alice was chopping up onions, and had been for an hour.

The second clause in (5.19) means "Alice had been chopping up onions for an hour", and we see that both the subject noun phrase and the phrasal verb have been deleted from (5.19) under co-ordinate identity conditions, leaving zero anaphors. We might compare (5.19) with

(5.20) Alice was chopping up onions, and had been chopping for an hour.

(5.21) Alice was chopping up onions, and had been up for an hour.

Neither of these sentences is interpreted like (5.19). From their second clauses only the subject noun phrase is deleted under identity conditions; neither 'chopping' in (5.20) nor 'up' in (5.21) can be interpreted as "chopping up".

So we conclude that phrasal verbs have more of the characteristics of conventional compounds than the characteristics of larger expressions such as phrases and clauses. And, like conventional compounds, phrasal verbs will be entered in the dictionary along with other lexemes. Their constituents are invariably words that recur as independent lexemes in the general vocabulary of the language, and on those grounds will be entered into the dictionary as a matter of course. However, there is at least one particle. *up*, which has a meaning in many phrasal verbs that it does not otherwise bear: compare the meanings of *cut* and *cut up*, *eat* and *eat up*, *close* and *close up*, *finish* and *finish up*. To all of these, and many other phrasal verbs, *up* brings a completive aspect[15] meaning roughly "completely". In its completive sense (which will obviously need to appear in the dictionary) *up* is productively compounded with verbs to coin new phrasal verbs.

4.6   Idioms

An idiom is a language expression whose meaning is not determinable from the meanings (if any) of its constituents. On this definition all lexicon items are idioms, cf. Charles Hockett *A Course in Modern Linguistics* 1958:172f. However, the particular set of idioms we discuss here is comprised of polylexemic expressions that must be entered in the dictionary (along with morphemes, lexical stems, and lexemes) because their meaning is autonomous from the meanings of their constituent lexemes. It is this need to have such idioms listed in the dictionary that has led many scholars[16] to claim that they are 'institutionalized'.

There are many idiomatic compounds which are members of a single lexical class, e.g. the nouns *hot-dog* 'frankfurter in a bun'', *red herring* "diversion from the point", *man-in-the-street* "(ordinary) person". The verbs *kick the bucket* "die" and *shoot the breeze* "chat idly" are compound lexemes that therefore cannot be subjected to grammatical processes normally applicable to verb-object phrases: e.g. they cannot be passivized, cf. **the breeze was shot by the boys*; individual constituents cannot be clefted from them, cf. *it was the bucket that Schwartz kicked* cannot mean "Schwartz died"; and co-ordinate deletion of a constituent is impossible, cf. *the cow kicked the milkmaid and the bucket* cannot mean "the cow kicked the milkmaid and died". Because idiomatic compounds are lexemes, they can be modified in a similar way to other lexemes in their class, cf. *a cold hot-dog, a very red herring* (= "something really off the point"), *the ordinary man-in-the-street, Jed kicked the bucket after a long illness, We had a smoke and shot the breeze for an hour.*[17] The phrase 'cats and dogs' in the idiom *rain cats and dogs* does not have the status of a compound adverb because it will not allow modification typical of adverbs, compare (6.1) with (6.2).

(6.1)
    a.   It rained very hard.
    b.   It rained harder.
    c.   It rained hardest of all.

(6.2)
    a.   *It rained very cats and dogs.
    b.   *It rained cats and dogser.
        ?*It rained more cats and dogs.[18]
    c.   *It rained cats(est) and dogsest of all.

Rain cats and dogs is a polylexemic idiom that must be entered in the dictionary as a whole, even though the verb 'rain' has its standard meaning.

Among polylexemic idioms (i.e. those that cannot be reckoned one lexical class) some have stable forms, and in this respect are rather like compounds, e.g. *by heart, to kingdom come, to do with the price of fish*. But many polylexemic idioms will submit to passivization, or being cleft apart, or co-ordinate deletion, all of which sets them apart from lexemes. Cf.

(6.3) It was Tom's leg, not his neck, that was pulled.

(Tom thought he was going to be hanged, but it turned out to be a practical joke on him.)

((6.4) Jim held his horses and Martha her breath.
        Martha held her breath, and Jim his horses.

(6.5) Tom's hair was pulled a little, and his leg a great deal.

An idiom like *pull someone's leg* is discontinuous, it can be passivized, cleft apart, and suffer co-ordinate deletion. Nevertheless, internal modification of the idiom is only possible if the figure is maintained or, better, heightened, or made more pertinent to the case in hand. This observation is a truism, because it seems to be impossible to legislate the boundaries of permissible modifications to idioms; but, e.g. *Tom had his left leg pulled* can only be taken literally, *Tom had his one remaining leg pulled* can be idiomatic if Tom has only one leg, and *Tom's leg was stretched to breaking point* might go through as an idiom if it can be recognized from context that the joke played upon Tom tormented rather than teased him. Many polylexemic idioms have a variety of forms anyway, cf. *blow the whistle/gaff on, this is not getting the baby its bonnet/bottle/dress, build castles/palaces in the air/clouds/heavens/sky*, etc. Since polylexemic idioms are figurative expressions, they encourage spontaneous variations – which have to be interpreted by relating them to a standard form of the idiom. This is one way in which idioms (or idiomlike expressions) leak out of the dictionary.

Obviously a dictionary cannot be expected to hold all the figurative expressions in a language, since novel ones are often produced: this is one of the more creative aspects of normal language use. *Bread and butter* has a literal meaning "bread and butter", and also a figurative meaning "source of income"; but it is uncertain whether the latter is an idiom, i.e. whether it should be entered into the dictionary. It is similarly doubtful whether all the figurative uses of, say, "strong" should be listed separately in a dictionary, cf. *strong candidate, strong beer, this magazine's strong stuff, he's strong on Sanskrit phonology*, etc. Whereas we have been able to refer to criteria for deciding which compound and phrasal verb lexemes should be listed in the dictionary, there are no clear criteria for distinguishing idiomatic from non-idiomatic polylexemic expressions. Perhaps we shall have to settle for a convention among scholars declaring which figurative polylexemic expressions are idioms to be listed in the dictionary. The meaning of other figurative expressions will have to be determined from the meanings of their constituents, the context of utterance, and background information.

4.7 Other ways of word-coining using the existing lexicon

4.7.1 Introduction

We have hitherto been discussing lexicon items derived from the existing stock of morphemes and lexemes in the language, and we have not yet exhausted the derivations possible from these sources. In §4.7 we shall briefly discuss clipping, hypocorisms, blends, acronyms, and the extension of proper names, as sources for new lexemes; and we consider whether the meanings of newly coined items are predictable from the meanings of their sources, or whether they are idiomatic so that the items have to be entered into the dictionary.

4.7.2 Clipping

Clipping is the abbreviation of a word to one of its parts. Perhaps because of this, new clippings are a mark of informal language; but after a time, clippings can become quite formal. For instance, *pants* from *pantaloons*, *taxi (cab)* from *taximeter (cab)*, and *cobweb* from Old English *ātor-coppe webbe*[19] are not thought of as clippings any more, and probably *bus* from *omnibus* isn't either. Foreclipped words are those with the first part of the original word cut off, e.g. *cobweb* and *bus*, *phone* from *telephone*, *plane* from *airplane*, and *roo* from *kangaroo*. More common are back-clippings (or 'end-clippings'), where the tail-end of the original has been shorn off, cf. *pants*,[20] *taxi*, *exam*, *math(s)*, *phys. ed.*, *tech*, *uni* are familiar in the educational field. Rarest are both fore- and backclipped words like *flu* from *influenza*. It can readily be seen that words derived by clipping retain the meaning of the word from which they are clipped. Any difference in meaning – if it should be called that – is a difference in formality rating: e.g. *exam* is less formal than *examination*, and so forth. Where the two forms are current they may be treated as variant forms of the same lexeme (i.e. as allolexes) for lexicographic purposes.

4.7.3   Hypocorisms

We get up to wakey-wakey and have brekky (probably a googie). If
you are good, Grannie will reward you with a bickie, chockie (be
careful, you might become a fattie) or even some chewie. When you
get older you are allowed to go to the footie. If you're a smartie,
you'll go early to get a good possie. If you go by tram your fare is
collected by a trammie or connie. Mummy reminds you to take a
hankie, and she puts on some lippy and goes window shopping at
Chaddy. Dad grabs a cab to go to the gee gees, he tips the cabbie
and puts money on a quaddie with his bookie. We get birthday
pressies and Chrissy pressies. We enjoy a barbie on Sundays shared
with the mozzies and blowies. We crack some tinnies, and if it turns
cold we go inside to watch the replays on the telly and abuse the
umpy. Our letters are delivered by a postie. We are attended on a
plane by a hostie. We have brickies, truckies and wharfies, who
probably love to play the pokies. The kiddies go to the pickies, the
parents go to the movies and the grandparents to the talkies to watch
the goodies and the baddies.

(The Age, Melbourne, 24th July 1981:12)

Hypocorisms like *Aussie*, *bookie*, *footy*, *looney*, *telly*, etc. are formed
by backclipping nouns then suffixing *-ie/-(e)y*. These are without
exception informal, and often have similar status to diminutives in
other languages. This kind of hypocorism exists in all major dialects of
English, but there is another kind peculiar to Australia, with an *-o*
suffix. Legend has it this came about from hawkers announcing their
wares, e.g. the rabbit seller *rabbit-o*, the milkman *milk-o*, the bottle
collector *bottle-o*, and each got to be named by his call. If that was the
origin, the habit has spread from occupation names, cf. *garbo*, *journo*,
muso[21] to many other nouns, e.g. *arvo* "afternoon", *nasho* "national
service", *smoko* "smoking-break (tea-break)", etc. In all of these, the
-o is suffixed to a backclipped noun. All hypocorisms are synonymous
with the standard words from which they derive and should probably
be included in the same lexicon entry, with some attached note of the
fact that they are generally excluded from formal discourse.

4.7.4   Blends

A blend is created by prefixing a whole word or a backclipped word to
a foreclipped word: e.g. *brunch* from *breakfast-lunch*, *motel* from

motor-hotel, *smog* from *smoke-fog*, *sexcapade* from *sex-escapade*, *cinemactress* from *cinema-actress*. It is notable that a blend combines the senses of the source words in a transparent fashion – given help from the context, and background information; for this reason, blending is productive (i.e. new blends are quite common). Nonetheless, many blends, such as *smog* or *fumble*, are idiomatic in that most English speakers do not recognize that they are derived forms, still less do they realize what the source lexemes are and what these contribute to the meaning of the blend. For this reason, blends should be treated in the same way as conventional compounds and entered in the dictionary. New blends, like novel compounds, are interpreted from the meanings of their supposed parts, the context, and background information.

4.7.5 Acronyms and abbreviations

Senator Edward Kennedy emceed a fund-raising "roast" of Arizona Congressman Morris Udall.

(*Time*, South Pacific edn., August 15, 1983:32)

Acronyms are words created from the initial letter or two of the words in a multiword name. E.g. RAdio Direction finding And Range gives *radar*, Light Amplification by Stimulated Emission of Radiation gives *laser*, Situation Normal All Fucked Up gives *snafu* (cf. *Time* May 16, 1983:59). True acronyms like *radar*, *laser*, *snafu* and *UNESCO* are all pronounced like genuine words, cf. /'reɪda·, 'leɪzə, 'sna·fu, ju'nɛskəʊ/. Abbreviations like *USA*, *lp*, *tv*, *MP*, *IOU*, *e.g.*, etc. are all pronounced as strings of letters, cf. /ju·ɛsɛɪ, ɛlpii, ti·vii/ etc. Abbreviations can be exploited to effect a double-meaning, e.g. the Women Against Rape organization use the abbreviation *WAR* to declare their militancy. Even if they are proper names (v. §4.7.7), acronyms and abbreviations have to be entered in the lexicon; neither can be left to have their meanings determined from the phrases of origin. Take the verb *emcee* in the quotation at the head of this section, which is a zero derivation from the noun *emcee* more familiar as *MC*, an abbreviation from Master of Ceremonies: the meaning of the verb *emcee* "act as MC at" transparently includes the meaning of the abbreviated noun *MC*, so the latter has to be specified in the lexicon.

4.7.6 The extension of proper names

Many types of wine are named after the places where the wine was first produced, e.g. *burgundy*, *champagne*, *port*[ugal], *sherry* [Jerez]. The transfer of place names to produce for which the place is famous is common with cheese (it is possible to buy Australian *gouda* and Kenyan *cheddar*) and carpets (you can also buy a Pakistani *Kerman*). Australian stores have a *manchester* department selling household linen. The scandal of the break in at the Watergate Hotel in 1972 by members of the campaign to re-elect U.S. President Richard Nixon became known simply as *Watergate*, and has often led to *-gate* being suffixed to names for political scandals since, e.g. U.S. President Jimmy Carter's brother Billy created a political scandal in dealings with Libyans in what was known as the *Billygate* affair.[22]

The names of people have been adopted and generalized to name things with which they are characteristically connected. E.g. *assassin* is from Arabic *hashishin* after a sect of moslem fanatics who reputedly used hashish to put them in the right frame of mind to carry out assassinations of crusaders and public figures. The verb *lynch* is thought to commemorate the act of Captain Lynch of Virginia who in 1782 took the law into his own hands and wrongly imprisoned some people; since then the meaning has shifted to "unlawful killing by a mob". Captain Charles Boycott was agent for Lord Earne's estates in County Mayo, Ireland where in 1879 the estate was *boycotted* by the peasantry and Boycott forced to leave Ireland. In 1818 Dr. T. Bowdler published an edition of Shakespeare expurgated of all the passages he found offensive, hence the verb *bowdlerize*. A *quisling* is named after Vidkun Quisling puppet head of state in occupied Norway during World War II. Inflated life-jackets issued to World War II flyers were reminiscent of actress Mae West's bosom, and so the jacket was named a *mae west*. The *blurb* on a book jacket is named after a fictitious personage: in 1906 American comic writer Gelett Burgess wrote some nonsense on the back of a jacket for one of his books beneath the picture of a model he called Belinda Blurb. A *jeep* is part acronym from General Purpose vehicle, and part named after a tough little creature called Eugene the Jeep in E.C. Segar's Popeye cartoon strip. People's names also live on in things they have found or created. Biological nomenclature often commemorates the discoverer's name in the name for a species or variety, but few such names enter common usage; *wisteria* named after Caspar Wister is one, *banksia* after Sir Joseph Banks, and *boronia* after Francesco Borone are others. Gauss, Ohm and Fahrenheit gave their names to units of measurement, another was named after Watt.

Schrapnel, Sandwich, MacIntosh and Brougham gave their names to inventions of theirs. And the English *bobby* is no longer called a *peeler*, but both names commemorate the founder of the British police force, Robert Peel.

The trade names of products often get generalized to other products of the same type, at least for a time. E.g. *biro* was for a long time used for all ball-point pens (at least in Britain and Australia), *hoover* for vacuum cleaners (also in Britain and Australia), *jandals* for rubber thonged shoes (in New Zealand), *kodak* for cameras of any kind (in North America), *kleenex* for tissues, *xerox* for dry photocopying. *Zipper* was the registered name for a boot fitted with a slide-fastener to which the name has transferred. It is notable that there are zero derived verbs *hoover*, *xerox*, and *zip*, but none such from, e.g. *biro*. There was no reason to coin a new verb for writing with a *biro*, since the action of using a biro is similar to the action of writing with a traditional pen; but the *hoover* cleaned in a spectacularly different way from the traditional brush or carpet-sweeper, and the new-fangled process apparently encouraged the coining of a special verb. Similar rationales can be argued for the verbs *xerox* and *zip*. Other influences on their coining may have been the relative length of the zero derived verb compared with some other appropriate verb, e.g. *xerox* is shorter than *photocopy* and *zip* shorter than *slide-fasten*; and in this area we should probably not overlook the effect of advertizing in keeping the product name salient.

The sources for trade names are proper names, blends of proper names, acronyms, derivations such as *Zipper* from the onomatopoeic adjective *zip*, borrowings like *Xerox* from Greek ξεϱος "dry" (the final *x* in place of *s* is to make the written name more memorable), and there are pure inventions like *Kodak* (whose spelling patterns like Xerox's). But what can we say about the meanings of words that have entered the vocabulary of the language as generalizations on proper names? Obviously, overall they are unpredictable. Although it is interesting to give the etymology of such words, each one will have to be entered into the dictionary and its meaning stated irrespective of its source.

4.7.7 In conclusion

In §4.7 we have discussed the meanings of words coined by clipping, hypocorism, blending, acronyming, and the extension of proper names. Clippings and hypocorisms have meanings almost identical with the meanings of their sources, and where these are current, the source word and the clipped or hypocoristic forms might reasonably be regarded as variants of the same lexeme; the clipped or hypocoristic forms being restricted to informal styles. Although many blends can be transparently linked with the source lexemes whose meanings as well as whose forms they blend, we decided that blends are idiomatic and therefore to be entered in the lexicon as independent lexemes. Acronyms and abbreviations, too, have to be entered in the dictionary; as do lexemes derived by extensions of proper names. And what should be done with proper names? Obviously these form part of the language and must be stored somewhere – presumably in the lexicon. We showed in §1.6.2 that proper names have no sense, but they might be glossed in some such way as the following:

John$_{proper\ name}$ J is called John → J is male

Robin$_{proper\ name}$ R is called Robin → (R is male) v (R is female)

Cairo$_{proper\ name}$ C is called Cairo → C is a city in Egypt

4.8   Borrowed words

Most of the vocabulary that comes from sources external to a given language is borrowed. Borrowing involves two languages, the source language L_s and the borrowing language L_b – some of whose speakers come into contact with L_s; L_s has an expression *e* denoting "x", and speakers of L_b adopt *e* (or some approximation to it) into their language in order to talk about "x". The motivation for borrowing is either (i) that "x" was previously unfamiliar to speakers of L_b, or (ii) that although L_b already has an expression *f* denoting "x", L_s is relatively more prestigious than L_b with respect to the area of vocabulary that includes *e* and *f* (i.e. the area of vocabulary dealing with phenomena like "x"). Sometimes these two motivations coincide. The languages of conquered peoples often supply vocabulary for features of the physical environment new to the conquerors; so, English has borrowed the following sorts of vocabulary from Australian aboriginal languages: place names. e.g. *Wagga Wagga*; names for topographical features, e.g. *billabong*; names for native flora and fauna, e.g. *waratah* and *kangaroo*; names for native institutions and artefacts, e.g. *corroboree* and *boomerang*. In the late middle ages, after the French governing class had established a new social order and new systems of government in England, English adopted French vocabulary in the areas of government and administration, the army, the church, learning, medicine, art, fashion, courtly manners, and food.[23] The cultural prestige of Latin and ancient Greek has made them the principal sources for learned and scientific terms in English, even though native terms could have been used – in German, for example, native terms are usual in these areas.[24] Italy's one-time dominance in music led to the borrowing of Italian musical terms (e.g. *tempo*, *andante*, *allegro*, *presto*). The earliest users were presumably motivated by the prestige they gained from knowing and using the Italian terms; but after a time these terms became standard and no special prestige now attaches to them.

The forms of borrowed words are usually adapted to the phonology of the borrowing language. It is easiest to see this in the mutation of English words borrowed by other languages: e.g. Hausa *sipirin* ‹ English [car] *spring*; Japanese *puraibashii* ‹ *privacy*, *suripā* ‹ *slippers*, *terebi* ‹ *television*; Melbourne Greek *fénsē* ‹ *fence*, *káro* ‹ *car*, *sampánia* ‹ *champagne*, *tsek* ‹ *cheque*.

The etymological connexion between the borrowed word in L_b and the source word in L_s is of no consequence to the generality of speakers of L_b, to whom its meaning is idiomatic. The semantics of borrowed lexemes obviously cannot be determined from their constituent parts. Nor can the meaning of a borrowed clause like *répondez s'il vous plaît* "please reply": it is idiomatic, and like the borrowed lexemes must be entered in the dictionary.

Expressions from a source language are sometimes translated instead of being borrowed, e.g. English *skyscraper* is the source for the 'loan-translations' *gratte-ciel* literally 'scrape-sky', in French and οὐρανοξύστης, literally 'skyscraper', in Greek. The English idiom *on the carpet* "in trouble with the boss" is a loan-translation from French *sur le tapis*. Loan-translations are typically lexemic, or otherwise idiomatic, and must therefore be entered into the dictionary. However, the expression *marriage of convenience*, although a loan-translation from French is not idiomatic on our definition (in §4.6) because its meaning can be determined from its constituents.

4.9 The effects of sound on word coining

4.9.1 Folk etymology

'Our father, in charge of heaven, . . .'

(6 year old's version of the Lord's prayer)

Speakers of a language occasionally reinterpret a relatively unfamiliar sounding morph in terms of a phonetically similar and familiar sounding morph – particularly if the latter happens to have a meaning compatible with the co-text in which the unfamiliar morph occurred. The phenomenon is known as 'folk etymology', cf. Gustaf Stern *Meaning and Change of Meaning (With Special Reference to the English Language)* 1965:234f., Stephen Ullmann *Words and Their Use* 1951:38f, *The Principles of Semantics* 1957:237, *Semantics: an Introduction to the Science of Meaning* 1962:102. A contemporary example of folk etymology is the mutation of the borrowed French compound *chaise longue* into *chaise lounge* in American and Australian English. Spelling has undoubtedly played its part here, but the real motivation comes from the fact that *lounge* was already used (in those dialects) for a piece of chairlike furniture where one can sit with one's legs up – as one can on a chaise longue/lounge. Around the 16th century, English transmuted Old French *crevice* into *crefyssh*, later *crayfish*: the crayfish being a water creature the semantic connexion with *fish* seemed obvious; but it wasn't there in the original French word. French *femelle* was the source for English *female*; the latter was made analogous to *male* (the French original is not) perhaps on the pattern of *woman* and *man*. Folk etymology reinterprets words of native origin, too. E.g. Old English *guma* "man" dropped out of use around the 16th century, and the compound *brȳdguma* "bride['s] man" was remodelled using the contemporary word for "lad" to give *bridegroom*. Expressions like *stark blind, stark dead*, in which 'stark' meant "completely" were the models for *stark naked*: this had been *start naked* "with no pants on", 'start' meaning "tail, bum, ass/arse"; and *stark* has come to mean "bare". Most folk etymologies have a semantic as well as phonetic motivation, but some are purely phonetically motivated, e.g. English *checkmate* (whose constituents are patently absurd) comes, via Old French *eschec mat*, from Persian *shah māt(a)* "the king is dead"; a *mayday* distress call is based on reinterpretation of French *m'aidez* "help me". There are two species of rhinoceros in Africa; one has a long tapered upper lip; the upper lip of the other one is blunt and wide – or *weit* in Afrikaans; and so English speaking folk called it the *white rhino*, and for contrast the other species was called the *black rhino*. Since both species are in reality the same grey colour, these names often confuse the uninitiated.

Not all these senseless changes are made to borrowed words: witness the use of *of* as a variant of auxiliary *have* after modals e.g. *could of, would of, should of done it*; some (adult) speakers actually pronounce it [ɒv], although the reinterpretation probably derives from the fact

that unstressed pronunciations of both *have* and *of* tend to be the same
– [əv] or just [v].

The primary cause of reinterpretation in folk etymology is phonetic
similarity between morphs; one morph gets mistaken for another, often
because the latter is more familiar; the mistake is easier to make when
the reinterpretation makes sense. It is clear that for lexicographic
purposes, words derived through folk etymology are idioms; and where
doublets like *chaise longue* and *chaise lounge* or *have* and *of* co-exist,
they will be entered in the dictionary as variants – perhaps with some
specified contextual constraint on their use.

4.9.2 Onomatopoeia

The sound must seem an echo to the sense.
(Alexander Pope *Essay on Criticism* 1.365).

Every language has some onomatopoeic words; words that – within the
limits of the phonological system of the language – deliberately mimic
the sounds they name, e.g. English *moo*, *miaow*, *murmur*, *susurrous*;
or else they name the source for the sound they mimic, e.g. English
cuckoo, Hausa *babur* or *butubutu* "motorbike", Hunanese *niao* "cat",
Tzeltal *lohp* "large swallow of liquid". It is often pointed out that
onomatopoeic words mimicking the same sound will differ from
language to language, e.g. roosters go *cockadoodledoo* in English,
cocorico in French, *kikeriki* in German, *kokekokko* in Japanese,
kukuryku in Polish.[25] But we should not make too much of the
differences; listed below is a handful of Tzeltal classifiers from Brent
Berlin *Tzeltal Numeral Classifiers: a Study in Ethnographic Semantics*
1968, appendix 2; the glosses are Berlin's, the English words for
comparison [in brackets] are mine. Tzeltal is a Mayan language spoken
in Mexico, and totally unrelated to English.

(Tzeltal) *b'ihš* "squirts of liquid" [English *piss*]; *čan* "sound emitted
from blows on metal objects" [*chang, clang*]; *čehp* "blows, cuts with
machete" [*chip*]; *čin* "sound emitted from vibrating object (e.g.
bells) due to blow" [*ching, ting*]; *čuh* "drops of liquid on a hot
object"; *c'ihp* "cries of ducks" [*cheep*]; *kan* "sound from blows on
metal" [*clang*]; *kič'* "action and sound of drawing bow across strings
of violin, etc." [*screech*]; *lehk'* "laps of liquid" [*lick*(ing waves)]; *lohp*
"large swallows of liquid" [*gulp*]; *mohč* "items crushed in fist"
[*mash*]; *pehp* "cries of geese, frogs" [*peep*]; *pihp* "sounds of horn,

trumpet" [*beep* cf. 'He beeped when he shoulda bopped']; *pohč'*
"pressing to form indentations in malleable objects" [*pouch*]; *pub'*
"blows with stick" [*bop*]; *pum* "blows accompanied by sound" [*bam*,
pummel]; *p'iʔ* "flatulations" [*burp*]; *p'iht* "jumps of small animals"
[*pitterpat*]; *p'oht* "sounds of popping corn, cracking cinders in fire"
[*pop*]; *ten* "blows of pounding" [*bang*]; *t'ehš* "blows with flat board"
[*bash*]; *t'oh* "blows with axe" [*chop*]; *wohč'* "blows in breaking up
cane, corn stalks" [*wack*].

Of course, the Tzeltal and English words differ from each other – they
are formed in different phonological systems. At the same time, there
are many phonetic similarities, because the words are onomatopoeic
and deliberately mimic natural sounds. Yet this a posteriori comparabi-
lity between the two totally unrelated languages in respect of certain
onomatopoeic words should not lead us to ignore that, e.g. the
meanings of the Tzeltal words could not be predicted (out of context)
by someone unfamiliar with Tzeltal. Onomatopoeic words need to be
listed in the dictionary; and only new coinings can be expected to be
interpreted from their phonetic form, their formal similarity with
established onomatopoeic words,[26] and the context of utterance.

4.9.3 Phonesthesia

Every language contains many sets of phonesthetic words such as the
following in English:

> glace, glade, glamour, glance, glare, glass, glaze, gleam, glimmer,
> glimpse, glint, glisten, glister, glitter, gloaming, gloom, gloss, glow,
> glower;

(nouns or verbs involving something "eyecatching" because of the
emission, reflexion, or passage of light)

> flack, flag, flail, flame, flap, flare, flash, flay, flee, flick, flicker, flinch,
> fling, flip, flirt, flit, flood, flop, flounce, flounder, flourish, flow,
> fluent, flurry, flush, fluster, flutter, flux, fly;

(mostly verbs; all suggest "a sudden or violent movement")

> clash, crash, dash, flash, gash, gnash, lash, mash, slash, smash,
> thrash;

(all verbs signifying "violent impact")

bumble, fumble, grumble, humble, mumble, rumble, stumble, tumble;
(verbs signifying "dull, heavy, untidy action")

batter, chatter, clatter, natter, patter, scatter, shatter, smatter(ing), spatter, splatter, tatter(ed), yatter;
flitter, fritter, glitter, jitter, litter, skitter, titter, twitter, witter;
clutter, flutter, scutter, sputter, splutter, stutter;
(all verbs signifying a "formless collation of iterated things, actions, events, etc."; in addition *-itter* words suggest "bittiness", and *-utter* words suggest "untidyness, ungainliness, imperfection").

Each of these sets of words is characterized by a recurring cluster of phonemes called a 'phonestheme'.[27] In English, phonesthemes are either initial consonant clusters, e.g. *gl-* and *fl-*, or rhymes, e.g. *-ash*, *-umble*, *-atter*, *-itter*, *-utter*, that recur in words from just one or two lexical classes. Phonesthetic words may be either monosyllabic or disyllabic, and the second syllable of disyllabic phonesthetic words is either a (syllabic) consonant or an unstressed vowel. Ignoring syllable boundaries, the general structure of phonesthetic words in English is as follows:

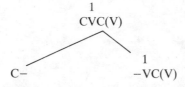

where 'C' is one or more consonants, 'V' is a stressed vowel, and '(V)' is an unstressed vowel if it is there at all. Either the onset C- or the rhyme -VC(V), or both, may be phonesthemes. It is notable that phonesthemes form incomplete syllables, and that no phonestheme may contain a morpheme boundary within it.

It seems probable that phonesthesia was first motivated by onomatopoeia: imitate a dog growling and you make a *gr* sound cf. *growl*, *grim*, *gripe*, *grizzle*, *groan*, *grouch*, *grouse*, *gruff*, *grumble*, *grumpy*, *grunt*, dialect *greet* "wail", and *grin* originally meant "bare the teeth in threat". But a phonestheme can function equally well from a purely arbitrary symbolic basis – e.g. the *gl-* phonestheme (seen above) must have developed in the pattern of the cardinal word. Whatever the original basis for the development of a phonestheme, the words instantiating it provide a pattern for new additions; and one member of a phonesthetic set can be responsible for the development of a subset centered on its peculiar semantics.

Linguists tend to be dubious about the morphological status of phonesthemes. Some say they are not morphemes, e.g. Peter Matthews *Morphology: an Introduction to the Theory of Word Structure* 1974:15f.; others, like Dwight Bolinger 'Rime, assonance, and morpheme analysis' 1950:130, and Hans Marchand *The Categories and Types of Present-Day English Word Formation* 1969:403, believe they are morphemes. Phonesthemes obviously contribute to the structure of words, and fall under the definition of the morpheme as 'the smallest individually meaningful element in the utterances of a language'.[28] However, phonesthemes fall into all the most troublesome areas of morphological analysis: (i) they have a vaguer and more subjective meaning than most morphemes; (ii) their phoneme sequences occur in many words with no hint of the relevant meaning; and (iii) they consist of incomplete syllables, and usually combine with word remnants that have no independent status as morphemes. Nonetheless, phonesthemes contribute to the structure and meaning of vocabulary items in a similar manner to (bound) morphemes, and need to be given similar status within the dictionary.

4.9.4 Reduplication

There is a small number of disyllabic colloquial words formed by reduplication, e.g. *booboo*, *byebye*, *dada*, *geegee*, *hush-hush*, *mama*, *night-night*, *tata*, *weewee*, *woop-woop*. Each of these is idiomatic.[29]

Colloquial informality, even playfulness, are also typical of quasi-reduplications. One kind of quasi-reduplication involves vowel alternation: e.g. *dilly-dally*, *fiddle-faddle*, *mishmash*, *riffraff*, *ding-dong*, *flip-flop*. The alternations, also called 'ablaut combinations', are mostly in the form [C₁C-CæC], less often [C₁C-CɒC], and any other alternation is exceptional (cf. *gewgaws*). The other kind of quasi-reduplication involves initial consonant alternations, cf. *fuddy-duddy*, *fuzzywuzzy*, *hankypanky*, *helter-skelter*, *holus-bolus*, *lovey-dovey*, *mumbo-jumbo*,[30] *nambypamby*, *rolypoly*, *super-dooper*. Almost all quasi-reduplications are nonserious, two exceptions are *walkie-talkie* and *hi-fi* – which is a compound of end-clippings!

All of these reduplicative words[31] are idiomatic. New coinings might sometimes be interpretable from pattern matching with existing reduplications, cf. *ding-ding*, *ding-dong*; or else from meanings assigned to one or both of the compounded constituents, cf. 'fiddle' in *fiddle-faddle*, 'knacks' in *knick-knacks*, or both parts of *lovey-dovey*.

4.9.5 Rhyming slang

The element of playfulness in many of these internally rhyming expressions is given greater rein in rhyming slang. Although rhyming slang is said to have begun as a secret language among 19th century Cockney navvies to confuse their Irish co-workers, it can only have remained secret at its first blush; surely its true *raison d'être* is the joy of word-play. Some examples are *apples 'n' pears* "stairs", *brass tacks* "facts", *charing cross* "horse", *dickie-bird* "word", *jimmy riddle* "piddle", *old pot 'n' pan* "old man (husband, father)", *plates o' meat* "feet", *the sweeney todd* "the flying squad". the last two are regularly abbreviated by knocking out the rhyme; and many of these expressions are better known in their abbreviated (end-clipped) forms: e.g. *berk* < *Berkeley Hunt* "cunt, stupid person," *boat* < *boat race* "face", *bristols* < *Bristol Cities* "titties, breasts", *(take) a butcher's* < *butcher's hook* "look", *china* < *china plate* "mate", *cobbler's* < *cobbler's awls* "balls", *(blow a) raspberry* < *raspberry tart* "fart" (transferred to a similar noise made by the lips), *titfer* < *tit for tat* "hat", *whistle* < *whistle 'n' flute* "suit". End clipped rhyming slang has the advantage of being utterly euphemistic (which probably helped *blow a raspberry* to change meaning); little old ladies who might think little of saying *He's a berk* or *That's a load of cobbler's*, would probably cringe from using the unabbreviated versions – should they know them – because of the suggestive power of the rhyme. Rhyming euphemism is a common means of avoiding taboo words,[32] cf. *ass* for *arse*, *crust* or *cripes* for *Christ*, *muck* for *fuck*, *pussy (cat)* for *twat*, *ruddy* for *bloody*, etc.

An innovative expression in rhyming slang relies on the rhyme for its proper interpretation; the rhyme must be matched (on the basis of phonetic similarity) with some other expression which makes sense in context. If a carpenter asks his apprentice to pass the *jimmy jammer* he probably wants a hammer;[33] if someone with a hangover says he was *Mozart* last night, he can rely on hearer's background knowledge and knowledge of English to supply an appropriate interpretation.[34]

How should the lexicographer deal with rhyming slang? The fact that there are dictionaries of rhyming slang in existence suggests that even well-established expressions are idiomatic. Although the meaning of end-clipped instances can often be determined from context and background information (as in the *Mozart* example above), it is clear that some expressions, e.g. *berk*, are perceived as idioms, and their origin in rhyming slang is unknown to many speakers, and not necessary to know. For the sake of consistency, then, the meanings of the expressions we have been discussing under the heading of rhyming slang should be entered into the dictionary.

4.9.6   Summing up the effects of sound on word formation

In §4.9 we have examined the effects of sound on word formation as exemplified through folk etymology, onomatopoeia, phonesthesia, reduplication, and rhyming slang. In each case we concluded that the words and expressions derived on what might loosely be called a phonetic basis, are idiomatic and must be listed in the dictionary. The only doubts arise in the case of polylexemic rhyming slang, and they have the same basis as our doubts about the boundaries between polylexemic idioms and nonidioms (cf. §4.6). We recognized, though, that new coinings can normally be interpreted from background information, context, and knowledge of the language – where the latter will, e.g. in the areas of onomatopoeia and phonesthesia, involve pattern matching with existing vocabulary of similar forms.

4.10   The composition of scientific names

It is instructive to compare the kind of spontaneous word coining we have been discussing hitherto, with the self-conscious procedure for the scientific naming of newly discovered or newly created phenomena. National language academies, like the Académie Française in France, have normally been ineffective in their attempts to regulate the acquisition of new vocabulary by the language community, as the mushrooming of franglais has proved.[35] The situation is different for most scientific disciplines where committees on nomenclature[36] have effectively controlled the so-called 'systematic naming' within their discipline, by establishing regulations that are internationally recognized. The concept behind the regulation is that there should be just one name, available to all members of the discipline whatever their native language may be, which will locate the denotatum in a taxonomic system by relating it via its morphemic representation to other phenomena within the system, so that the meaning of the name is

– as far as possible – self-explanatory.[37] To achieve this there are strict rules on combining morphemes: for example, the chemical with the trivial name *chloramphenicol* has the systematic name *2-(dichloro-acetylamino)-3-hydroxy-3-(paranitrophenyl)-propanol* which describes the composition of its chemical structure (cf. Adams 1973:209). Although the component morphs of systematic scientific names are ultimately arbitrary, there is a constraint on their forms, since they are required to be in neo-Greek or Latin. There are rules for abbreviation, e.g. *chloramphenical* derives by conventional abbreviation from *chlor-amide-phenyl-nitro-glycol*; there are rules for when to hyphenate, when to compound and when not to, rules for italicization, rules for ordering morphs. Such rules make scientific languages a subclass of natural languages: they are based on natural language, but are much more highly constrained.

Biological nomenclature is written in neo-Latin, often using Latin-ized transcriptions of Ancient Greek roots; and there are standard reference works to facilitate this (e.g Jaeger 1959, Woods 1966). The use of Latin is in part motivated by tradition. Taxonomic classification in biology began with Linnaeus's *Systema Natura* in 1735. Carl von Linné ('Carolus Linnaeus' in Latin) was a Swede; but he wrote in Latin because it was a contemporary language of scholarship in Europe, and had been since the time of the Roman Empire. Latin had the advantage then of being no-one's national language. Ancient Greek also has this advantage; and, like Latin, it is associated with scholarship. Natural taxa in biology are divided (in descending order) into phyla or divisions, classes, orders, families, genera, species, subspecies, varieties, subvarieties, forms and subforms. Thus, in botany, a kind of wheat might be described as *Triticum aestivum* ssp. *vulgare* giving the genus, species, and subspecies name respectively. Or one can make finer distinctions as with '*Saxifraga aizoon* [genus and species] var. *aizoon* subvar. *brevifola* forma. *multicaulis* subforma. *surculosa*.' In zoology a creature is identified by a binomial compound consisting of a genus name in the (Latin) nominative singular followed by a species name that will either be an adjective in nominative singular (c.f. Canis *familiaris*), or a noun in apposition (Canis *lupus*), a noun in the genitive (Raphidia *londoniensis*), or a genitive adjective derived from the name of a salient associated organism (e.g. 'Lernaea *lusei*' a parasite on 'Gadus *luscus*'). The binomial restriction may lead to unusual compounding such that the true Latin *Coluber novae hispanae* becomes zoo-Latin *Coluber novaehispanae*; this sort of constraint would be unlikely to apply in a natural language. But the rules governing the form of the species name are derived from regular

Latin constructions. The sources for names are: geological (in paleontology), geographical, the local common name (e.g. *Bandicota*), a personal name (often of the collector, but not necessarily), and frequently some salient characteristic of the organism (cf. Jaeger 1959: xvi-xxiv). Such resources are essentially similar to the ones found in ordinary naming in natural languages.

A difference, in zoological nomenclature, is that synonyms and homonyms are not permitted. For instance *Noctua variegata* is the name for both an insect and for a bird, but it is apparently not acceptable to differentiate them using the class names *Insecta* and *Aves*; instead the disambiguation is effected by appending the name of the zoologist(s) who created the names, cf. "*Noctua variegata* Jung" versus "*Noctua variegata* Quoy & Gaimard" cf. *International Code of Zoological Nomenclature* 1961:55. Natural language nomenclature never makes use of such a device.

We see from this sortie into the process of name creation in the sciences that it is a highly constrained refinement of normal word-coining procedures in natural languages. The constituent morphs of scientific names are arbitrary symbols, but their form is constrained in most sciences to selection from one of the neo-classical languages (Ancient Greek and Latin), and sometimes there are even standard abbreviations from these. The rules for combining the constituent morphs are strictly regulated so as to show the place of the denotatum within a natural system, such as biological taxonomy or atomic structure. In natural language nomenclature there is no such regulation, and any locating of the denotatum in a system as a consequence of its name would be accidental. Furthermore, natural languages develop synonyms and homonyms that cannot be expunged by fiat as those in scientific language must be.

4.11 The set of lexicon items

The set of lexicon items in language L comprises all the semantically primitive expressions in L whose meaning has to be defined in a dictionary because it cannot be determined in any other way. The meaning of an expression constructed from more than one lexicon item is computed from the combined meanings of its component lexicon items; if this should be impossible then the whole expression must itself be a lexicon item. In ch.4 we have been discussing the nature of word coining and the sources for creating new lexemes in English so as to discover which kinds of language expressions must be listed in the theoretical dictionary; we conclude that the set of lexicon items in English comprises the following:

all inflexional morphemes
all derivational morphemes, including phonesthemes
all lexical stems
all lexemes, including polylexemic idioms.

The types of lexicon items we have identified on linguistic grounds happens to be more or less identical with the set deemed by psycholinguists to exist in the mental lexicon, cf. Anne Cutler 'Lexical complexity and sentence processing' 1983 for a summary account and detailed references.

Among inflexional morphemes we count such compound morphemes as, e.g. (English) progressive aspect "be + V + present participle" (where 'V' is a variable for the verb inflected) and the passive "be/get + V + past participle". The ambiguity of, say, *The window was broken* is a matter of structural homonymy between (a) the passive inflexion of the verb "break", which is the construction "be/get + break + past participle" giving the nonstative interpretation "the window got broken", and (b) the stative phrase composed of the lexeme "be" and the lexeme "break + adjectival participle" given the interpretation "the window was [already in a] broken [state]".

We count as lexemes all the words that appear in standard dictionaries such as the *Oxford English Dictionary* and *Webster's New International Dictionary* (perhaps with a proviso that only the words current in English at some given period of time, e.g. the present, be included within the theoretical dictionary). Lexicon items include expressions of native origin, borrowed expressions, loan translations, expressions derived through folk etymology, blends, acronyms and abbreviations, proper names, extensions of proper names, onomatopoeic and reduplicative expressions, rhyming slang, conventional compounds, phrasal verbs, and idioms. There is a problem with those polylexemic idioms which are arguably (but not certainly) determinable from the meaning of the formally identical literal expressions, and we have suggested that a decision on their status as lexicon items could only be made by convention. We have also suggested that word pairs such as *exam/examination* or *bookmaker/bookie* do not warrant separate lexicon entries but should be treated as allolexes of the same lexeme.

The meaning of a nominalizing suffix like *-al* (cf. *proposal*) will be given in the lexicon entry for this item, cf. §4.12; but what should we do about zero derivation, which (by definition) does not utilize a derivational affix that could be listed as a lexicon item? The case of zero derivation is particularly interesting because the semantic difference between, e.g. the noun *waitress* and the verb *waitress* is wholly attributable to their different syntactic categorization: consequently, lexical class meaning ought to be represented in the lexicon. So it will be; but we do not need to propose that any syntactic categories as such are lexicon items, for the following reason. In §4.12 we propose that every lexicon item has, as part of its lexicon entry, a representation of its syntactic category, after the manner of traditional dictionaries; thus we might have *waitress*$_{noun}$ and *waitress*$_{verb}$. Although the labels 'noun' and 'verb' form part of the metalanguage, we show in §4.12 that translation between the object language (being described) and the metalanguage (used to describe it) is both possible and desirable; metalanguage 'noun' and 'verb' translate into the object language lexemes *noun* and *verb* – which are, necessarily, lexicon items semantically interpreted in their lexicon entries. Thus metalanguage 'noun' and 'verb' can be assigned meaning from the lexicon entries of their translations in the object language. In this way, we use the existing resources of the lexicon to semantically interpret the syntactic category descriptions used in the lexicon, by assuming that syntactic categories are assigned meanings through their names – either directly in the lexicon, if like *noun* and *verb* they are lexicon items, or by computation from the combined meanings of the lexicon items that compose them.[38]

4.12　Form and presentation in the theoretical dictionary

4.12.1　The ordering of items in the lexicon, and the ordering of information in a lexicon entry

A lexicon entry must include: (i) a representation of the phonological and graphological form of a lexicon item; (ii) a representation of its syntactic category and constraints on its syntactic distribution; (iii) a representation of its meaning. In principle, any of these three aspects could be adopted as the basis for ordering items and their entries within the lexicon, and there is psycholinguistic evidence that all three can be used to access items in the mental lexicon.[39] But since we take the view that linguists can only reasonably analyze data that arises from S's uttering U in language L to H in context C, we shall presume that the first step in recognizing a lexicon item in U is a matter of recognizing its form. In addition, though, we have to allow that formal boundaries may be indicated and are confirmed, heuristically, from observation of syntactic distribution within the utterance, and, ultimately, from the meaning of the item in context. In consequence, we assume: (i) that lexicon items are arranged within the theoretical dictionary in much the same way as in a traditional dictionary – according to the sequence of letters or phonemes in their formal representation;[40] and (ii) that each entry (again, like a traditional dictionary) gives formal, syntactic, then semantic information – in that order – about the lexicon item.

4.12.2 Formal presentation

Each lexicon entry will present the item in phonological and graphological form: the etic citation form for the emic item. The phonological representation will consist not only of sequences of phonemes (or a distinctive feature matrix), but also include the normal stress assignment for the item. Although the precise manner of representation is a matter for phonologists and beyond the scope of this book, we shall make some general observations on the assignment of stress patterns and prosodic structure. Following from the work of Mark Y. Liberman & Alan Prince 'On stress and linguistic rhythm' 1977 and Elizabeth O. Selkirk 'The role of prosodic categories in English word stress' 1980a and *On Prosodic Structure and Its Relation to Syntactic Structure* 1980b, we assume that prosodic structures analyze into paired sisters whose prominence is relative such that one of the sisters is strong, *s*, and the other is weak, *w*. Since a stressed syllable is by definition more prominent than a non-stressed one, all stressed syllables are *s* and all non-stressed ones fall under a *w* node, cf. Liberman & Prince 1977:265 (18). It follows that for a syllable to be stressed within a given language expression, it and all the prosodic nodes above it must be strong.

What makes a syllable strong? For a proper answer to this question the reader is referred to the works cited above, because it depends on the phonological representation of the item within the dictionary, and on the actions of phonological rules upon the constituents of that representation when the item is included within an utterance. It is not sufficient, for instance, to spell the lexicon item *conception* simply as /kən'sɛpʃn/ because the grammar needs to allow also for, e.g. 1 stress to fall on the first syllable of the word, as in *I said cónception not pérception* where the item is pronounced /'kɒnsɛpʃn/. Whatever the phonological entry for *conception* in the lexicon, it must allow for both these pronunciations, and possibly others. We do not attempt to specify the proper phonological representation of lexicon items here, but will discuss the notion of syllable strength in relation to the normal surface form of lexicon items. Syllable strength is determined by the quality of a syllable's vowel, and by the structure and distribution of the syllable. In English, consonantal syllables are all weak (cf. Liberman & Prince 1977:299), so are syllables with (short) [ə]. Word final open syllables terminating in short lax central vowels [ɪ, ɔ, ʌ] are also weak. Syllables with long vowels and with tense vowels are strong. Non-final syllables containing short lax vowels [ɪ, ɔ, ɛ, ʌ] may be either weak or strong, though they will be weak if they have a strong sister syllable containing a long or a tense vowel; where two such vowels occur in adjacent syllables, the leftmost is typically strong, cf. *mínim*. Obviously, these are only rough guidelines.

Not all strong syllables are stressed, although all stressed syllables are strong. Strong syllables which are not stressed have weak prosodic nodes dominating them. Selkirk groups syllables as constituents of what she calls 'stress feet'. A stress foot, π, will always dominate a strong syllable, σ_s, though π may be either *s* or *w* itself.[41] According to Selkirk there are three types of stress feet found in English:

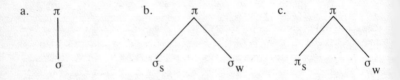

In (1) the syllable is strong by definition because it is the only syllable dominated by a stress foot; the strong/weak labelling defines a relation between sister nodes and an isolated *s* or an isolated *w* would violate the relational nature of these labels, cf. Liberman & Prince 1977:256. Stress feet types (b) and (c) have mirror images. Type (c) Selkirk calls a 'stress superfoot'. The general condition of foot strength is

Given sister feet π_1 and π_2, π_2 is strong if it branches, and otherwise it is weak.

Consider a sample of lexicon items with their normal stress patterns (next page). The lex *good* and the root *-vince* each consist of just one strong syllable and so each is dominated by a stress foot. The suffix *-ic* is always preceded by a stressed (hence strong) syllable, cf. *photográphic*, *éthnic*, *prosthétic* – each with a final trochaic foot. *Modest* (12.2.4) also

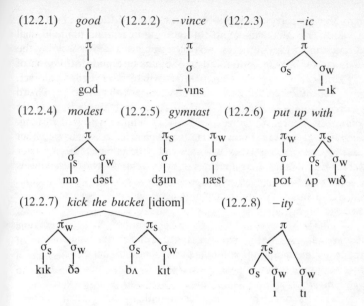

(12.2.1) *good*   (12.2.2) *−vince*   (12.2.3) *−ic*

(12.2.4) *modest*   (12.2.5) *gymnast*   (12.2.6) *put up with*

(12.2.7) *kick the bucket* [idiom]   (12.2.8) *−ity*

contains only one strong syllable, so it has only one stress foot; the /-dəst/ syllable is weak so if the word is uttered in isolation it is the strong /mɒ-/ syllable which is stressed. *Gymnast*, *put up with*, and *kick the bucket* each contain two strong syllables and so each has two stress feet, one strong, one weak. The strong foot dominates the 1 stress syllable. The weak foot of *gymnast*, for instance, dominates the strong syllable /-næst/ which is said to have secondary stress. *-ity* in (12.2.8) is always preceded by a stressed syllable, cf. *personálity*, *electrícity*, *ethnicity*, hence it forms part of a dactylic stress superfoot.

It is arguable that every σ_s has a degree of stress computable from the number of prosodic nodes dominating the lowest w dominating it, plus one: hence for *gymnast* the degree of stress on /dʒɪm-/ is one, i.e. this syllable takes primary stress; the degree of stress on /-næst/ is two, hence this syllable has secondary stress. We conclude that any σ_s, has a degree of stress greater than any σ_w, and its degree of prominance compared to any other $\sigma_s{}'$ will be computable from the s/w assignment of the prosodic nodes which dominate them in the prosodic structure of the language expression in which they appear. In practice, however, the phonetic differences between varying degrees of stress are such that there is no point distinguishing beyond three auditory levels at most, of which only two are communicatively functional. Because the lexicon is to be used by all components of the grammar, the phonological representations of lexicon must serve the criteria for the phonological component and also the criteria for the semantic component. We shall briefly consider degrees of stress with respect to both sets of criteria.

In a controlled psychoacoustic experiment conducted by Philip Lieberman, two competent phoneticians trained in the Trager-Smith tradition (cf. George L. Trager & Henry L. Smith *Outline of English Structure* 1951) were set to transcribe four levels of stress in a stretch of natural speech and in a parallel synthesized piece in which the constant vowel /a/ replaced all the phonemes in the utterance while retaining a fundamental frequency and envelope amplitude contour that varied in the same manner as the original natural language speech signal. Lieberman reports that

> [The] results suggest that in connected speech the fundamental
> frequency and amplitude contours of the speech signal can
> differentiate only two degrees of stress. These acoustic quantities
> (fundamental frequency, amplitude, and duration) can provide a
> physical basis for the listener's perception of stressed versus
> unstressed vowels. Vowel reduction phenomena may perhaps
> provide an acoustic basis for differentiating a third level of stress in
> connected speech.
>
> (Lieberman *Intonation, Perception and Language* 1967:128)

The three auditory levels of stress are

Unstressed weak syllables, σ_w.
Unstressed strong syllables, σ_s dominated at some level by a w node.
Stressed syllables, σ_s dominated by s nodes in prosodic structure.

Cf. also Lieberman 1967:159, Stanley S. Newman 'On the stress system of English' 1946, Henry Sweet *New English Grammar* 1891 §659. There is no good reason for phonological theory to admit any more than these three degrees of stress in phonological representations of lexicon items.

It is notable that these three auditory stress levels divide into two major categories: stressed versus unstressed, corresponding respectively to s and w sisters at a high level (? the highest level) in prosodic structure. It appears that only these two major categories are communicatively significant in English, cf. Gillian Brown, Karen Currie, & Joanna Kenworthy *Questions of Intonation* 1980:33, Michael A.K. Halliday *A Course in Spoken English: Intonation* 1970, Peter

Ladefoged *A Course in Phonetics* 1982:107, Kenneth L. Pike *The Intonation of American English* 1945:82. The division of unstressed segments between those consisting of inherently strong syllables versus those consisting of inherently weak syllables is (morpho)phonologically motivated but has no semantic consequences. In evidence of this take the example of the lex *photographic*.

(12.2.9)

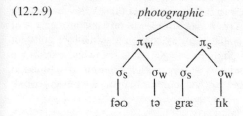

/græ/ bears primary stress and all other syllables are unstressed. /fəʊ/ is an unstressed strong syllable because it has a long vowel. /tə/ is an unstressed weak syllable because it contains /ə/; /fɪk/ is an unstressed weak syllable because the short lax vowel /ɪ/ is basically part of the *-ic* suffix (to which /f/ is prefixed in the phonological process of syllabification). To turn /fəʊ/ into an unstressed weak syllable it would have to undergo vowel reduction to /fə/ as in the lexeme /fə'tɒgrəfə/. To pronounce *photographic* as /fətə'græfɪk/ does not have any meaningful implications; but to shift the primary stress from /græ/ to any of the unstressed syllables in the word does have meaningful implications, because it focuses on the syllable chosen. For instance, to correct a mispronunciation one might say *It's [ˈfəʊtəgræfɪk] not [ˈfɔːtəgræfɪk]* placing 1 stress on the first syllable to give the prosodic structure in (12.2.10).

(12.2.10)   /ˈfəʊtəgræfɪk/

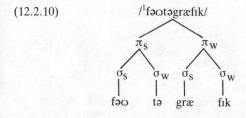

Note that this shift of the 1 stress has meaningful implications. Again, should S be orally correcting someone's spelling he might say *It's*

[fɑɒt'ɒgræfik] not [fəɒ'təəgræfik], putting the 1 stress on the second syllable instead of the third, once again with meaningful implications. To locate 1 stress on a normally unstressed syllable, and concomitantly to destress the normally 1 stressed syllable, produces a meaningful effect. But we have seen that to make a normally weak syllable an unstressed strong syllable, or vice versa, simply messes up the pronunciation of the lexicon item without creating any systematically meaningful effect. We therefore conclude that in giving an account of meaning in language, only two degrees of stress need be recognized in lexicon items: the 1 stress syllable, which is a strong syllable dominated by *s* nodes in the prosodic structure of the item; and unstressed syllables, which are syllables dominated by a *w* node at any level in prosodic structure.

The normal stress pattern for lexicon items is just the pattern which occurs most frequently and regularly and is thereby taken to be the unmarked form of the item. I have noticed in recent years that the 1 stress on the lexeme *employer* has shifted from the penultimate to the final syllable – apparently to ensure a clear phonological contrast between it and the word *employee*. *Employer* is an agentive nominal, and agentive nominals such as *eater*, *inspector*, *worker*, *putter-togetherer* are not normally stressed on the agentive suffix *-er*. *Employer* used not to be stressed on the final syllable either, cf. /ɛm'plɔiə/. The words *bargee*, *escapee*, *licensee*, *trustee*, (not to mention *Tennessee* and *settee*), are all stressed on their *-ee* suffix; so is *employee*. In order to ensure a contrast between *employer* and *employee* it has become usual (in Australian English at least) for the former to be pronounced /ɛmplɔ'əə/ with stress on the agentive suffix – which becomes a long, tense vowel.[42] Such alternative pronunciations of lexicon items should be represented in the lexicon as being both "normal" at the present time.

4.12.3   Syntactic information in the lexicon entry

There were five kinds of syntactic information proposed for lexicon entries in the kind of transformational grammar described by Noam Chomsky in *Aspects of the Theory of Syntax* 1965 and adopted by Jerrold J. Katz in *Semantic Theory* 1972 and other works (see ch.5). They are

category features, e.g. [+noun] (= is a noun)
rule features (cf. George Lakoff *Irregularity in Syntax* 1970 §2.2)
strict subcategorization features, e.g. [+ _NP] (= verb takes an object)

inherent features e.g. [+human] (= is human)
selectional features, e.g. [+[+animate]_[+abstract]] (= verb has an
   animate subject and an abstract object)

We require only the first two sorts of syntactic information to be
specified in the lexicon entries of our theoretical dictionary; that is to
say, (i) we label the syntactic category of the item – e.g. progressive
aspect, nominalizing suffix on verbs, conjunction, verb, or whatever;
and (ii) also such nonsemantic distributional information as, e.g. the
distribution of the phrasal verb particle, and the fact that a noun like
equipment cannot occur in countable noun phrases, etc.[43] The 'strict
subcategorization features', 'inherent features', and 'selectional features'
of lexical entries in transformational grammars are used in defining co-
occurrence relations between lexicon items within sentences, and these
are included within the semantic component of our lexicon entries. 'Strict
subcategorization features' identify notions such as transitivity in verbs
and the relational nature of nouns like *brother of* which are dealt with
via the syntactic structure of our semantic definitions. Semantic
definitions necessarily do have syntactic structure and there is no point
in duplicating this in the syntactic information given for a lexicon entry
(which is a fault in the semantic theories for transformational grammars
of the *Aspects* type, cf. ch.5). We assume that the information carried
by such supposedly syntactic 'inherent features' as [+human] for nouns
and [+active] for verbs is in fact nothing but semantic. Chomsky 1965
§2.3 admitted that there is a semantic basis for at least some of the
syntactic 'inherent features' of *Aspects* type transformational grammars
'Explorations in semantic theory' 1966, James D. McCawley in
'Concerning the base component of a transformational grammar' 1968
and 'The role of semantics in a grammar' 1968, and Ray Jackendoff in
Semantic Interpretation in Generative Grammar 1972, among many
others, have concluded that all inherent features are semantic. We also
take this view, and include the information supposedly carried by the
syntactic 'inherent features' of *Aspects* type transformational grammars
within the semantic component of the lexicon entry, seeing no reason
to copy this information as part of the syntactic component of the
entry. Because the 'selectional features' of one lexicon item refer to the
'inherent features' of other, co-current, items, and we have dispensed
with the syntactic 'inherent features', we have no place for syntactic
'selectional features' either. 'Selectional features' were postulated to
constrain anomaly, and we shall show in §5.2.4 why they are not
adequate to the task; but in any case, anomaly is a meaning relation
that should fall within the scope of the semantic component of lexicon

entries (if it falls within the domain of the lexicon at all). So we conclude that the syntactic component in a lexicon entry gives just two kinds of information: the syntactic category of the lexicon item; and any relevant information about constraints on the distribution of the lexicon item (or its constituent parts).

4.12.4 Use of the lexicon in the interpretation of new coinings

The formal and syntactic representations in the lexicon entry are primarily there to identify the lexicon item. Suppose, for the sake of argument, that our lexicon includes all the lexicon items in English; this does not exclude the possibility that S may, on occasion, coin a new item with the belief and intention that H will correctly interpret its meaning from his existing knowledge of the language. How, then, does H use the lexicon in determining the meaning of the new item? Take the following couple of sentences, and we will put ourselves in H's shoes.

(12.4.1) Haig, in Congressional hearings before his confirmatory, paradoxed his auditioners by abnormalling his responds so that verbs were nouned, nouns verbed and adjectives adverbized. He techniqued a new way to vocabulary his thoughts so as to informationally uncertain anybody listening about what he had actually implicationed.

    (London *Guardian* 'Alexander the Haigiographer' 3 Feb 1981)

Consider just 'abnormalling', 'nouned', and 'uncertain' from (12.4.1). It is up to syntacticians to tell us how to recognize that 'abnormalling' is the gerund of a verb *abnormal*, that 'nouned' is the (passive) past participle of the verb *noun*, and that 'uncertain' is the infinitive of a verb *uncertain*. However, having recognized these lexemes, we find they are not listed within the English lexicon. Our next step is to formally match them with items that do occur in the lexicon, i.e. with the adjectives *abnormal* and *uncertain*, and the noun *noun*. The meanings assigned in the entries of these lexicon items are then reinterpreted with the syntactic category meaning of the newly coined item, and this interpretation is essayed in context; if it seems to make sense the reinterpretation is assumed to be correct. Thus, the verb *abnormal* is taken to mean "cause X to be abnormal", the verb *noun* means "cause X to be a noun", the verb *uncertain* means "cause X to be uncertain" – all of which makes sense in the context of (12.4.1). If the deduced meaning of the newly coined lexicon item does not fit the context, the next step is to try matching it with an alternative homonym. Failing that, H must either abandon the lexicon search or assume that S has made a slip of the tongue or is indulging in language play (as with the Ladle Rat Rotten Hut story quoted in ex. (2.3.2) of ch.3); in such cases H will search for a formal similarity between the expression used by S and some lexicon item(s) whose meaning makes sense in context – but exactly how one should model a set of procedures for this kind of lexicon search I don't know.

4.12.5 The metalanguage for semantic definitions

The nub of a lexicon entry is the semantic definition of the item, and we have to decide what metalanguage to use for the purpose. The basic requirement is to satisfactorily communicate the meaning of item E_o from the object language, in terms of an expression E_m in the metalanguage, bearing in mind that the metalanguage is meant to be understood by human beings who normally communicate in a natural language of which they have fluent command. Thus, for instance, if you understood neither Polish nor Kiswahili there is little point using Kiswahili as a metalanguage for the semantic definition of Polish (or vice versa): e.g. to say *To jest pies* means "Ni mbwa" will not help you at all. Readers of this book must, perforce, know English; so we can use English as a metalanguage and say *To jest pies* (in Polish) means "It's a dog"; or we can say *To jest pies* means "Ni mbwa" in Kiswahili, which means "it's a dog" – here using English as a meta-metalanguage. To ensure that readers understand the semantic metalanguage used in this book it will have to be interpreted in English; in consequence we shall use English as either a metalanguage or a meta-metalanguage.

Ideally, a semantic metalanguage would be a formal language with a fully defined vocabulary and syntax. In other words, the vocabulary would be a specified set of symbols whose forms and correlated meanings are fully defined; all possible combinations of vocabulary items in the metalanguage would be generated from fully specified syntactic axioms and rules of syntax; and the meanings of syntactically well formed structures would be fully specified by semantic rules and axioms for the metalanguage. This is fine in principle, but such a metalanguage would be exactly equivalent to a natural language for two reasons: (i) the metalanguage is in effect a translation of the object language, and the object language is a natural language; (ii) in order for the metalanguage to be understood and used by human beings it must be translateable into a natural language. At best, then, a formal semantic metalanguage would be a deliberately contrived artificial language of the same notational class as a natural language; and although such a metalanguage would be a triumph for human ingenuity and might, as a by-product, reveal something about the nature of natural human languages, it will not in other respects be superior to a natural language as a semantic metalanguage. Consider a very simple example: if we use ($♀$) as the metalanguage expression for the predicate "be female" it is obviously, and by definition, equivalent in meaning to the English expression *be female*; furthermore, for ($♀$) to be correctly used and understood by human beings, it needs to be interpreted in English or some other natural language. To generalize: a metalanguage expression E_m used in the semantic definition of an expression E_o in the object language, which is a natural language, will always be equivalent to the natural language expression through which it is interpreted.

The advantages of a formal semantic metalanguage would be the explicit definition of primitives and, in general, a need to observe standards of rigour and exactitude that tend to be ignored when using an informal metalanguage such as a natural language. Furthermore, proper formalization of the metalanguage should permit proofs of particular conclusions about semantic structure and so prevent mistaken conclusions derived from faulty premises. However, none of these advantages of a formal system is necessarily unobtainable using an informal system like a natural language metalanguage for semantics. The disadvantage of the formal metalanguage is that it would have to be at least as comprehensive as a natural language (and to date no formal system comes close to achieving this goal), and in order to be used and understood by human beings it will have to be interpreted in terms of a natural language used as a meta-metalanguage.

In the view of Uriel Weinreich *On Semantics* 1980:50, 161, 300 a natural language can rightfully be its own metalanguage, but ideally the metalanguage would be a proper part of the natural language. More particularly, Weinreich proposed that a natural language metalanguage could be optimized by stratifying its vocabulary into a central core whose members are definable only circularly and by ostensive definition, with the next stratum out using items whose definitions contain only core items without (further) circularity, and each more peripheral stratum using items from the preceding stratum without circularity, and so forth for all lexicon items in the language, cf. Weinreich 1980:308f. Apart from the fact that we have rejected ostensive definition (such as "colour of the sky" in the entry for *blue*) from lexicon entries, no one has successfully described a method for identifying the core vocabulary for any language[44]. However, Anna Wierzbicka in *Semantic Primitives* 1972:15f has proposed a universal set of 'between ten and twenty' semantic primitives and lists the following fourteen:

> want, diswant (= don't want), feel, think of, imagine, say, become, be a part of, something, someone (being), I, you, world, this.

In the more recent *Lingus Mentalis* 1980 'feel' is omitted from the list. It is unclear what relationship these have to semantic metalanguage, however, because Wierzbicka's meaning descriptions use a lot of other items besides, cf.

'a cat = an animal thinking of which one would say "cat" ' (1972:22)
'hair = long thin flexible things growing on the skin and not being part of the body' (1972:26)
'hair – something that is on the skin, that is thought of as part of the body and that many long flexible things are parts of whose first parts are parts of the body' (1980:94)
'fur = thick stuff growing on the skin of an animal and not being part of the body' (1972:27)
'fur – something soft that is on an animal's skin, that is thought of as part of the body, and that many thin flexible things are parts of whose first parts are parts of the body' (1980:94)
'elbow – part of the arm where it bends
thigh – part of the leg above the knee
face – the front part of the head
ears – projecting parts of the body on the sides of the head' (1972:28, cf. 1980:80, 84)
'girl = young human being that one thinks of as becoming a woman.' (1972:41)
'A is walking along X. = A causes his body to be becoming supported [sic] by further parts of X, by causing movements of his legs which cause his legs to be becoming supported, first one, then the other (another), by further parts of X.
'A is running along X. = A causes movements of his legs which cause his body to be becoming first not supported by any part of X and then supported by further parts of X.' (1972:106)

It may be seen from these quotations that Wierzbicka does not envisage a metalanguage for semantics expressed only in terms of her 'semantic primitives', and she has yet to show, even, that the primitives form a core vocabulary (in Weinreich's sense) upon which all other metalanguage vocabulary is defined. There is, furthermore, the problem of defining a syntax for the metalanguage, though it appears that Wierzbicka uses something very close to English syntax in these examples.

One thing to avoid is using a semantic metalanguage which is simply a degenerate form of a natural language.[45] In 'Recent Issues in semantic theory' 1967:169 Jerrold J. Katz proposes the following semantic definition for the English verb *chase*:

(12.5.1) (((Activity of X) (*Nature*: (Physical)) (Motion) (*Rate*: (Fast)) (*Character*: (Following Y)) (*Intention*: (Trying to catch ((Y) (Motion)))

Nowhere does Katz define the vocabulary or syntax of his metalanguage and we have to try to comprehend it by matching our knowledge of the meaning of *chase* with our knowledge of the English expressions used in (12.5.1). This is made necessary by the fact that Katz's metalanguage is a degenerate form of English, and in order to interpret it we have to reformulate his metalanguage into natural English which uses the normal vocabulary of English structured by the familiar (if not well explicated) rules of English syntax. Reformulating (12.5.1) we get (12.5.2)

(12.5.2) "X is quickly following the moving object Y with the intention of catching it."

As we shall see in ch.5 there is no advantage to be gained from Katz's deformation of natural English: indeed, the deformation causes a reduction in comprehensibility which obscures the explication of meaning in the object language. Even lesser deformations of natural English than Katz's devalue a semantic metalanguage. Consider the following semantic definition of the English transitive verb *open* taken from Ray S. Jackendoff *Semantic Interpretation in Generative Grammar* 1972:41.

(12.5.3) [CAUSE (NP^1, [$\frac{\text{CHANGE}}{\text{physical}}$] (NP^2, NOT OPEN, OPEN))]

NP^1 corresponds to the transitive subject (i.e. the causer), and NP^2 to the direct object. Even so, it is only because we know the meaning of *open* and the meanings of the words used in this semantic definition of it, that we can interpret the metalanguage expression used in the definition. Like Katz, Jackendoff fails to describe the deformation rules he has applied to natural English in order to arrive at the metalanguage expression in (12.5.3), which we could reverse to reformulate the expression automatically in natural English. However, using our knowledge of English and a little ingenuity, we may assume that (12.5.3) is meant to be interpreted as (12.5.4).

(12.5.4) "NP^1 causes a physical change to come about, such that NP which was not open changes to being open".

We conclude that it is preferable to use the normal vocabulary and syntax of natural English for our semantic metalanguage.

It is notable that in interpreting the metalanguage used by Katz in (12.5.1) and by Jackendoff in (12.5.3) we were forced to interchange metalanguage expresions with object language expressions. And it might have been remarked from (12.5.3) or (12.5.4) that it is self-defeating to conclude in a lexicon entry that the meaning of the item *open* is "open" – however accurate this may be. The only grounds for this objection to giving the meaning of *open* in the object language as "open" in the metalanguage are the vicious circularity that results from the interchanging of an object language expression with its translation in the metalanguage when the two are identical. The interchange between identical expressions is felt to be intuitively unsatisfactory,[46] which would not be the case if the meaning of *open* were given as, e.g., "not shut". As we shall see in §4.12.6, trafficking between metalanguage and object language in a monolingual lexicon is thoroughly desirable. It is possible because of the necessary intertranslateability between them. For instance, suppose we say of *spinster*$_{noun}$

(12.5.5) F is a spinster $\longleftrightarrow$ (F is a woman) & (F has never married)

In (12.5.5) "F is a woman" is a metalanguage proposition, yet it corresponds to the identical expression in the object language; indeed the metalanguage implication in (12.5.6) corresponds to the object language implication expressed in (12.5.7) which is a more explicit and precise version of the colloquial tautology in (12.5.8)

(12.5.6) F is a spinster $\longrightarrow$ (F is a woman)

(12.5.7) F is a spinster semantically implies that F is a woman

(12.5.8) A spinster is a woman.

The analytic truth of (12.5.8) in the object language both justifies and is justified by the semantic relation defined in the metalanguage in (12.5.6) and this interchange is essential if we are to assume that the semantic metalanguage expresses meaningful properties and meaning relations which translate back into the object language and throw light on the meaning relations between expressions in the object language.

4.12.6 Semantic information in the lexicon entry

The semantic definitions used of lexicon items are expressed as synonyms wherever possible, and otherwise as conventional implicatures.[47] The noun *spinster*, for instance, is translated into the metalanguage expression 'F is a spinster' (in which 'F' is a variable) and its fully synonymous description is given as in (12.6.1).

(12.6.1) F is a spinster $\longleftrightarrow$ (F is a woman) & (F has never married)

On the righthand side of the double-headed arrow is the semantic definition whose constituents are implicational; it makes no sense to say that *spinster* is COMPOSED of "woman" and "never having married", cf. §3.5.3. The properties of 'being a woman' and 'never having married' are the necessary attributes of anyone properly called 'a spinster' – in other words, they are the salient perceived characteristics of the prototypical denotatum of *spinster*, cf. §2.9.10.

The semantic definition only gives the salient attributes of the prototypical denotatum, further implications such as for example that a spinster is a human being and a physical object can be determined from definitions elsewhere in the dictionary. These are accessible by interchanging metalanguage terms for object language terms and looking up the object language items in the dictionary. E.g. *F is a spinster* → *F is a woman*; if we take the metalanguage noun "woman" from the righthand side of this implicational statement and interchange it with the object language item *woman*$_{noun}$ we find

(12.6.2) F is a woman $\longleftrightarrow$ (F is female) & (F is adult) & (F is a human being)

Through the relation of transitivity we may reasonably deduce from the dictionary that

(12.6.3) F is a spinster → F is a woman → F is a human being ∴ F is a spinster → is a human being.

There is therefore no need for the dictionary to contain a special set of redundancy rules of the type proposed by Jerrold J. Katz & Paul M. Postal in *An Integrated Theory of Linguistic Descriptions* 1964:16 (cf. §5.2.6 below).

It is notable that the metalanguage translation of the lexicon item demonstrates a certain amount of syntactic information about it, including its syntactic category and one of the distributional possibilities (the rest being specified in the rules of syntax for the language).[48] If they are anywhere near satisfactory, semantic definitions in a metalanguage necessarily reveal certain kinds of syntactic information – we saw this even in (12.5.1) and (12.5.2) in the previous section. In particular, the metalanguage translation of the lexicon item reveals co-occurrence relations whose semantic nature is often elaborated upon in the semantic definition, or can be deduced from the implications of the semantic definition. E.g. in (12.6.1) we see that *spinster*$_{noun}$ is a one place predicate – i.e. 'being a spinster' is the property of one argument 'F'; compare this with the two place predicate *brother* which is a relation holding between two arguments:

(12.6.4) B is $\left\{ \begin{array}{l} \text{the brother of X} \\ \text{brother to X} \end{array} \right\}$ $\longleftrightarrow$ (B is male) & (B has at least one parent the same as X)

The semantic entry or its implications not only reveal how many arguments a predicate has, but also the roles of these arguments. For instance 'B' in *B is the brother of X* has an essive role, whereas 'X' is the possessor. The entry for *contain*$_{verb}$,

(12.6.5) C contains D $\longleftrightarrow$ D is in C

shows that 'C' has an inessive role and 'D' is essive. The entry for *kill*$_{verb}$,

(12.6.6) A kills B $\longleftrightarrow$ A causes B to die

shows that 'A' is the causer (or agent) and 'B' is the one that something happens to, called the affected object, or patient. We recognize this role because of the implication expressed in

(12.6.7) B dies $\rightarrow$ Something happens to B.

The role of causer or agent is more specialized than that of doer: e.g.

(12.6.8) A sits down $\rightarrow$ A does something

(12.6.9) *(A sits down $\rightarrow$ A causes something to happen)

Whereas *kill* is a causative verb, and the killer is a causer (or agent), *sit down* is simply an active verb, the doer (the sitter downer) is not an agent. But because

(12.6.10) A causes that B comes about $\rightarrow$ A does something it follows that a causative verb is a kind of active verb, and a causer (or agent) is a kind of doer.

Discussion of other kinds of roles, and further subcategorizations of verbs in English, belong in a semantic description of English and not in this description of lexicon entries. But it may be seen from the discussion about how such things will be determined in particular grammars. One thing that has not yet been specifically mentioned is that although the semantics of the predicate determines the roles that its arguments play in the utterance, recognition of these roles presupposes a concomitant recognition of the primary grammatical relations of the arguments. For instance, we said of (12.6.6) that 'A' is the causer or agent, and 'B' is the affected object or patient; but these remarks presuppose that 'A' is concomitantly recognized as the subject, and 'B' as the object of an active sentence (viz. *A kills B*). It is a convention in English, as in most languages, that the subject of an active sentence will be the agent or doer – if there is one in the proposition; and, concomitantly, the object of a transitive clause with an active predicate typically bears the role of affected object. Thus the determination of role relations goes hand in hand with a recognition of the grammatical relations held by various arguments of the predicate, cf. §7.8 for further discussion.

Before concluding this section we should briefly consider the nature of semantic entries for minor lexical categories, affixes, and stems. Take *the*_{article} as an example of a minor category item:

(12.6.11) the N(s) → a specified and unique entity or set of entities is holistically denoted by N(s) in W, such that no larger set is implied of which the set denoted is a subset (cf. §7.11.1)

And *-ize*_{verbalizing suffix on nouns & adj's} as an example of a bound morpheme:

(12.6.12) A N-izes → A causes or brings about (an) N

(12.6.13) A N-izes B → A causes or brings about that B has the property of being (an) N or of being N-like

Lastly, consider the stem *-juvenate*_{verb stem} in *rejuvenate*

(12.6.14) -juvenate ⟷ make young

Only a minimal entry for stems is necessary because they achieve propositional status within the lexemes which the syntactic part of their lexicon entry identifies as their conventional distributional domain.

4.12.7 Conclusions about form and presentation in the lexicon

We have concluded that the theoretical dictionary, or lexicon, is ordered like a traditional dictionary, according to the phonemic or graphemic sequence in the formal representation of lexicon items. Also like the traditional dictionary, a lexicon entry presents formal, syntactic, and semantic information. The phonological presentation shows the normal location of 1 stress (if any) on the item. The syntactic presentation lists the syntactic category of the item together with relevant distributional information. The formal and syntactic entries in the lexicon serve to identify a given lexicon item so as to match an appropriate utterance constituent with a lexicon entry for the purpose of semantically interpreting it. Neologisms are interpreted (where possible) by matching them as closely as possible with the formal representation of a lexicon item whose meaning – perhaps modified by syntactic recategorization – appears suitable in context. Semantic presentation in a lexicon entry is, wherever possible in terms of synonyms of the lexicon item, and otherwise in full statements of conventional implicatures; in either case the semantic definition describes the salient characteristics of the item's prototypical denotatum. The metalanguage used in the lexicon is a natural language; and a limited degree of translation back and forth between object language and metalanguage (in a monolingual lexicon) is permitted in order to exploit the resources of the lexicon when inferring the semantic implications of a particular item.

Chapter 5

The semantic interpretation of sentences:
a study of Katz's semantic theory and post-Katzian semantics

5.1 Introduction

We have said that the meaning of a sentence is projected up through the hierarchy of syntactic levels from the meanings of its constituent lexicon items. The meanings of the individual lexicon items are combined to give meanings for the constituent words in the sentence; the meanings of words are combined to give meanings for the constituent phrases in the sentence; and so forth up the hierarchy. But exactly how is this to be accomplished? The most comprehensive theory of semantics in natural language is that of Jerrold J. Katz, and Katz has offered an answer to the projection problem in semantics; so in §5.2 we examine Katz's work in detail. We find that Katz's theory does not, in fact, solve the projection problem, and that it turns out to have some serious flaws as a theory of linguistic meaning. In §5.3, therefore, we discuss some hypotheses proposed as alternatives to Katzian semantics; but find that these too are inadequate. In §5.4 we sketch another approach to the problem of relating the meaning of the sentence to the meanings of the lexicon items it contains.

5.2 Katzian semantics

> Semantic theory is taken to be an answer to the question 'What is meaning?'
>
> (Jerrold J. Katz *Semantic Theory* 1972:xxv)

5.2.1 The importance of Katz's contribution to linguistic semantics

The study of word meanings has a very long history whose practical effect has been the production of dictionaries. The meaning of some kinds of sentences – in particular those used to make statements – has been studied by logicians for more than two millenia. But serious investigation of the ways in which the meanings of lexicon items are combined into sentence meanings has blossomed only in the last 25 years, either inspired or provoked by the work of Jerrold J. Katz.[1] In Europe the study of meaning was not excluded from modern linguistics (cf. Ferdinand de Saussure *Course in General Linguistics* 1974:111, Jost Trier *Der Deutsche Wortschatz im Sinnberzirk des Verstandes die Geschichte eines sprachlichen Feldes* [German Vocabulary in the Conceptual Field of Knowledge and Understanding: the History of a Linguistic Field] 1931, John R. Firth 'The technique of semantics' 1935, Louis Hjelmslev *Omkring Sprogteoriens Grundlaeggelse* [Prolegemona to a Theory of Language] 1943:63, Stephen Ullmann *The Principles of Semantics* 1957) but no theory of meaning was developed. In America, Bloomfieldians had rejected the study of linguistic meaning on the grounds that it is not susceptible to scientific investigation (cf. Leonard Bloomfield *Language* 1933:140); and it was Uriel Weinreich who brought semantics out of the cold with his contribution to the 1961 Dobbs Ferry Conference on Language Universals 'On the semantic structure of language' (cf. Weinreich 1980 ch.3). Weinreich's writings on semantics (collected in *Weinreich On Semantics* 1980) contain many bright ideas whose appeal evaporates as we search for the foundation he failed to lay for them (cf. §5.3.2, Keith Allan 'Review of Weinreich on Semantics' 1981b). It was Katz's work, inaugurated in a paper written with Jerry A. Fodor 'The structure of a semantic theory' 1963 and comprehensively presented in *Semantic Theory* 1972, which established semantics as an integral part of modern linguistic analysis, and first set the goals for any satisfactory theory of sentence meaning (i.e. of sense).

Katz's approach to semantics stands in marked contrast to the informal collection of observations about meaning and meaning relations to be found in e.g. Ullmann's *The Principles of Semantics* 1957 or John Lyons' *Semantics* 1977. Katz sought to establish a theory of meaning that would accomplish the following:

(i)   to define what meaning (sense) is;
(ii)   to relate semantics to syntax and phonology by postulating semantic theory as an integral component of a theory of grammar;

(iii)   to establish a metalanguage in which semantic representations, properties and relations are expressed;

(iv)   to ensure that the metalanguage is universally applicable by correlating it with the human ability to conceptualize;

 (v)   to identify the components of meaning, and show how they combine to project meaning onto structurally complex expressions;

(vi)   to define the form of lexicon entries.

These goals should all be met by a theory of linguistic meaning, and they are met – in one way or another – in the theory of meaning proposed in this book. It is notable that Katz's theory is a theory of sense and sense relations, a theory of sentence meaning and not of utterance meaning. Katz believes that a theory of utterance meaning

> cannot be completed without systematizing all the knowledge about the world that speakers share and keeping such a systematization up-to-date as speakers come to share more knowledge. A limited theory of how socio-physical setting determines the understanding of an utterance is possible, but even such a theory blurs the distinction between the speaker's knowledge of his language (his linguistic ability) and the speaker's knowledge of the world (his beliefs about matters of fact).
>
> (Katz & Fodor 'The structure of a semantic theory' 1963:181)

We are more optimistic than Katz about the feasibility of postulating a theory of utterance meaning, cf. chs 1, 8, and 9 of this book. And we shall see when we come to examine Katz's work that his theory of sentence meaning leaks into pragmatics at various points, cf. §8.10.4. However, since our purpose in this chapter is to investigate the semantic interpretation of sentences, Katz's theory should be adequate to the task.

We want to extract from Katz's semantic theory his method for projecting the meanings of lexicon items onto structurally complex expressions up to the level of sentence, and in order to do so we shall examine the whole of his semantic theory. There are three reasons for this. The first is that Katz's semantic theory is the most comprehensive theory of sentence meaning available, and for that reason alone it is worthy of critical examination. The second is to consider his metalanguage and his presentation of lexicon items as possible alternatives to what was offered in ch.4 of this book. And the third reason we need to examine Katz's theory as a whole, is that his method for projecting the meanings of lexicon items onto sentences presupposes an understanding of his theory, its underlying assumptions, and the metalanguage used in it. We shall begin with the original statement of the theory in 'The structure of semantic theory' 1963, because many of the assumptions underlying Katzian semantics are to be found there; and some of the objections to the projection rules postulated in that paper led to a revision of Katz's solution to the projection problem – which is what we are most interested in, in this chapter.

5.2.2 'The structure of a semantic theory' (1963)

Semantics takes over the explanation of the speaker's ability to produce and understand infinitely many new sentences at the pont where grammar [= syntax] leaves off.

(Katz & Fodor 1963:172f)

Fundamental to an understanding of Katz's semantic theory is the assumption that the theory semantically interprets (i.e. assigns meanings to) the constituents of phrase markers (or, equivalently, labelled bracketings) generated by the syntactic rules in a transformational grammar of a type described by Noam Chomsky. In 'The structure of a semantic theory' (Katz & Fodor 1963) it was envisaged that the semantic theory would operate on the output of syntactic rules described in Chomsky's *Syntactic Structures* 1957; and in the definitive statement of the basic theory in Katz's *Semantic Theory* 1972, it was envisaged that the semantic component of a grammar operates on the output of rules of the syntactic base as described in Chomsky's *Aspects of the Theory of Syntax* 1965. Katz has not updated his semantic theory in line with later developments in transformational syntax – see Katz 1972 ch.8, his 'Chomsky on meaning' 1980, and *Language and Other Abstract Objects* 1981 for the reasons why. In order to understand Katz's theory, therefore, it will be necessary to describe certain of Chomsky's presumptions about the nature of syntax during the period 1957-1970.

Chomsky 1957 proposed that the syntactic component of a grammar should be autonomous and serve as input to both the phonological and semantic components. The kind of arguments advanced in support of the view that the semantic component should operate on the output of the syntactic component are the following. (i) Sentences containing identical lexicon items but different syntactic structures may have different semantic interpretations, cf.

(2.2.1) The hunters killed the crocodile.

(2.2.2) The hunter killed the crocodiles.

(2.2.3) The crocodile killed the hunters.

The differences in meaning between (2.2.1-3) can only be accounted for through reference to their respective syntactic structures, cf. §1.5.4. (ii) The noun lexeme *waitress* and the verb lexeme *waitress* differ in meaning because of the different syntactic categories they fall into; to assign them meaning, therefore, requires prior syntactic categorization. (iii) According to Chomsky 1957:100, in a sentence like (2.2.4) 'to' is a semantically empty word:

(2.2.4) I asked him to come over;

thus in (2.2.4) 'to' is described only in terms of syntax. Chomsky implies that in natural languages there are no instances of syntactically empty objects which are described only in terms of semantics,[2] and in consequence syntactic specification will need to precede semantic interpretation. At the time he wrote *Syntactic Structures* Chomsky did not believe that enough was known about semantics for a semantic component to be included as an integral part in the grammar; in this as in many other respects, the Chomsky of 1957 shows a close affinity with the Bloomfieldians he was later regarded as supplanting. He did presume that the output from the syntactic component would serve as input to the phonological component, but it was left to Katz & Fodor 1963 to describe a semantic component for the grammar which also operates on the output from the syntactic component, cf. 'A sentence and its grammatical description provide the input to a semantic theory' (Katz & Fodor 1963:193).

Chomsky in *Syntactic Structures* 1957, and subsequently, conceives of a grammar as a sentence generating device; each sentence generated is an individual, the grammar does not generate coherent texts, only single sentences at random. The syntactic component of the device is programmed with a small set of category symbols such as Σ, NP, VP, etc.[3] representing sentence constituents, and a set of rules for combining them. There are two kinds of rules. (i) Phrase structure or PS rules, which are rewrite rules of the form 'X $\rightarrow$ Y (Z) $\{{R \atop T}\}$' meaning "X consists of Y and optionally Z and either R or T but not both" and which thereby expand the category into its constituents. Together the PS rules generate phrase markers, which are labelled branching constituent structures trees rooted in Σ, whose nodes are labelled by category symbols. In the 1957 model the PS rules generate 'kernel sentence phrase markers' and in the 1965 (*Aspects*) model they generate 'base phrase markers', cf. §5.2.3. (ii) The other rules in the syntactic component are transformations, which perform operations of various kinds (deletion, reordering, etc.) on the output of the PS rules and on the ouput of earlier transformations, and whose output is a derived phrase marker. The last phrase marker generated by the syntactic component is known as the 'final derived phrase marker'. In the 1957 model of syntax, serving as input to the semantic component described in 'The structure of a semantic theory', lexicon items are introduced into the kernel sentence phrase marker by a rewrite rule of the same kind as the other PS rules. By these means the syntactic component can generate an infinite number of sentences from finite resources.

Consider the derivation of the sentence *the man hits the colourful ball* in a grammar of this kind. We choose this sentence because it is semantically interpreted by Katz & Fodor 1963:197ff. For various reasons the phrase marker we shall generate is trivially different from that found in 'The structure of a semantic theory'; this is partly because the PS rules in (PS.1) are more in line with *Syntactic Structures* than the rules Katz & Fodor must have used, and partly for the sake of simplicity in exposition. The PS rules are listed in (PS.1).

(PS.1)

$$
\begin{aligned}
\Sigma &\rightarrow \text{NP VP} \\
\text{VP} &\rightarrow \left\{ \begin{matrix} \text{Vb NP} \\ \textit{is} \text{ Adj} \end{matrix} \right\} \\
\text{NP} &\rightarrow \text{NP}_{sg} \\
\text{NP}_{sg} &\rightarrow \text{T N} \\
\text{Vb} &\rightarrow \text{Aux V} \\
\text{V} &\rightarrow \text{V}_{tr} \\
\text{Aux} &\rightarrow \text{Pres} \\
\text{T} &\rightarrow \textit{the} \\
\text{N} &\rightarrow \textit{man, ball} \\
\text{Adj} &\rightarrow \textit{colourful} \\
\text{V}_{tr} &\rightarrow \textit{hit}
\end{aligned}
$$

These PS rules generate two phrase markers which will subsequently be combined into one by transformation:

(PM.1)

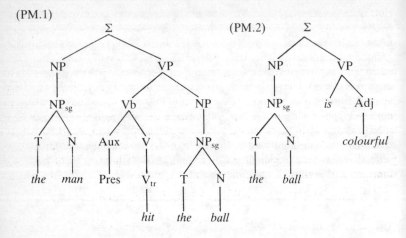

(PM.2)

The 'Auxiliary transformation' (Chomsky 1957:113) changes the V_{tr} constituent of (PM.1) into *hits*; and the 'Nominalizing transformation T_{Adj}' (Chomsky 1957:114) combines the two phrase markers (PM.1) and (PM.2) into the final derived phrase marker [= surface structure] (PM.3); cf. Katz & Fodor 1963:197.

(PM.3)

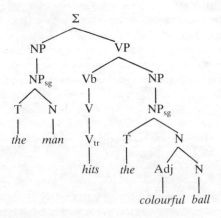

(PM.3) represents a sentence with its grammatical (i.e. syntactic) description (cf. Katz & Fodor 1963:193) to provide the input to the semantic component.

In 'The structure of a semantic theory' Katz & Fodor propose that each 'lexical formative' (lexicon item) in the final derived phrase marker is assigned a 'reading' (i.e. a semantic interpretation) from the lexicon, and then 'projection' rules combine these readings into one or more readings for the whole sentence. The lexicon and the projection rules together form the semantic component in Katz's semantic theory. Although the presentation of lexicon entries has changed over the years, entries have remained polysemous and Katz has retained the same set of descriptive categories within the entries:

(i)   a phonological or graphological representation of the lexicon item
(ii) a syntactic marker containing syntactic information about the item
(iii) a set of semantic markers (sort of semantic components) each enclosed in parentheses '(. . .)'
(iv) a distinguisher enclosed in square brackets '[. . .]'
(v)   a selection restriction enclosed in angled brackets '‹. . .›'

'The semantic markers and distinguishers are the means by which we can decompose the meaning of one sense of the lexical item into its atomic concepts, and thus exhibit the semantic structure IN the ditionary and the semantic relations BETWEEN dictionary entries.' (Katz & Fodor 1963:185f). In §5.2.5.1 we shall discuss the distinction made between semantic markers and distinguishers, but for the purposes of the discussion which follows, it may be assumed that a semantic marker represents a semantic property present in two or more lexicon items, i.e. it occurs in at least two readings in the lexicon, whereas a distinguisher is the bit of meaning left over when one particular sense of a lexicon item has been expressed as far as it can be in terms of semantic markers. The selection restriction is for use by the projection rules. The projection rules in Katz & Fodor 1963 apply recursively to 'amalgamate' the semantic readings of lexicon items under sister nodes (i.e. nodes branching from the same mother, thus in (PM.3) the Adj *colourful* and the N *ball* are sisters, and so are the subject NP and VP); these amalgamations progress up the tree, building up sensical interpretations for phrases, and ultimately for the sentence as a whole. The projection rules filter out anomalous amalgamations through action of the selection restrictions. The selection restrictions impose co-occurrence constraints on the amalgamation of readings for sister nodes by causing anomalous amalgamations to be discarded. The procedure for assigning semantic interpretations to sentences in Katz & Fodor 1963 is summarized in Figure 5.1.

The first step in the semantic interpretation of the final derived phrase marker (PM.3) is for the lexicon items to be associated with entries from the dictionary. This is done in the following manner: given that lexicon item λ in the FDPM (final derived phrase marker) is mothered by the syntactic category marker Γ (e.g. *colourful* is mothered by Adj), look in the lexicon for item λ with the syntactic marker Γ and enter material from the lexicon entry for λ under λ in the FDPM, cf. Katz & Paul Postal *An Integrated Theory of Linguistic Descriptions* 1964:18. (For those unfamiliar with Greek letters λ is called 'lamda' and Γ is 'gamma'.) In other words, the syntactic markers in the lexicon entry provide a necessary and sufficient condition for assigning a semantic reading to the lexicon item in the FDPM provided the latter specifies for the lexicon item a syntactic categorization identical with the one in the lexicon entry; this is determined by a simple matching process.

The readings Katz & Fodor give for the lexicon items in (PM.3) are as follows. (Each sense is given separately here, thus *ball*₁ refers to one sense of ball, *ball*₂ to another sense, and so forth. In §3.3.2 we proposed that each sense identifies a separate lexicon item, but Katz's lexicon items are polysemous like those of a traditional lexicographer.)

$ball_1$ → N → (Social Activity) → (Large) → (Assembly) → [For the purpose of social dancing]

$ball_2$ → N → (Physical Object) → [Having globular shape]

$ball_3$ → N → (Physical Object) → [Solid missile for projection by engine of war]

$colourful_1$ → Adj → (Colour) → [Abounding in contrast or variety of bright colours] ‹(Physical Object) v (Social Activity)›

$colourful_2$ → Adj → (Evaluative) → [Having distinctive character, vividness, or picturesqueness] ‹(Aesthetic Object) v (Social Activity)›

the → T → [Some contextually definite]

hit_1 → V$_{tr}$ → (Action) → (Instancy) → (Intensity) → [Collides with an impact] ‹SUBJECT (Higher Animal) v (Improper Part) v (Physical Object, OBJECT: (Physical Object)›

hit_2 → V$_{tr}$ → (Action) → (Instancy) → (Intensity) → [Strikes with a blow or missile] ‹SUBJECT: (Human) v (Higher Animal), OBJECT: (Physical Object), instrumental: (Physical Object)›

man → N → (Physical Object) → (Human) → (Adult) → (Male)

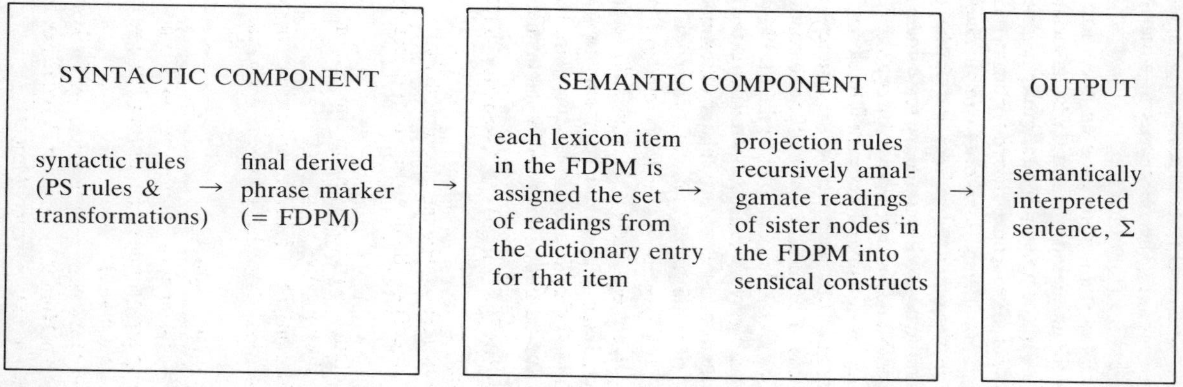

SYNTACTIC COMPONENT		SEMANTIC COMPONENT		OUTPUT
syntactic rules (PS rules & transformations)	→ final derived phrase marker (= FDPM)	→ each lexicon item in the FDPM is assigned the set of readings from the dictionary entry for that item	→ projection rules recursively amalgamate readings of sister nodes in the FDPM into sensical constructs	→ semantically interpreted sentence, Σ

Figure 5.1   The procedure for assigning semantic interpretations to sentences in Katz & Fodor 1963

Only one reading is given for *man*, although clearly there should be more; and no reading is given for the Present Tense in '*hits*'. These are infelicities we can ignore, however. The selection restriction, e.g. on *hit*₁, '<SUBJECT: (Higher Animal) v (Improper Part) v (Physical Object), OBJECT: (Physical Object)>', says that the lexicon entry for the subject NP on the FDPM (i.e. the NP mothered by Σ, or [NP, Σ]) must contain either the semantic marker (Higher Animal) or the marker (Improper Part) or the marker (Physical Object), and the lexicon entry for the object NP, i.e. [NP, VP, Σ] on the FDPM must contain the marker (Physical Object) otherwise the sentence will be anomalous. Thus, *the man hits*₁ *the ball*₂ is semantically well formed because *man* has the marker (Physical Object) and so does *ball*₂; but *the man hits*₁ *the ball*₁ is anomalous because *ball*₁ does not have the semantic marker (Physical Object) in its lexicon entry. The meaning of the arrows in these readings is mysterious – they are not equivalent to arrows in rewrite rules, however.

Once the dictionary entries have been associated with the lexicon items in (PM.3) the various readings are amalgamated by projection rules. Katz & Fodor describe the application of projection rules as follows.

> The general way in which the projection rule component works is by proceeding from the bottom to the top of a constituent structure tree and effecting a series of amalgamations. It [. . .] amalgamates sets of paths dominated by a grammatical marker [= syntactic category symbol], thus assigning a set of readings to the concatenation of lexical items under that marker by associating the result of the amalgamation with the marker, until it reaches the highest marker 'Sentence' and associates this with a semantic interpretation [. . .] Amalgamation is the joining of elements from different sets of paths under a given grammatical marker if these elements satisfy the appropriate selection restrictions represented by the material in angles.
>
> (Katz & Fodor 1963:197)

The procedure for amalgamation can be spelled out in relation to (PM.4) which is like (PM.3) but with extraneous nodes pruned away, and with the lexicon items replaced by their semantic readings, symbolized R1-R6.
The projection rules apply recursively to amalgamate the meanings of constituents in the following sequence; (2.2.5.e.) provides a semantic interpretation for the whole sentence, Σ.

(PM.4)

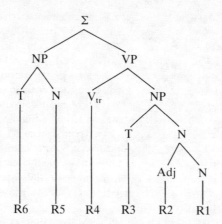

(2.2.5)
a. R2 + R1
b. R3 + (R2 + R1)
c. R4 + (R3 + (R2 + R1))
d   R6 + R5
e. (R6 + R5) + (R4 + (R3 + (R2 + R1)))

Amalgamation is the conjunction of readings for sister nodes. Applying the projection rules to the readings associated with the lexicon items in (PM.3) we begin by amalgamating the readings for *colourful* and *ball*. There are six combinations possible, but two are filtered out because the reading for *colourful*$_2$ is blocked by its selection restriction ⟨(Aesthetic Object) v (Social Activity)⟩ from amalgamating with the readings for *ball*$_2$ and *ball*$_3$. That leaves the following semantically well formed amalgamations to go through.

colourful$_1$ + *ball*$_1$ → N → (Social activity) → (Large) → (Assembly) → (Colour) → [[Abounding in contrast or variety of bright colours] [For the purpose of social dancing]].

colourful$_1$ + *ball*$_2$ → N → (Physical object) → (Colour) → [[Abounding in contrast or variety of bright colours] [Having globular shape]]

colourful$_1$ + *ball*$_3$ → N → (Physical Object) → (Colour) → [[Abounding in contrast or variety of colours] [Solid missile for projection by engine of war]]

colourful$_2$ +*ball*$_1$ → N → (Social Activity) → (Large) → (Assembly)
→ (Evaluative) → [[Having a distinctive character, vividness, or
picturesqueness] [For the purpose of social dancing]]

Projection rules then apply to amalgamate the reading for the article
the with those chosen for its sister noun *colourful ball*, to associate a
reading with the object NP. The next rule applies to amalgamate the
readings for the VP *hits the colourful ball*. The selection restrictions on
both readings for *hit* make them incompatible with the reading for
ball$_1$; so with the two remaining readings for *the colourful ball*, and the
two for *hit*, there are four readings for the VP. Finally, the reading for
the subject NP is determined and amalgamated with the VP readings to
give the following four semantic interpretations for the whole sentence.

The + *man* + *hits*$_1$ + *the* + *colourful*$_1$ + *ball*$_2$ → Σ → [Some
contextually definite] → (Physical object) → (Human) → (Male) →
(Action) → (Instancy) → (Intensity) → [Collides with an impact] →
[Some contextually definite] → (Physical Object) → (Colour) →
[[Abounding in contrast or variety of bright colours] [Having
globular shape]]

The + *man* + *hits*$_1$ + *the* + *colourful*$_1$ + *ball*$_3$ → Σ → [Some
contextually definite] → (Physical Object) → (Human) → (Adult) →
(Male) → (Action) → (Instancy) → (Intensity) → [Collides with an
impact] → [Some contextually definite] → (Physical Object) →
(Colour) → [[Abounding in contrast or variety of bright colours]
[Solid missile for projection by engine of war]]

The + *man* + *hits*$_2$ + *the* + *colourful*$_1$ + *ball*$_2$ → Σ → [Some
contextually definite] → (Physical object) → (Human) → (Adult) →
(Male) → (Action) → (Instancy) → (Intensity) → [Strikes with a
blow or missile] → [Some contextually definite] → (Physical Object)
→ (Colour) → [[Abounding in contrast or variety of bright colours]
[Having globular shape]]

The + *man* + *hits*$_2$ + *the* + *colourful*$_1$ + *ball*$_3$ → Σ [Some
contextually definite] → (Physical object) → (Human) → (Adult) →
(Male) → (Action) → (Instancy) → (Intensity) → [Strikes with a
blow or missile] → [Some contextually definite] → (Physical Object)
→ (Colour) → [[Abounding in contrast or variety of bright colours]
[Solid missile for projection by engine of war]]

It is our purpose here to exemplify the theory in operation rather than discuss the inadequacies of the particular examples given. But we might note in passing: (i) that the dictionary entry for *the* is pitifully inadequate; that *ball₃*, "a solid missile for projection by an engine of war", has globular shape just like *ball₂*; (ii) that the imagination needs quite a stretch to conceive of a man colliding with a cannon ball; and (iii) that, for many people, *the man hits the colourful ball* can also be interpreted "the man arrived at the colourful assembly for the purpose of social dancing".

Prior to the publication of *Semantic Theory* 1972, amalgamation of the type demonstrated above was the only form of projection rule exemplified in detail by Katz or his co-authors. As we see from (2.2.5) the readings of sister nodes are combined into Boolean conjunctions, the effect of which is to destroy the structure imposed by the phrase marker. This is obvious from the equivalence shown for each step in the amalgamation in (2.2.6)

(2.2.6)
  a. $R2 + R1 = R1 + R2$
  b. $R3 + (R2 + R1) = R3 + R1 + R2$
  c. $R4 + (R3 + (R2 + R1)) = R2 + R3 + R1 + R4$
  d. $R6 + R5 = R5 + R6$
  e. $(R6 + R5) + (R4 + (R3 + (R2 + R1))) = R4 + R2 + R5 + R1$
       $+ R6 + R3$

(2.2.6) shows that the process of recursive conjunction makes the bracketing superfluous, so that the reading for the sentence *the man hits the colourful ball* would turn out to be identical with the readings for all of the following – which should definitely not be the case.

(2.2.7)
  a.   the colourful ball hits the man
  b.   the ball hits the colourful man
  c.   the colourful man hits the ball
  d.   hits colourful man ball the the

(Cf. Uriel Weinreich 'Explorations in semantic theory' 1966:410). Katz has disputed this damning objection to his theory, and spoken of there being as many projection rules as there are grammatical relations between sister nodes. He gives as examples, 'subject-predicate, verb-object, modification, etc.' (*The Philosophy of Language* 1966:165). The only way in which these rules could possibly differ from one another is in their application to different nodes in the FDPM, and we have to assume that the method of amalgamation remains Boolean conjunction, since Katz has said nothing to the contrary. We therefore conclude that in the early accounts of Katzian semantic theory no satisfactory procedure exists for combining the semantic readings of lexicon items to give the meanings of sentences; Boolean conjunction destroys the structure that semantic interpretation rules supposedly derive from the structural description provided by the syntactic component.[4] The only constraint on the amalgamation of readings in Katz & Fodor 1963 is the selection restriction.

Katz & Fodor 1963 actually propose two kinds of projection rules. Those we have looked at they call 'type 1 projection rules', which apply to all kernel sentence phrase markers, and by convention to all transforms of kernel sentences that are meaning preserving. Sentences whose derivation includes the application of a meaning changing transformation were to be interpreted by 'type 2 projection rules', whose form was never specified. The *Syntactic Structures* model of transformational syntax generates only one clause at a time, and complex sentences are created by generalized transformations whose function is either to adjoin two clauses or to embed one within the other, thus effectively changing the meaning of the matrix sentence. There are also the optional singulary meaning changing transformations[5] which convert declarative kernels into the corresponding imperative, interrogative or negative sentences. Since the semantic theory operates on final derived phrase markers it is not obvious why two types of projection rule were proposed for the different kinds of sentences. Perhaps type 2 rules were deemed necessary to reconstruct understood elements for surface structures impoverished by deletion transformations (e.g. reconstructing the second person subject of an imperative such as *Be good!*). But because the form of type 2 projection rules was not described, one can only speculate on possible differences between them and the type 1 rules. The theoretical developments reported in Katz & Postal *An Integrated Theory of Linguistic Descriptions* 1964 and Chomsky's *Aspects of the Theory of Syntax* 1965 dispensed with the supposed need for type 2 projection rules anyway.

5.2.3   The semantic interpretation of underlying phrase markers

The syntactic component of a grammar must specify, for each sentence, *a deep structure* that determines its semantic interpretation and *a surface structure* that determines its phonetic interpretation.

(Chomsky *Aspects of the Theory of Syntax* 1965:16)

It was by no means obvious how kernel sentences were to be linked with those of their transforms in which meaning was preserved, in order to be assigned identical semantic interpretations. Katz & Fodor 1963:206 wrote: 'It would be most satisfying if we could take the position that transformations never change meaning.' In *An Integrated Theory of Linguistic Descriptions* 1964:157, Katz & Postal did take this position, at least with respect to singulary transformations; and once Chomsky 1965 had done away with the need for generalized transformations by allowing the conjunction and embedding of clauses through the phrase structure rules, all remaining transformations were singulary, and all transformations were therefore supposed to be meaning preserving. The kind of evidence offered in support of this view was that the (a) and (b) sentences in (2.3.1-7) are transformationally related and also mean the same, (or so it was claimed).

(2.3.1)
   a.   The dog chased the cat.
   b.   The cat was chased by the dog.

(2.3.2)
   a.   All the boys went to the movie.
   b.   The boys all went to the movie.

(2.3.3)
   a.   He looked up the number in the phone book.
   b.   He looked the number up in the phone book.

(2.3.4)
   a.   Eat the soup.
   b.   You will eat the soup.

(2.3.5)
   a.   John does not go home.
   b.   It is not the case that John goes home.

(2.3.6)
   a.   Who saw Celia?
   b.   I request that you answer 'X saw Celia.'

(2.3.7)
   a.   Did Dad sleep?
   b.   I request you answer whether or not Dad slept.

Cf. Katz & Postal 1964 chs 3 & 4. For some of these pairs it is disputable whether the two sentences do mean the same thing, but that is not the point at issue here; Katz & Postal, and most transformational grammarians at that time, did take such pairs to mean the same and to be transformationally related. The different forms in the (a)/(b) pairs arise because (a) is generated by a different set of transformations than (b). But because (a) means the same as (b), the different sets of transformations operate upon exactly the same Lexically specified Underlying Phrase Marker (LSUPM) for each of the pairs. Intead of having the semantic component operate on the FDPMs (final derived phrase markers) in (a) and (b) to assign them the same meaning, as was proposed in Katz & Fodor 1963, the later versions of Katz's semantic theory have the semantic component operate on a single LSUPM from which a number of FDPMs (perhaps more than just the two illustrated in the (a)/(b) pairs of (2.3.1-7)) might be generated by different sets of transformations. The distinction between deep and surface structure also offered a neat way to account for the ambiguity of certain surface sentences. For instance, *Roly hates boring students* can mean either "Roly hates students who are boring" or "Roly hates to bore students"; these two meanings are treated as the semantic interpretations of two different LSUPMs which are operated upon by different sets of transformations to derive the same final derived phrase marker – i.e. the same surface form. The advantages of semantically interpreting the LSUPM (deep structure) and having meaning preserving transformations derive one or more FDPMs (surface structures) from it, are summarised in Figure 5.2.

The convention that transformations are meaning preserving has been abandoned by everyone but Katz. In 'On the requirement that transformations preserve meaning' 1971, Barbara Hall Partee subjected the matter to detailed examination, and found that although a majority of transformations are meaning preserving, there is a small number of incorrigible exceptions. For instance, the following (a)/(b) pairs ought necessarily to mean the same if transformations are meaning preserving, but they don't.

(2.3.8)
    a.   Everyone in the room knows two languages.
    b.   Two languages are known by everyone in the room.

(2.3.9)
    a.   Many arrows didn't hit the target.
    b.   The target wasn't hit by many arrows.

(2.3.10)
    a.   John even kissed Kate!
    b.   Kate was even kissed by John!

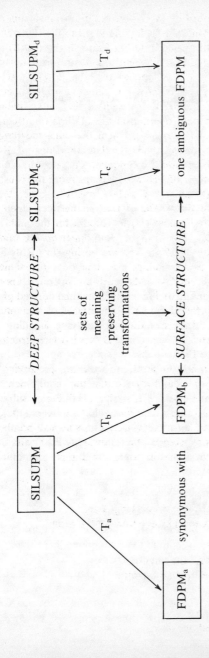

Figure 5.2   A summary sketch of the reasons for semantically interpreting deep structures

(SILSUPM = semantically interpreted (lexically specified) underlying phrase marker; FDPM = final derived phrase marker)

(2.3.11)
   a. I got some avocados for 20¢ each.
   b. *I got each of some avocados for 20¢.

(2.3.12)
   a. I am fated by having only one leg never to run normally.
   b. *Having only one leg fates me never to run normally.

(2.3.13)
   a. Maisie didn't shoot¹ her husband.
   b. Maisie didn't shoot¹ her husband.

(2.3.14)
   a. Excuse me? [= "What did you say?"]
   b. I request that you answer whether or not you will excuse me.

(2.3.15)
   a. Have a good time!
   b. You will have a good time.

(2.3.16)
   a. Few students are wealthy and few students support large
       families.
   b. Few students are (both) wealthy and support large families.

Katz 1972:436 has retorted that supposed counterexamples like (2.3.8-12), which involve a contrast between active/passive pairs, are inappropriate because the LSUPMs of the active and passive are distinct, cf. Katz & Postal 1964:72.[6] In respect of (2.3.13), Katz 1972 §8.4.1 has recognized that his theory is unable to accommodate the contribution of prosody to meaning because prosody is specified on FDPMs (surface structures);[7] he has therefore assigned the semantic interpretation of prosody to an unformulated 'rhetorical component' of the grammar. We can regard this response as ducking the issue. So far as I know Katz has not commented on such counterexamples as (2.3.14-16). In sum, Katz has hung on to the convention that transformations preserve meaning in the face of some evidence to the contrary, and effectively ignored the contribution of prosody to meaning. Consequently, his semantic theory requires that the semantic component of a grammar component operates in LSUPMs.

Katz sees his semantic theory as an integral part of a theory of transformational grammar that came to be known as the 'standard theory'. Standard theory TG is based on work reported in Katz & Postal 1964 and Chomsky 1965. The tripartite grammar has syntactic, semantic, and phonological components. Chomsky was largely responsible for the development of the syntactic and phonological components; Katz for developing the semantic component. A standard theory grammar is based on an autonomous syntactic component consisting of phrase structure rules which expand category symbols such as Σ, NP, VP etc. into their immediate constituents to generate phrase markers in much the same way as the earlier *Syntactic Structures* grammar did. In the 1957 model, lexicon items were introduced into the terminal nodes of phrase markers by the same kind of rewriting rules as expand category symbols into their immediate constituents, cf. (PS.1) in §5.2.2; but in the standard theory, lexical category nodes like N (noun) or Prep (preposition) get rewritten as dummy symbols (△). The resulting phrase marker is known as the 'base phrase marker'. Lexical substitution transformations replace the terminal dummy symbols of the base phrase marker by a complex symbol of phonological, syntactic, and semantic material that specifies the form and meaning of the lexicon item – i.e. it constitutes a lexicon entry. When the last △ has been replaced we have the LSUPM – lexically specified underlying phrase marker – on which the semantic projection rule operates. (For reasons that will become apparent, there is only one projection rule.) One or more semantic interpretations are projected onto the LSUPM after the insertion of lexicon items and before any other transformations take place, and at no other level of the grammar. This identifies the requirements for the semantic interpretation of sentences in the standard theory grammar of which Katz's semantic theory constitutes a proper part; they are summarized in Figure 5.3.

5.2.4 Problems with selection restrictions

In reality, an enormous range of features would be needed to express the full range of selection restrictions to be found in English.
(James D. McCawley 'Concerning the base component of a transformational grammar' 1968a:265)

McCawley's observation is, as we shall see, a serious understatement of the difficulties facing anyone who seeks to specify the set of selection restrictions required in either the syntactic or the semantic component of a grammar. The problem might more realistically be compared to counting the grains of sand in the Sahara Desert – it may be possible, it is certainly impracticable. Syntactic selection restrictions, which will be discussed in §5.2.4.1, are postulated to constrain lexical insertion,[8] with

SYNTACTIC BASE

PS rules generate a base phrase marker whose terminal symbols are △s hanging from lexical category nodes

LEXICAL SPECIFICATION

Lexical insertion transformations replace △s in the base phrase marker by lexicon entries consisting of
1. the phonological or graphological form of the lexicon item;
2. the syntactic marker consisting of (a) a category feature, (b) strict subcategorization features, (c) inherent features, (d) selectional features, (e) rule features;
3. the semantic description of the lexicon item in terms of (a) a set of semantic markers and/or distinguishers, (b) semantic selection restrictions. When all △s are replaced, lexical insertion is complete and the resulting phrase marker is called a lexically specified underlying phrase marker (= LSUPM).

PROJECTION RULE

The projection rule operates on the LSUPM to combine the readings of sister nodes progressively up the tree until there is at least one reading for Σ

Figure 5.3   The semantic interpretation of a sentence in Katz's semantic theory

the aim of generating only acceptable sequences of lexicon items within sentence constituents. A lexicon item λ may be inserted into a base phrase marker provided the constraints imposed by its syntactic marker, and the syntactic markers of other items in the tree, are satisfied: a significant portion of these constraints are expressed as selection restrictions. We have already encountered semantic selection restrictions in §5.2.2. Semantic selection restrictions constrain the action of the projection rule as it combines the readings for sister nodes in the LSUPM. Inappropriate sense (readings) of a given lexicon item λ will be discarded by the projection rule on the basis of the semantic selection restrictions in the readings for its sister lexicon items.

We shall see that it would be practically impossible ever to specify the set of either syntactic or semantic selection restrictions; consequently the grammarian is faced with a choice between two evils. (i) So as to generate all the acceptable lexical sequences in the language, he can allow the grammar to generate both acceptable and anomalous sequences, while admitting that there is no way for the grammar (including the semantic component) to distinguish between them. (ii) He can arbitrarily restrict the grammar by postulating a few selection restrictions so as to generate only acceptable sequences, while admitting that these will be only a proper subset of all acceptable lexical sequences in the language. With unwarranted optimism, Katz's semantic theory presupposes that the grammar will generate all and only the acceptable lexical sequences in a language, and that the well formedness conditions on lexical insertion can be specified; consequently his theory is weakened (though not destroyed) if the presumptions about the well formedness of the LSUPMs are false.

5.2.4.1 The problem of lexical insertion in a standard theory grammar

Colorless green ideas sleep furiously

(Chomsky 1957:15(1))

A prerequisite to the successful operation of Katz's semantic theory is a lexically specified underlying phrase marker (LSUPM). Lexical specification of the base phrase marker involves the insertion of entries from the lexicon, into its terminal $\triangle$ symbols, each entry being a complex of phonological, syntactic and semantic material of the kind described in Fig. 5.3. The literature on transformational grammar speaks of constraints on lexical insertion that will allow only acceptable sequences of lexicon items to appear in the LSUPM; if these well formedness conditions on lexical insertion are properly stated, the grammar should generate all and only the lexical sequences acceptable by speakers of the language. But in fact, the set of syntactic features which supposedly define these well formedness conditions cannot be specified, for reasons we shall examine below.

In the models of semantic theory presented in Katz & Fodor 1963 and Katz & Postal 1964 it was assumed that lexicon items were introduced into the terminal nodes of phrase markers by the same kind of rewriting rules as expand category symbols into their immediate constituents. Conventionally, one symbol to the left of the arrow is expanded into one or more to its right. Rules of this same kind were used to subcategorize lexical nodes such as Noun and Verb, and it was the fully subcategorized lexical nodes that provided the lefthand side of the rewrite formula introducing lexicon items, cf. (PS.1) in §5.2.2. But here was a problem. Take the simple instance of the cross-subcategorization of just four nouns given in (2.4.1.1)

(2.4.1.1)

$N_{count/animate} \rightarrow$ *cow*
$N_{mass/animate} \rightarrow$ *(live)stock*
$N_{count/inanimate} \rightarrow$ *pebble*
$N_{mass/inanimate} \rightarrow$ *sand*

To achieve these four composite subcategories there is a choice of rules (2.4.1.2) or (2.4.1.3)

(2.4.1.2)

a. $N_{count} \rightarrow \left\{ \begin{array}{l} N_{count/animate} \\ N_{count/inanimate} \end{array} \right\}$

b. $N_{mass} \rightarrow \left\{ \begin{array}{l} N_{mass/animate} \\ N_{mass/inanimate} \end{array} \right\}$

(2.4.1.3)

a. $N_{animate} \rightarrow \left\{ \begin{array}{l} N_{animate/count} \\ N_{animate/mass} \end{array} \right\}$

b. $N_{inanimate} \rightarrow \left\{ \begin{array}{l} N_{inanimate/count} \\ N_{inanimate/mass} \end{array} \right\}$

But, firstly, there is no principled reason for choosing between

(2.4.1.2) and (2.4.1.3) and, secondly, whichever is chosen entails a redundancy. Supposing we choose (2.4.1.2), then it is impossible to refer to the class of animate nouns except through the disjunct $N_{count/animate}$ or $N_{mass/animate}$. To choose (2.4.1.3) makes it impossible to refer to the class of mass nouns, except through a comparable disjunct.

To dispose of these problems Chomsky 1965 proposed a radical theoretical change, by including in the syntactic base a set of rules to generate complex symbols. In place of a lexicon entry being governed by subcategorization, as in (2.4.1.4), there was now something like (2.4.1.5), in which each subcategory was represented individually by a syntactic feature.

(2.4.1.4)

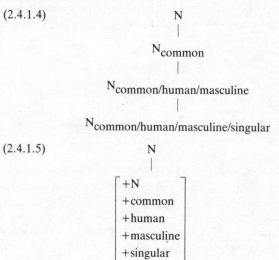

$$N$$
$$|$$
$$N_{common}$$
$$|$$
$$N_{common/human/masculine}$$
$$|$$
$$N_{common/human/masculine/singular}$$

(2.4.1.5)

$$N$$
$$|$$
$$\begin{bmatrix} +N \\ +common \\ +human \\ +masculine \\ +singular \end{bmatrix}$$

This made it possible to refer to the class of human nouns, for instance, as those bearing the syntactic feature [+human], and mass nouns as those bearing the feature [+mass]. As we shall see in a moment, (2.4.1.5) is a simplified version of what Chomsky actually proposed, but such simplified sets of features are common in the literature.[9] George Lakoff *Irregularity in Syntax* 1970:7ff exemplifies lexical insertion using the complex symbol as a matrix for a well formedness condition on the lexical item. He attributes to Paul Postal the notion that the complex symbol is generated together with a twin dummy node, as in (2.4.1.6), to be replaced by an entry from the lexicon, as in (2.4.1.7).

(2.4.1.6)

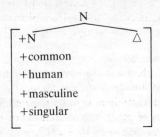

(2.4.1.7)

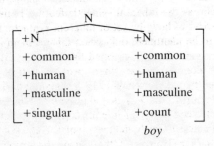

boy

Lexical substitution was random, and the degree of matching between the features in the complex symbol and those in the lexicon entry was thought to indicate degrees of grammaticality; therefore *Peter* would be more grammatical in the environment of (2.4.1.6) than would *Mary* because it would differ by only one feature, whereas *Mary* would differ by two. But the gross redundancy in this method of lexical insertion led to its being abandoned in favour of an alternative proposal from Chomsky 1965, that lexical categories mother only the dummy symbol, △. Lexical insertion transformations then replace the △s with a complex symbol consisting of a triple specifying (i) the phonological form of the lexical item, (ii) a set of syntactic features, and (iii) a set of semantic features which Chomsky apparently identified with dictionary readings, cf. Fig. 5.3 p. 294. The set of syntactic features comprises

(2.4.1.8)
    a.   category features, e.g. [+N] (= is a noun), [+V] (= is a verb)
    b.   strict subcategorization features, e.g. [+_NP] (= verb takes an object)
    c.   inherent features, e.g. [+human], (= is human), [+active] (= is active)

d.   selectional features, e.g. [+[+animate]−[+abstract]] (= verb
has an animate subject and an abstract object)
e.   rule features, e.g. [+particle shift] (= [phrasal] verb undergoes
particle shift)

(2.4.1.8. a-d) specify the well formedness conditions on lexical
insertion. (2.4.1.8. a-b) are defined by reference to the base phrase
marker into which the lexicon item is to be inserted. (2.4.1.8.d) refers
to the inherent features of other lexicon items. For instance the verb
kill has syntactic features such as [+V, +−NP, +−[+living]]; thus *kill*
can only be inserted under a Verb node that is sister to the direct
object NP whose head noun denotes an animal or plant, or something
similar, and which has the inherent syntactic feature [+living].

The question arises of how the set of inherent syntactic features of a
lexicon item are to be identified; only when this problem is solved can
the well formedness conditions described by (2.4.1.8.c, d) be defined.
All Chomsky has done is indicate them programmatically. Chomsky
1965 §2.3 admitted that there seems to be a semantic basis for at least
some syntactic features; for instance the syntactic inherent feature
[+human] in the lexicon entry for *boy* in (2.4.1.7) presumably reflects
the semantic characteristic of humanness which Katz would represent
by the semantic marker (Human). Others made the stronger claim that
all so-called syntactic features, including category features, are
semantic; cf. Weinreich 1966:432f: 'We intend the distinguishing
feature of each major morpheme class, e.g. [+Noun], to be taken as
semantic in the full sense of the word; more revealing names might be
"thingness" or "substantiality", "quality" (for [+Adjective]), and so
on.'[10] In 'Recent issues in semantic theory' 1967:152f Katz quite clearly
differentiated syntactic features from semantic markers on the basis
that the former were necessarily referred to in the lexical insertion
rules of the syntactic component, and the latter in spelling out
dictionary readings. This would appear to allow, as Chomsky did, that
syntactic features may pretheoretically be semantic. For instance Katz
1967:156 (1972:81) notes that in

(2.4.1.9) The ship met her doom on the rocks

'ship' has the syntactic feature [+feminine] to justify the use of the
pronoun 'her'; but it is not semantically female, because (2.4.1.9) does
not imply *The female met her doom on the rocks*. Although he is surely
right for this case, it is nonetheless true that the majority of English
nouns bearing the syntactic feature [+feminine] denote females, and
that the use of this feature with inanimates is a metaphorical extension.

Thus although Katz might hold that a syntactic feature is not a semantic component, we can still reasonably assume that syntactic features reflect semantic characteristics and are to be discovered through reference to meaning.[11]

In 'Concerning the base component of a transformational grammar' 1968a, James D. McCawley drew attention to an inadequacy following from Chomsky's discussion of double selectional features (Chomsky 1965:119). Chomsky argued from the data in (2.4.1.10) for the set of double selectional features on *command* given in (2.4.1.11)

(2.4.1.10)
  a. John commanded our respect.
  b. John commanded the platoon.
  c. John's resignation commanded our respect.
  d. *John's resignation commanded the platoon.

(2.4.1.11)
  a. [+[+human]_[+abstract]]
  b. [+[+human]_[+human]]
  c. [+[+abstract]_[+abstract]]
  d. [−[+abstract]_[+human]

McCawley writes:

> Chomsky's description of *command* in [(2.4.1.10)] as taking an abstract object does not correctly capture the restriction, since a wide variety of combinations of "abstract" noun phrases violate the selection restriction in question:
>   *Our respect commanded John's decision to resign.
>   *The fact that $2 + 2 = 4$ commanded our respect.
> In reality, an enormous range of features would be needed to express the full range of selectional restrictions to be found in English, as is clear from a consideration of the selectional violations in [(2.4.1.12)]
>   a. *That verb is in the indicative tense.
>   b. *Bernstein's theorem is nondenumerable.
>   c. *John diagonalized the differential manifold.
>   d. *That electron is green.
>   e. *I ate three phonemes for breakfast.
>   f. *He pronounces diffuseness too loud.
>   g. *My hair is bleeding.
>   h. *That unicorn's left horn is black.

(McCawley 1968a:265)

This passage is quoted in full because it raises a question that has never been answered: how are we to determine the set of features mentioned in selection restrictions? There are clearly many many times more of them than one sees dotted about in the literature; and many lexicon items have very specialized features indeed. For instance, in (2.4.1.12.a) both the grammatical terms 'indicative' and 'tense' have very restricted collocability within a noun phrase: *indicative* with *mood*, and *tense* with perhaps a dozen attributives, whose common syntactic feature escapes my ingenuity. McCawley, in 'The role of semantics in a grammar' 1968b:134, returns to this point: 'the verb *diagonalize* requires as its object a noun phrase denoting a matrix (in the mathematical sense), the adjective *benign* in the sense "non-cancerous" requires a subject denoting a tumor, and the verb *devein* as used in cookery requires an object denoting a shrimp or prawn.' However, there is nothing theoretically problematic in the fact that selectional features do not just indicate macroclasses like abstractness, animacy, or activity.

The problem lies with the fact that what governs collocability of lexicon items is just the requirement that the collocation denotes some possible denotation (be it substance, object, state, event, process, quality, metalanguistic statement or whatever) in W, the world spoken of. When we find a world in which the expression can reasonably denote, it ceases to be anomalous. In §3.2.2 we discussed some of McCawley's asterisked examples, namely those in (2.4.1.12.d, e, g, h), and for all of them found contexts in which the sentences make sense. For instance, (2.4.1.12.d) is presumably asterisked because electrons are theoretical constructs that cannot absorb or reflect light, and therefore cannot be predicated as green – even metaphorically. However, supposing an explanatory model of an atom were constructed in which the electron was represented by a green flash, it would be quite legitimate to say in reference to the model *That electron is green* without anomaly and therefore without any violation of a selection restriction. Obviously, the empirical evaluation of sequences of lexicon items is ultimately governed by pragmatic conditions. Strictly speaking, it is not the sequences of lexicon items that are being evaluated, but the denotational constructs they evoke, cf. Charles Fillmore 'Verbs of judging: an exercise in semantic description' 1971:274, Jackendoff *Semantic Interpretation in Generative Grammar* 1972:379, Philip N. Johnson-Laird 'Mental models of meaning' 1981:115. Empirical evaluations of normal, unusual, and impossible sequences have to be matched in the grammar by well formedness conditions – defined for standard theory largely on selectional features. But well formedness conditions could only be determined after a sequence of lexicon items has been judged for its efficacy in a particular context. To describe the full set of well formedness conditions would entail trying every conceivable combination of lexicon items in every conceivable context, within grammatical constraints loose enough to encompass such sequences as (2.4.1.13).

(2.4.1.13) But me no buts.

Such a task is at best impracticable, and at worst impossible.

There might appear to be a life-line for interpretative semantics through Jackendoff's 1972:21 proposal that lexical insertion be constrained only by category features. This would allow for perfectly legitimate sequences like (2.4.1.14) to be generated:

(2.4.1.14) Quang says his toenail sings five-part madrigals; I guess he's tripping out again.

But it would still block novel derivations such as we saw in 'Alexander the Haigiographer' in §4.3.2. ex. (3.2.16); e.g.

(2.4.1.15) This, it was suppositioned, was a new linguistic harbingered by NATO during the time he bellwethered it. But close observers have alternatived that idea. What Haig is doing they concept, is to decouple the Russians from everything they are moded to.

To accommodate (2.4.1.13) and (2.4.1.15) we can adopt Weinreich's 1966:434 suggestion that although lexical insertion under minor class nodes should be restricted by category features, insertion under major class nodes (noun, verb, adjective, adverb) should be free. Unfortunately this would allow the grammar to generate sentences like those in (2.4.1.16), cf. §3.2.2 ex. (2.2.6):

(2.4.1.16)
  a.   *The in anded some thes.
  b.   *This blue and on speak conferenced uply.
  c.   *Peter thated nine an equipment.

Notice that reclassified words take on the regular morphological characteristics of their adopted lexical category. Assuming that a grammatical description seeks to model a native speaker's knowledge of what is grammatical in his language, these sentences must be marked as horribly deviant. The obvious recourse is to Weinreich's 1966:466 semantic evaluator: 'The function of the semantic evaluator is primarily to compute a quantitative measure of the deviance of a sentence from normality.' This is to be accomplished by reference to the output of 'construal rules' that make the best sense possible of ill-matched semantic features[12] within the complex symbol associated with a lexicon item. Obviously, the semantic evaluator presupposes a statement of well formedness conditions for lexical sequences. The specification of these well formedness conditions faces exactly the difficulties that arise when trying to define well formedness conditions on lexical insertion. To describe the full set of such conditions would require trying every conceivable combination of lexicon items in every conceivable context – which is impracticable, if not impossible.

We conclude that there are very severe difficulties met with in describing lexical insertion conditions in a standard theory model of transformational grammar, such as is presupposed by Katz's semantic theory. At best, well formedness conditions on lexical insertion will have to be written in an arbitrarily over-restrictive manner, such that the grammar generates only a proper subset of the sentences of the language. If we were to adopt the Weinreich-Jackendoff line, lexical insertion would be restricted for minor class nodes, but otherwise constrained. In that case the grammar will generate all the sentences of the language together with an infinite number of nonsentences, without any means of distinguishing between them. Neither of these solutions will satisfy the goal of observational adequacy – that the grammar should generate all and only the sequences of lexicon items judged acceptable by speakers of the language. The fact that the set of LSUPMs generated by the syntactic component is inadequate in this respect is of significance to Katz's semantic theory, because they constitute the syntactic premise on which the theory is built. Although the semantic theory can be judged independently of the syntactic objects on which it operates, it suffers analogy with a house built on sand.

5.2.4.2 Problems with semantic selection restrictions

> Each reading in the dictionary must contain a *selection restriction*, i.e. a formally expressed necessary and sufficient condition for that reading to combine with others.
>
> (Katz & Postal 1964:15)

Syntactic selection restrictions are hypothetical constructs which are supposed to constrain lexical insertion by checking that the inherent syntactic features mentioned in the selection restriction of a given lexicon item λ are compatible with the inherent features present in the syntactic description of the relevant lexicon items already inserted in the base phrase marker. Semantic selection restrictions have no effect on lexicon insertion, they only come into play after lexicon items have been inserted. They are the (only) hypothetical constructs postulated to constrain the action of the projection rule, which they do by preventing the combination of incompatible readings for sister nodes that would give the mother constituent an anomalous reading. Because Katz's lexicon entries are polysemous, (like those in standard dictionaries), a lexicon item λ may be inserted into a phrase marker provided only one of its senses is appropriate (this will be indicated by its inherent SYNTACTIC features – which we saw in (5.2.4.1) are semantically determined by exactly this condition); any other inappropriate senses that λ may have will be discarded by the projection rule on the basis of the semantic selection restrictions in the readings for its sister lexicon items. For instance, we saw in §5.2.2 the selection restriction on the direct object of the verb *hits* given in Katz & Fodor 1963:202 is ⟨(Physical Object)⟩, this marker does not appear in the reading for one sense of *ball* (viz. *ball₁*) and so this sense is thrown out when the projection rule operates to amalgamate the meaning of the object NP *the colourful ball₁* with the meaning of *hit*; the readings for the other two senses of *ball* (viz. *ball₂* and *ball₃*) do contain the semantic marker (Physical Object) and these two senses are combined with the senses for *hit*, as we saw earlier.

Semantic selection restrictions operate in a manner exactly parallel to the way syntactic selection restrictions operate: the syntactic selection restriction determines the syntactic compatibility of the lexicon item λ with co-occurrent lexicon items; the semantic selection restriction determines the semantic compatibility of a particular sense of λ with the senses of co-occurrent lexicon items. It should be obvious that the same difficulty which we met in trying to define the set of syntactic selection restrictions has to be faced when trying to define the set of semantic selection restrictions. We earlier mentioned that Katz & Fodor's selection restrictions blocked "the man arrived at the colourful assembly for the purpose of social dancing" as a possible interpretation of *the man hit the colourful ball*. Novel combinations of lexicon items, like *the apple-juice seat* (cf. §4.4), superficial contradictions like *he's a tall short man* (meaning "he's tall for a supposedly short man"), and many poetic figures, would all be blocked by semantic selection restrictions even though they occur quite normally in language. It would only be possible to state semantic well formedness conditions in terms of selection restrictions after every conceivable combination of lexicon items had been tried in every conceivable context. It is an impracticable, if not impossible task to root out anomaly in this way, and consequently it is not feasible to state semantic well formedness conditions in terms of selection restrictions on each sense in a lexicon entry.

5.2.4.3 Summary remarks on selection restrictions

The primary function of language is to communicate meanings; this is done through combining the bits of meaning encapsulated in lexicon items into "larger meanings", and clearly a "larger meaning" will impose some sort of ordering relation on the lexicon items used in utterance.[13] It follows that languages could not function as they do if they permitted just any old sequence of lexicon items to be concatenated – i.e. there cannot be a language without syntax. Some of the constraints on the ordering of language constituents can be dealt with by such devices as phrase structure and transformational rules. This is not the place to question the efficacy of such rules in general, we are interested only in lexical insertion and projection rules, and more particularly the selection restrictions which constrain the operation of these rules. Both syntactic and semantic selection restrictions serve to condition the sets of readings (senses) of lexicon items that can be combined with one another: syntactic selection restrictions condition the insertion of lexicon entries and thereby the inclusion or exclusion of all the readings for a given item in the LSUPM; semantic selection restrictions allow only a subset (but not necessarily only a proper subset) of readings from a lexicon item in the LSUPM to be combined with readings from its sisters. It follows that, in order to determine the set of selection restrictions, the grammarian must be able to predict all of the "larger meanings" that speakers of the language could wish to communicate and then decide which of these would be acceptable and which would not. It should be obvious that such a task would defeat Hercules – it may be impossible, it is certainly impracticable for mortal speakers and mortal linguists. The purpose of a linguistic theory is to explicate linguistic data; it is pointless, therefore, for the theory to postulate certain constructs (such as selection restrictions) that are supposed to explicate language data if it does not also specify the means by which such constructs can be determined from the data or be shown to correspond with the data; otherwise, the theory is inapplicable to the very data it supposedly explicates, and it will be invulnerable to empirical validation. Suppose someone were to claim that selection restrictions are revealed to us by angels in dreams that we can never consciously recollect; since this hypothesis is immune from any correspondence with language data, it cannot be invalidated –

but nor can it be shown to say anything interesting about the nature of language. We face exactly the same problem with the selection restrictions postulated in the theory of grammar of which Katz's semantic theory is a component part.

5.2.5 Katz's metalanguage: semantic representations in the lexicon

The semantic markers and distinguishers are the means by which we can decompose the meaning of one sense of a lexical item into its atomic concepts, and thus exhibit the semantic structure IN the dictionary and the semantic relations BETWEEN dictionary entries.

(Katz & Fodor 1963:185f)

5.2.5.1 Semantic markers and distinguishers

The question arises whether the distinguisher will not keep receding toward the horizon until it vanishes altogether.

(Dwight Bolinger 'The atomization of meaning' 1965:558)

There has been a good deal of criticism of the differentiation between semantic markers and distinguishers, made originally by Katz & Fodor 1963 and subsequently by Katz in other publications, cf. Bolinger 'The atomization of meaning' 1965, Weinrich 'Explorations in semantic theory' 1966, and Manfred Bierwisch 'On certain problems of semantic representation' 1969. There is evidence that everything which would be included within a distinguisher could just as well be expressed in terms of one or more semantic markers; nonetheless, Katz has steadfastly held to the distinction between semantic markers and distinguishers even though he has changed the definitions of both over the years. Although Katz still believes there is a worthwhile distinction to be made (personal communication, 1981) he has ceased to use distinguishers in work published since *Semantic Theory* 1972.

According to Katz & Fodor 1963:188 a semantic marker must occur in more than one lexicon entry, or, more correctly, in more than one reading within the lexicon; i.e. semantic markers are used to show meaning overlap between lexicon items. Antonymous sets of semantic markers, e.g. (Male) versus (Female), are postulated in the definition of antonymous expressions, contradiction, and so forth. By contrast, a distinguisher only occurs in the semantic reading of one sense of one lexicon item, therefore distinguishers 'do not enter into theoretical relations within a semantic theory' (op.cit.). In this earliest version of the semantic theory distinguishers identify the entirely idiosyncratic elements of meaning in a lexicon item; for instance it might have been noticed that the different senses for *hit* given in §5.2.2 are distinct only in their distinguishers: they share the semantic markers (Action), (Instancy), (Intensity); but one sense is distinguished as [Collides with impact], the other as [Strikes with a blow or missile]. Two of the senses of *ball* also share the semantic marker (Physical Object) and are distinguished only by the distinguishers [Having globular shape], and [Solid missile for projection by engine of war]. The distinguishers seem to capture the essential ingredients of the sense of the lexicon item.

Although each distinguisher occurs only once in the dictionary this does not stop them entering into semantic relations, contrary to what Katz & Fodor 1963:188 said (see above). In fact in his paper 'Analyticity and contradiction in natural language' 1964a:532 Katz talks of colour names being 'distinguisher-wise antonymous'; that is, he ascribes the semantic difference between colour names solely to the distinguishers in their readings, e.g.

red – Adjective – (Colour) – [Red] – ‹SR›
green – Adjective – (Colour) – [Green] – ‹SR›

Thus semantic relations like antonymy and contradiction are stated in terms of distinguishers. The only difference between semantic markers and distinguishers is that semantic markers appear more than once in the lexicon, distinguishers only once; consequently we might conclude that distinguishers are semantic markers which appear only once in the dictionary, and this is a trivial distinction between the two categories.

In 'Recent issues in semantic theory' 1967:161 Katz redefined the different functions of distinguishers and semantic markers:

> We hold that distinguishers do not enter into *the system of inter-sense congruity relations reconstructed by selection restrictions*, but [. . .] holding this is perfectly compatible with holding, as we also hold, that distinguishers [. . .] can play a role in marking many of the semantic properties and relations of a sentence.

With these redefinitions, distinguishers appear only once in the lexicon and are not named in semantic selection restrictions; semantic markers recur more than once in the lexicon and appear in the statement of semantic selection restrictions. Both grounds for discriminating between semantic markers and distinguishers are open to objection. Firstly, some distinguishers will have to be named in selection restrictions. Consider that the NP *a pale black* is a lexically well formed sequence, i.e. must be permitted by the lexical insertion rules, because it has the sense "a lighter than usual black person". However the same sequence is semantically anomalous in the sense "*a pale black colour" although such sequences as *a pale yellow (colour)* or *a pale green (colour)* are not anomalous. Thus, there has to be a semantic selection restriction on *pale* that prevents the combination of its sense with the sense of *black (colour)*; this selection restriction will necessarily name the distinguisher [Black], because this is all that distinguishes between the reading for *black* and the readings for other colours such as *yellow* and *green*. Furthermore, in *Semantic Theory* 1972:88, Katz allows that distinguishers may in fact recur more than once in the lexicon; e.g. the items *red*, *scarlet* and *vermillion* share the common distinguisher [Red]; *viridescent* and *green* share the distinguisher [Green]; and *blue* and *azure* share [Blue]. The reason Katz revised the theory in this way was that he changed the bases for discriminating between semantic markers and distinguishers for the last time.

He wrote

> Distinguishers can be regarded as providing a purely denotative
> distinction which plays the semantic role of separating lexical items
> that would otherwise be fully synonymous, such as, for instance
> 'red', 'yellow', 'blue', 'green', etc. Unlike semantic markers, which
> represent conceptual components of senses of lexical items and
> expressions, distinguishers mark purely perceptual distinctions
> among the referents of conceptually identical senses. Presumably a
> psychological theory of the mechanisms of (visual, auditory, tactile,
> and so on) perception will define the perceptual distinctions which
> distinguishers mark at the linguistic level.
>
> (Katz 1967:159, 1972:84)

Distinguishers now represent percepts, while semantic markers identify concepts. But it is clear from the final sentence quoted that Katz is unsure what constitutes a percept, and thus unclear exactly how distinguishers differ from semantic markers. Perception is generally understood to be the mental act or reflex that uses knowledge as a filtering device to categorize cues from objects, states, events, and acts in the external world; cues that have been mediated through the senses of sight, touch, hearing, taste and smell. In addition there are proprioceptions such as the sense of balance, the sense of danger, and bodily sensations like pain; Katz does not say whether he regards the distinction between *headache* and *stomachache* as marked only by distinguishers in their respective radings, but he would appear to be committed to it. All perception involves conception in the filtering process that results in categorizing the sense data; though Katz obviously cannot understand perception in this way. To comprehend his notion of perception there is only his discussion of colour terms to go on. He regards, for instance, red, green, and blue as being conceptually identical, and represents this by the common semantic marker (Colour); they are, he says, perceptually differentiated and this is represented semantically by the distinguishers [Red], [Green], and [Blue], respectively. Katz justifies this point of view with the argument that a percept such as blue is apprehended through only one of the senses, whereas a concept such as roundness is apprehended by more than one (Katz 1972:87) – presumably by sight and touch. Here he seems to be making the same distinction as was made by the seventeenth century English philosopher John Locke. Katz's concepts are defined in much the same way as Locke's 'primary qualities' of solidity, extension, figure, motion or rest, and number – characteristics which are 'utterly inseparable from the body in what estate soever it be' (Locke *Essay on Human Understanding* 1690:II:viii.9). Locke's 'secondary qualities', colour, taste, smell and sound, 'in truth are nothing in the objects themselves, but powers to produce the various sensations in us' (op.cit. II.viii.10); which seems very like Katz's notion of the perceptual distinctions to be identified by distinguishers. However, there is the equivocation over colour. Locke includes colour among his 'secondary qualities'; but does he have in mind the differentiae of colour, corresponding to Katz's percepts, or does he mean what Katz identifies as the common concept (Colour)? The answer hardly matters. Because colour can only be apprehended by the sense of sight, by Katz's own criterion he should recognize it as a percept, corresponding to Locke's 'secondary quality'. In 'Classifiers' 1977:298, Allan showed cross-language evidence for an apprehension of the difference between the 'primary' and 'secondary qualities' of objects in the noun class systems of classifier languages. Nouns are invariably classified according to characteristics of their denotata which are perceivable by more than one of the senses alone; hence, there are no known languages where a classifier indicates one of the 'secondary qualities' of a noun's denotatum. If Katz's use of the notion 'conceptual distinction' correlates with Locke's 'primary quality', and his 'perceptual distinction' with Locke's 'secondary quality', then these different theoretical constructs might well turn out to mark a useful division in semantic analysis.

There is, however, an inconsistency in Katz's application of the term 'distinguisher' which makes any such correlation impossible. Katz

1972:87 writes, 'As worked out in early discussions on semantic theory [. . .] distinguishers [. . .] mark conceptually unanalyzable, purely perceived qualities.' But it is very difficult to see how this claim could possibly be true of distinguishers such as [Having the academic degree conferred for completing the first four years of college], [When without a mate during the breeding time], [Abounding in contrast or variety of bright colours], [Collides with an impact], to list but a few of the distinguishers that appear in his early discussions on semantic theory. None of them is conceptually unanalyzable, nor is it obvious that they mark purely perceptual qualities. So the revised definition of distinguishers in *Semantic Theory* simply does not obtain for all the earlier examples of them given – which has never been revised or retracted.

Furthermore, in his last published statement on the matter, Katz claimed that 'selection restrictions hold only between conceptual components of senses' (1972:84). But we have seen that at least one colour distinguisher, [Black], will have to be named in a selection restriction; this implies that [Black] should be a conceptual component of sense, and be represented by a semantic marker, not a distinguisher, viz. by (Black). If one colour term is differentiated by a conceptual component of sense, other colour terms ought to be, too. If colour terms are to be differentiated conceptually, and this is indicated in lexicon entries by the use of semantic markers such as (Black), (Red), (Green), etc., then Katz's only instantiation of the revised definition of distinguishers has gone. Furthermore, his distinction between conceptual and perceptual distinctions cannot be made to match with Locke's identification of 'primary' and 'secondary qualities' of objects. All in all, it is overwhelmingly evident that Katz's semantic theory would be better if distinguishers were dropped altogether.

How should distinguishers be disposed of? In 'The atomization of meaning' 1965, Dwight Bolinger demonstrated a method for dispersing distinguishers into semantic markers, using Katz & Fodor's own discovery procedure for markers. Although it is not exactly clear how Katz & Fodor 1963 light upon all the semantic markers presented in their paper, they do say that markers are the means by which disambiguations are effected. Consider three of the senses they give (p.186) for *bachelor*.

bachelor$_1$ – Noun – (Human) – (Male) – [who has never married]
bachelor$_2$ – Noun – (Human) – (Male) – [young knight serving under the standard of another knight]
bachelor$_3$ – Noun – (Animal) – (Male) – [young fur seal when without a mate during the breeding time]

Two senses of *bachelor*, *bachelor₁* and *bachelor₂*, differ only in respect of their distinguishers. However, the sentence *The old bachelor finally died* cannot be using 'bachelor' in the sense of *bachelor₂* because the sense "*the old young knight . . . finally died" would be contradictory; and at this time such semantic properties could be defined only on semantic markers, not on distinguishers; consequently, Katz & Fodor postulate a semantic marker (Young) to be included in the sense of *bachelor₂*. This same marker can also be used in the reading for *bachelor₃*. The resulting changes to the dictionary entry for *bachelor* are shown in Figure 5.4.

Bolinger 1965 points out that if the pattern of Katz & Fodor's extraction of the semantic marker (Young) from the distinguishers in *bachelor₂* and *bachelor₃* is used to effect all the disambiguations necessary in the semantic description of a language, 'the question arises whether the distinguisher will not keep receding towards the horizon until it vanishes altogether' (p.558, and cf. Weinreich 1966:398). To prove his point, Bolinger uses the Katz & Fodor disambiguation scheme to replace all the distinguishers in Figure 5.4 with semantic markers; his nifty arguments deserve to be quoted in full.

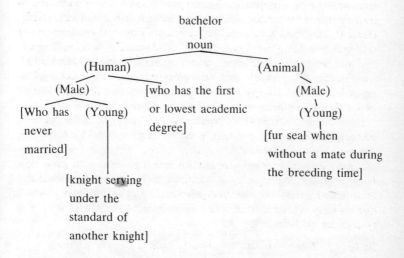

Figure 5.4   The revised entry for *bachelor* from Katz & Fodor 1963:190

1. *He became a bachelor*. This rules out 'the man who has never married' – it is impossible to become one who has never done something. We can extract the *-ever* part of *never* from the distinguisher and set up a marker (Nonbecoming).

2. *The seven-year-old bachelor sat on the rock*. The definition 'male who has never married' was deficient. It should have been something like 'adult male who has never married', and from that expanded distinguisher we now extract the marker (Adult).

3 *Lancelot was the unhappiest of all the bachelors after his wife died*. This seems to justify raising (Unmarried) to marker status and wipes out the distinguisher on one of the branches: *bachelor* – noun – (Human) – (Male) – (Adult) – (Non-becoming) – (Unmarried).

4. *That peasant is a happy bachelor*. Being a peasant is not compatible with being a knight. There must be a marker of status lying around somewhere. A knight has to be of gentle birth. Let us extract (Noble) from the distinguisher (leaving the degree of nobility for the moment undisturbed as still part of the knight's distinguisher).

5. *George is one bachelor who is his own boss*. This eliminates the knight, and turns 'serving under' into another status marker that might be called (Dependent).

6. *George is a bachelor in the service of the Queen*. This again eliminates the knight, and yields a marker that shows the direction of the (Dependency) relationship: it is to the person on the next higher rung of the (Nobility) ladder. I suggest (Proximate), dominated by (Dependent).

7. *Knight banneret Gawain is a bachelor*. This eliminates the lower status of the knight bachelor, and admits (Inferior) as a restriction on (Noble).

8. *At some time in his life every man is a bachelor*. This eliminates both the knight and the B.A., because status has no bearing. We can therefore add a generalized status marker to those other two meanings. I call it (Hierarchic).

9. *A bachelor is expected to fight*. This puts the hierarchy in its proper setting, with a superior marking (Military). There is now no distinguisher left on the knighthood branch; it reads *bachelor* – noun – (Human) – (Male) – (Military) – (Hierarchic) – (Noble) – (Inferior) – (Dependent) – (Proximate) – (Young).

10. *He's studying hard to be a bachelor*. Again there is suggested a possible hierarchic setting of some kind. I will use (Educand).

11. *Employers prefer married men who are at least bachelors; without the degree you hardly have a chance*. This confirms that the general status marker (Hierarchic) should be repeated on this path.

12. *At the age of twenty-five he ceased to be a bachelor, but he never married.* This has to refer to the knight, and points to a marker akin to the (Nonbecoming) that was added to the 'unmarried man' branch: one cannot become an unmarried man, but can cease to be one; one could both become and cease to be a knight bachelor; one can become but not cease to be a bachelor of arts. The position on the academic ladder is therefore (Permanent), and sets off *bachelor* from *sophomore*, for example. As we already have the marker (Inferior) on the knighthood branch, we can add it here and eliminate the distinguisher. The B.A. comes out *bachelor* – noun – (Human) – (Educand) – (Hierarchic) – (Permanent) – (Inferior).
13. *That pet of mine is always nuzzling me and barking and wagging his flippers.* I include this to show that the system will need, somewhere, to discriminate (Canine) and (Phocine), whence (Phocine) should be extracted from the distinguisher and set up on this path, beneath (Animal). Without going through another series of disambiguations, we can lay down the path *bachelor* – noun – (Animal) – (Phocine) – (Hirsute) – (Male) – (Adult) – (Young) – (Unmated) as an almost complete characterization of the seal by means of markers alone. [. . .]

Where it was sufficient to designate the human being as (Adult), since human beings do not rut and the whole of their adulthood is characterized by availability for mating, seals do have their season, and (Adult) is not sufficient; one can have a yong adult male fur seal without a mate which is still not a bachelor if the time is wrong. 'During the mating season' seems an unlikely candidate for a marker, until we realize that when we call someone – human or animal – a bachelor, we mean that he is without a mate at a time when he is expected to have one: incidentally the whole of adulthood in the human being, incidentally the mating season in the seal. The marker then is (Availability of Mating), or, to use a single appropriate term, (Nubile). If we find that *The migrating bachelors stopped to rest* is unambiguous because we know that the seal's migrating season does not coincide wth his mating season, and therefore the bachelors must be human, we are employing our 'knowledge of the world'. In other words, (Nubile) can be purified of its temporal associations just as *knight* can, by banishing them to our 'knowledge of the world', and the entry for *bachelor* can now be diagrammed with markers only, as in Figure [5.5].

(Bolinger 1965:558-60, 562-3).

314 *The semantic interpretation of sentences*

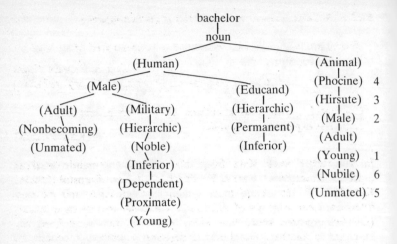

The numbers on the right are the order of which the markers appear in the dictionary definition: 1 – Young, 2 – Male, 3 – Fur, 4 – Seal, 5 – Without a Mate, 6 – During the Mating Season.

Figure 5.5   The dictionary entry for *bachelor* from Bolinger 1965:563

Thus did Bolinger demonstrate how distinguishers could be removed from semantic readings.[14] He advocates that distinguishers could be used to represent pragmatic rather than semantic information, to incorporate knowledge of the world (what Katz 1972:450-2 calls 'broad concepts') into the grammar. For instance they might portray such information as that *bachelor* in the sense [knight serving under the standard of another knight] would not, in the twentieth century, be a valent interpretation of the word out of some specialized medieval or lexicographical context. Bolinger also suggests that lists of possible referents be included in the distinguisher; e.g. *Julius*, *Augustus*, *Tiberius* etc. might appear in the distinguisher for *caesar*. Possibly distinguishers might carry such information as that cats miaow and purr, have sleek fur, and mostly have retractile claws. But it is dubious whether this kind of encyclopaedic information should be included within semantic theory at all; Katz has certainly rejected the notion (cf. Katz 1972:450-2). Whatever one's conclusion about the possible functions of distinguishers, nothing Katz has written justifies differentiating them from semantic markers within his semantic theory.

5.2.5.2   Semantic markers as concepts and as abstract objects

A semantic marker can be thought of as a certain kind of name of a universal concept.

> (Katz & Richard Nagel
> 'Meaning postulates and semantic theory' 1974:363)

Concepts [. . .] are abstract entities. They do not belong to the conscious experience of anyone.

> (Katz 1972:38)

In his earlier work Katz frequently said that semantic markers represent concepts, cf. Katz & Fodor 1963:210, Katz & Postal 1964:16, Katz 1972:37. He viewed these concepts as universal, and we may interpret them in terms of Aristotle's universal 'mental experiences' (*On Interpretation* §16a, 4) – which allow for translation from one language to another. We should understand a 'universal' concept as one which any human being can conceive, and not as one which necessarily exists in every human's mind. Katz's claim that semantic markers name universal concepts constitutes a claim that his meta-language for a semantic theory is applicable to all natural languages because its basic constructs are correlated with the human ability to conceptualize. Katz explains what he means by the conceptual content of semantic markers in the following passage.

> A semantic marker is a theoretical term that designates a class of equivalent concepts or ideas. Consider the idea each of us thinks of as part of the meaning of the words 'chair', 'stone', 'man', 'building', 'planet', etc., but not part of the meaning of such words as 'truth', 'togetherness', 'feeling', 'shadow', 'integer', 'departure', etc. – the idea that we take to express what is common to the meaning of the words in the former group and that we use to conceptually distinguish them from those in the latter. Roughly, we might characterize what is common to our individual ideas as the notion of a spatially and temporally contiguous material thing. The semantic marker (Physical object) is introduced to designate that notion. It provides a means of expressing the generalization that the words in the former group are semantically similar in this conceptual respect whereas they differ in meaning from the words in the latter group in the same respect. Such generalizations are expressed by including this semantic marker in the lexical readings for the words in the former group and excluding it from the readings for those in the latter.

> (Katz 1967:129-30)

It is clear from this that Katz's semantic markers are semantic components determined on the basis of intuition and reflexion, rather than on the basis of commutation within a distinctive feature matrix such as we find in Hjelmslev 1943:63, Harris 1948, or Lyons 1968:470ff – cf. §3.5.2.

Although Katz 1967 describes the conceptual content of the semantic marker as 'what is common to our individual ideas', in *Semantic Theory* he has already moved away from this psycholinguistic position towards the Platonist conception of linguistic theory that is argued for in *Language and Other Abstract Objects* 1981 and 'An outline of Platonist grammar' in press. The description which Katz 1972 gives of the content of semantic markers is somewhat confusing. While saying that a semantic marker represents a concept, he also says that a concept is not something any individual has in mind on any particular occasion (nor any number of people on any number of occasions), because 'Concepts [. . .] are abstract entities. They do not belong to the conscious experience of anyone' (Katz 1972:38). This unintentionally suggests that concepts are unknowable, which would make a concept a useless datum for a construct in semantic theory because it could have no explicative nor explanatory value. In any case, the content of semantic markers does fall within people's conscious experience, otherwise it could not be described and understood as Katz 1967:129f describes it (in the passage quoted above) to our understanding. What Katz would probably say nowadays, is that semantic markers represent abstract theoretical concepts in the metalanguage of a semantic theory i.e. they are emic constructs; they may or may not correspond to concepts in the object language, but they are not equivalent to concepts in the object language. I conclude that we should consider semantic markers to be abstract, emic, constructs whose etic counterparts are concepts in the minds of speakers of the object language.

5.2.5.3 The form and structure of semantic markers

> Although semantic markers are given in the orthography of a natural language, they cannot be identified with words or expressions of the language that is employed to give them suggestive labels.
>
>   (Katz 'Semantic theory and the meaning of "good" ' 1964b:744)

According to Katz, his semantic markers should not be taken at face value as words of English bounded by parentheses; it will become apparent that this is an empty claim. In the days when Katz believed that semantic markers represented concepts, he thought the concepts should be represented iconically, cf.

> [Semantic markers] have internal structure and can be components of other semantic markers, for they are intended to reflect, in their formal structure, the structure of the concepts represented by them. [. . .] For example, (Physical Object), although not presently definable, should eventually be replaced by some formal configuration of symbols whose internal structure represents the notion of some physical entity constituted of spatio-temporally contiguous parts which endures in form unless its permanence is terminated by outside influence.
>
> (Katz 1967:167f)

(Cf. also 'The advantage of semantic theory over predicate calculus' Katz 1977b:385.) An iconic representation of the notion 'physical object' in terms of a formal configuration of symbols is impossible to imagine – which probably accounts for the fact that nothing like it has been forthcoming. The closest thing to it is the form of words Katz used to describe a physical object, namely 'some physical entity constituted of spatio-temporally contiguous parts which endures in form unless its permanence is terminated by outside influence.' Now that Katz believes semantic markers to be abstract theoretical constructs this form of words should seem a perfectly adequate representation of the constitution of the notion physical object, one that might be compared with the formula H_2SO_4 as a description of the constitution of sulphuric acid: the difference is that one uses the vocabulary and syntax of English, the other uses the conventional vocabulary and syntax of chemical formulae. It is not uninteresting that the language of chemical formulae can be translated into a proper subset of English, but the converse doesn't hold. We mention chemical formulae at this point because Katz compared the formal constructs of his theory to them in 'Semantic theory and the meaning of "good" ' 1964b:744. His semantic markerese is like chemical formulae in that it translates into English; but it is unlike chemical formulae in having neither a conventional vocabulary nor a conventional syntax – as we shall demonstrate.

In §4.12.5 we discussed the properties necessary in a semantic metalanguage like semantic markerese pretends to be. We said that a formal metalanguage should have a specified vocabulary of symbols whose forms and correlated meanings are fully defined; that all the combinations of these vocabulary items acceptable within the metalanguage should be generated from fully specified syntactic axioms and rules of syntax; and that the meanings of all these syntactically well formed structures should be fully specified by semantic rules and axioms for the metalanguage. We further pointed out that the metalanguage would necessarily be exactly equivalent to a natural language. It follows then that to define the vocabulary, syntax and semantics of a metalanguage would be the same kind of task as describing the grammar for a natural language such as the object language which the metalanguage is being invented to describe! It is justifiable to escape from this paradox by deciding to use a natural language for a metalanguage, because the lexicon, syntax, and semantics of a natural language is already specified – albeit implicitly.

Since Katz has never specified a grammar for semantic markerese it does not constitute a formal metalanguage. In fact, semantic markerese is only interpretable in terms of the English expressions used in the semantic markers and – where relevant – the distinguishers, cf. §4.12.5 exx. (12.5.1-2). We can easily demonstrate that it is only through identifying semantic markers with the English expressions within them that they have any value whatsoever. Compare Figure 5.6 which reproduces the dictionary entry for *bachelor* from Katz & Postal 1964, with Figure 5.7 where all the semantic markers from Figure 5.6 are replaced by arbitrary proper names in a one-to-one correlation; the resulting would-be dictionary entry is nothing short of gibberish, even though the distinguishers are left intact.[15] It follows that unless we identify Katz's semantic markers with the English words employed in them, his dictionary entries are worthless; and we are led to conclude that semantic markerese is simply a notational variant of English, cf. Harrison 1974:601. Semantic markers may be theoretical constructs, but the claim that they are not to be identified with English expressions is an empty one.

Katz has not substantiated his claim that simply expressed semantic markers like (Human) and (Physical Object) have a complex internal structure, cf. Katz 1967:167, Katz & Nagel 1974:325 n.33. However, since the time of 'Semantic theory and the meaning of "good" ' 1964b:785f Katz has been writing complex semantic markers for verbs. Take the reading for *chase* given in Katz 1967:169.[16]

(2.5.3.1) (((Activity of X) (*Nature*: (Physical)) (Motion) (*Rate*: (Fast)) (*Character*: (Following Y)) (*Intention*: (Trying to catch ((Y) (Motion))) ⟨SR⟩

Here is a marker (or reading) containing other semantic markers within it. The marker (Activity of X) classes *chase* with verbs such as *eat*,

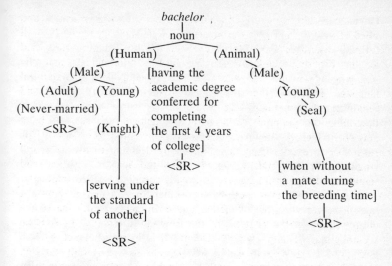

Figure 5.6 The lexicon entry for *bachelor* from Katz & Postal 1964:14

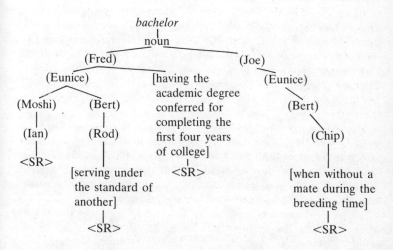

Figure 5.7 Katz & Postal's lexicon entry for *bachelor* with the semantic markers replaced by arbitrary proper names

speak, *walk* and *remember* as against state verbs like *sleep* or *wait*, and process verbs like *grow*, or *freeze*. The marker (*Rate*: (Fast)) distinguishes *chase* from *creep* and *walk*; (*Character*: (Following Y)) distinguishes it from *flee* or *wander*. The variables 'X' and 'Y' indicate where the readings for subject and object NPs should be inserted, thus imposing a structure onto the semantic interpretation projected onto the phrase marker by projection rules. This innovation, which leads to the embedding of one reading into another, counters objections from Weinreich and others that the amalgamation rules proposed in the earliest versions of the theory destroy syntactic structure through Boolean conjunction of all pairs of semantic readings, cf. §5.2.2 exx. (2.2.6-7).

In the 1966 and 1967 versions of the reading for the verb *chase* the grammatical relations held by arguments 'X' and 'Y' are informally indicated, and have to be determined by intuitions about English syntax. In *Semantic Theory* 1972 Katz formally represents these grammatical relations by categorizing the variables, i.e. identifying which NP node they must occupy on the LSUPM; cf. the reading for *chase* given in Katz 1972:106.

(2.5.3.2)

(((Activity) (((Physical))

$$((\text{Movement}) ((\text{Speed})^{(\text{Fast})} \quad (\text{Following} \begin{smallmatrix} [NP,VP,PP,\Sigma] \\ X \\ \langle(\text{Object})\rangle \end{smallmatrix})))$$

$$((\text{Purpose}) ((\text{To catch} \begin{smallmatrix} [NP,VP,PP,\Sigma] \\ X \\ \langle(\text{Object})\rangle \end{smallmatrix})))))$$

$$\begin{smallmatrix} [NP,\Sigma] \\ X \\ \langle(\text{Human}) \end{smallmatrix}_{v} (\text{Animal})\rangle)$$

The object being purposefully followed ('Y' in the earlier versions) is here identified as the argument holding the grammatical relation [NP,VP,PP,Σ), that is to say the NP daughter of the VP which is daughter of the PP (predicate phrase), which is the daughter of Σ.[17] The activity of chasing is carried out by an animate argument (human or animal) holding the relation [NP,Σ], i.e. the NP daughter of Σ – the subject NP. This convention for identifying tree relations was established by Chomsky 1965:71. It should be noted that although the introduction of categorized variables incorporates structural conditions into semantic interpretation as part of a semantic representation, the categorization refers to the structure of the LSUPM: otherwise we should not know which NP reading to substitute for the variable in the predicate.

The complex semantic marker for *chase* in (2.5.3.2) comprises the whole reading for one sense of the verb, and contains within it a supposedly structured set of constituent semantic markers. Thus it seems justifiable to treat complex semantic markers as readings.

It will be noted that each categorized variable is accompanied by a semantic selection restriction referring to a semantic marker required in the reading for whatever replaces the variable. As we have seen, selection restrictions establish semantic well formedness conditions on the combined reading for a predicate and its argument: the combination will be semantically well formed if the argument contains the semantic marker (or one of the disjunctions of semantic markers) named in the selection restriction on the categorized variable in the reading for the predicate; otherwise it will be ill formed. Under the reading for *chase* given in (2.5.3.2) *the clouds chased each other across the sky* will be deemed semantically ill formed because 'clouds' will have neither of the semantic markers (Human) or (Animal). A comparable judgement would be made of *the Phantom chased the Mig over the border*. In fact, both sentences are semantically acceptable so the selection restrictions stated on the subject NP of *chase* need revising. In view of what was said in §5.2.4 it would be surprising if the selection restrictions on *chase* could be stated satisfactorily.

It has been claimed that 'semantic markers have the formal structure of phrase markers: a semantic marker is a string of elements properly bracketed with labelled bracketing' (Katz & Nagel 1974:325). Without guidance from Katz it would be difficult to substantiate this claim. Although clearly some of the bracketing in the reading for *chase* is equivalent to tree structuring, it is not obvious what the rules for semantic tree construction would be. Doubts on this matter are not assuaged by the fact that Katz has offered two different tree structures for the semantic reading of *chase*; they are given in Figures 5.8 and 5.9. In *Semantics: Theories of Meaning in Generative Grammar*, Janet D. Fodor 1977:173 & 175, proposes two additional tree representations based on the parentheses in (2.5.3.2). This is no insignificant jibe; it points to the very real problem with Katzian semantic representations: that no rules for constructing semantic markers have been described. Katz has never properly discussed either the vocabulary or syntax of semantic markerese, so that we can only learn to interpret his metalanguage by induction from his examples; and it is disconcerting that the semantic representation of *chase*, for instance, has changed in

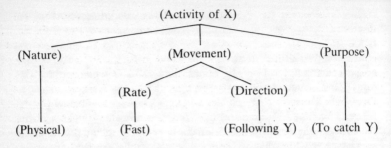

Figure 5.8   The semantic reading for *chase* from Katz & Nagel 1974:325

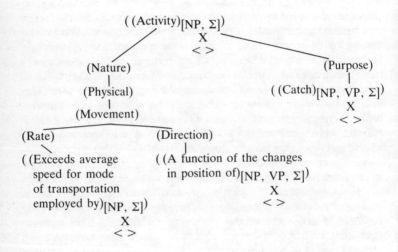

Figure 5.9   Semantic reading for *chase* in Katz *Propositional Structure and Illocutionary Force* 1977a:62

every published version (1966, 1967, 1972, 1974 and 1977a).

Although the structural conditions on complex semantic markers have never been stated, we might take as a starting point for discussion Katz's claim that they have the formal structure of phrase markers – by which he must mean syntactic phrase markers. Whereas it might be justifiable to say that his readings for *chase* are equivalent to tree structures, it is absurd to compare them with the phrase markers of, say, standard theory grammar which are generated by familiar rewrite rules, or alternatively by node admissibility conditions of the kind discussed by McCawley in 'On the base component of a transformational grammar' 1968a. To begin with, syntactic phrase markers are constituent structure trees: all nodes dominated by node Γ are constituents of Γ. For the most part the constituency is well established, by a tradition of parsing that goes back at least to Dionysios Thrax in the first century BC, and which is based on the formal, functional, and distributional characteristics of the syntactic constructs. But there is no set of discovery procedures for semantic parsing (as it were) that are relevant to the case in hand. Katz has not explained on what basis he decided that the semantic marker (Direction) is a constituent of (Activity) – if it is; nor why (Movement) is mothered by (Activity) in Fig. 5.8, but mothered by (Physical) in Fig. 5.9. However, he has written of Fig. 5.9 that 'the concept of physicalness is used to qualify the concept of activity' (Katz 1977a:65); and the relocation of (Movement) under (Physical) may therefore be justified because movement is a kind of physical activity. But this leaves the position of (Nature) and (Purpose) to be explained, since neither is a kind of activity. Nor are (Direction) and (Rate) kinds of movement. So there is no consistent relationship of this sort (nor, indeed, its converse) between semantic markers in the tree. Furthermore, there could be no comparing the relationship 'A is a kind of B, if B mothers A' with relations holding between nodes in a syntactic phrase marker. Given such a phrase marker in which Sentence mothers Noun Phrase which mothers Noun; it is not true to say that Noun is a kind of Sentence, or that the concept of nounness qualifies the concept of sentencehood; and the converse, Sentence is a kind of Noun, etc. is equally absurd. As if to confirm that he never intended (Movement) to be understood as a constituent of (Activity), Katz 1972:167 analyzes both these semantic markers in a way which fails to reveal any relationship between them:

(Activity) = (Performs a sequence of related acts from $[X]_{\langle\rangle}$ to $[X]_{\langle\rangle}$)

where the categorization of the variables is to be 'given in terms of grammatical relations between the tense constituent and the verb within the same predicate phrase and between temporal adverbials and the verb within the same predicate phrase' (Katz 1972:166f); and

(Movement) = (Covers the distance from $[X]_{\langle\rangle}$ to $[X]_{\langle\rangle}$)

where the categorization of the variables is to be 'given in terms of grammatical relations between locative adverbials and the verb within the same predicate phrase.' It is clear that in no sense does (Activity) contain (Movement). So, the tree representations of semantic markers and readings do not mark constituency relations; and to that extent they are significantly different from (syntactic) phrase markers.

The use of tree structures in semantic markers and readings does render them trivially similar to the tree structures of phrase markers. But tree structures can be used in the representation of taxonomies other than linguistic ones – e.g. biological taxa and genealogies can be represented on trees. Thus the structure of a semantic reading is trivially comparable with a family tree as well as a phrase marker.

We conclude that the structure of semantic markers and readings in Katzian semantics cannot be seriously compared to the structure of syntactic phrase markers, for the following reasons. (i) The vocabulary of category symbols used in the construction of phrase markers is, by and large, drawn from a standard, conventionally agreed upon set, with relatively few members; the vocabulary of semantic markerese is not. (ii) The nature of the rules for the construction of phrase markers is generally agreed upon, even though there is variation between models in the standard set of rules employed; but no standard set of rules for constructing semantic markers and readings has ever been proposed by Katz nor anyone else, nor is there any general agreement about the nature of such rules – as may be judged from the discrepancies between Katz's five published versions of the semantic marker (reading) for *chase*, and the additional two in Fodor 1977. (iii) Phrase markers indicate a hierarchy of constituent relations in the transitive daughter-of-Γ relation (or, conversely, the mother-of-Γ relation); but there is no firm evidence for comparable constituency relations in Katz's semantic trees.[18]

It is conceivable that semantic marker trees capture some other sort of relation. For instance Katz 1977a:68 writes of Fig. 5.9 that 'the notation provides a domain for entailment definition.' But he cannot be referring to an entailment relation defined on dominance relations between semantic markers in a tree, because, for example (Activity) does not entail (Physical), nor does (Physical) entail (Activity); similarly, (Purpose) does not entail (Catch), nor vice versa.

Writing of the earlier forms of complex semantic marker illustrated by the 1966, 1967 and 1972 readings for *chase*, where parenthesization was used instead of tree structuring, Katz says:

Instead of such parenthesization, we could use the standard notation of predicate calculi (see Bierwisch 1969). In certain cases, however, the parenthesis notation far better reflects the structure of complex concepts (e.g. the representation of processes, [. . .]), and, in general, the parenthesis notation is more convenient for the statement of rules.

(Katz 1972:166 n.21)

Cf. Katz 'The advantage of semantic theory over predicate calculus' 1977b. While his final comment may be true for Katz, there is no evidence that it holds for any other scholar, presumably because no one else knows the rules for constructing Katzian semantic readings (and even he is not consistent). It would be no recommendation for Katz's semantic theory if his semantic markers were equivalent to the calculi of predicate logic, because predicate logic is inadequate for the semantic representation of natural language; yet this is the logical system used in the only published translations of Katzian markers into logical form. Compare Katz's 1967 semantic marker for chase in (2.6.3.3) with Bierwisch's translation of it in (2.5.3.4).

(2.5.3.3) (((Activity of X) (*Nature*: (Physical)) (Motion) (*Rate*: (Fast)) (*Character*: (Following Y)) (*Intention*: (Trying to catch ((Y) (Motion)))

(Katz 1967:169)

(2.5.3.4) [Physical] Activity & [Fast] Motion]X & [Following]XY & [Trying]X ([Catch]XY) & [Motion]Y
(Manfred Bierwisch 'On certain problems of semantic representation' 1969:160 (8))

It is only in the vocabulary that there is any interesting similarity between the two; there is a striking difference in structure. Bierwisch has used the standard and conventional syntax of predicate logic, but the syntax of Katz's semantic marker is neither standard nor conventional. Katz has often claimed, but failed to demonstrate, that his metalanguage – semantic markerese – directly captures all the subtleties of natural language and offers a natural logic which is a better instrument for logical analysis than artificial metalanguages such as predicate calculus, quantificational logic, the intensional logics developed by Montague and Cresswell, and Carnap's meaning postulates, cf. 'Logic and language: an examination of recent criticisms of intensionalism' 1975a, 'The dilemma between orthodoxy and identity' 1975b, 'The advantage of semantic theory over predicate calculus in the representation of logical form in natural language'

1977b, 'Literal meaning and logical theory' 1981b. Because semantic markerese is supposedly a formal metalanguage which maps S's knowledge of his language without confusing it with S's use of his language, Katz believes it to be a better instrument for language philosophy than anything offered by the so-called 'ordinary language philosophers' such as the Wittgenstein of *Philosophical Investigations*, or Austin or Searle (cf. ch.8). However, this claim falls flat because Katz's semantic markerese is not in fact a formal metalanguage.

Nowhere has Katz presented and explicated the syntax of his semantic markers, or offered a satisfactory comparison of their structural mechanisms with either a logical system or the syntax of a natural language. All he has said is that 'their parts and the formal relations among them [sc. the parts] mirror the parts and logical relations among them in the concept [represented by the semantic marker]' (Katz 'The advantage of semantic theory over predicate calculus' 1977b:385). We have already criticized the notion that a semantic marker can be an iconic representation of meaning; and in any case it does not help in the interpretation of Katz's metalanguage. The only way to substantiate the claim that (2.5.3.3), for instance, represents the meaning of *chase* is to point out that we can go some way to understanding this semantic marker because it uses familiar lexicon items from English, and we try to match the combined meanings of these lexicon items with what we already know (as speakers of English) about the meaning of *chase*. Thus, we use the same technique in trying to comprehend Katzian semantic markers and readings as Katz, in 'Semi-sentences' 1964c, postulates for interpreting what he calls semi-sentences, e.g. *Man bit dog* or *Scientists truth the universe*. There he writes, 'A string is a semi-sentence of the language L if and only if it is not generated by an optimal grammar of L and has sufficient structure to be understood by the speakers of L' (p.410). This is as much as to say, that Katz's metalanguage is a degenerate form of English. We have argued here and in §4.12.5 that a natural language may function as its own metalanguage; so we might reformulate the semantic marker for *chase* given in (2.5.3.3) into something close to natural English such as in (2.5.3.5):

(2.5.3.5) X is quickly following the moving object Y with the intention of catching it.

This meaning description uses not only the standard and conventional vocabulary of English, it is also structured by the standard and conventional (if not fully specified) rules of English syntax. Consequently, as a metalanguage, it is superior to Katz's unconventional, nonstandard, and ill-explained metalanguage.

Having lambasted Katz's metalanguage it may appear fruitless to continue discussing the semantic theory that employs it; but this is not so, for two reasons. Firstly the complaint that Katz's metalanguage is simply a degenerate form of English is based on discussion of the 1964 dictionary entry for *bachelor* and the various semantic markers for *chase*; it could be either confirmed or disconfirmed by looking at some other, later uses of the metalanguage, and we shall proceed to examine it further. Secondly, whatever the faults of his metalanguage, the scope of Katz's semantic theory is wide, and it is salutory to consider some of the problems Katz has identified, and the ways in which he has sought to solve them. Heeding the adage not to throw out the baby with the bathwater, we shall continue discussing Katzian semantics.

5.2.5.4 Katz's metalanguage and the semantics of time, tense, and aspect

Any semantic theory will require some representation of time, in order to (a) describe tense and temporal adverbs; (b) to specify states – which don't change over time – and contrast them with processes, which do; and (c) to give a proper account of the meaning of a verb like *promise*, which undertakes a future obligation. Katz offers no new insight into the semantics of time and tense; his principal purpose was to develop a notation for the representation of time within the metalanguage of his semantic theory.

Simple past, present and future are represented by $(t^{(-n)})$, $(t^{(o)})$, and $(t^{(+n)})$ respectively; and we shall call these 'points of orientation for the clause'. (t) is 'some unspecified position on the time dimension' (Katz 1972:312); (o) is simultaneous with the moment of utterance; $(-n)$ is an unspecified number of time units before the moment of utterance; and $(+n)$ is an unspecified number of units after it. It transpires that 'a unit of time' is one second: 'I choose the "second" as the basic unit of time because it is the smallest temporal unit for which there is a simple name in common speech' (Katz 1972:324). This is an extraordinary choice for a semantic theory that pretends to model native speakers' conceptualizations: it has the effect of translating *the dynasty endured five centuries* into *the dynasty endured 15778800000 seconds*; which would almost certainly be inaccurate in fact, because *five centuries* is normally used as a vague time span rather than a precise one. Such absurdity is totally unnecessary; the notion 'unit of time' should be left unspecified. This criticism has even greater force if semantic theory treats language as an abstract object.

Perfect aspect is represented by the reading in (2.5.4.1).

(2.5.4.1)

$$[\text{T,Aux,PP},\Sigma] \qquad ([\alpha]) \qquad [\text{Asp,Aux,PP},\Sigma]$$
$$(\quad X \quad) \qquad X \qquad (\quad X \quad +(-r))$$
$$(t \quad \langle\;\rangle \quad), \; (\langle(\text{Event})\rangle \text{ at } (t \quad \langle\;\rangle \quad))$$

The first categorized variable is the lexical reading of the tense form. The second part of the formula is intended to pick out a member of the relevant class of time adverbials, one denoting an event such as *by Christmas*, or *by the time Cedric arrives*. The rightmost categorized variable picks out the aspect marker, whose point of orientation is determined by either the Tense constituent in the Auxiliary, or a temporal adverb. The point of orientation is modified by $(-r)$, indicating a number of time units prior to it. We can illustrate this with the sentences (2.5.4.2-3).

(2.5.4.2) John had left when Bill arrived.

(2.5.4.3) John will have left when Bill arrives.

The point of orientation identified by the temporal adverb in (2.5.4.2) is $(t^{(-n)})$, so the output of (2.5.4.1) applied to (2.5.4.2) is to give a time reading for 'had left' of $(t^{(-n+(-r))})$, i.e. sometime before Bill arrived. In (2.5.4.3) 'when Bill arrives' is semantically future, $(t^{(+n)})$, and so the output of (2.5.4.1) applied to (2.5.4.3) is $(t^{(+n+(-r))})$, i.e. sometime in the future before Bill arrives. One advantage of this system is that it enables an appropriate semantic reading to be assigned past nonfinites as in *To have won that battle would have won the war*. According to Katz 1972:319 (7.77) & 321, the semantic representation of the present perfect $(t^{(o+(-r))})$ reduced to $(t^{(-n)})$, the past. But a regrettable effect of this analysis is failure to distinguish between the pairs in (2.6.4.4-5).

(2.5.4.4)
  a. John has come.
  b. John came.

(2.5.4.5)
  a. John has been crying.
  b. John was crying.

The (a) and (b) sentences are not synonymous. And in fact the reduction of $(t^{(o+(-r))})$ to $(t^{(-n)})$ is illegitimate; it should be reduced to $(t^{(-r)})$, which could be taken to represent a retrospective viewpoint rather than a past, cf. William E. Bull *Time, Tense, and the Verb* 1960; Otto Jespersen *The Philosophy of Grammar* 1924:269, *A Modern English Grammar Part IV* 1931:2, 361; Hans Reichenbach *Elements of Symbolic Logic* 1947:290ff. This would much better account for the fact that the English perfect translates into say Manx, or Welsh, as it does;

(2.5.4.6)

a. V'ad   er   n'gholl   gys   Albin.   [Manx]
   were   they   after   going to Scotland
   'They had gone to Scotland'

b. Mae   John   wedi   cicio   Bill.   [Welsh]
   is   John   after   kicking   Bill
   'John has kicked Bill'

c. Mae   Bill   wedi   cael   ei   cicio   gan   John. [Welsh]
   is   Bill   after getting his   kicking   by   John
   'Bill has been kicked by John'

Katz 1972:314 represents the semantics of *after* by $(-r)$, which would account for the synonymy between such English pairs as

(2.5.4.7)

a. The up train came in when the down train had left.
b. The up train came in after the down train left.

However, it might appear that (2.5.4.8) ought, on this analysis, to be contradictory:

(2.5.4.8) The up train came in before the down train had left.

But this is to overlook the fact that the prospective 'before' is not defined on the same time point as the retrospective 'had left'; in fact the retrospective functions as the reference point to which 'before' is prospective. This is clarified if we put in some explicit time points:

(2.5.4.9) The up train came in at 5, before the down train had left,

$$\text{which it did at} \begin{cases} 5.01 \\ 6. \\ *4. \\ *5. \end{cases}$$

It is not clear exactly how Katz would formally describe the temporal relations demonstrated here.

The progressive aspect is represented as in (2.5.4.10)

(2.5.4.10) $(t^{\S u)}) \rightarrow ((t^{(\S u+(-r_1))}),.\ .\ .,(t^{(\S u)}),.\ .\ .,(t^{(\S u+(+r_2))}))$

The symbol '$(t^{(\S u)})$' is the reading for past, present or future, '$\S$' being a variable over the signs '$+$' and '$-$'; 'u' a variable over 'o' and 'n'. The time specification for (2.5.4.11) is (2.5.4.12).

(2.5.4.11) John was eating soup.

(2.5.4.12) $((t^{(-n+(-r_1))}),.\ .\ .,(t^{(-n)}),.\ .\ .,(t^{(-n+(+r_2))}))$

(This is also the time specification, Katz 1972:320f tells us, for *John has been eating soup*.) The point of orientation for the progressive aspect is clearly $(t^{(\S u)})$ from which the event is viewed both retrospectively, indicated by the $(-r_1)$ superscript, and prospectively by the $(+r_2)$ superscript; in other words the point of orientation is located within the event, after its commencement and before its conclusion. This view of the progressive is close to Jespersen 1931 §12.5. But it is by no means certain that the English progressive invariably describes an event that has commenced at the point of orientation; consider the examples in (2.5.4.13-14).

(2.5.4.13)
   a.   He was writing after I entered.
   b.   He was writing as soon as I entered.

(2.5.4.13.a) is ambiguous, it can denote either an event of writing that began before the speaker entered; or, like (2.5.4.13.b), an event that began after the speaker entered. Both sentences can imply that the writing is a continuation of something begun earlier, but this is not necessarily so, cf. *He hadn't written a word all day; been down at the pub more than likely! But after I got home he was writing; oh yes, anything rather than talk to me*. The present progressive is regularly used in denoting future events, cf. (2.5.4.14).

(2.5.4.14)
   a.   I am going now.
   b.   We are dining with the Smiths unless you've made other
         arrangements.

(2.5.4.14.a) is generally used to signal that S is about to leave, even though it can be used when he is on his way out (in which circumstance it is more usual to say *I'm on my way*). Thus (2.5.4.14.a) is ordinarily used to signal something that has not yet begun. (2.5.4.14.b) has to be understood in terms of an anticipated event; to suggest that the point of orientation is sometime after the dining has begun is ludicrous. In *The Verb System of Present-Day American English* 1966, Robert Allen says that the progressive denotes a process that is incomplete at the point of orientation; which allows for it not even to have begun at that point.

Katz explicitly omits analysis of the habitual present, the historic present, and the future present (1972:315). But he does offer accounts of temporal adverbs such as *before* and *after*, *while*, *during*, and *repeatedly*, using the notation for temporal relations sketched here. We will take one example, the reading for *during* as in *John kicked George during the time Bill was sleeping*. The reading for 'during' is (2.5.4.15), cf. Katz 1972:323.

$$(2.5.4.15) \quad \upsilon[T^s] = ((t^{(\S u + (-r_i))}),.\,.\,.,(t^{(\S u)}),.\,.\,.,(t^{(\S u + (+r_j))}))$$
$$\upsilon[T^s] \rightarrow ((t^{(\S u + (-r_i))}),.\,.\,.,\upsilon[T^m],.\,.\,.,(t^{(\S u + (+r_j))})), \langle\,\rangle$$

The symbols $\upsilon[T^s]$ and $\upsilon[T^m]$, represent, respectively, the temporal specification of the subordinate clause 'Bill was sleeping' and the main clause 'John kicked George'. The arrow indicates the change effected on the semantics of the subordinate clause proposition by the adverb. It is notable that the temporal specification for the subordinate clause is, as is usual, taken to be the point of orientation for the main clause.

In addition to specifying the semantic analysis of temporal adverbs, Katz offers a description of the concepts 'state' and 'process'. Roughly speaking the notion of state is, according to Katz 1972:304, that which is the case at some given time, or during a given time interval. He apparently thinks that the concept (State) can be defined solely by reference to time. But it should rather be defined in terms of something unchanging over time. More successful, though not uncontroversial from a philosophical point of view, is Katz's definition of (Process) in terms of changes of states over time, i.e. a progression from State$_1$ to State$_2$. . .to State$_n$. This definition (Katz 1972:336) is complex, and better read in the original than simply reproduced here. What we can do, is to interpret a semantic marker in which the representation of process appears. Take the reading of the transitive verb *open*, given in Figure 5.10

We shall more fully discuss this reading in §5.2.5.5 but for the present purpose it can be paraphrased as in (2.5.4.16).

(2.5.4.16) The subject NP (i.e. [NP,Σ] on the LSUPM) causes that (state$_1$) a barrier to an enclosure which is positioned to prevent passage between inside and outside at H_1 through H_3, or at H_2, or at

open [+ – – –NP, . . .];   [NP, Σ]
                                    X
                  ($_{<\text{(Physical object) v (Physical event)}>}$ (Causes)

(((Condition)   (Positioned to prevent passage between inside and outside
            [NP, PrepP, VP, PP, Σ]   [NP, VP, PP, Σ]
    of   X   )   of   X
            <(Enclosure)>   <(Barrier)>
      [Tense, Aux, PP, Σ]$_{/H_1, H_2, H_4, \ldots,(\ldots}$ [Tense, Aux, PP, Σ]$_{/H_3, H_2, H_5), \ldots}$),
      at   X   X
            <(. . . t . . .)>   <(. . . t . . .)>
  ((Condition)   (Positioned to allow passage between inside and outside
[NP, PrepP, VP, PP, Σ]   [NP, VP, PP, Σ]   [Tense, Aux, PP, Σ]
    of   X   )   of   X   at   X $/H_6$)))
  <(Enclosure)>   <(Barrier)>   <(. . . t . . .)>

Figure 5.10   The lexicon entry for the transitive verb *open*, Katz
1972:358

H_4 through H_5, (becomes state$_2$) a barrier to an enclosure which is
positioned to allow passage between inside and outside at H_6.

The period H_1 through H_3 is relevant when the time point for the
clause is simple past or present; in those circumstances state$_1$ holds
retrospectively for a period between $((-r_1) + (-r_2))$ – which can be
glossed "further back in time" – and $(-r_1)$, "(not so far) back in time".
When the point of orientation is simple future 'it is not known whether
the state in question [state$_1$] occurred in the past, present, or future'
(Katz 1972:337). This may indeed be true, but nonetheless the
(punctual) H_2 which appears first in the condition (along with H_1 and
H_4 in Fig. 5.10), should be marked as temporally prior to the H_2 in the
second half of the condition (the H_2 that lies between H_3 and H_5). The
period represented as between H_4 and H_5 is relevant to progressive
aspect. H_4 is equivalent to '$(t^{(\S u+(-r_1))})$', and H_5 to '$(t^{(\S u)})$', in the
semantic reading for the progressive, given in (2.5.4.10). Thus the
period of duration for state$_1$ can be paraphrased "at some time prior to
the point of orientation for the clause". The time point represented by
H_6 is prospective from the last time unit of state$_1$: for simple past or
present, it is equivalent to the point of orientation for the clause (i.e.
$(-r_1)$ is deleted from H_3). For the simple future, it is the future

$(t^{(+m)})$. For the progressive, it is the prospective '$(t^{(\S u+(+r_2))})$' component of the progressive reading in (2.5.4.10). But this is inaccurate. In *Max was opening the door very carefully* 'the door' ceases to be closed at the point of orientation $(t^{(\S u)})$ and subsequently. This means that H_5 should in fact be immediately retrospective to the point of orientation, and H_4 retrospective to that.

It is possible to rectify the inadequacies noted in Katz's representations of the semantics of aspect constituents in the Aux node of the LSUPM using his notation. $(t^{(\S u)})$ will be retained to stand for any of $(t^{(-n)})$, $(t^{(o)})$, or $(t^{(+m)})$ – past, present, and future respectively. However, $(-r)$ and $(+r)$ will be used to mark retrospective and prospective temporal viewpoints; that is, "looking to the past" and "looking to the future", as distinct from 'being in the past' or 'being in the future.' The four inflexional aspectual possibilities in English can be represented as follows:

(2.5.4.17)

simple	$(t^{(\S u)})$
perfect	$(t^{(\S u+(-r))})$
progressive	$((t^{(\S u)}), (t^{(\S u+(+r))}))$
perfect-progressive	$((t^{(\S u+(-r))}), (t^{(\S u)}))$

The simple and the perfect are represented very much as before; the only difference being that the $(-r)$ constituent of the perfect marks retrospective. The progressive and perfect-progressive are quite different: they almost mirror one another, the progressive being prospectively oriented, the perfect-progressive being retrospectively oriented. While this neatly accounts for such sentences as those in (2.5.4.14) a number of apparent counter-examples spring to mind. For example there are many instances of the progressive where the event referred to is already in progress, giving rise to such pairs of paraphrases as the following.

(2.5.4.18)
   a.   Max was telling his story when he was stopped.
   b.   Max was in the course of telling his story when he was stopped.

(2.5.4.19)
   a.   They were eating their dinner when a stranger called.
   b.   They were in the middle of eating their dinner when a stranger called.

(2.5.4.20)
   a.   Cedric was chatting up Penelope when her husband interceded.
   b.   Cedric was in the process of chatting up Penelope when her
        husband interceded.

(2.5.4.21)
   a.   The chairman was being shouted down by the shareholders.
   b.   The chairman was in the position of being shouted down by the
        shareholders.

(2.5.4.22)
   a.   Pluto was caught tearing up the leaflet.
   b.   Pluto was caught in the act of tearing up the leaflet.

The (a) and (b) sentences of (2.5.4.18-22) mean more or less the same,
and it seems obvious that the progressive forms in the (a) sentences
denote ongoing events; it is the use of the marker $(t^{(\S u)})$ as the initial
component in the semantic reading for the progressive which allows for
this fact. The use of this marker for the simple aspect in (2.5.4.23-27)
certainly does.

(2.5.4.23)
   a.   Will is hunting for deer.
   b.   Will is on a hunt for deer.

(2.5.4.24)
   a.   Percy is holidaying in France.
   b.   Percy is on holiday in France.

(2.5.4.25)
   a.   The parcel is coming/going.
   b.   The parcel is on its way.

(2.5.4.26)
   a.   He's telephoning her now.
   b.   He's on the telephone to her now.

(2.5.4.27)
   a.   Susan is crying.
   b.   Susan is in tears.

The use of the simple aspect, represented by the marker $(t^{(\S u)})$, in the
(b) sentences of (2.5.4.23-27) does not militate against our understanding that the event is in progress; this is because the marker gives no
commitment on the commencement of the event (i.e. makes no

commitment on retrospectiveness). That is exactly why the progressive can be used of events that have yet to come about:

(2.5.4.28)
    a.   Elspeth is coming to dinner this evening.
    b.   *Elspeth is in the middle of coming to dinner this evening.

(2.5.4.29)
    a.   He was writing as soon as I entered the room.
    b.   *He was in the process of writing as soon as I entered the room.

Thus the progressive is prospective oriented, which is why Allen 1966 and others claim it indicates an incomplete event. All the examples of the progressive so far considered instantiate this characteristic; but there are apparent counterexamples. Consider (2.5.4.30).

(2.5.4.30) Ed was writing, but stopped when I entered.

There is something odd about this (perfectly grammatical) sequence, a feeling that the first clause ought to be perfect-progressive: *Ed had been writing*. The reason for this is that S's report is expected to be retrospective from his own point of entry, and the information reported in the first clause is based on circumstancial evidence. Notice that (2.5.4.30) is more extraordinary than (2.5.4.31), which we might contrast with (2.5.4.32).

(2.5.4.31) I was writing, but stopped when Joan came in.

(2.5.4.32) I had been writing, but stopped when Joan came in.

In (2.5.4.31) there are two points of orientation: one associated with S's writing – with the strong implication that it was interrupted by Joan's entry before completion; and the other with Joan's entry. In (2.5.4.32), however, Joan's entry is the point of orientation from which the event of S's writing is looked at retrospectively. If we look back to (2.5.4.30) it is now clear why the retrospective is preferred. *Ed had been writing but stopped when I entered* views the events from the point of S's entry, which is the expected viewpoint; but (2.4.5.30) has two points of orientation, just like (2.5.4.31). The difference is that S is involved in both events in (2.5.4.31), and in the second event only in (2.5.4.30): S is excluded from the first event of (2.5.4.30), 'Ed was writing', which leaves us wondering how S could know about it other than retrospectively from his own point of entry – i.e. S appears to violate the co-operative maxim of quality, cf. §1.2.3.3. The facts relevant to this discussion of (2.5.4.30-32) surely arise only if the progressive involves a prospective expectation that the event is to continue (though it may in fact not do so): whereas the perfect-progressive indicates a retrospective on an event continuing up to the point of orientation.

The perfect-progressive is oriented towards a retrospective view of the event, continuing up to the point of orientation. But just as $(t^{(\S u)})$ is uncommitted on retrospectiveness, so too is it uncommitted on prospectiveness. Thus the perfect-progressive is compatible both with events that are going to go on, and events which have come to an end; as we see from (2.5.4.33-34).

(2.5.4.33)
  a.   John has been working all day; I wish he'd stop soon.
  b.   Elspeth had been working all morning and continued throughout the afternoon.
  c.   Max will have been teaching all morning, but he won't stop until nightfall.

(2.5.4.34)
  a.   Give John your chair, he's been working all day.
  b.   Elspeth had been working all day and was dead tired when she got home.
  c.   Max will have been packing all day, I don't think he'll be up to dancing at a disco all night.

The form of Katz's semantic representation of temporal relations has permitted useful discussion of the semantics of time, tense, and aspect. And although his notation could be simplified, his metalanguage seems basically sound in this area.

5.2.5.5   Interpreting Katz's lexicon entry for the transitive verb *open*

Looking again at Figure 5.10 (p. 332) it is obvious that Katz's notation for the semantics of temporal relations is difficult for the average reader to follow. That can be excused provided the notation is a necessary part of the metalanguage for semantics. Let's look at Katz's lexicon entry for *open* to judge its efficacy in terms of its rigour, clarity, simplicity, and explanatory value.[19]

The conditions on the LSUPM indicated by the categorized variables in the entry are given in (PM.5.10), where parentheses indicate semantic markers.

There is nothing much to say about the formal presentation of the lexicon item: '*open*' is the normal orthographic form; there is no

(PM.5.10)

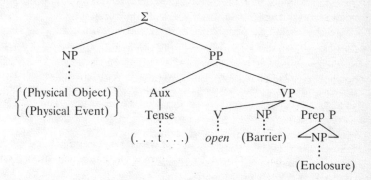

phonological information, not even the location of primary stress is given. But these are matters which could easily be rectified.

The contents of the square brackets to the immediate right of '*open*' constitute the syntactic marker which is intended to serve as a set of well formedness conditions on the insertion of this and co-occurrent entries into the LSUPM by lexical insertion rules. We established in §5.2.4.1 that we should not expect the complete set of features in this syntactic marker to be specified.

The semantic reading proper opens with a categorized variable, for the NP which is the subject in the LSUPM. The interesting thing about this variable is the semantic selection restriction, which turns out to be both over-restrictive and not restrictive enough: (2.5.5.1) exemplifies the over-restrictive nature of the selection restriction on the subject of transitive *open*.

(2.5.5.1)
  a. His work opened my eyes to new possibilities in artistic creation.
  b. Macchiavelli's ideas opened my mind to new ways of thinking about the exercise of power.
  c. The ghost opened the coffin lid and stepped out.
  d. Let my love open the door. [Song title].
  e. Having a hit opened the door to success.

All the examples in (2.5.5.1) are semantically sound, yet they would be classed as anomalous by the semantic theory because they violate the selection restriction imposed on the subject NP. It follows from the discussion in §5.2.4.2 that simply trying to patch up the selection restriction in this instance is unlikely to prove successful. One solution for Katz would be to claim that there are many more senses to the transitive verb *open* than are represented in Fig. 5.10, and each sense will have its appropriate selection restrictions. This solution takes no cognizance of the obvious danger that the differentiations of senses could be boundless as more and more selection restrictions were found; cf. Weinreich 1966:411, Bernard Harrison 'Critical notice of *Semantic Theory*' 1974:605f.

Katz completely overlooks the fact that, to a certain extent, selection restrictions on one argument of a predicate affect the interpretation of the whole clause. It is relevant in some of the examples in (2.5.5.2) where the subject NPs all conform to the stated selection restriction (and the other arguments also conform to the restrictions stated on them), yet the sentences are apparently anomalous. The stated selection restrictions on the arguments of *open* are nowhere near restrictive enough to account for this state of affairs.

(2.5.5.2)
 a. The soup opened the door.
 b. The ravioli opened the bank safe.
 c. A filing cabinet opened the gate.
 d. A clipping from my little toe opened the book at page 92.
 e. In 1386 the vibrating of my alarm clock opened the hatch in a submarine under the North Sea.
 f. The wind opened my mind to suggestions about what should be done with thalidomide side-effects.

In view of what was said in §5.2.4 it is not surprising that difficulties arise when trying to state the proper set of selection restrictions for the transitive verb *open*.

The semantic marker (Causes) means exactly what the simple present tense form of the verb "cause" regularly means in English (and as such is perhaps the most efficient part of the semantic reading).

The partial semantic marker reproduced in (2.5.5.3) is, in contrast to (Causes), extremely difficult to interpret.

(2.5.5.3) (Positioned to prevent passage between inside and outside of

$$[NP,PrepP,VP,PP,\Sigma] \qquad [NP,VP,PP,\Sigma]$$
$$X \qquad) \quad of \quad X$$
$$\text{‹(Enclosure)›} \qquad \text{‹(Barrier)›}$$

$$[Tense,Aux,PP,\Sigma] \qquad [Tense,Aux,PP,\Sigma]$$
$$at \qquad X \qquad /H_1,H_2,H_4,\ldots, \qquad X \qquad /H_3,H_2,H_5),\ldots,$$
$$\text{‹(. . .t. . .)›} \qquad \text{‹(. . .t. . .)›}$$

If we use the selection restrictions ‹(Enclosure)› and ‹(Barrier)› to indicate the essential content of their respective NPs, and paraphrase the temporal specification as "at some time prior to the point of orientation for the clause", (2.5.5.3) can be interpreted in terms of (2.5.5.4).

(2.5.5.4) Positioned to prevent pasage between inside and outside of an enclosure, of a barrier, at some time prior to the point of orientation for the clause.

I.e. a barrier to an enclosure is shut at some time prior to the point of orientation for the clause. Is it necessary that (2.5.5.3) be so complicated? Since Katz claims that the English words used in semantic markers have only mnemonic value, *shut* could be used instead of 'positioned to prevent passage between inside and outside', the only reason for not doing this would be where the circumlocution has more explanatory power than the simple word *shut* – and it is far from obvious that it does. 'Positioned to prevent passage between inside and outside' is a regular sentence of English whose understood subject is "a barrier to an enclosure". That being so, one wonders exactly why the subject NP follows the rest of the clause in (2.5.5.3). And the sequence "of an enclosure, of a barrier" is also somewhat baffling. There seems no clear reason for not using the more readily interpretable, natural order of presentation in (2.5.5.5).

(2.5.5.5)

$$[NP,VP,PP,\Sigma] \quad [NP,PrepP,VP,PP,\Sigma]$$
$$(\quad X \quad to \quad X \quad being\ shut$$
$$\text{‹(Barrier)›} \quad \text{‹(Enclosure)›}$$
$$[Tense,Aux,PP,\Sigma]$$
$$at\ some\ time\ prior\ to \quad X$$
$$\text{‹(. . .t. . .)›}$$

In the original reading, it is obviously intended that the barrier be defined as the one to the enclosure, but the categorization of the enclosure variable does not properly specify the relationship with the barrier. As it stands, the variable could properly be replaced by any of the emphasized NPs in (2.5.5.6).

(2.5.5.6)
a. Harry opened the can beside *the box*.
b. Harry opened the door with *a scabbard*.

    c.   Harry opened the jewelbox in *his room*.
    d.   Harry opened the safe on *the wall*.

In consequence these sentences will be assigned the wrong semantic interpretation, because in none of (2.5.5.6) is the direct object NP the barrier to the enclosure denoted by the emphasized NP. This particular problem will not arise from (2.5.5.5), where the relation between the two is clearly indicated by 'to'.

The semantic marker identifying the reading for what was called state$_2$ in (2.5.4.16) above, namely

$$[NP,PrepP,VP,PP,\Sigma] \quad [NP,VP,PP,\Sigma] \quad [Tense,Aux,PP,\Sigma]$$
$$X \qquad) \text{ of } \qquad X \qquad \text{at} \qquad X \qquad /H_6))$$
$$\langle(Enclosure)\rangle \qquad \langle(Barrier)\rangle \qquad \langle(...t...)\rangle$$

is now readily interpretable, and may be paraphrased by (2.5.5.8).

(2.5.5.8) The barrier to the enclosure is no longer shut at the point of orientation for the clause.

Here the gloss 'no longer shut' is used rather than 'open' because in a sentence like (2.5.5.9) the former obtains while the latter is incorrect.

(2.5.5.9) Max was opening the door very carefully.

Katz's lexicon entry for *open*, given in Figure 5.10, can be compared with the entry offered by Jackendoff in *Semantic Interpretation in Generative Grammar* 1972, reproduced as Figure 5.11. The first element in Jackendoff's entry is, like Katz's, the normal orthographical form of the lexicon item. The second and third elements of Jackendoff's dictionary entry are syntactic features referring to nodes on the LSUPM: the category feature +V; and a strict subcategorization feature +[NP$_1$–NP$_2$] defining the verb *open* as transitive. There are no

$$\left[\begin{array}{l} open \\ +V \\ + [NP^1 \underline{\quad\quad} NP^2] \\ CAUSE\ (NP^1, \left[\begin{array}{l} CHANGE \\ physical \end{array} \right]\ (NP^2, NOT\ OPEN, OPEN)\ ) \end{array} \right]$$

Figure 5.11   The lexicon entry for *open* from Jackendoff 1972:41

syntactic selectional features as there are in Katz's standard theory, and no inherent features; so the full set of syntactic markers in Jackendoff's dictionary entries presumably CAN be specified, whereas this is not possible for standard theory, as was shown in §5.2.4.1. Where Katz uses categorized variables to identify the nodes of phrase markers, Jackendoff uses superscripts on simple representations of single category symbols. These are a notational equivalent of the categorized variable, and they have the huge advantage of being very much easier to read and write. Generally speaking Jackendoff does not place semantic selection restrictions on arguments, but instead postulates an undescribed filtering device to semantically evaluate the lexical sequences generated by the grammar; it was shown in §5.2.4 that this device is open to the same objections as were raised against Katz's semantic selection restrictions. The only selection restrictions Jackendoff includes in a lexicon entry act like distinctive features to differentiate one predicate from another; e.g. *buy* and *sell* are distinguished from *barter* by the fact that money changed hands; so one of their arguments should denote money (even though no such argument need in fact appear in the LSUPM). This is not the way in which Katz uses selection restrictions.

Coming to the semantic content of the dictionary entry: Jackendoff's semantic components are English words written in upper case, e.g. 'CAUSE', and this is obviously a notational equivalent to Katz's simple semantic markers, e.g. (Causes), written within parentheses. Jackendoff 1972:42 protests 'the need for more specific and highly structured semantic representations', but this looks like a typical academic disclaimer against the criticism that the entry is not definitive. There are a number of criticisms to be made of Jackendoff's lexicon entry. The syntax of his metalanguage has not been described, and the reading must therefore be interpreted intuitively on the basis of our existing knowledge of the meaning of *open* and the combination of terms within the reading, cf. §4.12.5. That is to say, we have to educe a paraphrase something like *NP¹ causes a physical change to come about, such that NP² which was not open, changes to being open*. Thus, Jackendoff's metalanguage, like Katz's is a degenerate version of English. Jackendoff uses the predicate 'CHANGE' to indicate the change of state where Katz, for no good reason, leaves it implicit. The sub-categorization of this predicate distinguishes physical change from other types such as e.g. locational or psychological change. Where Katz has the direct object NP 'positioned to prevent passage between inside and outside', Jackendoff has it 'NOT OPEN'. Where Katz has 'positioned to allow passage between inside and outside', Jackendoff has 'OPEN'. Here Katz is longwinded but correct; Jackendoff should have used NOT SHUT for reasons exemplified in (2.5.5.9). For consistency, where Jackendoff has 'NOT OPEN', it would now be preferable to have SHUT. Of course Jackendoff might claim that 'OPEN' is not identical with the ordinary English word *open* (as George Lakoff 1972:605 does in a parallel case) and so the objection raised in respect of (2.5.5.9) is invalid. But this would be an equivocation, destroying the pretence that the English words used to represent semantic content have only mnemonic value; and it would lead to the requirement that every single semantic component be itself semantically defined before being used (as in a formal metalanguage). Jackendoff's entry for *open* does not specifically mark the relevance of time, which is implied within the predicate 'CHANGE', and could easily be made explicit. Unlike Katz, Jackendoff does not restrict transitive *open* to direct objects that are barriers to enclosures, thus excluding the opening of books, minds, eyes, windows, fêtes, etc.

Jackendoff's lexicon entry for *open* was adduced to highlight the felicities and infelicities of Katz's entry. The most noticeable difference between them is readability: Jackendoff's is much easier to interpret. The question is, is Katz's dictionary entry more complicated because it is more exact? Jackendoff's entry is inferior to Katz's to the extent that Jackendoff uses 'OPEN' where he should use 'NOT SHUT', and he fails to indicate relevant temporal specifications; however, were these failings rectified, Jackendoff's manner of presentation would still be clearer than Katz's and equally rigorous. This suggests that Katz's dictionary entries could be made a whole lot simpler with no loss in explicitness. Katz can justifiably be accused of making his semantic readings look more formidable than they need be. They lack clarity, they lack simplicity; and we have seen that they are not as rigorous as they might be.

5.2.6   The projection rule

With the introduction of categorized variables into the readings for lexicon items which are logically predicates, the structure-destroyed amalgamation rules of Katz & Fodor's original projection rule component were no longer necessary. Categorized variables structure semantic readings through being substituted by readings for the arguments of the predicate in which they appear. For example, suppose we have the (oversimplified) LSUPM in (2.6.1).

(2.6.1)

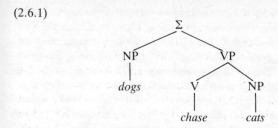

Here 'chase' is the predicate and 'dogs' and 'cats' are its arguments; thus the readings for 'dogs' and 'cats' have to be located within the reading for 'chase'. The reading for *chase* we shall use is the one in Figure 5.9. The semantic reading for the NP 'dogs' is inserted in place of the variable 'X' categorized [NP,Σ] in two places in the reading for 'chase' (at the top and at the bottom left); and the reading for the NP 'cats' is inserted in place of the variable 'X' categorized as [NP,VP,Σ], also in two places in the reading for 'chase'. This replacement of the categorized variables by readings for the arguments of the predicates in which they appear is effected by the projection rule. The projection rule substitutes the appropriate readings for the categorized variable, and forms a conjunction of the readings for sister nodes (as in the

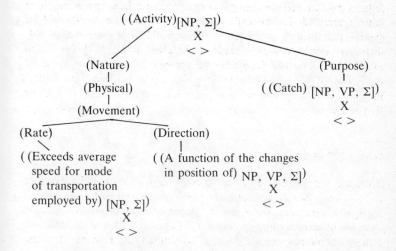

Figure 5.9   Semantic reading for *chase* in Katz *Propositional Structure and Illocutionary Force* 1977a:62

earlier amalgamation rule). Like earlier projection rules, this new rule works from the lowest order constituents to the highest, cumulatively adding in all the readings of daughter constituents to derive the readings of their mothers.

There is a problem that arises with categorized variables. In the reading for *chase* given in Fig. 5.9 there are four occurrences of categorized variables; two referring to the subject, and two to the direct object; both defined in terms of a single clause, viz. $[NP,\Sigma]$ and $[NP,VP,\Sigma]$ respectively. But suppose the clause containing *chase* is embedded, for example in (2.6.2)

(2.6.2) After his castration, Felix began to try to want to chase mice again, but all enthusiasm seemed to have gone out of him.

The subject of "chase" in (2.6.2) actually holds the grammatical relation $[NP,\Sigma,NP,VP,\Sigma,VP,\Sigma,VP,\Sigma]$ within the LSUPM under interpretation. To cope with the discrepancy between the categorized variable in the dictionary entry and its instantiation in the LSUPM, we need a rule to expand categorized variables in readings. Informally, what such a rule must do is proceed from the rightmost Σ in the categorization, through its mother and each supersequent mother node, until the highest (matrix) Σ is reached. More formally, this is stated by the rule in (2.6.3).

(2.6.3)

$$[\alpha_i,\ldots,\Sigma_i] \quad [\alpha_i,\ldots,\Sigma_i,X_j,\ldots,\psi_n,\ \Sigma\#\#]$$
$$X \quad \rightarrow \quad X$$
$$\langle\,\rangle \qquad\qquad \langle\,\rangle$$

(2.6.3) must form one of the clauses in the projection rule. The rest of the rule is given in (2.6.4).

(2.6.4) Given an underlying phrase marker U in which there is a segmentation[20] or bracketing that satisfies the conditions

(a) there is a node N that directly dominates the nodes N_i and N_j,

(b) the substring of the terminal string of U that is dominated by N_i bears the grammatical relation H to either the substring of the terminal string of U that is dominated by N_j or some constituent of it,

(c) either (i) N has no set of readings assigned to it but N_i and N_j have a maximal set of readings assigned to them, the sets R_i and R_j respectively, or (ii) N has a maximal set of readings R_i

assigned to it and there is an N_j that has a maximal set of readings R_j assigned to it, form the possible combination pairs of readings from the sets R_i and R_j, i.e., (r_{i_1}, r_{j_1}), (r_{i_1}, r_{j_2}),. . .,(r_{i_m}, r_{j_n}), and then, for each such pair (r_i, r_j), replace each occurrence of the variable categorized for H in one with the other member of the pair just in case it satisfies the selection restriction contained in the angles under the categorized variable. In case there is no categorized variable in these readings, simply form the union of them. The result of doing this for each combination pair will be a set of *potential derived readings*. If N directly dominates nothing besides N_i and N_j, then assign the potential derived readings as derived readings of the constituent dominated by N. If N directly dominates another node N_k, repeat the process with the combination pairs whose first member is a reading from the potential derived readings and whose second is a reading from the set assigned to the constituents dominated by N_k. Repeat until all nodes dominated by N are exhausted.

(Katz 1972:114f).

The projection rule is language universal, and for that reason need not be included within the grammer of a particular language. In consequence the semantic component of the grammar of any particular language will consist of two subcomponents: the set of dictionary readings that form part of the lexicon entry (supposedly) inserted into the LSUPM by lexical substitution rules; and the semantic redundancy rules.

Katz & Postal 1964 had proposed a simplification of dictionary entries by postulating for the dictionary a general set of redundancy rules stating implication relations between semantic markers.

The implication holds between a pair of semantic markers when the category represented by one is a subcategory of that represented by the other. For example the semantic marker (Human) represents a conceptual category that is included in the categories represented by (Animate), (Higher Animal), (Physical Object), etc., but the category that the semantic marker (Physical Object) represents is not included in any of these aforementioned categories.

(Katz & Postal 1964:16)

The semantic redundancy rules reduce the number of semantic markers needed in a dictionary entry, because, for instance, where an entry contains the marker (Human) it need not in addition contain the markers (Animate) or (Higher Animal) or (Physical Object), all of which will be specified by the redundancy rules as being necessarily implied by (Human). Thus semantic redundancy rules will expand the readings for lexicon items in the manner illustrated in (2.6.5).

(2.6.5) (Human) → (Physical Object) & (Sentient) & (Capable of Movement)

A full specification is necessary on two counts. Firstly, Katz's semantic theory aims at an exhaustively explicit representation of meaning. Secondly, a semantic marker implied by a marker in the dictionary reading but not itself present in the reading may be the one named in a selection restriction governing well formedness conditions on the combination of that reading with another.

By way of illustrating this, and other aspects of Katz's semantic theory in operation, consider the LSUPM in Figure 5.12.

Semantic redundancy rules will operate to expand the readings for *bachelor* and *spinster* as demonstrated in (2.6.5). This constitutes the domain of the projection rule. Applying the projection rule to the LSUPM partially represented in Figure 5.12, we first assign a reading to [NP, VP, Σ], then proceed to assign one to [VP, Σ], followed by [NP, Σ], and finally to Σ. The reading for [NP, VP, Σ] will be (2.2.6).

(2.6.6) {(The) & (Human) & (Physical Object) & (Sentient) & (Capable of Movement) & (Adult) & (Female) & (Single)}

v

{(The) & (Human) & etc.}

For convenience, we shall represent these hereafter as {(The Spinster)$_\alpha$ v (The Spinster)$_\beta$}. In the derived reading for [VP,Σ] this set of disjunctive readings will replace the appropriate categorized variable in the semantic marker for *chase*, given their compliance with the selection restriction ‹(Capable of Movement)›. Since the semantic redundancy rules introduced this marker into the readings for *spinster*, the selection restriction is complied with; and so the variable is replaced. The semantic reading for Tense will also be inserted in the appropriate place within the semantic marker for the verb. There are two substitutions for variables on this occasion, but there is no reason to order them; hence the reading for VP will be (2.6.7).

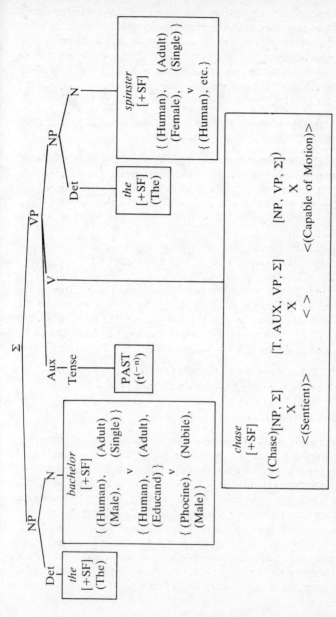

The symbol [+SF] stands for the unspecified set of syntactic features.

Figure 5.12 A lexically specified underlying phrase marker

(2.6.7)

$$((\text{Chase})_{[NP,\Sigma]} \quad [T,Aux,VP,\Sigma] \quad [NP,VP,\Sigma] \quad)$$
$$X \quad , \quad (t^{(-n)}) \quad , \quad \{(\text{The Spinster})_\alpha \text{ v}$$
$$\langle(\text{Sentient})\rangle \quad\quad\quad\quad (\text{The Spinster})_\beta \}$$

The readings for $[NP,\Sigma]$ are then combined to give three readings which we shall designate $\{(\text{The Bachelor})_\alpha \text{ v } (\text{The Bachelor})_\beta \text{ v } (\text{The Bachelor})_\gamma\}$ where the latter, for example, is an abbreviation for (2.6.8).

(2.6.8) $\{(\text{The}) \& (\text{Phocine}) \& (\text{Physical Object}) \& (\text{Sentient}) \& (\text{Capable of Movement}) \& (\text{Male}) \& (\text{Nubile})\}$

The full reading for Σ involves the combination of the subject NP reading with the reading for VP; which in effect means inserting the subject reading within the semantic marker for *chase*. The selection restriction on the categorized variable $[NP,\Sigma]$, is $\langle(\text{Sentient})\rangle$, and because (Human) and (Phocine) both entail this marker, causing it to be introduced by semantic redundancy rules, all readings for *bachelor* are appropriate interpretations of the subject NP for *chase*. The final semantic interpretation for the sentence specified by the phrase marker in Fig. 5.12 is, therefore, (2.6.9)

(2.6.9)

$$(\text{Chase})_{[NP,\Sigma]} \quad\quad\quad\quad [T,Aux,VP,\Sigma] \quad [NP,VP,\Sigma]$$

$$\left\{ \begin{array}{l} (\text{The Bachelor})_\alpha \text{ v} \\ (\text{The Bachelor})_\beta \text{ v} \\ (\text{The Bachelor})_\gamma \end{array} \right\}, \quad (t^{(-n)}) \quad , \quad \left\{ \begin{array}{l} (\text{The Spinster})_\alpha \text{ v} \\ (\text{The Spinster})_\beta \end{array} \right\}$$

Katz would disclaim (2.6.9) as a full semantic interpretation for the sentence *The bachelor chased the spinster*, because it presents only some aspects of the semantic properties of the sentence. A full specification requires not only the reading for the Σ node, but the whole of the semantically interpreted underlying phrase marker, Σ, and in addition statements that it is determinable, not analytic, not tautologous, not contradictory, meaningful, an assertion, six ways ambiguous, etc. An abbreviated version of the semantically interpreted underlying phrase marker from Figure 5.12 is given in Figure 5.13.

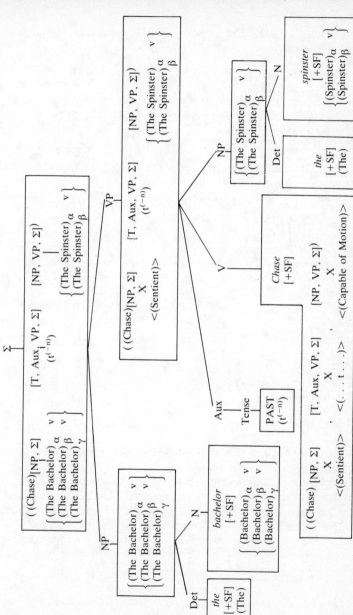

Figure 5.13 A semantically interpreted underlying phrase marker

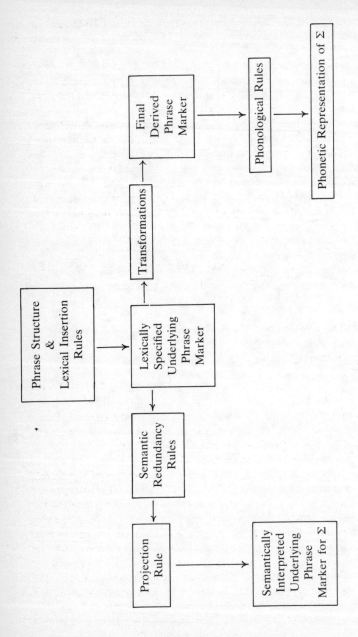

Figure 5.14   Correlating meaning and form in Katz's semantic theory

5.2.7 On relating the surface sentence with its meaning in Katzian semantics

In Katzian semantics there is no direct correlation between the surface form of a sentence and its semantic interpretation. The surface forms are not even generated using semantically interpreted constituents. Thus, form and meaning are very sharply divided, and can only be correlated through their derivational history to a common LSUPM, cf. Figure 5.14 (and Katz 1972:390). The LSUPM is a theoretical construct, not open to empirical validation. Thus on Katz's theory, the correlation of meaning and form depends on accurate theorems framed in terms of a highly valued syntactic theory. The theory Katz presupposes is what Chomsky calls 'standard theory', which is based on his book *Aspects of the Theory of Syntax*. The theory outlined in that book has been controversial since it was published in 1965: and since about 1969 has been rejected by its creator. Without wishing to engage in an argument about syntactic theory, it should be obvious that for Katz to rely on a controversial syntactic theory in relating meaning to form must raise grave doubts about the efficacy of his semantic theory.

5.2.8 A final assessment of Katz's theory as a theory of Σ's meaning

> Semantic theory is taken to be an answer to the question 'What is meaning?'
>
> (Katz 1972:xxv)

A cursory sortie through Katz's works can lead to the conclusion that meaning is syntactically degenerate English expressions in a typographical jungle. This is too hasty a judgement of Katz's contribution to semantics (as should be evident from §5.2.1), but Katz has failed to give a convincing account of what linguistic meaning is. The building blocks of his semantic theory are semantic markers. They supply the theoretical vocabulary for the representation of meaning, and for the statement of semantic properties and relations.[21] The theoretical vocabulary supposedly includes distinguishers as well; but the lack of any semantically significant distinction between semantic markers and distinguishers has been universally remarked upon. Katz has offered various descriptions of semantic markers and distinguishers over the years, deciding in *Semantic Theory* that distinguishers represent percepts, whereas semantic markers represent concepts; we suggest in §5.2.5.1 that this is an untenable demarcation. We have shown that both semantic markers and distinguishers (a) appear more than once in the lexicon, (b) are used in stating semantic relations and properties, (c) are used in stating selection restrictions – i.e. they have similar distribution within the constructs of Katz's semantic theory. Nowadays Katz believes that semantic markers represent abstract objects rather than concepts, and it may be presumed that distinguishers also represent abstract objects, so there are really no grounds left for maintaining a distinction between them. In publications following *Semantic Theory* 1972, Katz makes no mention of distinguishers. As early as 1965, Bolinger showed that distinguishers can be justifiably resolved into semantic markers, and this is undoubtedly the best thing to do with them.

The vocabulary of Katz's metalanguage is English. He has often claimed that this is simply a mnemonic device and the words used in semantic markers and readings should not be identified with the English words they appear to be. It was shown in Fig. 5.7 and during the discussion in §5.2.5.3 that this is an absurd claim. Semantic markerese can only be understood in terms of the English expressions it employs. But Katz has failed to define, or even indicate, which subset of English words constitutes the vocabulary of markerese. He has also failed to establish the structural principles on which the vocabulary within a marker or a reading is supposed to be combined. He has said that the form of semantic markers is intended to model the formal structure of concepts, but no convincing evidence has been given. Instead, it seems that the readings succeed in representing the meaning of an expression by courtesy of our pre-existing knowledge of that meaning. For instance, the favoured sense of *bachelor* is given the reading {(Human), (Adult), (Male), (Single)} in Katz & Nagel 1974:324. Aware that *bachelor* means, inter alia, "a man who has never married", we match this with the English expressions in the reading to concoct a feasible paraphrase of it, such as "male, adult human being who is single." This paraphrase has the conventional vocabulary and syntax of English. Katz's semantic markers and readings are, by contrast, couched in an unconventional metalanguage whose vocabulary and syntax have not been satisfactorily described; but because it uses English vocabulary, approximates English syntax, and so is interpretable via our competence in natural English, it can justifiably be described as a degenerate version of English.

The unconventional metalanguage Katz uses leads to difficulties with the interpretation, but more especially with the construction of semantic markers and readings. Furthermore, many of those exemplified in Katz's work may be criticized for lacking clarity and simplicity.

It might be thought these complications arise because we are dealing with the constructs of a formal theory of semantics; but this line of argument has no force. Formalism, especially unconventional formalism, can only be justified if it increases explicitness of statement, rigour of analysis, and leads to clarity of expression. But we found that Katz's semantic markers and readings have none of these properties. His metalanguage is obscurantist, and cannot be said to explain meaning. We have seen in Chs 3 and 4 that it is possible to achieve the same or a greater degree of explicitness and rigour, with a good deal more clarity and greater explicative value, by using a natural language such as English for a metalanguage.

Our principle concern in ch.5 is to determine a theoretical procedure for projecting the meanings of lexicon items up through the hierarchy of syntactic levels to give meanings for sentences. Katz's theory identifies three devices which are involved in the combining of semantic readings. (i) Semantic selection restrictions are intended to state well formedness conditions on sequences of readings: it has been argued that it would be either impossible, or impracticable, to identify the set of all selection restrictions needed. (ii) Categorized variables are a structure dependent device for locating one reading within the scope of another. A categorized variable is located within the structure of a predicate reading to identify which argument reading is to be inserted there: the argument is identified by the category node it occupies in the LSUPM. (iii) The projection rule effects the movement of argument readings into the scope of predicate readings, and forms a Boolean conjunction of readings for sister nodes. It, too, is a structure dependent device, that works progressively up the LSUPM. If one takes a skeptical look, what it does in practice is to place sets of meaning descriptions side by side, to provide a metalanguage paraphrase of the natural language constructions. Since Katz's metalanguage is syntactically degenerate English, we end up with a degenerate English paraphrase of a natural language expression; and that does not constitute an explication of its meaning. We therefore conclude that Katzian semantic theory has not solved the projection problem for a theory of linguistic meaning.

5.3 Some alternatives to Katzian semantics

5.3.1 Introduction

Having found that Katz cannot satisfactorily explain how meaning is projected up through the hierarchy of syntactic levels onto sentences, we turn to some alternatives to Katzian semantics. In §5.3.2 we discuss the work of Uriel Weinreich. Weinreich's criticisms of Katz & Fodor 1963 and Katz & Postal 1964 apparently led Katz to introduce categorized variables into semantic readings, and consequently to revise the projection rule; although this did not save his theory, it did greatly improve it. It was Weinreich who suggested to William Labov that he should conduct experiments on the denotational scope of lexemes, giving rise to the work reported in Labov's 'Denotational structure' 1978 – which we discussed in §2.9.4. Weinreich also inspired Edward H. Bendix whose analysis of *have*-related verbs is presented in *Componential Analysis of General Vocabulary* 1966; in some of his analyses, Bendix uses rules of inference similar to the ones used in this book. Some of Weinreich's ideas were a major influence on the development of generative semantics, which we discuss in §5.3.3. Roughly speaking, generative semantics is a theory of transformational grammar which takes the deepest structure to consist of a vocabulary of semantic atoms, functioning as recursive predicates on variables representing denotata; these are located in a syntactic structure which is a hybrid of predicate logic and familiar categories from natural language syntax such as Σ, V, and NP. In Katz's semantic theory lexicon items together with their semantic descriptions are mapped onto base phrase markers by transformations, and then the meanings of the items within the LSUPM are combined by the projection rule to give meanings for phrases, clauses, and sentences. In generative semantics, the initial structure lays out the entire semantic structure for all syntactic levels up to Σ, and transformations map lexicon items onto this semantic structure at various points during the derivation of surface sentences. There is, therefore, no projection problem in generative semantics – but, as we shall see, there are other difficulties instead. In §5.3.4 we round off the discussion of alternatives to Katzian semantics with a few observations on so-called 'case grammars'. Because case grammars did not, strictly speaking, pretend to offer an alternative to Katzian grammar, we shall not have much to say about them. We concentrate on their claim that semantically relevant participant roles (such as agent, instrument, beneficiary, etc.) were completely ignored in standard theory grammars; in response to this claim Katz has felt the need to indicate how participant roles can be represented within the semantic component of the grammar. The way he does it is, in principal, comparable with the way we did it in §4.12.6.

In §5.3.5 we conclude that none of the theories of meaning proposed within the framework of transformational generative grammar, nor any other decompositional theories of meaning within linguistic semantics, seem to have solved the projection problem for semantics.

5.3.2 Weinreich on semantics

> Since the main purpose of speech is meaningful communication, there is hardly a more significant study than the clarification of how the coding of meanings takes place within the limitations of phonological and grammatical structure. For the problem to be amenable to scientific analysis, it is necessary to operate, not with intuitive notions of meanings, but with explicit, verbalized, validated *meaning-descriptions*. The significance of the project lies in its search for a satisfactory methodology for obtaining and evaluating such meaning-descriptions.
>
> (Winreich 'Draft proposal: on the semantic structure of natural language' 1980:390)

The work of Uriel Weinreich on theoretical and applied semantics has been collected in *Weinreich on Semantics* 1980, edited by William Labov & Beatrice S. Weinreich. As we have already remarked, it was Weinreich who brought semantics out of the cold where it had been stored during the Bloomfieldian period, and conceived the aim of 'bridging the present abyss between semantic theory and semantic description as contained in dictionaries and grammars' (Weinreich 1980:385, cf. pp.14, 39, 297). Weinreich alloted priority to establishing a semantic theory for standard, prosaic uses of language; but what set him apart from semanticists like Katz, was seeking to show in addition how semantic theory might encompass cliché, idiom, figurative speech, and other kinds of deviance (cf. Weinreich 1980:10, 43, 269ff, 208ff). He wrote (see above) that semantic analysis should not operate 'with intuitive notions of meaning, but with explicit, verbalized, validated *meaning-descriptions*' (emphasis in original) – i.e. with a formal metalanguage; but, as we shall see, he did not succeed in creating one.

In Weinreich's view the metalanguage should be based on natural language (1980:55, 161, 300). He thought such a metalanguage could be developed by stratifying the natural language vocabulary into a central core, and – like onion rings – into increasingly peripheral strata. The central core would be defined circularly and by ostension (e.g. the meaning of *blue* is ostensively given as "the colour of the sky"); then each more peripheral stratum would be defined using terms from more central strata without further circularity (1980:308f). Yet Weinreich warned that natural language vocabulary probably would not yield to such stratification in practice, and in §4.12.5 we saw that his pessimism was justified. This has the undesirable consequence that the semantic metalanguage will be informal; but the desirable consequence that we have to use the full resources of the natural language as a metalanguage.

Weinreich often expressed the opinion that lexicography should be based on semantic theory (1980:14, 363-7); but his contribution to a theoretical foundation for lexicography does not advance so far as we have in chs 4 and 5 of this book. In 'Problems in the analysis of idioms' 1969/1980 Weinreich distinguished between a 'simplex dictionary' from which entries are inserted into underlying phrase markers by lexical insertion transformations; and a 'complex' dictionary' which assigns readings to idioms, and 'familiarity ratings for complex words and clichés', as they appear in the final derived phrase marker (1980:257). The idea of having two lexica arose because idioms cannot be treated like lexes or single words for the reasons that: (a) they may contain variable slots into which other readings must fit, cf. *pull NP's leg*; and (b), an idiom such as *shoot the breeze* meaning "chat" could not be inserted in toto under a verb node, because then there would be no way of restricting verb morphology to 'shoot' rather than have it apply to the whole idiom; nor could such idioms reasonably be inserted directly under the nonterminal Verb Phrase node in a phrase marker without upsetting the whole system of phrase structure rules and lexical insertion. Certain phraseological units, such as the adjective *spic and span* whose conjoined components never occur separately, and the adverb *to kingdom come* which violates regular syntactic categorization, are entered in the simplex dictionary, however. Weinreich concludes that because the constituents of idioms are, by and large, subject to regular morphosyntactic processes, it is preferable to generate the constituents by the regular phrase structure and lexical insertion rules within a lexically specified underlying phrase marker, and then check this or a derived phrase marker to see whether or not an idiom has been generated. Because many idioms block certain transformations, it would have been ideal for the 'idiom matching rule' to have applied to the LSUPM; but the 'matching rule' also assigns familiarity ratings to phrases to distinguish between e.g. the normal *bread and butter* and the unusual *butter and bread*, or the normal *hair brush* as against *brush for the hair*; and because Weinreich believes that e.g. *hair brush* derives transformationally from a sentence corresponding to '*The brush is* Prep *hair*' (1980:256), familiarity ratings must be assigned post-transformationally, i.e. to final derived phrase markers.

Hence the matching rule operates to match FDPMs with entries in the 'complex dictionary' to assign idiom readings and familiarity ratings from the dictionary. Weinreich does not say how the matching rule is to be defined;[22] nor does he describe how the complex dictionary might be compiled. Although he sketches differences between the simplex dictionary and the complex dictionary, the radical proposal that the grammar should have two lexica has not been convincingly argued for.

Weinreich raises the question of the degree of specification needed in a lexicon entry. To pose the problem, consider the *Oxford English Dictionary* reading for one sense of the familiar noun *carrot*: 'An umbelliferous plant (*Daucus Carota*) having a large tapering root, which in cultivation is bright red, fleshy, sweet, and edible.' The fact that carrots are umbelliferous (this describes the nature and appearance of the plant's flowering system) will constitute part of the meaning for botanists, as will the Latin name which places the carrot in plant taxonomy. But these aspects of the meaning of *carrot* are probably irrelevant to nonbotanists, and unknown to most of them – i.e. so far as most people are concerned, they do not form part of the meaning of the lexicon item. Unfortunately Weinreich offers no discussion of the ways in which the degree of specificity should be objectively determined for the practical purpose of writing a dictionary entry for a particular public – including theoretical semanticists.

The semantic content of Weinreich's lexicon entries is bipartite: there is a description of the item's sense (which we shall discuss shortly), and an ostensive description – such as "colour of the sky" in the entry for *blue* (1980:301f). Whereas ostensive information would be useful in the familiar dictionary that sits on one's bookshelf, it has no place in the theoretical dictionary that forms part of the theory of linguistic meaning: even though statements like *The sky is blue*, *Grass is green*, and *Snow is white* are held to be generally true, they provide only instances of the use of the colour adjectives *blue*, *green*, and *white*, and do not define their meanings.

Weinreich has proposed three different ways of representing semantic information in the lexicon: sets of conditions for denotation (1980:76, 302ff)[23] – which recognizes the link between sense and denotation lacking in, e.g. Katz's work; semantic features (cf. 'Explorations in semantic theory' 1966/1980); and analytic sentences stating definitions (1966:445, 1980:160). It is not clear how these different proposals are intended to relate one with another. Weinreich has suggested that semantic features such as [+Animate], [+Male] or [+Adult] are abbreviations for sets of conditions on denotation. Certainly, we showed in §3.5.3 that such semantic features correspond to the predicates in *X is animate*, *Y is male* and *Z is adult* respectively; but the features do not constitute the 'explicit, verbalized, validated meaning-descriptions' which Weinreich claimed are essential in semantic analysis (1980:390, 101). To carry out his stated intentions, Weinreich should have done what we did in §3.5.3 and §4.12.6, rather than just jot down semantic features.

Meaningful properties and meaning relations are poorly dealt with in Weinreich's work by comparison with, say, Katz 1972. Although polysemy is more frequently discussed in his work than any other property or relation, Weinreich did not describe criteria for distinguishing polysemy from homonymy (cf. §3.3. above), even though this is a matter of considerable lexicographical significance. And Weinreich has an unusual notion of synonymy: 'Let us define *synonymy* not as identity, but as "likeness of meaning" ' (1980:288). This reduces synonymy to a relation of semantic overlapping, and nothing more; thus any pair of items whose senses differ by one component are said to be immediate synonyms (1980:77). Weinreich talks about there being 'first degree synonymy' between *end* and *beginning*, instead of a relation of antonymy, 1980:307f. On p. 163 he defines antonymy as follows:

Given *X is a Y which Z*, & also *V is a Y which ~Z*, then *X* and *V* are antonyms.

Making substitutions for the variables: *an end is something which terminates*, and *a beginning is something which does not terminate*; hence *end* is antonymous with *beginning*, according to Weinreich's definition of antonymy. But because he has said that *end* and *beginning* are first degree synonyms, first degree synonymy must be the same as antonymy – which is an unhappy conclusion for Weinreich's definitions to lead to.

In 'On the semantic structure of language' Weinreich wrote: 'The structure of the designata of the signs of a language [i.e. the structure of the senses of language expressions] is the topic of its semantic description in the strict sense' (1980:40). The rules for combining meaning components were discussed in 'Explorations in semantic theory' 1966/1980 §3.2. Weinreich proposed four kinds of combinatorial rules: linking, nesting, delimitation, and modalization, none of which was adequately elaborated, cf. James D. McCawley *Grammar and Meaning* 1973:198. Linking is the type of meaning relation holding between 'subject nouns and main verbs, subject nouns with predicate nouns and predicate adjectives, main verbs with manner adverbials, descriptive adverbs with adjectives [e.g. *astonishingly white*].' Nesting is the type of meaning relation that holds between 'Main Verb + (object) NP and Preposition + (object) NP [. . .] the temporal and locative phrases which accompany "verbs of duration" and "verbs of movement" [e.g. *walk home*, *last hours*].' Delimitation is the type of semantic relation imposed by the functions of quantifiers and deictics, and perhaps intensifiers (e.g. *very*, *completely*). And finally, modalization is the type of relation imposed by modal verbs and adverbials, verbs of seeming and resembling, etc. Weinreich offered virtually no discussion of the semantic differences between these four types of combinatorial rules – perhaps because there is not much to say. We are, after all, considering the syntax of the semantic metalanguage, and it is noticeable that linking and nesting are both defined on syntactic relations in natural language, and delimitation and modalization on the semantic functions of certain classes of language expressions. In any case it is unclear just how committed Weinreich was to just these four types of semantic combination; he seems also to allow that there may be as many combinatorial mechanisms in semantics as there are in natural language syntax, because he wrote: 'every relation that may hold between components of a sentence also occurs among the components of meaning of a dictionary entry' (1966:446, 1980:159); and 'we may set ourselves a goal of reformulating the phrase-structure component of a syntax in such a way as to contain the same number of nonterminal nodes as there are (independently arrived [sic]) semantic functions' 1980:262 n.8. These views lead directly to generative semantics, cf. §5.3.3. Given that Weinreich approved the use of a natural language as a semantic metalanguage, it would seem that the syntactic resources of the natural language metalanguage might all be required in describing the meanings in the object language.

Weinreich made a radical revision to the standard theory phrase structure rules by proposing that the terminal symbols in the base phrase marker consist of three kinds of dummies: one for major classes (dominated by N, V, Adj, etc.); another for minor classes (dominated by Det, Prep, Number, etc.); and one for semantically empty morphs like Verbal Number which are not replaced from the dictionary. Although lexical insertion under minor class nodes is restricted by category features, insertion under major class nodes is unconstrained (1966:434, 1980:145) – which has interesting morphological conse- quences Weinreich does not discuss. Not only would this have desirable effects such as properly generating *But me no buts*, which is interpretable, it would also license sequences like *the in anded some thes*, *this blue and on speak conferenced uply*, *Peter thated nine an equipment*, etc. Weinreich postulates a 'semantic calculator' to assign a deviance quotient to sentences; but he does not suggest how it could be programmed to carry out this task, and his proposal falls to the same objections that we advanced against the statement of selection restrictions in §5.2.4. Weinreich proposes that lexicon entries include transfer features in place of selection restrictions; of this proposal he writes: 'The two approaches have been contrasted informally as follows: Chomsky and Katz match a square peg against a round hole and state that it does not fit. My theory presses the peg into the hole to see whether the peg is thereby tapered, or the hole stretched' (1980:263 n.13). E.g. the adjective *pregnant* will transfer the feature [+Female] to any argument headed by a concrete noun; thus in *my neighbour is pregnant* the subject NP is semantically [+Female] by transfer of this feature from *pregnant*. Thus transfer features represent the contextual effect of the meaning of one expression on another. It seems that transfer features are abbreviations for inferences, just like other semantic features. The transfer feature from *pregnant* operates according to the following scheme:

(3.2.1) If F is pregnant and F is animate, then F is necessarily female
(at least in part[24]).

Obviously inferences of this kind can operate across sentence boundaries. In a sentence like *the pencil is pregnant* Weinreich's semantic theory would transfer a feature [+Female] to *pencil*, and the semantic calculator, via the construal rule and the semantic evaluator, would have to assign a deviance quotient to the result – though the manner of its doing so remains a mystery.

Weinreich wrote 'The investigation of discourse in its logical aspects is [. . .] one of the most important frontiers of linguistics for the decades ahead' (1980:43); and on p.64 he says that a sentence may be disambiguated by one that precedes it. But without apology, he contradicts himself with the following: 'We do not [. . .] propose to hold semantic theory accountable for resolving the ambiguity of *jack* ("1. lifting device; 2. metal toy for playing jacks") in the sentence *I realized we had no jack* by association with, say, *car* and *break* in the adjacent sentence (*On a deserted road that night our car broke down*). Such phenomena are in principle uncoded and beyond the scope of linguistics' p.94 n.38. Doubtless Weinreich felt constrained by Chomsky's syntactic theory, which was inadequate to cope with anything above sentence level.

In all his works prior to 'Explorations in semantic theory', Weinreich adhered to the structuralist doctrine of the autonomy of syntax from semantics. However in 'Explorations' he changed his mind. He came to believe that syntax and semantics are interdependent; and, e.g., so-called syntactic features are in fact semantic: 'We intend the distinguishing feature of each major morpheme class, e.g. [+Noun], to be taken as semantic in the full sense of the word; more revealing names might be "thingness" or "substantiality", "quality" (for [+Adjective]), and so on' (1966:432f, 1980:143). Weinreich's views on these matters contributed to the development of generative semantics, as we shall see. He introduced semantic features on nonterminal nodes in the phrase marker, and we shall look at one example of this, namely the marking of countability on NPs. In English, countability is marked syntagmatically in singular NPs; and in plural NPs morphologically, and occasionally syntagmatically as well. But uncountability is never marked, cf. §2.9.8. The conventional wisdom that countability is a characteristic of nouns, to be accounted for by a feature [±Count] in the lexicon, is therefore descriptively inadequate: as Weinreich noticed, it 'fails to account for the ability of English words [sic] to be used as *either* count *or* mass nouns' (1966:435, 1980:146). He suggested three alternative solutions. One was to create separate countable and uncountable lexicon entries for the same noun; but this was rejected because it almost doubles the number of nouns in the lexicon, and because it fails to show that some nouns are more countable than others. His second suggestion was to make countability a feature on determiners to be transferred to the (countability-neutral) noun 'by a concord-type rule'; but without discussing the interesting possibilities of such an hypothesis, Weinreich rejected it on the grounds that determiners like *the*, *any*, *this*, and *my* are countability-neutral. The solution he adopted was to maintain the conventional binary marking for countability on the lexical entries for nouns, and in addition to mark NP nodes for countability. This bipartite proposal requires the use of a semantic calculator to resolve the various effects of locating a [±Count] noun in a [±Count] NP; but this is an unwelcome complication to the grammar of countability, and my own analysis in Allan 'Nouns and Countability' 1980 shows it to be unnecessary. Weinreich's proposal contains two additional flaws. Although his model demanded it, he offered no solution to the problem of determining whether a given noun is countable or uncountable: e.g., on what grounds would he decide the countability of *cake*, and what would be the grounds for agreeing or disagreeing with him? His adherence to the conventional view of countability as a binary feature on the lexical class of nouns renders the problem insoluble. The second, and less serious flaw in Weinreich's proposal is the lack of explicit justification for his substantially correct claim that countability is a feature of NPs.

It is typical of Weinreich that good ideas are left incompletely explored. He often referred to the abyss between lexicography and semantic theory; but he never actually bridged it. He dabbled with a formalism for semantics in 'On the semantic structure of language' and in 'Explorations', but on careful inspection it turns out to be useless. He saw the inadequacy of using Boolean conjunction as the only combinatorial mechanism in semantics; but he didn't exhaustively explore the alternatives. He postulated five different kinds of semantic representation: (i) sets of conditions for denotations; (ii) semantic features; (iii) analytic sentences stating definitions; (iv) semantic components combined by linking, nesting, delimitation, and modalization; (v) semantic components combined by natural language syntax. He has suggested that (ii) is an abbreviation for (i); and presumably (v) could contribute to (i) and (iii); but it is not clear how (i), (iii) and (iv) are related, if they are; nor how (iv) relates to (v), if it does. Weinreich has identified five vehicles for conveying representations of meaning, but no traffic rules. Adopting the interdependence of syntax and semantics in passing, he didn't seriously discuss the ramifications. The semantic calculator, although intuitively satisfying, remains a pie-in-the-sky notion because Weinreich omits to explain how it is to be programmed. Similarly hard to pin down are the notions of a complex dictionary and a matching rule that assigns idiom senses and familiarity ratings to derived phrase markers: like many of Weinreich's bright ideas, these have too little substance. None of his theoretical constructs is explicitly and rigorously described, nor exhaustively discussed.

Consider, on the other hand, some positive aspects of Weinreich's contributions to a theory of linguistic meaning. He has said that senses should be expressed in terms of conditions on denotation – which is close to our own conclusion in ch.2 that sense reflects the salient characteristics of the prototypical denotatum. He has said that lexical class meaning should be noted within a grammar, which is a return to the traditional view, cf. §2.9.9. He has said that both the vocabulary and the syntax of a natural language can function as the vocabulary and syntax of the metalanguage for semantics. Weinreich was the original inspiration for such investigations of meaning as are reported in William Labov's 'Denotational structure' 1978, discussed in §2.9.4; and for the work of Edward H. Bendix *Componential Analysis of Vocabulary* 1966, which we referred to in §4.12.6; and, as was mentioned earlier, his ideas on the interdependence of syntax and semantics influenced the generative semanticists we discuss in §5.3.3.

5.3.3 Generative semantics

From a generative semantic point of view, this problem of the morphemic identity or difference of two forms may seem to be a pseudo-problem. Thus, for example, a generative approach which includes both form and meaning might contain rules for rewriting metalinguistic symbols which stand for meanings or components of meaning as the corresponding object-language forms.

(Edward Bendix *Componential Analysis of General Vocabulary* 1966:12)

The standard theory notion was that a grammar should have a level of deep structure at which the meaning of a sentence, and each of its constituents, is specified; and, distinct from it, a level of surface structure at which the form of the sentence is specified. This leads naturally to the view that in pairs of formally distinct expressions such as *A caused B to die* and *A killed B*, or *X reminds me of Y* and *X strikes me as similar to Y*, or *my mother* and *the woman who bore me*, the different surface forms derive by different sets of transformations (including different lexical insertion transformations) from the same deep structure. The next theoretical development was to propose that the initial structures in a grammar are semantic rather than solely syntactic; and that the forms of sentences and their constituents are generated by transformational processes from these underlying seman- tic structures. This was the theoretical basis for 'generative semantics'.

Thus, generative semantics grew directly out of the work that led to Katz & Postal's *An Integrated Theory of Linguistic Descriptions* 1964 and Chomsky's *Aspects of the Theory of Syntax* 1965. One of the earliest works in generative semantics (though when it was written it was conceived of as an extension of standard theory) is George Lakoff's *On the Nature of Syntactic Irregularity* 1965, later published as *Irregularity in Syntax* 1970; in the Introduction, Lakoff gives credit to Paul Postal for ideas which apparently led to the development of generative semantics. One such idea can be found in Katz & Postal 1964:

Given a sentence for which a syntactic derivation is needed; look for simple paraphrases of the sentence which are not paraphrases by virtue of synonymous expressions; on finding them, construct grammatical rules that relate the original sentence and its paraphrases in such a way that each of these sentences has the same sequence of underlying P-markers [viz. the same deep structure]. Of course, having constructed such rules, it is necessary to find *independent syntactic justification* for them.

(Katz & Postal 1964:157, emphasis in original)

Note the emphasis here on syntactic justification: argumentation within generative semantics was heavily biased towards syntax, and not without good reason; it was primarily a theory of syntax and not a theory of semantics; consequently, there was little serious investigation of the nature of meaning, other than a considerable interest in the structuring of meaningful elements. For example Lakoff 1965/1970 postulated phrase markers whose terminal nodes consist of feature bundles (in line with the Chomsky 1965 proposal which came to be rejected in standard theory TG); Lakoff differed from Chomsky by proposing that lexicon items would be inserted into only some of these terminal nodes, the others would function only as well formedness conditions on lexical insertion and semantic interpretation. Lakoff 1965/1970 takes lexical insertion to precede any other kind of transformation.

Also in 1965, Jeffrey Gruber submitted *Studies in Lexical Relations* as a doctoral thesis at MIT; the original version was published in 1970 and a substantially revised version in 1976. Gruber's prelexical structures have most of the syntactic characteristics of standard theory phrase markers, but they have terminal nodes (at least some of) which are semantic components.[25] Gruber argued that certain movement and deletion transformations need to operate on prelexical structure before lexical insertion takes place, and also that lexicon items can be inserted over more than one terminal node in the prelexical phrase marker. The semantic components in prelexical structures do not give a full semantic specification of lexicon items, and Gruber assumes that semantic interpretation is effected on the LSUPM before further transformations derive the FDPM. Thus in Gruber's theory, semantics and syntax are interdependent.

Weinreich 1966 proposed that the acceptability of lexical sequences is semantically determined, so that well formedness conditions on lexical insertion in a grammar should be semantically governed. He also said, in effect, that syntactic structure is the skeleton for semantic components so that semantic structure has the same kinds of categories and syntactic relations that are to be found in natural language syntax.

In 'Lexical insertion in a transformational grammar without deep structure' 1968c, James D. McCawley assumed that semantic structure is just like syntactic structure and that the initial structures in a grammar are semantic structures. The constituents of a sentence, Σ, are a predicate represented by 'V' and arguments represented by 'NP'; in initial structure the V consists of a semantic component (or, 'atom'), and NPs consist of either the recursive Σ (sentence node), or, terminally, a variable symbolizing the denotatum. All natural language syntax can (he appears to have assumed) be represented by these few structural symbols. He also allowed that certain movement transformations could precede lexicalization; and he proposed that lexicon items be inserted, where appropriate, over more than one predicate node. All these assumptions typified generative semantics for as long as it lasted.

Language is the pairing of meaning with form. Generative semantics starts with meanings and maps forms onto it. It begins with a set of symbols representing semantic components and sets them in structures based on a hybrid of predicate logic and natural language syntax. These structures can be rearranged in various ways by transformations before having forms mapped onto them from the lexicon. Then transformations may rearrange or perhaps delete nodes in an intermediate (derived) phrase marker, until the final derived phrase marker gives the surface form of the corresponding sentence, together with its structural description. Because the starting point for a generative semantics grammar is the meaning of a sentence, and form is mapped onto that, there is no projection problem: the meaning of the sentence is not determined from the meanings of the lexicon items but directly from the initial semantic structure. The problem for the generative semanticists is to give consistent semantic descriptions for lexicon items, phrases, clauses, etc. as they occur in different sentence environments, in such a way that the meaning for any sentence constituent can be determined from the initial semantic structure. We shall evaluate generative semantics as a theory of meaning in §5.3.3.4 after examining it in more detail.

5.3.3.1 The notion of hypothetical verbs from Lakoff 1965/1970

The three sentences (3.3.1.1-3) mean more or less the same, according to Lakoff, and have very similar (though not quite identical) LSUPMs.

(3.3.1.1) It came about that the sauce was thick.

(3.3.1.2) The sauce became thick.

(3.3.1.3) The sauce thickened.

All three have a LSUPM like (PM.1), the difference being in the terminal node of V_1.

(PM.1)

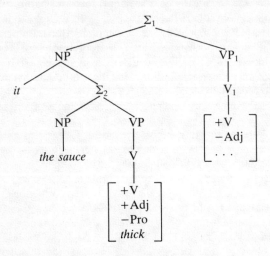

For (3.3.1.1) the features under V_1 are given in (i) below, for (3.3.1.2) they are given in (ii), and for (3.3.1.3) they are given in (iii):

$$
\text{(i)} \begin{bmatrix} +V \\ -Adj \\ +Pro \\ +Inchoative \\ \textit{come about} \end{bmatrix}
\quad
\text{(ii)} \begin{bmatrix} +V \\ -Adj \\ -Pro \\ +Inchoative \\ \textit{become} \end{bmatrix}
\quad
\text{(iii)} \begin{bmatrix} +V \\ -Adj \\ +Pro \\ +Inchoative \end{bmatrix}
$$

Before discussing the derivation of (3.3.1.1-3) from the LSUPM, one or two comments are in order. Notice that tense and the copula are omitted: this is common in generative semantics literature, because generative semanticists are usually more interested in putting across the major innovations proposed in their theory rather than in elaborating a grammar which would explicitly generate acceptable surface sentences starting from Σ.[26] Lakoff treats both verbs and adjectives as members of the same lexical category, verb, symbolized $+V$ (cf. 1970:10). This is incorrect: although both verbs and adjectives typically function as predicates, they nevertheless constitute different lexical classes, cf. Allan 'Complement noun phrases and prepositional phrases adjectives and verbs' 1973:378-80. We may take it for the present purposes that $[\pm Adj]$ indicates the lexical distinction between verbs and adjectives.[27] The feature $[-Pro]$ indicates lexical verbs such as (i), (ii), and *thick*;

and hypothetical verbs such as the unlexicalized (iii) are [+Pro].

Lakoff suggests the following derivational process using, for the most part, transformations which were thought at the time to be well justified. Extraposition puts Σ_2 as right sister to VP_1, this will give the FDPM for (3.3.1.1). For both (3.3.1.2-3), *It* Substitution copies the subject NP from Σ_2 in place of the *it* under the subject NP of Σ_1 (this rule was later known as Subject Raising); Identical NP Deletion removes the copied subject NP from Σ_2 giving (PM.2).

(PM.2)

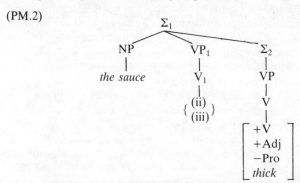

(PM.2) is the FDPM for (3.3.1.2). To derive (3.3.1.3) the predicate of Σ_2 is raised by the Inchoative transformation onto V_1 the transformation being triggered by the features [+Pro, +Inchoative] under V_1. The features [+V, −Adj, +Inchoative] are retained from (iii), but the feature [+Pro] converts to [−Pro]; Σ_2 and all nodes under it are pruned away. Thus the FDPM for (3.3.1.3] will be (PM.3).

(PM.3)

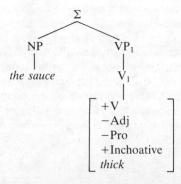

A spelling rule will later be triggered by the [+Inchoative] feature and it will add *-en* onto *thick* to give *thicken*.

Lakoff's proposals here are based on the belief that the number of lexicon items in a language is larger than the number of semantic specifications necessary in a dictionary; hence there will be a semantic specification of *thick* but not of *thicken*, which means (according to Lakoff) "thick + inchoative" – similarly for *hard/harden, black/ blacken*, etc. We have presented a different view in ch.4 where we said that all lexemes and morphemes, and even stems in the language, should be entered separately into the lexicon, largely because the inconsistencies and unsystematic nature of derivational morphology do not generally allow the meanings of derived lexemes to be predicted. This is one reason why generative semantics was unsatisfactory.

Consider another example from Lakoff 1965/1970, this time on the meaning of *kill*. Lakoff believed that both *kill* and *die* could have their meaning specified on the basis of the semantic specification for *dead*, together with [+Inchoative] in the meaning of *die* and [+Causative, +Inchoative] in the meaning of *kill*. The lexicon entry for *kill* is therefore located in the LSUPM where the entry for *dead* would be expected, and moved successively onto first an Inchoative hypothetical [+Pro] verb and then a Causative hypothetical verb required in the LSUPM. Omitting tense (as usual) the LSUPM for (3.3.1.4) is (PM.4).

(3.3.1.4) John killed Bill.

The feature bundle that is inserted along with *kill* refers to the meaning of the adjective *dead*, viz. [+V, +Adj, −Pro, DEAD]; 'R(Inchoative)' indicates that the Inchoative rule must apply: 'SD(Causative)' means that the phrase marker must contain a hypothetical Causative, as (PM.4) does, and it presupposes an SD(Inchoative); 'R(Causative)' says that the Causative rule must apply (this is comparable with the Inchoative rule, as we shall see).

To generate (3.3.1.4) from (PM.4) we first go through the same series of transformations as generate (PM.3) from (PM.1): Extraposition makes Σ_3 the daughter of Σ_2; *It* Substitution (Subject Raising) copies the subject NP of Σ_3 under the subject NP node of Σ_2; Identical NP Deletion deletes the original from Σ_3; the Inchoative transformation raises the V from Σ_3 onto the V of Σ_2, and after pruning we get (PM.5).

(PM.4)

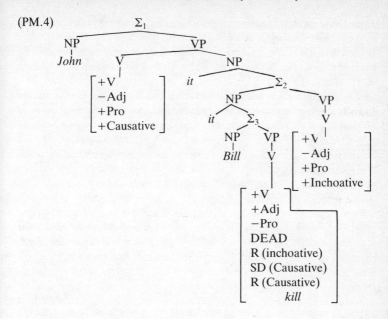

(PM.5)

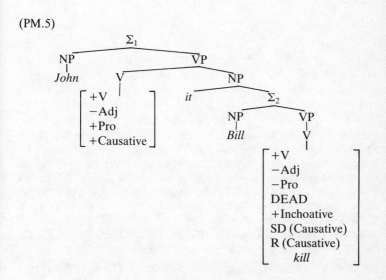

Σ_2 in (PM.5) can be glossed "Bill die" or "Bill become dead", and so Σ_1 means "John cause Bill die" or "John cause Bill become dead"; however, the phrase marker cannot give rise to a surface sentence of that form because the causative is a hypothetical [+Pro] verb and not the lexical [−Pro] verb *cause*. (PM.5) gives rise to (3.3.1.4) via an *It* Deletion transformation which removes the 'it' sister to Σ_2; then the Causative transformation raises the verb of Σ_2 onto the verb of Σ_1 to give (PM.6).

(PM.6)

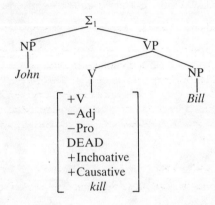

This is lexically *John kill Bill* (no tense indicated), and semantically "John kill Bill" or "John cause Bill to die" or "John cause+become+ dead Bill".

Lakoff's proposal does show the semantic relation between *kill, die,* and *dead* (respectively, a causative verb, an inchoative verb, and a stative adjective). However, he also suggests that the superficially simple sentence *A kill B* is complex in underlying structure, i.e. at least as complex as *A cause B to die*. In 'Three reasons for not deriving "kill" from "cause to die" ' 1970, Jerry A. Fodor points out that the simple sentence refers to only one event, a complex sentence to two events; thus, e.g., (3.3.1.5) is acceptable but (3.3.1.6) is not.

(3.3.1.5) John caused Bill to die on Sunday by stabbing him on Saturday.

(3.3.1.6) *John killed Bill on Sunday by stabbing him on Saturday.

Then, again, in (3.3.1.7) it has to be Sue and not Jo who takes the pills:

(3.3.1.7) Sue killed Jo by taking the pills.

But in the more complex (3.3.1.8) it could be Jo who takes the pills (it can also be Sue):

(3.3.1.8) Sue caused Jo to die by taking the pills.

A rather similar situation holds with the following pair: in (3.3.1.9) it is Fred's bad luck that S refers to, in (3.3.1.10) it could be either Fred's or Joe's:

(3.3.1.9) Fred killed Joe, though it was bad luck he did so.

(3.3.1.10) Fred caused Bill to die, though it was bad luck he did so.

It is therefore misleading to suggest that a superficially simple sentence like *A kill B* derives from a complex sentence like *A cause B to die*. Notice that where we have said in ch.3 that *A kills B at time T* $\longleftrightarrow$ *A causes B to die at time T* this states a semantic equivalence, not a derivational relationship. A semantic equivalence does not necessarily imply a derivational relationship – contrary to what generative semanticists believed.

5.3.3.2 Jeffrey Gruber's Studies in Lexical Relations 1965/1970/1976

Syntax and semantics will have the same representations at the prelexical level.

(Gruber 1970:2, 1976:3)

Gruber postulated a prelexical structure consisting of constituent structure rules that generate trees whose terminal symbols are not dummies ($\triangle$s) as in the standard theory transformational grammar, but semantic components. It seems that these semantic components do not fully specify the meanings of lexicon items (as a rule), but serve as semantic entry conditions for lexical insertion; thus they serve the same kind of function as selection restrictions in a standard theory grammar. Gruber envisaged a full semantic specification of lexicon items and higher sentence constituents along the lines described by Katz, after lexical insertion takes place.

On the basis that the (a/b) pairs in (3.3.2.1-3) are synonymous, Gruber argued that *cross* and *go across* should be mapped onto semantically identical nodes in prelexical structure.

(3.3.2.1)
   a. Ed crossed the street
   b. Ed went across the street.

(3.3.2.2)
   a.   The little boy crossed on his own.
   b.   The little boy went across on his own.

(3.3.2.3)
   a.   The wire crosses the front of the house.
   b.   The wire goes across the front of the house.

The relevant part of the prelexical structure onto which *cross* or *go across* will be mapped is given in (3.3.2.4):

(3.3.2.4)

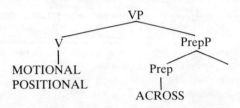

Lexical insertion will put either the verb *go* under the V node and the preposition *across* under the preposition node, or alternatively map the single verb *cross* into a combination of both the V and Prep nodes. The latter was a radical innovation in contemporary transformational theories.

In 'Look and see' 1967, Gruber argued that the verb *see* should be mapped onto a verb node semantically specified as SEE, MOTIONAL in combination with a preposition node specified as TO. We shall not discuss this analysis except to question Gruber's grounds for categorizing *see* as a MOTIONAL verb, which are: ' "John's gaze goes to the cat" is sufficiently close in meaning to "John sees the cat" to justify the procedure semantically' (1967:941). A very dubious similarity between the ordinary sentence *John sees the cat* and the completely abnormal *?*John's gaze goes to the cat* is not in fact sufficient justification for treating *see* as a motional verb (spelled out by the 'goes to' in the abnormal sentence). Sloppy would-be synonymies of this kind were too often taken to justify analyses in generative semantics, analyses that sometimes reveal more about the grammarian's ingenuity than they do about the semantic structure of language.

5.3.3.3 James D. McCawley rejects the distinction between syntax and semantics

1. Syntactic and semantic representations are of the same formal nature, namely labelled trees.
2   There is a single system of rules (henceforth 'transformations') which relates the semantic representation to surface structure through intermediate stages.
3. In the 'earlier' stages of the conversion from semantic representation to surface structure, terminal nodes may have for labels 'referential indices' [variables standing for the denotata of arguments].

> (McCawley 'Lexical insertion in a transformational grammar without deep structure' 1968c)

In papers published in 1967 and 1968 McCawley moved a long way from standard theory transformational grammar, inspired partly by predicate logic, and partly by the work of Weinreich, Postal, Lakoff, and Gruber, among others. The most significant contributions McCawley made to generative semantics have been collected in *Grammar and Meaning* 1973, which contains extensive self-critical footnotes on each of the papers in it. (We could add 'Syntactic and logical arguments for semantic structures' 1972/1973). McCawley conceived of syntactic structure as constituted from little more (if any more) than the following minimal set of constituent structure rules:

(CS.1)

$$\Sigma \rightarrow \text{VP NP (NP)}$$
$$\text{NP} \rightarrow \{ \begin{matrix} \Sigma \\ \text{[Variable]} \end{matrix} \}$$
$$\text{V} \rightarrow \text{[Semantic predicate]}$$

It is clear that this syntactic structure owes a great deal to predicate logic: V represents a predicate and the NPs its arguments; the arguments may be either variables representing denotata, or other sentences (propositions); the predicates are 'semantic atoms'. Among the semantic atoms which appear under V nodes in generative semantics grammars are:

verbs	–	BECOME, BOMB, CAUSE, DO, FORGIVE, HOLD, INTEND, INVENT, REQUEST
adjectives	–	ALIVE, CLOSED, FEMALE, OBNOXIOUS, RED, TEMPORARY
quantifiers	–	TWO, FEW, MANY, SOME, ALL

nouns   –   ACTION, AGENT, NAIL, OFFSPRING,
                RESULT
prepositions – IN, ON
conjunction – AND
negator   – NOT

It is often obvious why these may be said to be predicates, but not always, and the matter is not argued for in the generative semantics literature. More to the point, there is no explanation offered for the fact that these predicates end up in a variety of lexical classes. Generative semantics argumentation cheerfully disregarded the details of the rules required for generating surface structures from some very abstract deep structures.

It may be seen from (CS.1) that V is first among the immediate constituents of Σ. In 'English as a VSO language' 1970, McCawley argued that the superficial subject-verb-object order typical of English declarative clauses arises by transformation from an underlying constituent order in which predicates appear first; it was also assumed, but not discussed, that subjects precede objects. The order of these constituents is not of any concern to us. What is of interest to us, is that lexicalized NPs are predicated on variables representing their denotata, which is in line with the semantic analysis presented in this book: cf. *A is a bachelor*, *D is sugar*, *Y is (called) John*. A difference would be that in generative semantics the lexicon item *bachelor* would be mapped over a set of semantic atoms recursively predicating the variable A, as we shall see.

In 'Lexical insertion in a transformational grammar without deep structure' 1968c/1973.[28] McCawley discusses the meaning of *kill* which he resolves into the semantic atoms *CAUSE BECOME NOT ALIVE*. He quite rightly says that this is insufficient to account for the meaning of the predicate *kill*, which requires two arguments 'one of whom causes the event in question, the other of whom dies in that event' (1973:157). He represents this in (PM.1).

There is a noticeable difference between the surface structures in (3.3.3.1-7), some of which are unacceptable, but all of which can be derived from (PM.1): so there is some reordering necessary of the phrase marker if the FDPM is to carry acceptable lexical structures.

(3.3.3.1) X kills Y.

(3.3.3.2) X causes Y to die.

(3.3.3.3) X causes Y to cease to be alive.

(PM.1)

(3.3.3.4) ??X causes Y to become dead.

(3.3.3.5) *X causes Y to become not alive.

(3.3.3.6) *X causes to become Y not alive.

(3.3.3.7) *X causes to become not alive Y.

McCawley argued for a Predicate Raising transformation which adjoins a predicate to the next highest predicate in the tree, and the stranded argument gets raised, too. The notion of Predicate Raising is borrowed from Lakoff 1965/1970, but there is a difference: Lakoff raised lexical [−Pro] predicates onto hypothetical [+Pro] verb nodes; McCawley raises lower semantic predicates onto higher semantic predicates. E.g. (PM.1) might be converted into either (PM.2) or (PM.3) by Predicate Raising.

(PM.2)

(PM.3)

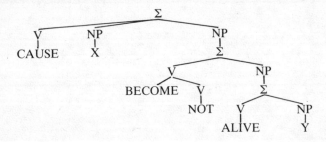

In (PM.2) ALIVE is raised to NOT to form the complex predicate NOT ALIVE which might be lexicalized to *dead*; thus, like Gruber 1965/1970, McCawley proposes that lexical items may be mapped onto more than one semantic terminal node in prelexical structure. If all other predicates in (PM.2) are lexicalized one to one, and certain reordering transformations operate, it would give rise to the extremely dubious (3.3.3.4). In (PM.3) the predicate NOT is raised onto BECOME to form the complex predicate BECOME NOT which, McCawley suggests 1973:158, might be lexicalized to *cease*, and after the operation of various other transformations (PM.3) could give rise to (3.3.3.3).

The complex predicate NOT ALIVE in (PM.2) can be raised to BECOME, forming the complex BECOME NOT ALIVE, which could be lexicalized to *die*, cf. (3.3.3.2); alternatively this predicate could be raised to CAUSE giving (PM.4)

(PM.4)

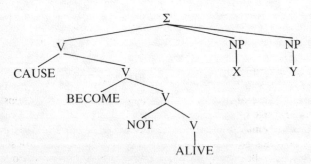

The complex predicate CAUSE BECOME NOT ALIVE, or more precisely the subtree in (3.3.3.8), is found in the lexicon entry for *kill*:

(3.3.3.8)

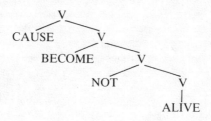

The item *kill* will thereafter be mapped onto the relevant part of the tree in (PM.4), such that after certain transformations operate, (PM.4) may generate (3.3.3.1).

5.3.3.4 An evaluation of generative semantics as a theory of sentence meaning

A full account of generative semantics would review a much wider range of literature than we have offered here.[29] However, we have presented sufficient of the theory to evaluate it as a theory of meaning. Generative semantics decomposes the meaning of lexical items into semantic components which are represented by vocabulary items from English (or some other natural language). Both Lakoff, 'Linguistics and natural logic' 1972:605, and McCawley, 'Syntactic and logical arguments for semantic structures' 1972:66 have suggested that there is a distinction between e.g. a semantic component such as CAUSE and the English verb *cause*; but, as we pointed out for Katz's semantic markerese in §5.2.5.2, these are unsubstantiated assertions, and in fact the representations of semantic components would be uninterpretable were they not assumed to be English (or whatever natural language) vocabulary items. So let us suppose that the componential vocabulary of generative semantics is taken from the vocabulary of a natural language.

The semantic components are located in structures based on those of predicate logic spiced with category symbols from natural language syntax. These are both well established conventional systems, so the metalanguage of generative semantics is superior in its conventionality to Katz's semantic markerese. It is, however, very seriously flawed in that no rules governing the insertion of semantic predicates under V nodes have been proposed. In a theory which purports to generate semantic structure, it should be obvious that there must be some constraints on the structures generated if they are meant to match acceptable semantic structures in a natural language. Consequently there must either be selection restrictions governing the entry of predicates into an array under the V nodes of a phrase marker, and these would be as impracticable or impossible to determine in generative semantics as in standard theory grammar, cf. §5.2.4; or, alternatively, semantic predicates could be freely inserted under V nodes, after which phrase markers would have to be checked through a filtering device such as Weinreich's 'semantic evaluator'; and we were just as pessimistic about the definition of a semantic evaluator as about determining the set of selection restrictions, cf. §§5.2.4.1 & 5.3.2. As generative semantics has been described, there are no well formedness conditions on semantic structures other than those imposed by the intuitions of the grammarian who write the nodes into a phrase marker.

One problem with generative semantics was alluded to at the end of §5.3.3.1 in the discussion of Fodor 1970's objection that *A kills B* is a simple sentence denoting one event, whereas *A causes B to die* – from which it supposedly derives – is a complex sentence denoting two events. Fodor's objection may not apply to a derivation like McCawley's, where a claim for the semantic equivalence between *kill* and *cause to die* might be thought different from the claim for their syntactic equivalence (as if the latter were at the level of surface structure): thus one line of defense for McCawley might be to claim that it is postlexical clauses which denote events, and not prelexical ones. However, this is contrary to the spirit of generative semantics

(3.3.4.1)

where meaning is defined prelexically. A preferable line of defense might be that, e.g. in *X cause Y to die on Sunday by stabbing him on Saturday* the scope of the adverbial acts as a constraint on lexicalization. For instance, *X cause on Saturday that Y die on Sunday* would have a structure something like (3.3.4.1). Obviously BECOME NOT ALIVE cannot here be Predicate Raised to CAUSE because of the intervening ON SUNDAY, so the conditions for introducing the lexical item *kill* don't arise. However, there is against this defense the argument that one interpretation of (3.3.4.2) is given in (3.3.4.3), cf. McCawley 'Syntactic and logical arguments for semantic structures' 1972:63.

(3.3.4.2) X almost killed Y.

(3.3.4.3)

As it stands this reads something like "X caused something to come about, namely that Y almost died", but somehow – it is not specified how – ALMOST can get moved up beyond CAUSE so that no predicate intervenes between CAUSE BECOME NOT ALIVE, which is lexicalized to *kill* in (3.3.4.2). Why shouldn't the (admittedly very different) adverbial in (3.3.4.1) also be moveable? Notice that although *X nearly killed Y* has the same ambiguity as (3.3.4.2), *X more than just killed Y [he mutilated him]* will not permit an interpretation based on the semantic structure in (3.3.4.3).

Consider pairs like the following:

(3.3.4.4)
- a.   A died in agony.
- b.   *A ceased to be alive in agony.

(3.3.4.5)
- a.   A died emaciated.
- b.   *A ceased to be alive emaciated.

I don't know of any way that the (b) sentences could be blocked in a generative semantics grammar except by a requirement that the array of predicates BECOME NOT ALIVE be lexicalized to *die*. Might this not be a sufficiently good reason to treat *die* as a semantic component?

In §3.5.3 we argued against semantic decomposition below the level of lexicon items. Suppose that lexicon items are the minimal semantic components in a language. Prima facie even decompositional theories like Katzian semantics and generative semantics utilize lexicon items (in fact lexes) in representations of meaning; they do, however, assume that the meanings of lexicon items can be expressed in terms of structured sequences of lexicon items in the metalanguage. We have shown that these are essentially equivalence relations based on inference. E.g.

(3.3.4.6) If it is true that X dies, then it is true that X ceases to be alive. And if it is true that X ceases to be alive, then it is true that X dies.

There is, however, no reason to assume from these facts that *die* is based on the meaning spelled out in *cease to be alive* rather than vice versa. In fact, there is no reason to think that either is in any sense, including a generative semantic sense, derived from the other. An equivalence relation does not necessarily imply a derivational relation in a grammar; take the meaning of 'four' in

(3.3.4.7) I have four children.

All the following are arithmetically, and, so far as I can tell, semantically, equivalent; though under the most likely of circumstances, only (a) would not violate the co-operative maxim of manner.

(3.3.4.8)
- a.   four children ⟷
- b.   one child & one child & one child & one child ⟷
- c.   two children & (another) two children ⟷
- d.   one child & three children ⟷
- e.   one less than five children ⟷

f. six less than ten children ⟷
g. one more than three children ⟷
h. three more than one child ⟷
i. four times one child ⟷
j. two times two children ⟷
k. two-squared children ⟷
l. the square-root-of-sixteen children ⟷
m. the same number of children as there are 25s in 100.

Obviously one could continue adding to this list. The point is that it would be absurd to suggest that (a) is in any way a lexicalization on a semantic structure comparable in form to any of (b-m). It is equally absurd to map *die* onto a semantic structure comparable to *cease to be alive*, or to map *kill* onto a semantic structure comparable to *cause to die*. Although there is usually synonymy between *kill* and *cause to die*, there doesn't have to be. Take the case where Max parks his car and fails to pull on the handbrake before he gets out. The car is parked on an incline and starts to roll downhill, gathering speed as it goes; toward the bottom of the hill it mounts the pavement and strikes down three children, killing two of them. Notice we have said that the car killed the two children (consider a newspaper heading: 'Runaway car kills two children'), and undoubtedly it caused their death. But whereas Max could be charged with causing the death of the two children, he could hardly be charged with killing them. In fact, what caused the death of the children was Max's negligence in not pulling his car handbrake on. If we assume only a semantic equivalence and not a derivational relationship between *kill* and *cause to die* we can appeal to a general condition that synonymous propositions are not substitutable for one another under all circumstances; in other words synonymy is not absolute. In a derivational relationship, where *kill* and *cause to die* have a common semantic structure, as in generative semantics theory, appeal to this general condition on the nonabsoluteness of synonymy cannot be made.

Semantic complexity postulated of lexicon items such as *bachelor* "man who has never married" and *kill* "cause to die" has been shown in psycholinguistic experiments to be nonexistent in the cognitive processing of these (and other similar) items. Janet Fodor, Jerry Fodor, & Merrill Garrett reported in 'The psychological unreality of semantic representations' 1975 that NPs containing purely definitional negatives – like the 'never' in the semantic representation of *bachelor* – are significantly easier to process than comparable NPs containing explicit negatives. Jerry Fodor, Garrett, Walker, & Parkes in 'Against definitions' 1980 used different techniques to evaluate processing difficulty, and came to the conclusion that

> b) The [. . .] results clearly indicated that [the causative verbs] "kill", "break", etc. are deep simplex verbs if any verbs are; viz. that the semantic representation of "John killed Mary" is something like "John killed Mary".
>
> c) This indicates, in turn, that causative verbs are undefined; psychological reality apparently cannot be claimed for the definitional structures that have been widely alleged to underlie such verbs [e.g. John caused Mary to die].
>
> d) Since causatives seem to be the 'best cases' for definition, the results suggest that there may few or no causes of psychologically real definitions.
>
> (Fodor, Garrett, Walker, & Parkes 1980:308)

What this means is that from a cognitive viewpoint lexicon items are semantic atoms, they do not decompose into semantic structures. Thus the language user does not understand, say, *kill* in terms of "cause to die"; but if asked to give the meaning of *kill* it would violate the co-operative principle (in particular the maxim of quantity) to say ' "Kill" is the meaning of *kill*'; instead, the language user will offer a semantically equivalent expression, such as in 'The meaning of *kill* is "cause to die." ' The linguist is in a similar position to any other language user, thus we criticised Jackendoff in §4.12.5 for using OPEN in specifying the meaning of *open*. It is a mistake to assume that a semantic description offers semantic decomposition, because all a linguist can offer by it is a semantic equivalence (at best). As Fodor, Garrett, Walker, & Parkes say 'there is no logical form *inside lexical items*' (1980:311, their emphasis). This directly refutes the claims of generative semantics.

Jerrold J. Katz has claimed in *Language and Other Abstract Objects* 1981a:95-114 (see also Katz 'The real status of semantic representations' 1977c) that the psychological reality or unreality of semantic descriptions is irrelevant to semantic theory. It is possible for a generative semanticist to claim that his metalanguage is an abstract representation and any coincidence with cognitively real structures is an irrelevance. In a sense, this is true. But then we must ask how generative semantics answers the question 'What is meaning?' The answer must be 'Meaning is a logically structured array of semantic atoms, such as we saw in (PM.1) of §5.3.3.3.' This answer is unsatisfactory; as we showed in ch.2, the meaning of language expression E_o (or rather its 'sense' because that is what we are talking about) is a language expression E_m describing the prototypical denotatum of E_o. Ideally, E_o and E_m are translation equivalents. But generative semanticists do not regard, e.g. *kill* and CAUSE BECOME NOT ALIVE as translation equivalents because *kill* is transformationally derived from CAUSE BECOME NOT ALIVE by the processes described in §5.3.3.3. If we were right in ch.2 about what meaning is, then generative semantics gives a false answer to the question 'What is meaning?' (or 'What is sense?') and therefore we should reject it as a theory of meaning. In view of its other infelicities, which have led to its demise, this is a welcome conclusion.

5.3.4 Schemes for marking participant roles in a grammar

The terms 'agent' and 'patient' – denoting respectively "the person acting" and "the person affected" – have been used in the western grammatical tradition at least since the time of Apollonius Dyscolus in the 2nd century A.D. (cf. Householder 1981). These two terms will distinguish the participant roles in

(3.4.1)   The farmer shot the dingo.

(3.4.2)   The dingo was shot by the farmer.

In both sentences 'the farmer' is agent and 'the dingo' is the affected object or patient. Because Bloomfieldian linguistics and early transformational grammars concentrated on syntactic structure to the virtual exclusion of semantics, they ignored even these traditional participant roles. In fact, every argument within a proposition plays some kind of role as a participant in the activity, event, or state which is denoted by the predicate. Because Gruber's *Studies in Lexical Relations* 1965 examined the semantics of motional verbs, Gruber was forced to recognize that their different arguments play different roles; thus he named the argument which moves 'theme', the location it moves from 'source', and the location it moves to 'goal'. Hence, in

(3.4.3)   X went to Y

'X' is theme and 'Y' is goal. In either of

(3.4.4)   A gave B to C

(3.4.5)   C got B from A

'A' is the source, 'B' the theme, and 'C' the goal. Gruber represented roles as nodes dominating NP or Prepositional Phrase arguments.

The same manner of representation was used by Charles Fillmore in 'The case for case' 1968, the paper which launched a school of case grammars – that is, grammars which represent participant roles in terms of 'deep case' nodes in underlying phrase markers. Fillmore pointed out that roles are often indicated by surface cases in a language like Finnish, and by prepositions in a language like English (e.g. 'goal' is typically indicated by *to*, and 'source' by *from*). One problem for so-called case grammars has been trying to decide how many roles a grammar should specify. In a grammar which seeks to generate all possible sentences in language L by expanding an initial symbol Σ, it is obviously necessary to specify the set of all possible roles for arguments within the proposition defined on Σ, as well as the possible combinations of roles with one another and with the predicate within the proposition. In §4.12.6 we saw that the lexicon entries for predicates permit participant roles to be determined by inference rules; and because of the nature of our analytical procedure, there is no need for any constraint on the number of roles that might be recognized. The combinations of roles with one another and with a given predicate will be decided by the normal conditions on inferences from the data.

Ray Jackendoff in *Semantic Interpretation in Generative Grammar* 1972 ch.2 recognized that some participant roles are complex. Take the similarities and dissimilarities between (3.4.6) and (3.4.7).

(3.4.6) A buys B from C.

(3.4.7) C sells B to A.

These sentences have in common that 'A' is goal, 'B' is what Gruber calls theme, and I prefer to call affected object, and 'C' is source. The sentences differ in that 'A' is agent in (3.4.6) whereas 'C' is agent in (3.4.7). Thus 'A' is both agent and goal, i.e. agentive goal, in (3.4.6); 'C' is both source and agent, i.e. agentive source, (3.4.7). In

(3.4.8) A was sold B by C

'A' is still agent, but it is also an affected object here – i.e. 'A' is an affected goal; 'B' is an affected object; and 'C' is the agentive source. In sentences like

(3.4.9)   John sat down

(3.4.10) Max left

the subject NP plays the role of both doer and affected object – a dual role spelled out in e.g. *John sat himself down* and *Max took himself off*. Comparing

(3.4.11) Ed fell over a cliff, it was a terrible accident.

(3.4.12) Harry fell over the cliff so realistically it looked like it wasn't a stunt at all.

'Ed' has the role only of the affected object in (3.4.11) whereas 'Harry' has the role of doer and affected object in (3.4.12). Even in something like
(3.4.13) Joe gave Mac a book

'Mac' may have the dual role of recipient and beneficiary; in (3.4.14), however, these two roles are separately assigned:

(3.4.14) Cathy gave Ro a book for her sister.

Here 'Ro' is the recipient, and 'her sister' the beneficiary. Note that these terms are more precise than Gruber's 'goal'. We won't pursue these matters any further here.

Case grammar was not conceived as an alternative to Katz's semantic theory, but simply as a hypothesis about the necessity for representing participant roles in the underlying phrase marker. Both Gruber and Fillmore expected something like Katz's semantic component would assign meanings to the underlying phrase markers in which their role indicators were located. Katz, for his part, has rejected the representation of deep case markers in underlying structure, preferring to treat case as a property bestowed on arguments by the semantic properties of the verb, cf. *Semantic Theory* 1972:112f, *Propositional Structure and Illocutionary Force* 1977a:84f.

5.3.5 Last words on the alternatives to Katzian semantics

We embarked on the examination of Katz's semantic theory in §5.2 because Katz has claimed to solve the projection problem for semantics; that is, he has claimed to model the way in which meaning is projected up through the hierarchy of syntactic levels from the meanings of lexicon items to give meanings (senses) for sentences. We found that Katz has not been successful in this venture, and so we turned to some alternative theories. We have not discussed any of the theories of linguistic semantics being worked on in Europe, and we have not further discussed Anna Wierzbicka's *Lingua mentalis* 1980 (which was briefly mentioned in §4.12.5), the reason being that there is nothing there to compare in scope with Katz's work. We did, however, discuss the work of Uriel Weinreich, some of which was specifically written to offer an alternative to Katzian theory; and we discussed generative semantics – which was also created in direct competition with Katz's semantic theory. We have not offered a detailed survey such as may be found in Janet D. Fodor's *Semantics: Theories of Meaning in Generative Grammar* 1977, largely through lack of space, but partly because we should have ended up repeating the kinds of criticisms already made. We found that Weinreich's work contains many interesting ideas which are not sustained or sustainable within a semantic theory in a way that is applicable to language data. We found that generative semantics, although it seems to solve the projection problem, does so in an unacceptable way, by taking a decompositional approach to meaning – a criticism which could be levelled at all theories discussed in ch.5. Neither Weinreich's work nor that of the generative semanticists compares in scope with Katz's semantic theory. But if none of these theories is adequate, what can we offer instead? This question is answered (somewhat tentatively) in §5.4.

5.4   Inferential semantics and the relationship between the meaning of a sentence and the meanings of the lexicon items it contains

In the kind of inferential semantics presented in this book we take the form of the sentence Σ to be given in S's utterance U (recall that U consists of Σ spoken with prosody Φ). We have already given meanings for sentences in ch.3; for instance, the meaning of *Robin is a woman*:

(3.11.1.10) Robin is a woman $\longleftrightarrow$ (Robin is female) & (Robin is adult) & (Robin is a human being)

Further inferences can be drawn from *Robin is a woman* that are not spelled out in (3.11.1.10), e.g. the inference that "Robin is the name of an individual." However, we are not interested here in an exhaustive account of the meaning of one particular proposition, but in the relationship between the meaning of a sentence and the meanings of the lexicon items which it contains.

In order to examine this relationship compare the meanings of the following sentences, paying particular attention to our understanding of 'lamb'.

(4.1) The black lamb was dead.

(4.2) Yesterday, two white lambs were gambolling in the field.

In both these sentences the lexeme "lamb" denotes young sheep; but the other attributes of the denotatum/denotata vary with each sentence, as the lex 'lamb' falls into the scope of a different stack of predicates. To illustrate this, take the denotatum of 'lamb' in (4.1). The denotatum is named as lamb; it might be any sort of lamb, but in fact it is something described as 'black lamb': thus we have two attributes for the denotatum, it is lamb and it is black. Looking to the rest of the NP in (4.1) we see that it is not just any black lamb, but 'the black lamb' – we shall discuss the meaning of *the* in §7.11.1 and nothing more will be said about it here, instead we will rely on the reader's knowledge of English to carry the point. Finally, the black lamb, which could have been doing anything, or to which anything could have happened, was in fact dead at some time (perhaps more precisely identifiable from extrasentential context) in the past. This, incidentally, determines that the NP could not be denoting meat – although once the lamb was defined was being black this was already unlikely.[30] We see that our understanding of 'lamb' in (4.1) is progressively defined by the predicates into whose scope it falls. In all languages scope relations are a function of syntax, determined by the respective syntactic categories of the semantic predicate and its scope, and either their relative position within syntactic structure, or morphosyntactic marking, or both these. In English, constituent order predominates as an indicator of scope relations, whereas in other languages, e.g. Polish or Warlpiri, morphosyntax predominates in this function. For instance, in (4.1) the stack of recursive predicates 'black', 'the', 'was dead', is structured as shown in the following diagram, where the scope of the predicate is pointed by an arrow.

(4.1′)

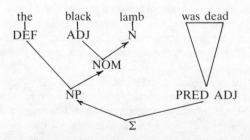

We shall analyze the PRED ADJ construction shortly. The structure, of course, contributes to the meaning. Although both (4.1) and (4.3) denote something which was a lamb, which was black, and which was dead, they do not convey the information in the same way:

(4.3) The dead lamb was black.

Only (4.1) is appropriate in context C_1, whereas only (4.3) is appropriate in C_3 (see ch.7 for more on information structure).

C_1:   Some while ago my favourite ewe gave birth to a black lamb and a white one. Last night there was a commotion in the paddock and when I went out there, the black lamb was dead.

C_3:   The ewe gave birth to twins, but one died shortly after. The dead lamb was black.

There are different assumptions arising from the different stacking of predicates, thus the structure in (4.3′) is different from that in (4.1′).

(4.3′)

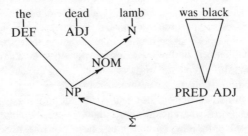

A similar pattern of analysis emerges from (4.2). Here the denotatum of the subject NP is once again lamb, and it might be any sort of lamb but because 'lamb' falls within the scope of the plural morph '-s' we know that there is more than one lamb. Again, they might be any sort of lambs but in fact they are white; and there may be any number of white lambs (greater than one) but there are exactly two. The two white lambs might have been doing anything – or anything might have happened to them – but in fact they were gambolling. The event of the two white lambs gambolling is presented as an essive argument of the prepositional predicate 'in', which locates this event in 'the field': thus, the field, which could have been mentioned for any purpose (e.g. because it was overgrown, or it was burning, or whatever) is in fact attributed by the predicate 'in' with the participant role of inessive location. This event of the two white lambs

playing in the field which could have been located at any time in the
past (see (4.5) below) in fact took place yesterday. Thus, the
structuring of the semantic predicates in (4.2) is as shown in (4.2′).[31]

(4.2′)

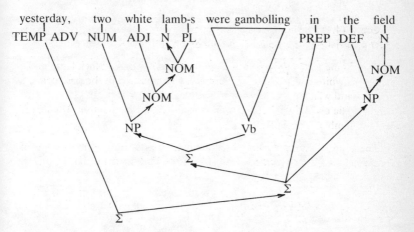

In result of the various predicates under whose scope 'lamb' falls, our
understanding of the denotation of this lex in (4.2) is very different
from our understanding of the identical lex in (4.1).

We have not attempted to give an exhaustive account of the meaning
relations within (4.1-2). For instance, in (4.1′) we have left the PRED
ADJ node unanalysed. Although the matter needs more investigation
it appears that the following parsing is justified.

(4.4)

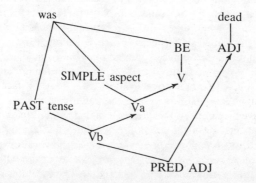

In determining the scope of covert constituents such as tense and aspect within portmanteau expressions like *was* morphology has its part to play, although for the most part, constituent order and the respective syntactic categories of the predicate and its scope are the predominant determinants of scope relations in English.

Again, in (4.2′) we did not analyze Vb; it should subsume the structure in (4.5).

(4.5)

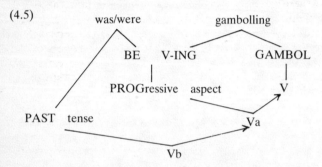

In the analyses above, our implicit claim is that the meanings of lexicon items contribute to the meanings of sentences via sets of recursive predicate structures. As can be seen from the sequences of meaning descriptions given for (4.1-2), recursive predication delimits the denotative scope of a lexicon item, or combination of lexicon items. The justification for our analysis is the following. Any lexicon item in the language has a potentially very large, perhaps infinitely large, denotative range if it is considered as an isolate, outside of a phrase or sentence. Locating a lexicon item within a sentence severely constrains its denotative range, which nevertheless remains virtually boundless until the sentence is located within an utterance – where, in the interests of effective communication, and under the constraints of the co-operative principle, it is normally reduced to a unique denotation. The recursive predicate structure properly captures the first stages of this reduction in denotative scope.

The recursive predicate structures that we identify are evidently indicated by natural language syntax. They also bear more than a passing resemblance to the kinds of structures proposed in generative semantics, but without the unacceptable semantic decomposition. Although we identify a common predicate function among a variety of lexical categories, it should be obvious that each lexical category has its own co-occurrence constraints: e.g. prepositions take a different range of arguments from verbs or nouns, conjunctions a different set from either of these.[32] Most nouns and adjectives are one place predicates, some are two place. Most prepositions are two place predicates unless they fall within the scope of a verb, adjective, or quantifier (as in e.g. *give NP to NP*, *fond of NP*, *all of the men*), in either case their semantic effect is typically on the noun phrase to their right. Verbs may have between one and four arguments (cf. *John died* and *Jo gave the ticket to Ed for Max*), though perhaps most verbs are two place predicates. There are also semantic types among the different lexical categories: nouns typically name, adjectives typically attribute properties, and verbs typically predicate acts; although there is a good deal of variation in this area, it tends to be with peripheral members of the category. All this confirms the need to recognize lexical categories when determining meaning, as well as recursive predicate structure; and that is what we have done.

Even so, the syntactic structures we have identified here do not correlate precisely with traditional accounts of syntactic structure – although there is, naturally, a large degree of overlap. However, on the assumption that the only motivation for syntax is to structure semantic relations between lexicon items, we conclude that the traditional syntactic analyses need to be revamped. Unfortunately it is beyond the scope of this book to explain how this might be done. Incidentally, we should not expect there to be a simple one-to-one relationship between surface syntactic structure and semantic structure: although syntax exists to structure semantic relations between lexicon items, it has its own peculiar features, not all of which transparently serve such a purpose in the contemporary language.

The meanings of phrases, clauses, and sentences are built up from the recursive predications of lexicon items on one another in a manner revealed through the syntactic structure of the construction in question, in a way that delimits the denotational scope of the lexicon items within the construction. When the sentence is used by S in his utterance U, its denotational scope, and that of its constituents, will usually be restricted to exactly what S has in mind to speak of in W, without ambiguity for the hearer H.

Notes to Volume 1

Chapter 1   Beginning an account of linguistic meaning

1. Cf. Noam Chomsky *Syntactic Structures* 1957:15.
2. Language is not all speech, but speech is the primary medium of linguistic communication, and for this reason we shall talk of the speaker and hearer. Almost everything said about S applies to the writer as well, mutatis mutandis, and almost everything said about H applies to the reader; where important differences come to light, they will be pointed out. How much of what I have to say about S and H is relevant to signing deaf people, I don't know.
3. For the sake of simplicity in exposition, it is generally assumed that both S and H are male. My apologies to any readers who might be offended by this.
4. *The Oxford Companion to Law* (David Walker 1980:1038) has as its entry for 'reasonable man': 'The standard of foresight of the reasonable man eliminates the personal equation and is independent of the idiosyncrasies of the particular person whose conduct is in question. [. . .] The standard provided by consideration of the "reasonable man" is objective and impersonal, but varies with circumstances, the known characteristics of the thing involved, the magnitude of any risk, the practicality of precautions, the customary practice in the circumstances, the existence of emergency and the like.' Lord Justice Greer in the Hall *v.* Brooklands Club case, said: 'The person concerned is sometimes described as "the man in the street", or "the man in the Clapham omnibus", or as I recently read in an American author, "the man who takes the magazines at home, and in the evening pushes the lawn mower in his shirt sleeves". Such a man taking a ticket to see a cricket match at Lord's would know quite well that he was not going to be encased in a steel frame which would protect him from the one in a million chance of a cricket ball dropping on his head.' (*Law Reports, King's Bench Division. Vol. I* 1933:224).
5. Cf. Kent Bach & Robert M. Harnish *Linguistic Communication and Speech Acts* 1979:12ff. Not all noises and graphic marks used in human communication are linguistic, but those that are can be distinguished from non-linguistic ones fairly readily: e.g.hieroglyphs are distinguishable from pictures, even when they are in an unknown language. Unintentional utterances do, of course, occur from time to time, but they are parasitic on intentional ones and present no difficulties for the exposition of meaning given in this book. Nor does the fact that a machine can be programmed to speak or write.
6. Cf. Stephen Schiffer *Meaning* 1972:30ff, Herbert H. Clark & Catherine

Marshall 'Definite reference and mutual knowledge' 1981, Neil Smith (ed.)
Mutual Knowledge 1982.
7. As I can leave the reader to figure it out for herself or himself.
8. The notions of politeness touched on here are discussed in detail in §1.2.3.3.
9. The fact that psycholinguistic experiments have shown subjects take longer
   to process implausible, grammatically degraded sentences, than to process
   plausible grammatical sentences of equal length and complexity, is
   explicable if the subject – as hearer or reader – spends time (a few
   centiseconds) trying to figure out a plausible interpretation in accordance
   with the communicative presumption, before rejecting them. Cf. Kenneth I.
   Forster & Leonie A. Ryder 'Perceiving the structure and meaning of
   sentences' 1971; Kenneth I. Forster 'The role of semantic hypotheses in
   sentence processing' 1974, 'Levels of processing and the structure of the
   language processor' 1979:75ff.; Patrice French 'Semantic and syntactic
   factors in the perception of rapidly presented sentences' 1981; Wayne S.
   Murray *Sentence Matching: The Influence of Meaning and Structure* 1982;
   Jan Ratcliff 'An investigation of the plausibility effect' 1978.
10. A convention is a regularity in behaviour to which, in a given situation,
    almost everyone within a population conforms and expects almost everyone
    else to conform – moreoever, almost everyone prefers this state of affairs to
    an alternative. This is not to say that the convention is immutable: if people
    cease to conform to a particular regularity and prefer to cease to conform to
    it, it will cease to remain a convention; and if they gradually adopt another
    regularity in behaviour this will become a convention when almost everyone
    in the population conforms to it, and almost everyone comes to prefer this
    state of affairs to the alternative. See David Lewis *Conventions* 1969:78 for
    a tighter definition of convention, and Dieter Wunderlich *Foundations of
    Linguistics* 1979:7ff for a discussion of language conventions.
11. Cf. Brown & Levinson 1978:66. This discussion of face is deeply indebted to
    Brown & Levinson's work.
12. Cf. Brown & Levinson 1978:79. The numbers (1-4) are included for
    expository purposes only; they are not intended to correlate wth *D*, *P*, and
    R ratings.
13. Bronislaw Malinowski 'The problem of meaning in primitive languages'
    1949:315.
14. Or whatever 'free goods' might be appropriately mentioned in the situation
    of utterance.
15. Conventions vary in different cultures. 19th century Europeans were
    repulsed by the positive face affect among many East African tribes of
    spitting on a departing stranger when farewelling him, as a mark of
    friendship; in European cultures spitting on someone is highly insulting to
    their negative face. Cf. Charles Miller *The Lunatic Express* 1973:90, 417.
16. Cf. Howard Giles & Peter F. Powesland *Speech Style and Social Evaluation*
    1975 ch.9.
17. These are normally accompanied by head movements and other
    paralinguistic signs of attention from the interlocutor.
18. Exx. (2.3.2.3) and (2.3.2.5) are from Brown & Levinson 1978:118, 119.
19. Cf. Charlotte Baker 'This is just a first approximation, but . . .' 1975.
20. See §8.6.1.
21. There is an extensive literature on choosing which language to use in a
    multilingual situation, cf: Gilbert Ansre 'The influence of English on West

African languages' 1971, Jan-Petter Blom & John J. Gumperz 'Social meaning in linguistic structures: code-switching in Norway' 1972; Nigel Denison 'Some observations on language variety and pluralism' 1972; Joshua A. Fishman 'The sociology of language: an interdisciplinary social science approach to language in society' 1971, 'The relationship between micro- and macro-sociolinguistics in the study of who speaks what to whom and when' 1972; John T. Platt 'The relation between accommodation and code-switching in a multilingual society: Singapore' 1980.

22. There seems a general tendency among the socially inferior to appear linguistically incompetent in front of their social superiors; e.g. in 'The logic of nonstandard English' 1969 William Labov argues that American Black children who appear to suffer a language deficit when speaking to white investigators may be extremely articulate among peer group Blacks.

23. Cf. Brown & Levinson 1978:192, 272.

24. Something we have not discussed is that the comparative ages and sexes of S and H are important factors determining the modes of address and general character of S's language usage. The comparative ages of S and H can as a rule be accommodated within the measure of social distance (D); in many societies S's seniors, even his senior siblings, must be treated with respect. In most societies, men's and women's language is rather different, one general characteristic being that women are typically more polite than men (i.e. their language will more often be marked by formal characteristics). It is possible that the parameter of sex is almost as significant as social distance in determining the manner of address. In some Australian aboriginal communities there are so-called 'mother-in-law' languages, used when S is the opposite sex from his or her spouse's parent, and also to cross cousins of the opposite sex (cf. Robert M.W. Dixon *The Dyirbal Language of North Queensland* 1972:32); the 'mother-in-law' language is lexically distinct from the language used with other kinsfolk.

25. Sino-Japanese terms are used to mark more formal and polite language, cf. Ide 1982.

26. Cf. James Collins 'Athapaskan classifiers, person, and deference' 1979:58.

27. Cf. Wesley Jacobsen 'The semantics of spontaneity in Japanese' 1981:114.

28. Data from an unpublished ms by Frances Snyder & Andrew Pawley 'The reduction principle in conversation' 1974.

29. Cf. Robin Lakoff 'The logic of politeness; or minding your p's and q's' 1973.

30. Supplications sound more humble when imperative than they do when interrogative, compare *Grant me one last wish, my lord* versus *Will you grant me one last wish my lord?*

31. We earlier (in §1.2.3.1) spoke of a meet-and-speak convention: if X meets Y and doesn't speak to him, X is likely to be thought unfriendly; it is polite to speak on meeting someone. We are now saying that for X to address Y is potentially an imposition upon Y and therefore impolite to Y. When X meets Y there is, therefore, a dilemma: should X appear unfriendly towards Y by not speaking to him, or should he risk imposing on Y by speaking to him? Phatic communion exists to solve this dilemma: it satisfies the meet-and-speak requirement without imposing S's ideas and opinions, and so forth, upon H. If H appears receptive to serious conversation, this can follow on the phatic communion.

32. Cf. Brown & Levinson 1978:203ff.

33. Cf. George Lakoff 'Hedges: a study of meaning criteria and the logic of fuzzy concepts' 1972.
34. For readers unfamiliar with Shakespeare (the master of *double entendre*) I will gloss some of the *double entendres* here, using the superscript [a-h] as reference points: *a*: There is a play on Pistol's name; and also play on the word 'charge' in the sense "fill" – thus, 'charge you with a cup of sack' means "fill you with a cup of wine". *b*: 'Discharge upon mine hostess' plays on Pistol's name; it openly means "pay the hostess", but in view of what follows there is perhaps a sexual innuendo, too. *c*: A play on 'bullets' meaning "little balls". *d*: "For no man's pleasure I' has the double meaning "I won't do it for anybody" and "I'm not a whore". *e*: Doll Tearsheet is a whore and Pistol's offer to 'charge' her, i.e. "fill" her, is undoubtedly a sexual innuendo, though openly he is offering her some wine. *f*: Here 'charge' takes the added sense of "demand money", hence Doll's anger and abuse – after all, whores don't pay for copulation, they get paid for it! *g*: 'Meat for your master' means both "good enough for your master" and "your master's whore, not yours". *h*: A play on 'know' meaning "acquainted with" and "have carnal knowledge of".
35. Credit must be given to the usefulness of Grice's original analysis of the communicative conventions; but over the years some inadequacies have come to light and we can now improve on Grice's pioneering work.
36. I am grateful to Edina Eisikovits for bringing this to my attention.
37. Cf. Grice 1975:46 – 'Under the category of QUALITY falls a supermaxim – "Try to make your contribution one that is true" – and two more specific maxims:
    1. Do not say what you believe to be false.
    2. Do not say that for which you lack adequate evidence.'
38. It might therefore be appropriate to say that S exploits the maxims in different ways to gain different effects.
39. Thus – though it is vacuous to say so – the text consists of E and its co-text.
40. The situation may be much more complicated. Suppose S writes a novel at time t_1 in place l_1 and sends it to a publisher, who utters the book at time t_2 in place l_2; the book is bought and read aloud onto a tape at time t_3 in place l_3; H listens to the tape at time t_4 in place l_4. In such circumstances we take the dichotomy to hold between the writer, S at t_1 in l_1 and hearer H at t_4 in l_4.
41. Cf. William E. Bull *Time, Tense, and the Verb* 1960; Robin T. Lakoff 'Tense and its relation to participants' 1970: Hans Reichenbach *Elements of Symbolic Logic* 1947:288. The temporal adverbials which form sets with *now*, *today*, etc. are also deictically oriented to the moment of utterance.
42. Cf. Emile Benveniste 'Structure des relations de personne dans le verbe' 1946 [= 'Relationships of person in the verb' 1971].
43. Cf. Penelope Brown & Stephen Levinson 'Universals in language usage: politeness phenomena' 1978:209.
44. Cf. David Thomas 'Three analyses of the Ilocano pronoun system' 1955:208.
45. Dell Hymes 'Models of the interaction of language and social life' 1972:60 calls this 'scene'.
46. Cf. William Marslen-Wilson & Lorraine K. Tyler 'Towards a psychological

basis for a theory of anaphora' 1980.

47. See Keith Allan 'Nouns and countability' 1980 where it is argued that the grammatical category of countability is characteristic of noun phrases rather than the lexical class of nouns.

48. Cf. Keith Allan 'Interpreting from context' 1981 for further discussion.

49. Cf. Emile Benveniste 'La nature des pronoms' 1956 [= 'The nature of pronouns' 1971]

50. Some additional examples of zero anaphora occur in:

    (a) Phyllis is thought to be, and Sue definitely is pregnant.
    (b) Mimi has and Flo will see the play.
    (c) Max plays the piano and Anna the flute.
    (d) Anyone who can, should get the hell out of there.
    (e) Max borrowed my car when his got stolen.

H's problem in recognizing that a constituent is missing is a semantic one; but his problem identifying which constituent it is, is a syntactic one. However, the two problems fall together, as we can see when we replace the zero anaphor of (a)-(e) with *something* (used as either noun or verb):

    (a′) Phyllis is thought to be *something*, and Sue definitely is pregnant.
    (b′) Mimi has *somethinged* and Flo will see the play.
    (c′) Max plays the piano and Anna *somethings* the flute.
    (d′) Anyone who can *something*, should get the hell out of there.
    (e′) Max borrowed my car when his *something* got stolen.

The zero anaphors, replaced here by *something*, are, then, interpreted from the co-text just like filled co-denotational anaphors, according to conventions that we leave to syntacticians to describe.

    Some of the more signifiant works discussing anaphora (of all kinds) are: Peter T. Geach *Reference and Generality* 1968; Ray Jackendoff 'Gapping and related rules' 1971; Paul M. Postal 'On co-referential complement subject deletion' 1971a, *Cross-over Phenomena* 1971b; Michael A.K. Halliday & Ruqaiya Hasan *Cohesion in English* 1976; Richard A. Hudson 'Conjunction reduction, gapping, and right-node raising' 1976; Anneke Neijt *Gapping* 1979; Jody Kreiman & Almerindo E. Ojeda *Papers from the CLS Parassession on Pronouns and Anaphora* 1980; Noam Chomsky *Lectures on Government and Binding* 1981, *Some Concepts and Consequences of the Theory of Government and Binding* 1982.

51. On quantifier scope, see §7.3.

52. Cf. Gerald Gazdar *Pragmatics* 1979:4 where he says that if D is the set of sentences of L, M is the set of contexts, and E the set $D \times M$, then U the set of utterances in L bears the relation $U \subset E$; i.e. utterances are 'sentence-context pairs'.

53. The words *gives* and *gave* consist respectively of the lexeme "give" + "3rd person singular subject agreement" morpheme and the lexeme "give" + "past tense", cf. §1.5.2 for discussion of the relationships between words, lex(eme)s, and morph(eme)s.

54. Cf. Charles F. Hockett 'Problems of morphemic analysis' 1947.

55. Cf. §3.4 for details. Analytic sentences, in which the meaning of the predicate is wholly included in the meaning of one of the arguments, e.g. *A cow is a mammal*, would seem to have a value independent of any utterance in which they are used. However, values are defined in relation to context C

and sentences are by definition contextless, therefore sentences cannot have values – whatever may appear to be the case.

56. Cf. David Brazil, Malcolm Coulthard, & Catherine Johns *Discourse Intonation and Language Teaching* 1980 ch.2.

57. We take *scissors* to be the citation form, despite the existence of the morph 'scissor' in *scissor-movement*. Most pluralia tantum nouns are immutably plural in form.

58. E.g. *black*, *newly-wed*, *oral*.

59. Cf. §4.3.2.

60. In my dialect the idiomatic sense of *is an old woman* must be predicated of a man, but many Australians allow this to be used of a woman, too.

61. There is no general convention governing the use of terminology here, and I use the terms *denote*, *denotation*, *denotatum* (= "that which is denoted", plural *denotata*) only after much soul-searching and trials of other terms. The same comment holds for the use of *designate*, *designation*, and *designatum* below; but the use of *refer*, *reference*, and *referent* is in line with the dominant convention. However, Charles W. Morris in *Foundations of the Theory of Signs* 1938:5 uses 'designation' as we shall use *denotation* and 'denotation' as we shall use *reference*.

62. I.e. objects, people, places, actions, events, states of affairs, etc.

63. I.e. the etic counterpart to a sentence.

64. Cf. Bach & Harnish 1979:29.

65. It is of no relevance to the claim that proper names have no 'sense' (in our terms) that they can be etymologically associated with meanings, e.g. *Colin* 'amiable', *Peter* 'stone', *Norman* 'man from the north' or Asante (southern Ghana) *Akua* 'female born on Wednesday', *Kofi* 'male born on Friday', etc. There are no circumstances under which a language would permit one to substitute *Peter* for *stone* or vice versa – nor anything like it.

Chapter 2   What is meaning?

1. See ch.4 for detailed discussion of lexicon semantics.

2. E.g. The use of *She sells sea-shells on the sea-shore* as a tongue twister has nothing to do with its meaning and everything to do with the phonetic similarity of the syllable initial /ʃ/ and /s/.

3. Cf. Moritz Schlick 'Meaning and Verification' 1949, Alfred J. Ayer's introduction to *Language, Truth and Logic* 1946. Bloomfieldianism was the counterpart in linguistics to verificationism, see Leonard Bloomfield 'A set of postulates for the science of language' 1926. Bloomfield's theory of meaning is discussed in §2.2.5 below.

4. *S-R* theory was motivated by Pavlov's experiments with dogs. It will be recalled that Pavlov noticed dogs salivate when they see food (this is an unconditioned response to the stimulus), and he trained them to salivate at the sound of a bell rung prior to the presentation of food (a conditioned response, reinforced by the food); eventually they would salivate at the sound of the bell even if there was no reinforcement in the form of food. This simple cause and effect model was thought to work for·any organism, with more complicated behaviour explained in terms of *S-R* chains, with

each intermediate response functioning as stimulus to the next link.

5. This may have been what provoked Bloomfield to write 'The statement of meanings is [. . .] the weak point in language-study and will remain so until human knowledge advances very far beyond its present state.' (Bloomfield 1933:140).

6. Although the behaviourist theory of language was much refined in B.F. Skinner's *Verbal Behaviour* 1957, nowhere does Skinner meet the kind of objections raised here against Bloomfield's account of meaning (cf. Chomsky's 'Review of B.F. Skinner's *Verbal Behaviour*' 1959).

   I have not discussed the work of Charles Morris, in particular his *Signs, Language, and Behaviour* 1946 which presents a much more complex behaviourist account of meaning than Bloomfield's, (a) because the significant characteristics of such an account have been dealt with already, and (b) because I concur with the following critical summary of Morris's work:

> Morris builds upon an excessively narrow basis of 'behavioural' primitive terms; the inadequacy of these terms as building blocks leads him to introduce metaphorical usages which are neither 'behavioural', well understood, nor epistemologically primitive; and the resulting vagueness of his terminology allows him to make, with unjustified confidence, a series of critical decisions on debatable questions which are presented with no better foundation than his own pronouncements. (Max Black *Language and Philosophy* 1949:185)

7. Aristotle's other two sentence constituents, *onoma* 'nominal' and *rhema* 'predicate', would both represent "ideas" or complexes of "ideas".

8. Cf. Ferdinand de Saussure *A Course in General Linguistics* 1974:9.

9. Cf. Noam Chomsky *Aspects of the Theory of Syntax* 1965:4.

10. Throughout §2.8 we shall speak as if the naturalist hypothesis is about word meaning, even though it was conceived as a theory of naming.

11. Cf. Bloomfield's 'A set of postulates for the science of language' 1926 §11.

12. Cf. Herbert H. Clark & Eve V. Clark *Psychology and Language: an Introduction to Psycholinguistics* 1977 ch.8; Jerry A. Fodor, Thomas G. Bever, & Merrill F. Garrett *The Psychology of Language* 1974 ch.8; David McNeill *'Developmental psycholinguistics'* 1966:47.

13. Cf. *McNeill 1966:22ff.*

14. See also Dwight Bolinger *Aspects of Language* 1975:84, Leonard Bloomfield 1926 §9, *Language* 1933:161; Victoria Fromkin & Robert Rodman *An Introduction to Language* 1978:143; Rodney Huddleston *An Introduction to English Transformational Syntax* 1976:28; John Lyons *Introduction to Theoretical Linguistics* 1968:180ff.

15. This is equivocation since the distinction between a free morpheme and a bound morpheme is exactly that a free morpheme can function as a word.

16. Cf. Charles K. Ogden & Ivor A. Richards *The Meaning of Meaning* 1949:27f.

17. Cf. ch.1 footnote 10.

18. Ovoμα is usually translated "name", but it seems to have been used much as I have been using 'word'.

19. Whether his explanations are correct or not is irrelevant to the point at issue.

20. My translations owe a considerable debt to Harold N. Fowler's edn. of the

Cratylus 1926, and that of Benjamin Jowett 1953; but they are intended to be free enough to get across the author's point without additional commentary.

21. Until the coining of the word *phoneme* in the late 19th century *letter* was used to mean both "letter" and its pronunciation, hence, roughly speaking "phoneme".

22. There was a Latin word *gerones* "carriers".

23. Socrates describes πυρ "fire" as a word of foreign origin, when it is in fact a native Greek word – or, at least, part of Greek's Indo-European heritage.

24. Ironically, the Greek roots of *onomatopoeia* mean "word creation".

25. Tzeltal is a Mayan language (spoken in Mexico). The letter 'c̓' is the alveolar affricate [ts], and 'c̓' ' the ejective alveolar affricate.

26. Onomatopoeia is discussed in more detail in §4.9.2 and phonesthesia §4.9.3.

27. Cf. Charles Osgood & Ivor Richards *The Meaning of Meaning* 1949:11, Stephen Ullmann *Words and Their Use* 1951:52, *Semantics: An Introduction to the Science of Meaning* 1962:55, John Lyons *Semantics* 1977:96.

28. Cf. Geoffrey Bursill-Hall *Speculative Grammars of the Middle Ages* 1971:349, 352. Fig. 2.1 is based particularly on the work of Thomas of Erfurt whose *Grammatica Speculativa* was written between 1300-1310 (cf. Bursill-Hall 1972:27) and Siger de Courtrai whose *Summa Modorum Significandi* was written between 1309-1320 (cf. Bursill-Hall 1971:32).

29. Cf. George Miller & Philip Johnson-Laird *Language and Perception* 1976, Michael Posner *Cognition: An Introduction* 1973.

30. Cf. Jeremy Anglin *Word, Object, and Conceptual Development* 1977:1; and Charles W. Morris *Foundations of the Theory of Signs* 1938:24.

31. Cf. Anglin 1977:181.

32. In 'Denotational structure' 1978:234 William Labov has a detailed discussion of the denotational scope of a child's noun *cat*.

33. Sense data, are, of course, the data coming from some phenomenon (object, state, act, etc.) to the senses of sight, touch, hearing, taste, or smell.

34. The patterns may be lineal, configurational, aural, olfactory, functional, temporal, etc.

35. If the expectancies invoked in the process of perceiving are based on past, experience, how do new born children perceive? In *Origins of Knowledge and Imagination* 1978:17 Jacob Bronowski writes that 'the eye is ready-wired to see straight boundaries or curved boundaries, contrasts of light, and so on', thus it has a built in search mechanism that begins to categorize visual data even before the information from the eye reaches the brain. Eleanor Gibson's exhaustive study of perception during ontogenetic development, *Principles of Perceptual Learning and Development* 1969, leaves no doubt that the human infant can perceive certain distinctive phenomena shortly after birth, and categorize them well enough on first acquaintance to recognize them another time. Human neonates must therefore be born with innate knowledge – probably of a rather primitive kind, and comparable to that found in varying measure in neonates of all species.

36. This explains the difficulties experienced by exotic cultural groups faced with the, to them, unknown pictorial conventions familiar to us, cf. A.C. Holmes *Health Education in Developing Countries* 1964; W. Hudson 'Pictorial depth perception in sub-cultural groups in Africa' 1960; B. Shaw

Visual Symbols Survey: Report on the Recognition of Drawings in Kenya 1969.

37. Perhaps *carrot* should only be assigned a value close to 1, because not everyone agreed that it is the best instance of a Vegetable (only 316 out of 442); this would leave open the possibility that the perfect instance could be found. However, given that the set of vegetables is defined by Battig & Montague's list, we shall assign *carrot* the value 1.

38. Members of fuzzy sets which have a value close to zero are known as 'peripheral' members of the set, those with a value close to 1 are known as 'core' members. In the speech of very young children, peripheral members of categories are less likely to be included under the category label than are core members; thus Anglin in *Word, Object, and Conceptual Development* 1977 ch.5 found that for young children a cow is an animal, but a praying mantis is not.

39. The 329 chips supplied by the Munsell Color Co. of Baltimore, Maryland are in a rectangular array: 8 degrees of brightness by 40 equally spaced hues red-yellow-green-blue-purple, all at maximum saturation; and 9 chips of neutral hue (achromatic) white-grey-black.

40. Many languages have a single term for the composite of green and blue – or 'grue' as it has come to be known. Nevertheless, Berlin & Kay 1969:10 say that 'the only language for which we have reliable data' on the focus of grue is Tzeltal – an admission which, in view of the evidence they give for the dual focus of grue, completely undermines their single stable focus doctrine.

41. These are the chromatic primary colours. Primary colours are labelled in SMALL CAPITALS in this discussion of basic colour terms. Achromatic BLACK and WHITE are perceived by a different neurophysiological system – or, more correctly as a psychophysical response to degrees of reflectance; see below and Kay & McDaniel 1978:626f.

42. Light wavelengths are measured in *nanometers* (nm). A nanometer is 10^{-9} of a meter, i.e. 0.000000001m.

43. For those unfamiliar with set theory: suppose we have two sets of letters
$$\{a, c, f, n, w\} \quad \text{and} \quad \{g, e, n, t, w\}$$
We can represent these two sets in a Venn diagram.

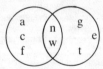

The intersection set $\{a, c, f, n, w\} \cap \{g, e, n, t, w\} = \{n, w\}$ The union of the two sets $\{a, c, f, n, w\} \cup \{g, e, n, t, w\} = \{a, c, f, n, w, g, e, t\}$.

44. Recall that young children's overgeneralizations of the denotational scope of words are not the result of a perceptual deficiency either.

45. Cf. Allan 1977:299ff.

46. Cf. §2.9.3. above, and Allan 1977:297f.

47. Cf. Roger Brown & Eric Lenneberg 'Studies in Linguistic relativity' 1959:14.

48. Cf. Keith Allan 'Classifiers' 1977.

49. E.g. Otto Jespersen *A Modern English Grammar on Historical principles, Part II* 1914 §§3.1-3, 4; H. Poutsma *A Grammar of Late Modern English, Part II Section IA* 1914:250-56; Henry Sweet *A New English Grammar Part*

II 1898 §1966-69; R. Zandvoort *A Handbook of English Grammar* 1972 §226c, 259.
50. Cf. Keith Allan 'Collectivizing' 1976.
51. For more extensive discussion of these matters cf. Allan 1980.
52. Sentences (i) and (ii) are more marked than sentences (iii) and (iv) because they have superficial number discords:

  (i) The herd are gathered by the river.
 (ii) The two elephant were close to our tent.
(iii) The herd is down by the river
(iv) The two elephants were close to our tent.

The discordant elements are the plural NP-external number registration in (i) and the collectivized $N_\emptyset$ noun in (ii). It is these discordant elements that provide the focus for number denotation. Viz. a herd is composed of a set or collection of individual animals and it is this plurality of members of the single set which is focused upon in (i). In (ii) there are two elephants denoted, but the collectivized $N_\emptyset$ noun indicates that they are perceived to be significant not as individual elephants but rather as two instantiations of the elephant species. The focusing effect of the discord does away with any suggestion that there is a contradiction between the $N_\emptyset$ NP heads and their plural external number registration.
53. Cf. Nicolas Beauzée Preface to *Grammaire Générale, ou Exposition Raisonnée des Eléments Nécessaires du Langage Pour Servir du Fondement à l'Etude de Toutes les Langues* 1767.
54. Cf. Noam Chomsky *Aspects of the Theory of Syntax* 1965, *Cartesian Linguistics* 1966.
55. Cf. John Bernard & Arthur Delbridge *Introduction to Linguistics: an Australian Perspective* 1980:159.

Chapter 3   Meaningful properties and meaningful relations

1. Cf. James D. McCawley 'Concerning the base component of a transformational grammar' 1968:265.
2. John L. Austin *How to Do Things With Words* 1975:144.
3. We are not speaking of indeterminability for a particular individual H that is due to his limited knowledge, a memory lapse, or whatever – if we were, the expression could be anomalous to him but not to others. We take it that E is determinable or indeterminable in the language, i.e. for any language user familiar with the context.
4. I had this piece from the late David DeCamp and have not been able to discover its source.
5. In many dialects of English there is a systematic phonetic difference between auxiliary *can* and the main verb *can* when they are juxtaposed. Not only would the auxiliary be unstressed /kn̩/ but even when stressed /ˈkæn/ the vowel will be shorter than the vowel in main verb /kæ·n/, cf. [kʰn̩kʰæ·n] [kʰn̩ ˈkʰææn] [ˈkʰæn kʰæ·n].

6. On the theoretical dictionary or lexicon see §1.5.3 and ch.4.
7. The form of entries in the lexicon is not quite as listed here, cf. §4.12.
8. Defining the predominant sense of *bachelor* as "an unmarried man" – which is common in dictionaries – is open to the objection that it fails to adequately distinguish the status of being a bachelor from that of being a male divorcee, or widower. Furthermore, suppose a man legally a bachelor has a common-law wife, in the eyes of the lay community he is probably only a fairly marginal member of the fuzzy set of bachelors.
9. Cf. Stephen Ullmann *Words and Their Use* 1951:54.
10. Cf. §4.9.5.
11. Cf. Peter Strevens *British and American English* 1972.
12. I.e. their inflexional characteristics and syntactic distribution, co-occurrence conditions, etc.
13. The two words, both originally pronounced /kʌnɪ/, were cognates deriving via Latin from a root meaning "tunnel".
14. Cf. Peter Paul 'Homonyms, semantic divergence and valency' 1982.
15. For detailed discussion see James D. McCawley *Everything that Linguists have Always Wanted to Know about Logic* 1981 ch.12; Nicholas Rescher *Many-valued Logic* 1969.
16. Evidence that truth is treated as a convention may be had from the fact that the South African Ministry of the Interior may reclassify a person's race. In one year 'A total of 101 colored people became white; one Chinese became white; two whites received colored classification; six whites became Chinese; two whites became Indian; 10 colored people became Indians; 10 Malays became Indians; 11 Indians became colored; four Indians became Malays; three coloured people became Chinese, while two Chinese were reclassified as coloured people.' (*The Age*, Melbourne, 30 July 1983:9).
17. The term 'set' is used to include both what are standardly called sets and also what Harry C. Bunt calls 'ensembles', cf. his 'The formal semantics of mass terms' 1976 and 'Ensembles and the semantic properties of mass terms' 1979. Mass terms like *water*, *lightning*, *sugar*, etc. which head uncountable NPs, denote 'ensembles' of phenomena in W, the world spoken of. According to Bunt, ensembles may be partitioned into 'parts' which correspond to subsets of sets; but they do not have constituents which correspond to members of sets. In other respects, however, ensembles are comparable with sets: their parts may be null (cp. null sets) or proper parts (cp. proper subsets) or equal to the ensemble itself (cp. every set is a subset of itself). Bunt has not described a notion of fuzzy ensembles to compare with the notion of fuzzy sets, but there is no reason to doubt their existence. We have established that natural language does not distinguish between members of sets, and subsets of sets that consist of what, mathematically, would be individual members; consequently in natural language there is no relation of set membership distinct from the relation 'subset of' – the relation corresponding to 'part of an ensemble'. Hence we deduce that the notion 'degree of membership in a fuzzy set' is equivalent to "degree of subsethood in a fuzzy set", and this corresponds directly to 'degrees of participation in a fuzzy ensemble'. For instance, the nouns *heavy water* and *brine* name fairly peripheral parts of the fuzzy ensemble of Water by comparison with the central H_2O. Because in natural language semantics the relation 'member of' is not distinct from the relation 'subset of', the significant difference between sets and ensembles disappears, so that in

natural language, sets have the theoretical properties of ensembles. Consequently there is no reason to distinguish between the two terms, and we shall use the term 'set' to refer to both sets and ensembles, and the term 'subset' to refer to both subsets and parts of ensembles.

18. Such analyses were developed by Prague School linguist Roman Jakobson and propagated after he emigrated to America in such works as Jakobson, Gunnar Fant & Morris Halle *Preliminaries to Speech Analysis* 1952, Jakobson & Halle *Fundamentals of Language* 1956, and Chomsky & Halle *Sound Pattern of English* 1968.

19. This title contains one of the earliest uses of the term 'componential analysis'.

20. For another contemporary analysis of verbal subcategories in terms of semantic components cf. William Wonderley 'Semantic components in Kechua person morphemes' 1952.

21. Kinsfolk are described in orientation to 'ego'. Thus, in English for example, ego's female parent is his or her *mother*; taking the mother as ego, her male child is her *son*, her female child her *daughter* and so forth.

22. Wilkins identifies six 'genera' or fundamental categories, the same number as we find in *Roget's Thesaurus* (first published in 1852), though the two lists are not identical. The manner of classification is similar in the two works; and in both, the fundamental categories are superordinate to multitudinous subdivisions. Indeed, Roget's preface acknowledges a debt to Wilkins. However Roget's purpose in compiling the Thesaurus differed from that of Wilkins in his *Essay*. The Thesaurus lists together expressions related in meaning, to help the user find the "right" word or phrase when it refuses to come to mind of its own accord; the classification of experience is incidental to this; Wilkins, on the other hand, was creating a universal language whose content necessarily reflects our experience; consequently the classification in his 'philosophical tables' is crucial to his endeavour.

23. However, cf. Tom McArthur *Longman Lexicon of Contemporary English* 1981 which uses groups of topics to organize the 15,000 vocabulary items in the lexicon. For fragmentary studies cf. Thomas T. Ballmer & Walteraud Brennenstuhl *Speech Act Classification* 1981, also 'An empirical approach to frame theory: verb thesaurus organization' 1981; D. Metzing 'Frame representation and lexical semantics' 1981; F. Neubauer & J.S. Petöfi 'Word semantics, lexicon systems, and text interpretation' 1981. In addition there is an extensive psychological literature on associative networks, cf. George A. Miller & Philip N. Johnson-Laird *Language and Perception* 1976 §4.4.1.

24. Jost Trier *Der deutsche Wortschatz im Sinnbezirk des Verstandes: die Geschichte eines sprachlichen Feldes* [German Vocabulary in the Conceptual Field of Knowledge and Understanding: the History of a Linguistic Field] 1931. For critical discussions of Trier's work see Stephen Ullmann *Principles of Semantics* 1957:158f; John Lyons *Semantics* 1977 §8.4; Adrienne Lehrer *Semantic Fields and Lexical Structure* 1974:15-19.

25. Carnap's 'meaning postulates' were expressly invented to state axioms and rules for so-called 'nonlogical vocabulary'. Like James D. McCawley in *Everything that Linguists have Always Wanted to Know about Logic* 1981:xii I can see no grounds for singling out meaning postulates or distinguishing 'logical' from 'nonlogical' vocabulary.

Philip N. Johnson-Laird in 'Mental models of meaning' 1981 claims that the theory of meaning postulates (and presumably what he says ought to apply to our model, too) cannot satisfactorily deal with predicates like *be on the right of*, which would have to be treated as transitives, e.g.

> B is on the right of X,
> X is on the right of Y,
> Y is on the right of Z.
> Therefore B is on the right of Z.

Johnson-Laird points out that this works for linear order, but not if B, X, Y, and Z are equally placed in a circle. He overlooks the fact that the conclusion 'B is on the right of Z' is logically correct if all four are ranged in a circle, but it is grossly misleading to say so – in fact it violates the co-operative maxim of manner. Thus Johnson-Laird's argument against the kind of semantic analysis presented in this chapter fails to find its mark.

26. Some one place predicates are implicitly relational, e.g. *tall* and *small*. Thus *A is tall* means "A is taller than the average A within a given context"; and *a small elephant* is one that is smaller than the average elephant (but still larger than a big ant). See §3.8.

27. Cf. Gottlob Frege 'On sense and reference' 1966.

28. A kill B → A die, if A = B.

29. Cf. Grice 'Further notes on logic and conversation' 1978; Ruth Kempson *Presupposition and the Delimitation of Semantics* 1975; Lauri Karttunen & Stanley Peters 'Conventional implicature' 1979; Gerald Gazdar *Pragmatics: Implicature, Presupposition and Logical Form* 1979; Stephen Levinson *Pragmatics* 1983 ch.3.

30. The implicature is still there even if the window had been previously mentioned, but not so obviously: the window would still be the only one in context. There is a discussion of definiticity in ch.7.

31. Charles E. Osgood *Focus on Meaning* 1976:5.

32. This must be why taboo homonyms displace their non-taboo counterparts, cf. §§3.3.3 and 3.12.4.

33. Cf. George A. Miller 'The magical number seven plus or minus one or two, or, some limits on our capacity for processing information' 1956.

34. For alternative classifications of meaning change see Gustaf Stern *Meaning and Change of Meaning* 1965, and Stephen Ullmann *The Principles of Semantics* 1957 ch.4, and *Semantics: an Introduction to the Science of Meaning* 1962 ch.8.

35. For convenience in this discussion a lexeme is represented by its etic citation form.

36. Standard dictionaries treat *crane* as polysemous in this respect and not as a pair of homonyms. But lexicographers are notably inconsistent in their distinctions between homonymy and polysemy, cf. Uriel Weinreich 'Lexicographic definition in descriptive semantics' 1980 and '*Webster's Third*: a critique of its semantics' 1980. The basis for such distinctions in most standard dictionaries is usually etymology: if two senses derive from a common etymological source they are treated as polysemes rather than homonyms except where they have come to be spelled differently – as with *flower* and *flour* or *poison* and *potion*. These are not the criteria relevant to differentiating polysemy and homonymy in a linguistic theory of meaning, as we have made clear in §3.3 above.

37. Cf. §4.4.

38. Cf. Otto Jespersen *Negation in English and Other Languages* 1917 ch.3,

Gustaf Stern *Meaning and Change of Meaning* 1965:263, Stephen Ullmann
Semantics: an Introduction to the Science of Meaning 1962:198.

Chapter 4   Lexicon semantics

1. Cf. Mark Aronoff *Word Formation in Generative Grammar* 1976, Peter
   Matthews *Morphology: an Introduction to the Theory of Word Structure*
   1974, Elizabeth O. Selkirk *The Syntax of Words* 1982.
2. I.e. the emic categories are represented by their etic citation forms.
3. Thus a derivational morpheme does not necessarily add meaning to the
   stem, as an inflexional morpheme does, though it will cause a meaning
   change.
4. Pluralia tantum nouns are those whose citation form is plural, cf. *trousers*,
   scissors, *pliers*, *glasses* ("spectacles"), *greens* ("green vegetables"), etc.
5. There is nothing unusual about the noun phrases *a well-acted play*, *a rarely
   acted play*, *an as yet unacted play* but simply *?an acted play* is decidedly odd
   because it normally violates the co-operative maxim of quantity (cf.
   §1.2.3.3): one expects plays to be acted. It is therefore only appropriate to
   use *an acted play* when, for some reason, the play in question is not
   expected to be acted.
6. A.J.F. Zieglschmid in 'Is the use of *wesan* in the periphrastic actional
   passive in Germanic languages due to Latin influence?' 1929 mentions
   instances of stative and nonstative participles in a number of Indo-European
   languages, including Armenian, Old English, Old Friesian, Gothic, Old
   Icelandic, Popular Latin, Lithuanian, and Old Saxon.
7. The contrast between the inconsistencies of derivational morphology and
   the comparative consistencies of inflexional morphology was remarked by
   the Stoics 2000 years ago. Circa 45 BC Marcus Terentius Varro in *De
   Lingua Latina* IX, 35 wrote: 'in voluntary derivations [derivational
   morphology] there is inconsistency, and in natural derivations [inflexional
   morphology] there is consistency'.
8. Despite the fact that *poss*- derives from the Latin root *potis* "able".
9. Even if the meaning of a newly derived lexeme is defined by whomever
   coins it, the meanings of its derivational components and the context of use
   will contribute to establishing the meaning of the new lexeme.
10. Downing also offers an inventory of the 12 most common relationships she
    found between the constituents of a compound (p.828): whole-part, half-
    part, part-whole, composition, comparison, time, place, source, product,
    user, purpose, occupation. The inventory is no better than the ones we have
    dismissed already. She also identifies (p.831) certain interesting tendencies
    in the salient perceived characteristics of different kinds of phenomena such
    as that plants and animals tend to be named according to appearance and
    habitat, natural objects according to inherent characteristics, and artefacts
    according to their purpose; although these tendencies narrow the probable
    meanings of compounds, they leave the precise meaning for any given
    compound to be determined by other means.
11. In this case, Berkeley students with a mean age of 25 years.
12. Such expressions sometimes occur as nonce terms.

13. Cf. Alan J. Lerner *My Fair Lady* 1959:23.
14. Cf. John Osborne *The Hotel in Amsterdam* 1973:297.
15. Cf. Arthur Capell 'Ups and downs' 1979.
16. On idioms see Uriel Weinreich 'Problems in the analysis of idioms' 1969, Bruce Fraser 'Idioms within a transformational grammar' 1970, Quang Phuc Dong 'The applicability of transformations to idioms' 1971, Adam Makkai *Idiom Structure in English* 1972, Chitra Fernando 'Towards a definition of idiom, its nature and function' 1978.
17. There is no reason to assume that the idiom *kick the bucket* should have a distribution identical with that of the verb *die*. (Near) synonyms rarely, if ever, have identical distribution.
18. I think this might be acceptable as a jocular expression with the sense "It rained hard again" provided it followed an antecedent *It rained cats and dogs*.
19. Cf. Hans Marchand *The Categories and Types of Present-Day English Word Formation* 1969:444.
20. When pluralia tantum nouns are back-clipped the final *-s* is usually left behind.
21. *Wino* "an alcoholic" is not of this set.
22. *Time*, South Pacific edn., February 7, 1983:20 carried a story entitled 'Liffeygate: Scandal rocks Fianna Fail': the first paragraph reads as follows:

> A country's onetime Chief Executive is mired in a widening scandal that has already claimed several top aides and threatens to force his own resignation. It is a tale of taps on journalists' phones, of a secret tape recording of a political discussion, apparent conspiracies and controversy involving high-ranking public figures. And then there is a dogged investigative reporting and at least one "Deep Throat". Sound familiar? Well, yes, but this is Dublin 1983, not Washington 1973. The central character is former Prime Minister Charles Haughey; the scandal is Liffey-gate, after the River Liffey that bisects Ireland's capital city.

23. Some of the terms borrowed are *government*, *parliament*, *tax*, *exchequer*, *revenue*, *public*, *office*, *sir*, *madam*, *religion*, *sermon*, *clerk*, *parson*, *charity*, *judge*, *crime*, *prison*, *army*, *navy*, *enemy*, *peace*, *fashion*, *dress*, *frock*, *coat*, *jewel*, *diamond*. For an appreciation of the full extent of the borrowing a history of English should be consulted.
24. Cf. German *Entwässerung* lit. 'drying' for "dehydration", *Fernsprecher* "farspeaker" for "telephone", *Fersehen* 'farsee' for "television", *Fleischfresser* 'meateater' for "carnivore", *Stickstoff* 'stickystuff' for "nitrogen".
25. Cf. Dwight Bolinger *Aspects of Language* 1975:232; Ronald W. Langacker *Language and Its Structure* 1968:25; Stephen Ullmann *Semantics: an Introduction to the Science of Meaning* 1962:86.
26. I.e. onomatopoeic words listed in the dictionary.
27. The term *phonesthesia* was apparently coined by John R. Firth in 'The use and distribution of certain English sounds' 1935, but it has been propagated by Dwight Bolinger in 'Rime, assonance, and morpheme analysis' 1950, and *Aspects of Language* 1975.
28. Charles F. Hockett *A Course in Modern Linguistics* 1958:123.
29. The iconicity of *fifty-fifty* and *half-half* is peculiar to these words alone.
30. Although the *Oxford English Dictionary* claims that *mumbo-jumbo*

originated in West Africa it bears an uncanny resemblance to the usual Kiswahili greeting *Jambo!* "Hello, how's things?" whose plural form is *mambo* "events, affairs", cf. *mambo leo* "today's news". Kiswahili /a/ and English /ʌ/ are both low central vowels, and it would be no surprise to find the one substituted for the other. Given 18th century English views of Africans, *mumbo-jumbo* is probably a bowdlerization of an African greeting that was not recognized as such but thought to be gibberish, and later attributed, through folk etymology, to an imagined African deity elsewhere on the Dark Continent. It is not impossible that *mumbo* was linked with *mumble*, too.

31. Cf. Nils Thun *Reduplicative Words in English: a Study of the Types Ticktick, Hurly-burly and Shilly-shally* 1963.
32. A British mid-evening television drama series called *Hazel* shown on British and Australian networks had one man say to another 'I suppose you were out with your rumble and grunt last night': without the rhyming euphemism no network would have carried such a line.
33. Cf. Julian Franklyn *A Dictionary of Rhyming Slang* 1961:28.
34. In case the reader is still puzzled, *Mozart* means "drunk": *Mozart and Liszt* "pissed".
35. Cf. Josette Rey-DeBove & G. Gagnon *Dictionnaire des Anglicismes* 1981.
36. For instance there is The International Code of Botanical Nomenclature 1956, The International Code of Nomenclature of Bacteria and Viruses 1958, The International Code of Zoological Nomenclature 1961.
37. The closest analogue in the outside community is the family name component of a personal proper name.
38. In the case of e.g. $noun_{noun}$ this appears to lead to an inherent circularity in the language; but we would break free from the circle by limiting to one the number of translations allowed for any given expression between the metalanguage and the object language.
39. No one admits to being certain how the three aspects of lexical storage correlate within the mental lexicon. In 'Malapropisms and the structure of the mental lexicon' 1977:514-6 David Fay & Anne Cutler say that lexicon items 'are arranged by phonemic structure, in a left to right manner, and based on a distinctive feature system. The major partitioning of the dictionary, however, seems to be by the number of syllables, with the stress pattern as a second categorization within syllable categories. Words may also be arranged by syntactic category'. Semantic storage is thought to be organized into associative networks of items within the same semantic field, cf. Lorian Baker *The Lexicon: Some Psycholinguistic Evidence* 1974, Herbert H. Clark 'Word associations and linguistic theory' 1970, Allan M. Collins & M. Rose Quillian 'Retrieval time from semantic memory' 1969, Fay & Cutler 1977, Victoria Fromkin *Speech Errors as Linguistic Evidence* 1973, George Miller & Philip Johnson-Laird *Language and Perception* 1976, Sibout G. Nooteboom 'The tongue slips into patterns' 1969. The dominating organization principle, however, is formal, cf. Cutler & Fay 'One mental lexicon, phonologically arranged' 1982.
40. This is apparently how the mental lexicon is arranged, too, cf. Anne Cutler & David Fay 'One mental lexicon, phonologically arranged' 1982. However, there is a deal of evidence that rhyme is also an important feature of formal representation: why else should we have utilized it in rhyming slang, in reduplicative words, in song and verse, and as a linking mechanism in word

association tasks (cf. Lorian Baker *The Lexicon: Some Psycholinguistic Evidence* 1974:93f)?

41. Where we use π as the symbol for a stress foot, Selkirk uses Σ which we have pre-empted for "sentence".

42. Dwight Bolinger 'Contrastive accent and contrastive stress' 1961:89 notes a comparable stress shift from *rétail* to *retáil*, cf. *whólesale*, and *extravérted* or *íntroverted* from *éxtraverted* and *íntroverted*.

43. Keith Allan 'Nouns and countability' 1980 shows that there are eight levels of countability for English nouns as measured by their different sensitivities when heading NPs: (a) with plural external number registration; (b) with a fuzzy plural denumerator, e.g. *a few*, ranging over the noun; (c) with a unit denumerator, e.g. *one*, ranging over the noun; (d) with *all* ranging over the noun in a genus denoting singular NP (e.g. *all wheat is nourishing*, **all car is the best mode of transport*); (e) with denumerators like *two* ranging over the noun. Representative nouns, ranked from most countable (*car*) to least countable (*equipment*), were: car_7, oak_6, $cattle_5$, $Himalayas_4$, $scissors_3$, $mankind_2$, $admiration_1$, $equipment_0$. All nouns can be used in uncountable environments on at least some occasions, though this is very rare for level 7 nouns; on the other hand, level 0 nouns can never (in standard English) be used in countable environments. The different levels correlate with distributional possibilities in the various types of NPs listed in (a-e) above, cf. Allan 1980:562.

44. In *Componential Analysis of General Vocabulary* 1966, Edward H. Bendix identified what he believed was a fragment of core vocabulary in analyzing a set of *have*-related verbs, e.g. *get*, *find*, *give*, *lend*, *lose*, *keep*, *take*. And in 'Some semantic universals of German adjectivals' 1967 Manfred Bierwisch identified what some might consider core vocabulary for spatial structure in analyzing such adjectives as *long*, *short*, *wide*, *high*, etc.

45. We have more to say about this in ch.5.

46. This is an important criterion. Albert Einstein *Ideas and Opinions* 1973 makes it quite clear that the conclusions of any scientific theory have to be judged for their value on the basis of one's intuitions about their explanation of the data.

47. Cf. Edward H. Bendix *Componential Analysis of General Vocabulary* 1966:8.

48. Cf. Bendix 1966:7.

Chapter 5   The semantic interpretation of sentences

1. More recently some linguists have become interested in the possiblity of extending a logic devised by philosopher Richard Montague to achieve this goal (cf. Richard Montague *Formal Philosophy* 1974, Michael Bennett *Some Extensions of a Montague Fragment of English* 1975, Barbara Hall Partee *Montague Grammar* 1976, Steven Davis & Marianne Mithun *Linguistics, Philosophy, and Montague Grammar* 1979). The interests of logic and linguistics have therefore reconverged over the last two decades. I

say reconverged because they have been intertwined in the past. In the western classical tradition theoretical linguistics (as contrasted to pedagogical or applied linguistics) was included within the scope of philosophical logic by the ancient Greeks, cf. Plato *Sophist* §261e-263; Aristotle *Categories* and *On Interpretation*; Diogenes Laertius *The Lives of the Philosophers, Book VII: Life of Zeno*. The medieval scholastic grammarians (approx 1250-1320A.D.) also analyzed language from a philosophical point of view, cf. Geoffrey L. Bursill-Hall *Speculative Grammars of the Middle Ages* 1971, as did the rationalist grammarians of the 17th and 18th centuries, cf. Claude Lancelot & Antoine Arnaud *Grammaire Generale et Raisonée* 1660, Noam Chomsky *Cartesian Linguistics* 1966. See also Robert H. Robins *A Short History of Linguistics* 1979.

2. Chomsky is undoubtedly wrong about this. Take for instance the fact that *aunt* is semantically feminine, yet this semantic property is not syntactically realized (or not to any greater extent than 'to' in (2.2.4) is semantically consequential).

3. We shall use 'Σ' as the symbol for "sentence" in line with our practice so far. Chomsky and his followers, including Katz & Fodor, systematically use 'S' which for us symbolizes "the speaker".

4. Weinreich commented, in 'Explorations in semantic theory' 1966:411, 'One would have thought that with the development of the calculus of many-place predicates, the logic of Boolean (one-place) predicates would be permanently dropped as a model for natural language.'

5. A singulary transformation performs some kind of operation on a single phrase marker, which in the *Syntactic Structures* model of TG meant on a single clause. It contrasts with a generalized transformation which, in that model, served to combine two phrase markers into one.

6. Although it is a fact that Katz & Postal 1964 and Chomsky 1965 do specify different LSUPMs for active/passive pairs, the idea that corresponding active/passive pairs derive from a common LSUPM seems to have been tenaciously recounted in almost all contemporary linguistic literature.

7. Cf. Chomsky 'Deep structure, surface structure, and semantic interpretation' 1971.

8. Lexical insertion rules are syntactic transformations, hence any constraints on lexical insertion are syntactic constraints.

9. Cf. Diane Bornstein *An Introduction to Transformational Grammar* 1977, Rodney Huddleston *An Introduction to English Transformational Syntax* 1976:150, Roderick A. Jacobs & Peter S. Rosenbaum *English Transformational Grammar* 1968.

10. See also James D. McCawley 'Concerning the base component of a transformational grammar' 1968a, 'The role of semantics in a grammar' 1968b; Ray S. Jackendoff *Semantic Interpretation in Generative Grammar* 1972, $\bar{X}$ *Syntax: A Study of Phrase Structure* 1977.

11. Katz has commented (personal communication 1981) 'what does it matter if they are discovered through Madam Zaza and her crystal ball?' The answer is that a linguistic theory is meant to explicate linguistic data, and Madam Zaza's crystal ball won't do that. In §5.2.4.1 we aim to discover what inherent syntactic features are, and whether they have any place in an empirically verifiable theory of language. See §5.2.4.3 for further discussion on the correlation between theoretical postulates and empirical data.

12. Semantic features can be regarded as equivalent to semantic components in

the sense of §3.5, and as comparable in function with Katz's semantic markers and distinguishers.

13. It would be more accurate to say that "larger meanings" impose a structuring relation, of which the ordering relation is the part which interests us here.

14. Katz & Fodor 1963:190 wrote:

> The addition of new semantic markers, as in Figure [5.4], is for the sake of increasing the precision and scope of a semantic theory, but in doing so it also increases the complexity of the theory's conceptual apparatus. Since allowing more complexity often coincides with greater precision and scope, the decision should be made on the basis of a strategy which seeks to maximize systematic economy: the greatest possible conceptual economy with the greatest possible explanatory and descriptive power. If such decisions are optimally made, there should eventually come a point when increasing the complexity of a semantic theory by adding new markers no longer yields enough advantage in precision and scope to warrant the increase. At that point, the system of semantic markers should reflect exactly the systematic features of the semantic structure of the language.

The question arises, how do we know when enough semantic markers have been identified? The decision is surely arbitrary, and so should not form part of a theory which claims ab initio to be a complete theory of semantics.

15. It is irrelevant to the point being made that Fig. 5.6 represents an obsolete version of the dictionary entry for bachelor.

16. This differs trivially from the version in Katz 1966:167

(((Activity) (Nature:(Physical)) of X), ((Movement) (Rate:Fast)) (Character:Following)), (Intention of X:(Trying to catch ((Y) ((Movement) (Rate:(Fast)))) [*sic*]

17. Katz 1977 omits the PP node and has VP directly dominated by Σ.

18. It is not relevant to this discussion on the structure of semantic markers & readings that both syntactic phrase markers and semantic marker trees can be used to identify certain functions. E.g. Chomsky 1965 §2.2. claims that the functional notion 'subject of' is indicated by the configuration [NP,Σ] "NP mothered by Σ". McCawley, and others, have suggested that in the configuration $_\Sigma$[V NP NP] the 'V' functions like a predicate ranging over the arguments 'NP' and 'NP' cf. §5.3.3. These are functions defined on constituent structure trees. Katz's semantic marker trees are not constituent structure trees. They do, however, allow for certain semantic functions to be assigned to readings for argument (NP) nodes on the LSUPM in a manner which is comparable with the use of labels like 'Agentive', 'Instrumental', and 'Locative' for these same argument nodes by Charles Fillmore in 'The case for case' cf. §5.3.4. E.g. instead of the label 'Agentive', Katz used the configurations

```
(Act)           or   (Activity)
    [NP]                  [NP]
     X                     X
  ‹(Sentient)›         ‹(Sentient)›
```

These effectively mean that a sentient subject NP of an active verb is an agent (where 'subject NP' is defined on the LSUPM), cf. Katz 1977a:84f & 145f. The fact that a certain configuration on a tree structure can be used to define functional relations of one kind or another is a property of tree structures and not of phrase markers as such nor of semantic markers as such.

19. To be fair, this entry is not presented as complete, and it would be better to discuss a completely specified reading; but in nearly twenty years of work, Katz has never presented one completely specified reading! For reasons discussed in §5.2.4-5 it is probable that there never can be a completely specified reading. So, we may as well take a Fig. 5.10 as a typical example, and make critical appraisal of it.

20. Katz 1972:115 writes:

> The segmentation referred to in the statement of the conditions for the application of [2.6.4] are those that divide words into their component morphemes, for example, "re-" and "sell" in the verb "resell" and "in-" and "distinct" in the adjective "indistinct". For the sake of simplicity in the statement of [2.6.4], we are establishing the convention that there is a grammatical relation that holds between such components. Whether we need one grammatical relation connecting each of the components of a word or a number of grammatical relations (one for the relation of a prefix to a stem, one for the relation of a suffix to a stem, etc.) does not need to be decided here and now. If, as we argued earlier, the specification of a grammatical relation is a choice from among the set of possible relations among substrings of the terminal string of an underlying phrase that are formally definable on the basis of the rules of the base component, and if the choice is semantic in the sense that it depends on the requirements of the projection process whereby derived readings are formed, then such new grammatical relations are a natural extension of those already recognized.

21. We have not discussed the definitions of meaningful properties and meaning relations to be found in Katz 1972. They seem to be acceptable given the assumptions and metalanguage of Katz's theory; and divergences from the definitions given in this book derive principally from differences between Katz's assumptions and metalanguage and ours.

22. Ironically only four pages after discussing the undefined matching rule Weinreich writes 'We would do well to guard against a loosening of the notions "theory" and "rule", lest linguistics be debased to a pseudo-science comparable to the interpretation of dreams' (1980:261). Weinreich's 'matching rule' must rate as one of the loosest rules ever proposed in linguistics.

23. Cf. Charles W. Morris *Foundations of the Theory of Signs* 1938:24.

24. This should cover bisexual earthworms and their ilk.

25. In the 1970 version, Gruber also has nodes that express semantic relations mothering category nodes – but these are removed from the 1976 version and we shall ignore them here. See §5.3.4 however.

26. In fact Lakoff included the copula in the original for this set of examples (1970:36f) but not tense.

27. But cf. Lakoff 1970:102 where certain prepositions are said to be [+V, +Adj].

28. We have been using 'deep structure' in a different sense from what

McCawley means by it in this title. We assume that deep structure is the
initial phrase marker – in a transformational grammar – whatever its
composition, and whatever happens to it subsequently. McCawley was using
'deep structure' in this title to refer to the standard theory notion of deep
structure as a lexically specified underlying phrase marker which is to be
semantically interpreted by the semantic component of the grammar.

29. Cf. Janet D. Fodor *Semantics: Theories of Meaning in Generative Grammar*
    1977; Frederick J. Newmeyer *Linguistic Theory in America* 1980; Peter
    Seuren *Semantic Syntax* 1974; George Lakoff 'On generative semantics'
    1971, 'Linguistics and natural logic' 1972; James D. McCawley 'A program
    for logic' 1972; Paul M. Postal 'On the surface verb "remind" ' 1970; John
    R. Ross 'Act' 1972.

30. Since the use of the definitive article *the* usually presupposes that H knows
    the NP's denotation (cf. §7.11.1), there need never have been any ambiguity
    on this score.

31. Notice that what is traditionally called the head constituent of a construction
    falls within the scope of its modifiers: check the head V of the Vb phrase in
    (4.4) and (4.5), and the head ADJ of the PRED ADJ construction in (4.4).
    Similarly the head N 'lamb' in (4.2'), and the head N 'house' in (i) below;
    note also the relationship between the intensifier 'very' and the adjective
    'old' in this construction.

(i)

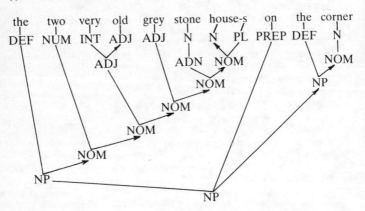

32. By tradition, conjunctions are not predicates, though McCawley 1981 has
    treated them as such; but they do assign a relation between the
    constructions they conjoin, and in this respect they are predicate-like. They
    are unlike other predicates in that their arguments come from a wide variety
    of syntactic categories, provided the elements conjoined are syntactically
    and semantically homogeneous; and it is at least arguable that they can have
    a boundless number of them (alternatively, each conjunction demands two
    arguments and all conjunctions but the last can be omitted from a string of
    linked conjoined elements). Consider (i):

(i)

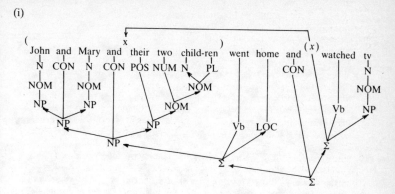

References

Adams, Valerie. 1973. *An Introduction to Modern English Word-Formation*. London: Longman.

Akmajian, Adrian, Richard A. Demers, & Robert M. Harnish. 1979. *Linguistics: an Introduction to Language and Communication*. Cambridge MA: MIT Press.

Allan, Keith. 1971. A note on the source of *there* in existential sentences. *Foundations of Language* 7:1-18.

Allan, Keith, 1973. Complement noun phrases and prepositional phrases, adjectives and verbs. *Foundations of Language* 10:377-97.

Allan, Keith 1976. Collectivizing. *Archivum Linguisticum* 7:99-117.

Allan, Keith. 1977a. Classifiers. *Language* 53:285-311.

Allan, Keith. 1977b. Singularity and Plurality in English Noun Phrases: A Study in Grammar and Pragmatics. Unpublished Ph.D. Thesis, Edinburgh University.

Allan, Keith. 1979. Number registration in English: concord and discord. *Talanya* 6:1-13.

Allan, Keith. 1980. Nouns and countability. *Language* 56:541-67.

Allan, Keith. 1981a. Interpreting from context. *Lingua* 53:151-73.

Allan, Keith. 1981b. Review of 'Weinreich on Semantics' ed. by William Labov & Beatrice S. Weinreich (1980). *Language* 57:941-8.

Allan, Keith. 1983a. Anaphora, cataphora, and topic focusing: functions of the object prefix in Swahili. *Current Approaches to African Linguistics* ed. by Ivan R. Dihoff, 323-35. Dordrecht: Foris.

Allan, Keith. 1983b. Review of 'Language and Other Abstract Objects' by Jerrold J. Katz (1981). *Language* 59:678-83.

Allen, Robert L. 1966. *The Verb System of Present-Day American English*. The Hague: Mouton.

Anderson, Stephen R. 1971. *On the Linguistic Status of the Performative/Constative Distinction*. Bloomington: Indiana University Linguistics Club.

Anglin, Jeremy M. 1977. *Word, Object, and Conceptual Development*. New York: W.W. Norton.

Ansre, Gilbert. 1971. The influence of English on West African languages. *The English Language in West Africa* ed. by John Spencer, 145-64. London: Longman.

Aristotle. *The Categories and On Interpretation* (tr. by Harold P. Cooke). Loeb Classical Library. London: Heinemann. 1938.

Aristotle. *Rhetoric* (tr. by W. Rhys Roberts). New York: Random House. 1954.

Arkell-Hardwicke, A. 1903. *An Ivory Trader in North Kenya.* London: Longmans, Green & Co.

Aronoff, Mark. 1976. *Word Formation in Generative Grammar.* Cambridge MA: MIT Press.

Austin, John L. 1963. Performative-Constative. *Philosophy and Ordinary Language* ed. by Charles E. Caton, 22-54. Urbana: University of Illinois Press. Reprinted in Searle (ed.) 1971:1-12.

Austin, John L. 1975. *How To Do Things With Words.* (2nd ed. by J.O. Urmson & Marina Sbisa. Oxford: Oxford University Press.

Ayer, Alfred J. 1946. *Language, Truth and Logic.* (2nd edn) London: Gollancz.

Bach, Emmon. 1968. Nouns and noun phrases. In Bach & Harms (eds) 1968:90-122.

Bach, Emmon & Robert T. Harms (eds). 1968. *Universals in Linguistic Theory.* New York: Holt, Rinehart & Winston.

Bach, Kent. 1975. Performatives are statements too. *Philosophical Studies* 28:229-36. Reprinted slightly amended in Bach & Harnish 1979:203-8.

Bach, Kent & Robert M. Harnish. 1979. *Linguistic Communication and Speech Acts.* Cambridge MA: MIT Press.

Bacon, Francis. 1605. *The Advancement of Learning.* London.

Baker, Charlotte. 1975. This is just a first approximation, but. . . *Papers from the Eleventh Regional Meeting of the Chicago Linguistic Society,* 37-47.

Baker, Lorian N. 1974. *The Lexicon: Some Psycholinguistic Evidence.* Working Papers in Phonetics 26. Los Angeles: U.C.L.A.

Ballmer, Thomas T. & Waltraud Brennenstuhl. 1981a. *Speech Act Classification: A Study in the Lexical Analysis of English Speech Activity Verbs.* Berlin: Springer-Verlag.

Ballmer, Thomas T. & Waltraud Brennenstuhl. 1981b. An empirical approach to frame theory: verb thesaurus organization. In Eikmeyer & Reiser (eds) 1981:297-319.

Battig, William F. & William E. Montague. 1969. Category norms for verbal items in 56 categories. *Journal of Experimental Psychology Monograph* 80.

Bazell, Charles, E., John C. Catford, Michael A.K. Holliday, & Robert H. Robins (eds). 1966. *In Memory of J.R. Firth.* London: Longmans.

Beattie, Geoffrey W. 1980. The role of language production processes in the organization of behaviour in face-to-face interaction. In Butterworth (ed.) 1980:68-107.

Beaugrande, Robert de. 1980. *Text, Discourse, and Process: Toward a Multidisciplinary Science of Texts.* Norwood NJ: Ablex Publishing Corp.

Beauzée, Nicolas. 1767. *Grammaire Générale, ou Exposition Raisonnée des Éléments Necessaires du Langage pour Servir du Fondement a l'Étude de Toutes les Langues.* Paris.

Beckett, Samuel. 1965. *Waiting for Godot.* (2nd edn) London: Faber & Faber.

Beech, Mervyn W.H. 1918. *Aids to the Study of Ki-Swahili.* London: Kegan Paul, Trench & Trubner.

Bendix, Edward H. 1966. *Componential Analysis of General Vocabulary.* Bloomington: Indiana University Press.

Bennett, Michael R. 1975. *Some Extensions of a Montague Fragment of English.* Bloomington: Indiana University Linguistics Club.

Benveniste, Emile. 1946. Structure des relations de personne dans le verbe. *Bulletin de la Société de Linguistique* 43:(1-12. [= Relationships of person in the verb, in Benveniste 1971:195-204].

Benveniste, Emile. 1956. La nature des pronoms. *For Roman Jakobson*, ed. by Morris Halle, Horace G. Lunt, Hugh McLean, & Cornelius Schooneveld, 34-7. The Hague: Mouton. [= The nature of pronouns, in Benveniste 1971:217-22].

Benveniste, Emile, 1971. *Problems in General Linguistics*. Coral Gables: University of Miami Press.

Berlin, Brent. 1968. *Tzeltal Numeral Classifiers: A Study in Ethnographic Semantics*. The Hague: Mouton.

Berlin, Brent & Elois A. Berlin. 1975. Aguaruna color categories. *American Ethnologist* 2:61-87.

Berlin, Brent, Dennis E. Breedlove & Peter H. Raven. 1974. *Principles of Tzeltal Plant Classification*. New York: Academic Press.

Berlin, Brent & Paul Kay. 1969. *Basic Color Terms: Their Universality and Evolution*. Berkeley & Los Angeles: University of California Press.

Berman, Arlene & Michael Szamosi. 1972. Observations on sentence stress. *Language* 48:304-25.

Bernard, John & Arthur Delbridge. 1980. *Introduction to Linguistics: An Australian Perspective*. Sydney: Prentice-Hall.

Bierwisch, Manfred. 1967. Some semantic universals of German adjectivals. *Foundations of Language* 3:1-36.

Bierwisch, Manfred. 1969. On certain problems of semantic representation. *Foundations of Language* 5:153-84.

Bierwisch, Manfred. 1970. Semantics. In Lyons (ed.) 1970:166-84.

Black, Max. 1949. *Philosophy and Language: Studies in Method*. Ithaca: Cornell University Press.

Bloch, Bernard & George L. Trager. 1942. *Outline of Linguistic Analysis*. Baltimore: Linguistic Society of America.

Blom, Jan-Petter & John J. Gumperz. 1972. Social meaning in linguistic structures; code-switching in Norway. In Gumperz & Hymes (eds) 1972:407-34.

Bloomfield, Leonard. 1914. *An Introduction to the Study of Language*. New York: Holt, Rinehart & Winston.

Bloomfield, Leonard. 1926. A set of postulates for the science of language. *Language* 2:153-64. Reprinted in Joos (ed.) 1957/1971:26-31.

Bloomfield, Leonard. 1933. *Language*. New York: Holt, Rinehart & Winston.

Boas, Franz. 1911. *Handbook of American Indian Languages. Volume 1*. Washington, D.C.: Smithsonian Institution.

Bock, J. Kathryn. 1982. Toward a cognitive psychology of syntax: information processing contributions to sentence formulation. *Psychological Review* 89:1-47.

Bolinger, Dwight. 1950. Rime, assonance, and morpheme analysis. *Word* 6:117-36.

Bolinger, Dwight. 1958. A theory of pitch accent in English. *Word* 14, 109-49.

Bolinger, Dwight. 1961a. Contrastive accent and contrastive stress. *Language* 37:83-96.

Bolinger, Dwight. 1961b. Ambiguities in pitch accent. *Word* 17:309-17.

Bolinger, Dwight. 1965. The atomization of meaning. *Language* 41:555-73.

Bolinger, Dwight, 1971. *The Phrasal Verb in English*. Cambridge MA: Harvard University Press.

Bolinger, Dwight. 1972. Accent is predictable (if you're a mind-reader). *Language* 48:633-44.

Bolinger, Dwight. 1975. *Aspects of Language* (2nd edn) New York: Harcourt, Brace, Jovanovich.

Bolinger, Dwight. 1978. Intonation across languages. *Universals of Human Language 2: Phonology* ed. by Joseph H. Greenberg, 471-524. Stanford: Stanford University Press.

Bolinger, Dwight. 1982. Intonation and its parts. *Language* 48:505-33.

Bolinger, Dwight & Louis J. Gerstman. 1957. Disjuncture as a cue to constructs. *Word* 13:246-55.

Boomer, Donald S. 1965. Hesitation and grammatical encoding. *Language and Speech* 8:148-58.

Bornstein, Diane D. 1977. *An Introduction to Transformational Grammar*. Cambridge MA: Winthrop.

Boucher, Jerry & Charles E. Osgood. 1969. The pollyana hypothesis. *Journal of Verbal Learning and Verbal Behavior* 8:1-8.

Brazil, David, Malcom Coulthard, & Catherine Johns. 1980. *Discourse Intonation and Language Teaching*. London: Longman.

Breivik, Leiv E. 1981. On the interpretation of existential *there*. *Language* 57:1-25.

Bresnan, Joan. 1971. Sentence stress and syntactic transformations. *Language* 47:257-81.

Bresnan, Joan. 1972. Stress and syntax: a reply. *Language* 48:326-42.

Bronowski, Jacob. 1978. *The Origins of Knowledge and Imagination*. New Haven: Yale University Press.

Brown, Gillian. 1978. Understanding spoken language. *TESOL Quarterly* 12:271-83.

Brown, Gillian, Karen L. Currie, & Joanne Kenworthy. 1980. *Questions of Intonation*. London: Croom Helm.

Brown, Gillian & George Yule. 1983. *Discourse Analysis* Cambridge: Cambridge University Press.

Brown, Penelope & Stephen Levinson. 1978. Universals in language usage: politeness phenomena. *Questions and Politeness: Strategies in Social Interaction* ed. by Esther N. Goody, 56-289. Cambridge: Cambridge University Press.

Brown, Roger & Eric Lenneberg. 1954. A study in language and cognition. *Journal of Abnormal and Social Psychology* 49:454-62.

Brown, Roger & Eric Lenneberg. 1959. Studies in linguistic relativity. *Readings in Social Psychology* ed. by E.E. Maccoby, T.M. Newcomb & E.L. Hartley, 9-18. London: Methuen.

Brown, W.P. 1978. A cross-national comparison of English-language category norms. *Language and Speech* 21:50-68.

Bruner, Jerome & Leo Postman. 1949. On the perception of incongruity. *Journal of Personality* 18:216-23.

Bull, William E. 1960. *Time, Tense and the Verb*. Berkeley & Los Angeles: University of California Publications in Linguistics 19.

Bunt, Harry C. 1976. The formal semantics of mass terms. *Papers from the Third Scandinavian Conference on Linguistics* ed. by Fred Karlsson, 81-94. Turku: Academy of Finland.

Bunt, Harry C. 1979. Ensembles and the formal semantic properties of mass terms. In Pelletier (ed.) 1979:249-77.

Bursill-Hall, Geoffrey L. 1971. *Speculative Grammars of the Middle Ages: the Doctrine of the 'partes orationis' of the Modistae*. The Hague: Mouton.

Bursill-Hall, Geoffrey L. (ed.) 1972. *Thomas of Erfurt's Grammatica Speculativa*. London: Longman.

Butterworth, Brian. 1980a. Evidence from pauses in speech. In Butterworth (ed.) 1980b:155-76.

Butterworth, Brian (ed.) 1980b. *Language Production 1: Speech and Talk*. New York: Academic Press.

Capell, Arthur. 1979. Ups and downs. *Talanya* 6:14-27.

Carnap, Rudolph. 1956. *Meaning and Necessity*. (2nd edn) Chicago: Chicago University press.

Carroll, John B. 1958. Process and content and psycholinguistics. *Current Trends in the Description and Analysis of Behavior*, 175-200. Pittsburgh: University of Pennsylvania Press.

Carroll, Lewis. 1965. *The Works of Lewis Carroll*, ed. by Roger L. Green. Feltham: Hamlyn (Spring Books).

Chafe, Wallace L. 1970. *Meaning and the Structure of Language*. Chicago: Chicago University Press.

Chafe, Wallace L. 1976. Givenness, contrastiveness, definiteness, subjects, topics and point of view. In Li (ed.) 1976:25-55.

Chamber's Encyclopaedia. 1966. Oxford: Pergamon Press.

Chomsky, Noam. 1957. *Syntactic Structures*. The Hague: Mouton.

Chomsky, Noam. 1959. Review of 'Verbal Behavior' by Burrhus F. Skinner (1957). *Language* 34:26-58. Reprinted in Fodor & Katz (eds) 1964:547-78.

Chomsky, Noam. 1965. *Aspects of the Theory of Syntax*. Cambridge MA: MIT Press.

Chomsky, Noam. 1966. *Cartesian Linguistics*. New York: Harper & Row.

Chomsky, Noam. 1971. Deep structure, surface structure, and semantic interpretation. In Steinberg & Jakobovits (eds) 1971:183-216. Reprinted in Chomsky 1972:62-119.

Chomsky, Noam. 1972. *Studies on Semantics in Generative Grammar*. The Hague: Mouton.

Chomsky, Noam. 1975. *The Logical Structure of Linguistic Theory*. New York: Plenum press.

Chomsky, Noam. 1981. *Lectures on Government and Binding*. Dordrecht: Foris.

Chomsky, Noam. 1982. *Some Concepts and Consequences of the Theory of Government and Binding*. Cambridge MA: MIT Press.

Chomsky, Noam & Morris Halle. 1968. *The Sound Pattern of English*. New York: Harper & Row.

Christophersen, Paul. 1939. *The Articles: A Study of Their History and Use in English*. Oxford: Oxford University Press.

Clark, Eve V. 1973. What's in a word? On the child's acquisition of semantics in his first language. In Moore (ed.) 1973:65-110.

Clark, Eve & Herbert H. Clark. 1978. Universals, relativity, and language processing. *Universals of Human Languages Vol.1: Method and Theory* ed. by Joseph H. Greenberg, 225-77. Stanford: Stanford University Press.

Clark, Herbert H. 1970. Word associations and linguistic theory. In Lyons (ed.) 1970:271-86.

Clark, Herbert H. & Thomas B. Carlson. 1982. Hearers and speech acts. *Language* 58:332-73.

Clark, Herbert H. & Eve V. Clark. 1977. *Psychology and Language: An Introduction to Psycholinguistics*. New York: Harcourt Brace.

Clark, Herbert H. & Catherine R. Marshall. 1981. Definite reference and mutual knowledge. In Joshi, Webber, & Sag (eds) 1981:10-63.

Cohen, L. Jonathon. 1964. Do illocutionary forces exist? *Philosophical Quarterly* XIV No.55:118-37. Reprinted in Rosenberg & Travis (eds) 1971:580-99.

Cole, Peter (ed.). 1978. *Syntax and Semantics 9: Pragmatics*. New York: Academic Press.

Cole, Peter (ed.). 1981. *Radical Pragmatics*. New York: Academic Press.

Cole, Peter & Jerry L. Morgan (eds). 1975. *Syntax and Semantics 3: Speech Acts*. New York: Academic Press.

Coleridge, Samuel T. 1958. *The Poems*. London: Oxford University Press.

Collins, Allan M. & M. Rose Quillian. 1969. Retrieval time from semantic memory. *Journal of Verbal Learning and Verbal Behavior* 8:240-47.

Collins, James. 1979. Athapaskan classifiers, person and deference. *Proceedings of the Fifth Annual Meeting of the Berkeley Linguistics Society*, 49-62.

Conklin, Harold C. 1967. Lexicographical treatment of folk taxonomies. *Problems in Lexicography* ed. by Fred W. Householder & Sol Saporta, 119-41. Bloomington: Indiana University Press.

Creider, Chet. 1979. On the explanation of transformations. In Givón (ed.) 1979b:3-21.

Cruttenden, Alan. 1981. Falls and rises: meanings and universals. *Journal of Linguistics* 17:77-92.

Crystal, David. 1969. *Prosodic Systems and Intonation in English*. Cambridge: Cambridge University Press.

Crystal, David. 1975. *The English Tone of Voice*. London: Edward Arnold.

Cutler, Anne. 1983. Lexical complexity and sentence processing. *The Process of Language Understanding* ed. by G.B. Flores d'Arcais & R.J. Jarvella, 43-79. New York: Wiley.

Cutler, Anne & David Fay. 1982. One mental lexicon, phonologically arranged: comments on Hurford's comments. *Linguistic Inquiry* 13:107-13.

Dahl, Östen. 1975. On generics. *Cambridge Colloquium on Formal Semantics of Natural Language* ed. by Edward L. Keenan, 99-111. London: Cambridge University Press.

Davidson, Donald. 1971. Truth and meaning. In Rosenberg & Travis (eds) 1971:450-65. First published in *Synthese* 17, 1967:304-23.

Davidson, Donald, 1973a. In defense of convention T. *Truth, Syntax and Modality* ed. by Hugues Leblanc, 76-86. Amsterdam: North Holland.

Davidson, Donald. 1973b. Radical interpretation. *Dialectica* 27:313-28.

Davidson, Donald. 1976. Reply to Foster. *Truth and Meaning* ed. by Gareth Evans & John McDowell, 33-41. Oxford: Clarendon Press.

Davidson, Donald & Gilbert Harman (eds). 1972. *Semantics of Natural Language*. Dordrecht: Reidel.

Davis, Steven. 1980. Perlocutions. In Searle, Kiefer & Bierwisch (eds) 1980:37-55.

Davis, Steven & Marianne Mithun (eds). 1979. *Linguistics, Philosophy, and Montague Grammar*. Austin: University of Texas Press.

Dawkins, Richard. 1976. *The Selfish Gene*. Oxford: Oxford University Press.

Denison, Nigel. 1972. Some observations on language variety and pluralism. In Pride & Holmes (eds) 1972:65-77.

Dik, Simon. 1978. *Functional Grammar*. Amsterdam: North Holland.

Dionysios Thrax. The grammar of Dionysios Thrax, tr. by Thomas Davidson. *Journal of Speculative Philosophy* 8, 1874:326-39.

Dixon, Robert M.W. 1972. *The Dyirbal Language of North Queensland*. Cambridge: Cambridge University Press.

Donnellan, Keith S. 1966. Reference and definite descriptions. *Philosophical Review* 75:281-304. Reprinted in Steinberg & Jakobovits (eds) 1971:100-14.

Donnellan, Keith S. 1978. Speaker reference, descriptions and anaphora. In Cole (ed.) 1978:47-68.

Downing, Pamela. 1977. On the creation and use of English compound nouns. *Language* 53:810-42.

Drake, Glendon F. 1980. The social role of slang. In Giles, Robinson & Smith 1980:63-70.

Duncker, Karl. 1939. The influence of past experience upon perceptual properties. *American Journal of Psychology* 52:255-65.

Eikmeyer, Hans-Jurgen & Hannes Rieser (eds). 1981. *Words, Worlds, and Contexts: New Approaches in Word Semantics*. Berlin: W. de Gruyter.

Einstein, Albert. 1973. *Ideas and Opinions*. London: Souvenir Press.

Ertel, Suitbert. 1977. Where do the subjects of sentences come from? In Rosenberg (ed.) 1977:141-68.

Fay, David & Anne Cutler. 1977. Malapropisms and the structure of the mental lexicon. *Linguistic Inquiry* 8:505-20.

Fernando, Chitra. 1978. Towards a definition of idiom, its nature and function. *Studies in Language* 2:313-43.

Fillenbaum, Samuel & Amnon Rapoport. 1971. *Structures in the Subjective Lexicon*. New York: Academic Press.

Fillmore, Charles J. 1968. The case for case. In Bach & Harms (eds) 1968:1-88.

Fillmore, Charles J. 1971. Verbs of judging. In Fillmore & Langendoen (eds) 1971:273-89.

Fillmore, Charles J. & Terence D. Langendoen (eds). 1971. *Studies in Linguistic Semantics*. New York: Holt, Rinehart & Winston.

Firbas, Jan. 1974. Some aspects of the Czechoslovak approach to functional sentence perspective. *Papers on Functional Sentence Perspective* ed. by František Daneš, 11-37. The Hague: Mouton.

Firth, John R. 1935a. The use and distribution of certain English sounds. *English Studies* 17. Reprinted in Firth 1957.

Firth, John R. 1935b. The technique of semantics. *Transactions of the Philological Society*, 36-72. Reprinted in Firth 1957.

Firth, John R. 1957. *Papers in Linguistics, 1934-1951*. London: Oxford University Press.

Firth, John R. 1968. *Selected Papers of J.R. Firth, 1952-1959* ed. by Frank R. Palmer. Bloomington: Indiana University Press.

Fishman, Joshua A. 1971. The sociology of language: an interdisciplinary social science approach to language in society. *Advances in the Sociology of Language 1* ed. by Joshua A. Fishman, 217-404. The Hague: Mouton.

Fishman, Joshua A. 1972. The relationship between micro and macro-sociolinguistics in the study of who speaks what language to whom and when. In Pride & Holmes 1972:15-32.

Fodor, Janet D. 1977. *Semantics: Theories of Meaning in Generative Grammar*. New York: Thomas Crowell.

Fodor, Janet D., Jerry A. Fodor, & Merrill F. Garrett. 1975. The psychological unreality of semantic representations. *Linguistic Inquiry* 6:515-31.

Fodor, Jerry A. 1970. Three reasons for not deriving "kill" from "cause to die". *Linguistic Inquiry* 1:429-38.

Fodor, Jerry A., Thomas G. Bever, & Merrill F. Garrett. 1974. *The Psychology of Language: An Introduction to Psycholinguistics and Generative Grammar*. New York: McGraw Hill.

Fodor, Jerry A., Merrill F. Garrett, E.C.T. Walker, & C.H. Parkes. 1980. Against definitions. *Cognition* 8:263-367.

Fodor, Jerry A. & Jerrold J. Katz (eds). 1964. *The Structure of Language: Readings in the Philosophy of Language*. Englewood Cliffs: Prentice-Hall.

Ford, Marilyn. 1982. Sentence planning units: implications for the speaker's representation of meaningful relations underlying sentences. *The Mental Representations of Grammatical Relations*. ed. by Joan Bresnan, 797-827. Cambridge MA: MIT Press.

Forster, Kenneth I. 1974. The role of semantic hypotheses in sentence processing. *Problèmes Actuels en Psycholinguistique* ed. by F. Bresson & Jacques Mehler, 391-408. Paris: Editions du CNRS.

Forster, Kenneth I. 1979. Levels of processing and the structure of the language processor. *Sentence Processing* ed. by N.E. Cooper & E. Walker, 27-84.

Forster, Kenneth I. & Leonie A. Ryder. 1971. Perceiving the structure and meaning of sentences. *Journal of Verbal Learning and Verbal Behavior* 10:285-96.

Fowler, Harold N. 1926. *Plato: Cratylus, Parmenides, Greater Hippias, Lesser Hippias*. Loeb Classical Library No.167. London: Heinemann.

Franklyn, Julian. 1961. *A Dictionary of Rhyming Slang*. London & Boston: Routledge & Kegan Paul.

Fraser, Bruce. 1970. Idioms within transformational grammar. *Foundations of Language* 6:22-42.

Fraser, Bruce. 1974a. An examination of the performative analysis. *Papers in Linguistics* 7:1-40.

Fraser, Bruce. 1974b. *An Analysis of Vernacular Performative Verbs*. Bloomington: Indiana University Linguistics Club.

Fraser, Bruce. 1975. Hedged performatives. In Cole & Morgan (eds) 1975:187-210.

Frege, Gottlob. 1966. On sense and reference. *Translations from the Philosophical Writings of Gottlob Frege* ed. by Peter Geach & Max Black, 56-78. Oxford: Blackwell. First published as 'Uber Sinn und Bedeutung' *Zeitschrift fur Philosophie und philosophische Kritik* 100, 1892:25-50.

French, Patrice. 1981. Semantic and syntactic factors in the perception of rapidly presented sentences. *Journal of Psycholinguistic Research* 10:581-91.

Friedrich, Paul. 1970. Shape in grammar. *Language* 46:397-407.

Fromkin, Victoria (ed.). 1973. *Speech Errors as Linguistic Evidence*. The Hague: Mouton.

Fromkin, Victoria & Robert Rodman. 1978. *An Introduction to Language*. (2nd edn) New York: Holt, Rinehart & Winston.

Fry, D.B. 1955. Duration and intensity as physical correlates of linguistic stress. *Journal of the Acoustical Society of America* 27:765-8.

Fry, D.B. 1958. Experiments in the perception of stress. *Language and Speech* 1:126-52.

García, Erica. 1975. *The Role of Theory in Linguistic Analysis*. Amsterdam: North Holland.

Garner, Richard. 1971. "Presupposition" in philosophy and linguistics. In Fillmore & Langendoen (eds) 1971:23-42.

Gazdar, Gerald. 1979. *Pragmatics: Implicature, Presupposition, and Logical*

Form. New York: Academic Press.

Gazdar, Gerald & David Good. 1982. On a notion of relevance: comments on Sperber & Wilson's paper. In Smith (ed.) 1982:88-100.

Geach, Peter T. 1968. *Reference and Generality* (Emended edn) Ithaca: Cornell University Press.

Gibson, Eleanor J. 1969. *Principles of Perceptual Learning and Development*. New York: Appleton-Century-Crofts.

Giles, Howard & Peter F. Powesland. 1975. *Speech Style and Social Evaluation*. New York: Academic Press.

Giles, Howard, W. Peter Robinson, & Philip M. Smith (eds.) 1980. *Language: Social Psychological Perspectives*. Oxford: Pergamon Press.

Givón, Talmy. 1976. Topic, pronoun, and grammatical agreement. In Li (ed.) 1976:151-88.

Givón, Talmy. 1979a. *On Understanding Grammar*. New York: Academic Press.

Givón, Talmy (ed.). 1979b. *Syntax and Semantics 12: Discourse and Syntax*. New York: Academic Press.

Givón, Talmy. 1979c. From discourse to syntax: grammar as a processing strategy. In Givón (ed.) 1979b:81-112.

Glanzer, Murray & Anita R. Cunitz. 1966. Two storage mechanisms in free recall. *Journal of Verbal Learning and Verbal Behavior* 5:351-60.

Goffman, Erving. 1955. On face-work: an analysis of ritual elements in social interaction. *Psychiatry* 18:213-31. Reprinted in *Communication in Face to Face Interaction* ed. by John Laver & Sandy Hutcheson, 1972:319-63. Harmondsworth: Penguin.

Goldman-Eisler, Freda. 1968. *Psycholinguistics: Experiments in Spontaneous Speech*. New York: Academic Press.

Goodenough, Ward H. 1956. Componential analysis and the study of meaning. *Language* 32:195-216.

Gordon, David & George Lakoff. 1971. Conversational postulates. *Papers from the Seventh Regional Meeting of the Chicago Linguistics Society*, 63-84. Reprinted in Cole & Morgan (eds) 1975:83-106.

Gowers, Sir Ernest. 1948. *Plain Words: A Guide to the Use of English*. London: His Majesty's Stationery Office.

Green, Georgia. 1970. Review of 'Abstract Syntax and Latin Complementation' by Robin Lakoff (1968). *Language* 46:149-67.

Green, Georgia. 1975. How to get people to do things with words. In Cole & Morgan (eds) 1975:107-42.

Greenbaum, Sidney. 1969. *Studies in English Adverbial Usage*. London: Longman.

Gregory, Richard L. 1966. *Eye and Brain: the Psychology of Seeing*. London: Weidenfeld & Nicholson.

Grice, H. Paul. 1957. Meaning. *Philosophical Review* 66:377-88. Reprinted in Rosenberg & Travis (eds) 1971:436-44, and Steinberg & Jakobovits (eds) 1971:53-9.

Grice, H. Paul. 1968. Utterer's meaning, sentence meaning, and word-meaning. *Foundations of Language* 4:225-42.

Grice, H. Paul. 1969. Utterer's meaning and intentions. *Philosophical Review* 78:147-77.

Grice, H. Paul. 1975. Logic and conversation. In Cole & Morgan (eds) 1974:41-58.

Grice, H. Paul. 1978. Further notes on logic and conversation. In Cole (ed.) 1978:113-27.

Grimes, Joseph E. 1975. *The Thread of Discourse*. The Hague: Mouton.

Grosz, Barbara J. 1981. Focusing and description in natural language dialogues. In Joshi, Webber, & Sag (eds) 1981:84-105.

Gruber, Jeffrey S. 1965. *Studies in Lexical Relations*. Ph.D. Thesis, Massachusetts Institute of Technology. Published by the Indiana University Linguistics Club (Bloomington) in 1970. Revised version in *Lexical Structures in Syntax and Semantics*, 1976:1-210. Amsterdam: North Holland.

Gruber, Jeffrey S. 1967. 'Look' and 'see'. *Language* 43:937-47.

Gumperz, John J. 1982. *Discourse Strategies*. Cambridge: Cambridge University Press.

Gumperz, John J. & Dell Hymes (eds). 1972. *Directions in Sociolinguistics: The Ethnography of Communication*. New York: Holt, Rinehart & Winston.

Gundel, Jeannette K. 1974/1977. *Role of Topic and Comment in Linguistic Theory*. Bloomington: Indiana University Linguistics Club.

Gunderson, Keith (ed.). 1975. *Language, Mind, and Knowledge*. Minneapolis: University of Minnesota Press.

Guy, Gregory & Julia Vonwiller. 1984. The meaning of an intonation in Australian English. *Australian Journal of Linguistics* 4:1-17.

Hadding-Koch, Kerstin. 1961. *Acoustico-Phonetic Studies in the Intonation of Southern Swedish*. Lund: Gleerup.

Hadding-Koch, Kerstin & M. Studdert-Kennedy. 1964. An experimental study of some intonation contours. *Phonetica* 11:175-85.

Halliday, Michael A.K. 1967a. *Intonation and Grammar in British English*. The Hague: Mouton.

Halliday, Michael A.K. 1967b. Notes on transitivity and theme in English, Part II. *Journal of Linguistics* 3:199-244.

Halliday, Michael A.K. 1970a. *A Course in Spoken English: Intonation*. Oxford: Oxford University Press.

Halliday, Michael A.K. 1970b. Language structure and language function. In Lyons (ed.) 1970:140-65.

Halliday, Michael A.K. & Ruqaiya Hasan. 1976. *Cohesion in English*. London: Longman.

Hammel, Eugene A. (ed.). 1965. *Formal Semantic Analysis*. Menasha WI: American Anthropological Assn.

Harnish, Robert M. 1975. The argument from *Lurk*. *Linguistic Inquiry* 6:145-54.

Harnish, Robert M. 1979. Meaning and speech acts. [Review of Katz 1977a] *Lingua* 49:331-54.

Harnish, Robert M. 1979. A projection problem for pragmatics. *Syntax and Semantics 10: Selections from the Third Groningen Round Table*, ed. by Frank Heny & Helmut S. Schnelle, 315-42. New York: Academic Press.

Harris, Zellig S. 1948. Componential analysis of a Hebrew paradigm. *Language* 24:87-91.

Harris, Zellig S. 1951. *Methods in Structural Linguistics*. Chicago: University of Chicago Press.

Harrison, Bernard. 1974. Review of 'Semantic Theory' by Jerrold J. Katz (1972). *Mind* 83:599-606.

Hawkins, John A. 1978. *Definiteness and Indefiniteness*. London: Croom Helm.

Heider, Eleanor. 1972. Probabilities, sampling and ethnographic method: the case of Dani color names. *Man* 7:448-66.

Henderson, Alan, Freda Goldman-Eisler, & Andrew Skarbek. 1965. Temporal patterns of cognitive activity and breath control in speech. *Language and Speech* 8:236-42.

Heringer, James T. 1971. *Some Grammatical Correlates of Felicity Conditions and Presuppositions*. Ph.D. Thesis, Ohio State University. Published by Indiana University Linguistics Club (Bloomington), 1972.

Hickerson, Nancy P. 1971. Review of 'Basic Color Terms: Their Universality and Evolution' by Brent Berlin & Paul Kay (1969). *International Journal of American Linguistics* 37:257-70.

Hjelmslev, Louis. 1943. *Omkring Sprogteoriens Grundlaeggelse*. Copenhagen. Tr. by Francis J. Whitfield as *Prolegemona to a Theory of Language*, 1961. Madison: University of Wisconsin.

Hockett, Charles F. 1947. Problems of morphemic analysis. *Language* 23:321-43. Reprinted in Joos (ed.) 1957:229-42.

Hockett, Charles F. 1958. *A Course in Modern Linguistics*. New York: MacMillan.

Holmes, Alan C. 1964. *Health Education in Developing Countries*. London: Nelson.

Householder, Fred. W. 1957. Accent, Juncture, intonation, and my grandfather's reader. *Word* 13:234-45.

Householder, Fred W. (ed.). 1981. *The Syntax of Apollonius Dyscolus*. Amsterdam: John Benjamins.

Huddleston, Rodney. 1976. *An Introduction to English Transformational Grammar*. London: Longman.

Hudson, Richard A. 1976. Conjunction reduction, gapping, and right-node raising. *Language* 52:535-62.

Hudson, W. 1960. Pictorial depth perception in sub-cultural groups in Africa. *Journal of Social Psychology* 52:183-208.

Hymes, Dell. 1972. Models of interaction of language and social life. In Gumperz & Hymes (eds) 1972:35-71.

Ide, Sachiko. 1982. Japanese sociolinguistics: politeness and women's language. *Lingua* 57:357-85.

International Code of Zoological Nomenclature. 1961. London: International Trust for Zoological Nomenclature.

Jackendoff, Ray S. 1971. Gapping and related rules. *Linguistic Inquiry* 2:21-35.

Jackendoff, Ray S. 1972. *Semantic Interpretation in Generative Grammar*. Cambridge MA: MIT Press.

Jackendoff, Ray S. 1977. *X̄ Syntax: A Study of Phrase Structure*. Cambridge MA: MIT Press.

Jacobs, Roderick A. & Peter S. Rosenbaum. 1968. *English Transformational Grammar* Waltham MA: Blaisdell-Ginn.

Jacobsen, Wesley. 1981. The semantics of spontaneity in Japanese. *Proceedings of the Seventh Annual Meeting of the Berkeley Linguistics Society*, 104-115.

Jaeger, Edmund C. 1959. *A Source-Book of Biological Names and Terms*. (3rd edn, revised) Springfield: Thomas.

Jakobson, Roman. 1936. Beitrag zur allgemeinen Kasuslehre. *Travaux du Cercle Linguistique de Prague* 6:240-288.

Jakobson, Roman, Gunnar Fant, & Morris Halle. 1952. *Preliminaries to Speech Analysis*. Technical Report 13, MIT Acoustics Laboratory. Cambridge MA: MIT Press.

Jakobson, Roman & Morris Halle. 1956. *Fundamentals of Language*. The Hague: Mouton.

Jespersen, Otto. *A Modern English Grammar on Historical Principles: Part I. Sounds and Spellings*, 1909; *Part II. Syntax. First Volume*, 1914; *Part III. Syntax. Second Volume*, 1927; *Part IV. Syntax. Third Volume*, 1931; *Part V. Syntax. Fourth Volume*, 1940; *Part VI. Morphology*, 1942; *Part VII. Syntax*, 1949. London: Allen & Unwin.

Jespersen, Otto, 1917. *Negation in English and Other Languages*. (2nd edn, 1966) Copenhagen: Ejnar Munksgaard.

Jespersen, Otto. 1924. *The Philosophy of Grammar*. London: Allen & Unwin.

Johnson, Samuel. 1755. *Dictionary of the English Language*. London.

Johnson-Laird, Philip N. 1981. Mental models of meaning. In Joshi, Webber, & Sag (eds) 1981:106-26.

Jones, Daniel. 1932. *An Outline of English Phonetics*. Cambridge: Heffer.

Joos, Martin. 195⁻. *Readings in Linguistics*. Washington, D.C.: American Council of Learned Societies. Reissued as *Readings in Linguistics I* 1971. Chicago: Chicago University Press.

Joos, Martin. 1961. *The Five Clocks*. New York: Harcourt, Brace & World.

Jowett, Benjamin. 1953. *The Dialogues of Plato (Vols I-IV)*. (4th edn) Oxford: Clarendon Press.

Joshi, Aravind K., Bonnie L. Webber, & Ivan A. Sag (eds). 1981. *Elements of Discourse Understanding*. Cambridge: Cambridge University Press.

Kafka, Franz. 1961. *Metamorphosis and Other Stories*. Harmondsworth: Penguin.

Kaplan, David. 1978. Dthat. In Cole (ed.) 1978:221-43.

Karttunen, Lauri & Stanley F. Peters. 1979. Conventional implicature. *Syntax and Semantics 11: Presupposition* ed. by Choon-Kyu Oh & David A. Dinneen, 1-56. New York: Academic Press.

Katz, Jerrold J. 1964a. Analyticity and contradiction in natural language. In Fodor & Katz (eds) 1964:519-43.

Katz, Jerrold J. 1964b. Semantic theory and the meaning of "good". *Journal of Philosophy* 61:739-66.

Katz, Jerrold J. 1964c. Semi-sentences. In Fodor & Katz (eds) 1964:400-16.

Katz, Jerrold J. 1966. *The Philosophy of Language*. New York: Harper & Row.

Katz, Jerrold J. 1967. Recent issues in semantic theory. *Foundations of Language* 3:124-94.

Katz, Jerrold J. 1972. *Semantic Theory*. New York: Harper & Row.

Katz, Jerrold J. 1975a. Logic and language: an examination of recent criticisms of intensionalism. In Gunderson (ed.) 1975:36-130.

Katz, Jerrold J. 1975b. The dilemma between orthodoxy and identity. *Philosophia* 4:287-98. Reprinted in *Language in Focus* ed. by Asa Kasher, 1976:165-75. Dordrecht: Reidel.

Katz, Jerrold J. 1977a. *Propositional Structure and Illocutionary Force*. New York: Thomas Crowell. Reprinted 1980. Cambridge MA: Harvard University Press.

Katz, Jerrold J. 1977b. The advantage of semantic theory over predicate calculus in the representation of logical form in natural language. *New Directions in Semantics* ed. by R.B. Marcus, *The Monist* 60/3:380-405.

Katz, Jerrold J. 1977c. The real status of semantic representations. *Linguistic Inquiry* 8:559-84.

Katz, Jerrold J. 1980. Chomsky on meaning. *Language* 56:1-41.

Katz, Jerrold J. 1981a. *Language and Other Abstract Objects*. Totowa: Rowman & Littlefield.

Katz, Jerrold J. 1981b. Literal meaning and logical theory. *Journal of Philosophy* 78:203-33.

Katz, Jerrold J. & Jerry A. Fodor. 1963. Structure of a semantic theory. *Language* 39:170-210.

Katz, Jerrold J. & Richard I. Nagel. 1974. Meaning postulates and semantic theory. *Foundations of Language* 11:311-40.

Katz, Jerrold J. & Paul M. Postal. 1963. Semantic interpretation of idioms and sentences containing them. *Quarterly Progress Report* 70:275-82. Cambridge MA: MIT Research Laboratory of Electronics.

Katz, Jerrold J. & Paul M. Postal. 1964. *An Integrated Theory of Linguistic Descriptions*. Cambridge MA: MIT Press.

Kay, Paul. 1975. Synchronic variability and diachronic change in basic color terms. *Language in Society* 4:257-70.

Kay, Paul & Chad McDaniel. 1978. The linguistic significance of the meanings of basic color terms. *Language* 54:610-46.

Kempson, Ruth M. 1975. *Presupposition and the Delimitation of Semantics*. London: Cambridge University Press.

Kempson, Ruth M. 1977. *Semantic Theory*. London: Cambridge University Press.

Kingdon, Roger. 1958. *The Groundwork of English Intonation*. London: Longmans.

Kiparsky, Paul & Carol Kiparsky. 1971. Fact. In Steinberg & Jakobovits (eds) 1971:345-69.

Krámský, Jiři. 1972. *The Article and the Concept of Definiteness in Language*. The Hague: Mouton.

Kreiman, Jody & Almerindo E. Ojeda (eds.). 1980. *Papers from the Parasession on Pronouns and Anaphora*. Chicago: Chicago Linguistics Society.

Kroeber, Alfred L. 1909. Classificatory systems of relationship. *Journal of the Royal Anthropological Institute* 39:77-84.

Kruisinga, E. 1932. *A Handbook of Present Day English*. Groningen: Nordhoff.

Kuno, Susumu. 1972a. Pronominalization, reflexivization, and direct discourse. *Linguistic Inquiry* 3:161-95.

Kuno, Susumu. 1972b. Functional sentence perspective. *Linguistic Inquiry* 3:269-20.

Kuno, Susumu. 1976. Subject, theme, and the speaker's empathy – a re-examination of relativization phenomena. In Li (ed.) 1976:417-44.

Kuno, Susumu. 1979. On the interaction between syntactic rules and discourse principles. *Explorations in Linguistics: Papers in Honor of Kazuko Inoue* ed. by George Bedell, Eichi Kobayashi, & Masatake Muraki, 279-304. Tokyo: Kenkyusha.

Kuno, Susumu & Etsuko Kaburaki. 1977. Empathy and syntax. *Linguistic Inquiry* 8:627-72.

Labov, William. 1969. The logic of nonstandard English. *Georgetown Monographs in Languages and Linguistics* 22, ed. by James E. Alatis, 1-43. Washington, D.C.: Georgetown University.

Labov, William. 1978. Denotational structure. *Papers from the Parasession on the Lexicon*. ed. by Donka Farkas, Wesley M. Jacobsen, & Karol W. Todrys, 220-60. Chicago: Chicago Linguistic Society.

Ladd, D. Robert. 1980. *The Structure of Intonational Meaning*. Bloomington: Indiana University Press.

Ladefoged, Peter. 1982. *A Course in Phonetics* (2nd edn) New York: Harcourt, Brace, Jovanovich.

Lakoff, George. 1965. *On the Nature of Syntactic Irregularity*. Report NSF-16, The Computation Laboratory of Harvard University. Reprinted as Lakoff 1970.

Lakoff, George. 1968. Instrumental adverbs and the concept of deep structure. *Foundations of Language* 4:4-29.

Lakoff, George. 1970. *Irregularity in Syntax*. (Reprint of Lakoff 1965) New York: Holt, Rinehart & Winston.

Lakoff, George. 1971a. On generative semantics. In Steinberg & Jakobovits (eds) 1971:232-96.

Lakoff, George. 1971b. The role of deduction in grammar. In Fillmore & Langendoen (eds) 1971:63-70.

Lakoff, George. 1972a. Linguistics and natural logic. In Davidson & Harman (eds) 1972:545-665.

Lakoff, George. 1972b. The global nature of the nuclear stress rule. *Language* 48:285-303.

Lakoff, George. 1972c. Hedges: a study of meaning criteria and the logic of fuzzy concepts. *Papers from the Eighth Regional Meeting of the Chicago Linguistics Society*, 183-228. Revised version in *Contemporary Research in Philosophical Logic and Linguistic Semantics* ed. by D. Hockney, W. Harper, & B. Freed, 221-71. Dordrecht: Reidel.

Lakoff, Robin T. 1968. *Abstract Syntax and Latin Complementation*. Cambridge MA: MIT Press.

Lakoff, Robin T. 1969. Review of 'Grammaire Générale et Raisonnée' ed. by Herbert H. Brekle (1966). *Language* 45:343-64.

Lakoff, Robin T. 1970. Tense and its relation to participants. *Languge* 46:838-49.

Lakoff, Robin T. 1972. Language in context. *Language* 48:907-27.

Lakoff, Robin T. 1973. The logic of politeness: or, minding your p's and q's. *Papers from the Ninth Regional Meeting of the Chicago Linguistic Society*, 292-305.

Lakoff, Robin T. 1975. *Language and Woman's Place*. New York: Harper Colophon.

Lamb, Sydney, M. 1965. Kinship terminology and linguistic structure. In Hammel (ed.) 1965:37-64.

Lambrecht, Knud. 1982. *Topic, Antitopic and Verb Agreement in Non-Standard French*. Amsterdam: John Benjamins.

Lancelot, Claude, 1644. *Novelle Méthode pour Comprendre, facilement et en peu de temps, la Langue Latine*. Paris.

Lancelot, Claude & Antoine Arnaud. 1660. *Grammaire Générale et Raisonnée*. Paris. Facsimilie, 1967. Menston: Scolar Press.

Lane, A. 1700. *A Key to the Art of Letters*. London. Facsimile, 1969. Menston: Scolar Press.

Langacker, Ronald W. 1968. *Language and Its Structure*. New York: Harcourt, Brace & World.

Law Reports. King's Bench Division. Vol.1. 1933. London: Incorporated Council of Law Reporting.

Lawler, John. 1972. Generic to a fault. *Papers from the Eighth Regional Meeting* of the Chicago Linguistic Society, 247-58.

Leech, Geoffrey. 1981. *Semantics: A Study of Meaning.* (2nd edn) Harmondsworth: Penguin.

Lehiste, Ilse. 1970. *Suprasegmentals.* Cambridge MA: MIT Press.

Lehrer, Adrienne. 1974. *Semantic Fields and Lexical Structure.* Amsterdam: North Holland.

Lehrer, Adrienne & Keith Lehrer (eds). 1970. *Theory of Meaning.* Englewood Cliffs: Prentice-Hall Inc.

Lenneberg, Eric & J.M. Roberts. 1956. *The Language of Experience: A Study in Methodology.* Bloomington: Indiana University.

Lerner, Alan J. 1959. *My Fair Lady.* Harmondsworth: Penguin.

Levi, Judith. 1978. *The Syntax and Semantics of Complex Nominals.* New York: Academic Press.

Levinson, Stephen C. 1983. *Pragmatics.* Cambridge: Cambridge University Press.

Lewis, David, 1969. *Convention.* Cambridge MA: Harvard University Press.

Lewis, David. 1970. General semantics. *Synthese* 22:18-67. Reprinted in Davidson & Harman 1972:169-218.

Li, Charles N. (ed.). 1976. *Subject and Topic.* New York: Academic Press.

Li, Charles N. & Sandra A. Thompson. 1976. Subject and topic: a new typology of language. In Li (ed.) 1976:459-89.

Liberman, Mark & Alan Prince. 1977. On Stress and linguistic rhythm. *Linguistic Inquiry* 8:249-336.

Liberman, Mark & Ivan Sag. 1974. Prosodic form and discourse function. *Papers from the Tenth Regional Meeting of the Chicago Linguistic Society,* 416-27.

Lieberman, Philip. 1967. *Intonation, Perception, and Language.* Cambridge MA: MIT Press.

Linde, Charlotte. 1979. Focus of attention and the choice of pronouns in discourse. In Givón 1979b:337-54.

Linde, Charlotte & William Labov. 1975. Spatial networks as a site for the study of language and thought. *Language* 51:924-39.

Linnaeus, Carolus. 1735. *Systema Naturae.* Leyden. Facsimile, 1964. Nieuwkoop: B. de Graaf.

Locke, John. 1690. *Essay Concerning Human Understanding* ed. by Peter H. Nidditch. Oxford: Clarendon Press.

Loman, Bengt. 1967. *Conversations in a Negro American Dialect.* Washington D.C.: Center for Applied Linguistics.

Longacre, Robert E. 1983. *The Grammar of Discourse.* New York: Plenum Press.

Lounsbury, Floyd G. 1956. A semantic analysis of the Pawnee kinship usage. *Language* 32:158-94.

Lyons, John. 1966. Firth's theory of 'meaning'. In Bazell et al. (eds) 1966:288-302.

Lyons, John. 1968. *Introduction to Theoretical Linguistics.* London: Cambridge University Press.

Lyons, John (ed.). 1970. *New Horizons in Linguistics.* Harmondsworth: Penguin.

Lyons, John. 1977. *Semantics (Vols 1-2).* Cambridge: Cambridge University Press.

Makkai, Adam. 1972. *Idiom Structure in English.* The Hague: Mouton.

Malinowski, Bronislaw. 1949. The problem of meaning in primitive languages. In Ogden & Richards (eds) 1949:296-336.

Marchand, Hans. 1969. *The Categories and Types of Present-Day English Word-Formation*. (2nd edn) München: C.H. Beck'sche.

Marslen-Wilson, William & Lorraine K. Tyler. 1980. Towards a psychological basis for a theory of anaphora. In Kreiman & Ojeda (eds) 1980:258-86.

Matthews, Peter H. 1974. *Morphology: An Introduction to the Theory of Word Structure*. Cambridge: Cambridge University Press.

Maydon, H.C. (ed.). 1951. *Big Game Shooting in Africa*. (Reprint) London: Seeley Services & Co.

McArthur, Tom. 1981. *Longman Lexicon of Contemporary English*. London: Longman.

McCawley, James D. 1968a. Concerning the base component of a transformational grammar. *Foundations of Language* 4:243-69.

McCawley, James D. 1968b. The role of semantics in a grammar. In Bach & Harms (eds) 1968:124-69.

McCawley, James D. 1968c. Lexical insertion in a transformational grammar without deep structure. *Papers From the Fourth Regional Meeting of the Chicago Linguistic Society*, 71-80.

McCawley, James D. 1970. English as a VSO language. *Language* 46:286-99.

McCawley, James D. 1972a. A program for logic. In Davidson & Harman (eds) 1972:498-544.

McCawley, James D. 1972b. *Syntactic and Logical Arguments for Semantic Structures*. Bloomington: Indiana University Linguistics Club. Also in *Three Dimensions of Linguistic Theory* ed. by Osamu Fujimura, 1973:259-376. Tokyo: TEC Co.

McCawley, James D. 1973. *Grammar and Meaning*. Tokyo: Taikushan.

McCawley, James D. 1977. Remarks on the lexicography of performative verbs. *Proceedings of the Texas Conference on Performatives, Presuppositions, and Implicatures* ed. by Andy Rogers, Robert Wall, & John Murphy, 13-25. Arlington: Center for Applied Linguistics. Reprinted in McCawley 1979:151-64.

McCawley, James D. 1979. *Adverbs, Vowels, and Other Objects of Wonder*. Chicago: University of Chicago Press.

McCawley, James D. 1981. *Everything that Linguists have Always Wanted to Know about Logic, but were ashamed to ask*. Chicago: University of Chicago Press & Oxford: Basil Blackwell.

McCawley, Noriko. 1973. Boy! Is syntax easy! *Papers from the Ninth Regional Meeting of the Chicago Linguistic Society*, 369-77.

McNeill, David. 1966. Developmental psycholinguistics. *The Genesis of Language* ed. by Frank Smith & George miller, 15-84. Cambridge MA: MIT Press.

Macquarie Dictionary. 1980. St. Leonards, NSW: Macquarie Library Pty.

Metzing, D. 1981. Frame representation and lexical semantics. In Eikmeyer & Rieser (eds) 1981:320-42.

Miller, Charles. 1973. *The Lunatic Express*. New York: Ballantine.

Miller, George. 1956. The magical number seven plus or minus one or two, or, some limits on our capacity for processing information. *Psychological Review* 63:81-96.

Miller, George & Philip N. Johnson-Laird. 1976. *Language and Perception*. Cambridge MA: Harvard University Press.

Milligan, Spike. 1972. *The Goon Show Scripts*. London: Woburn Press.

Milsark, Gary L. 1976. *Existential Sentences in English*. Bloomington: Indiana University Linguistics Club.

Montague, Richard. 1974. *Formal Philosophy* ed. by Richmond Thomason. New Haven: Yale University Press.

Moore, Timothy E. (ed.). 1973. *Cognitive Development and the Acquisition of Language*. New York: Academic Press.

Moreland, Floyd L. & Rita M. Fleischer. 1977. *Latin: An Intensive Course*. Berkeley: University of California Press.

Morris, Charles W. 1938. *Foundations of the Theory of Signs*. International Encyclopedia of Unified Science, Vol.1, No.2. Chicago: University of Chicago Press.

Morris, Charles W. 1946. *Signs, Language, and Behavior*. Englewood Cliffs: Prentice-Hall Inc.

Murdock, B.B. 1962. The serial position effect of free recall. *Journal of Experimental Psychology* 64:482-8.

Murray, Lindley. 1795. *English Grammar*. London.

Murray, Wayne S. 1982. *Sentence Matching: The Influence of Meaning and Structure*. Unpublished Ph.D. Thesis, Monash University.

Naipaul, V.S. 1981. A new king for the Congo: Mobutu and the nihilism of Africa. *The Return of Eva Peron*. Harmondsworth: Penguin.

Neijt, Anneke. 1979. *Gapping: A Contribution to Sentence Grammar*. Dordrecht: Foris.

Neubauer, F. & J.S. Petöfi. 1981. Word semantics, lexicon systems, and text interpretation. In Eikmeyer & Rieser (eds) 1981:343-77.

Newman, Stanley S. 1946. On the stress system of English. *Word* 2:171-87.

Newmeyer, Frederick J. 1980. *Linguistic Theory in America: The First Quarter Century of Transformational Generative Grammar*. New York: Academic Press.

Nida, Eugene A. 1951. A system for the description of semantic elements. *Word* 7:1-14.

Nooteboom, Sibout G. 1973. The tongue slips into patterns. In Fromkin (ed.; 1973:144-56.

O'Connor, J.D. & G.F. Arnold. 1961. *Intonation of Colloquial English*. London: Longmans, Green & Co.

Ogden, Charles K. & Ivor A. Richards. 1949. *The Meaning of Meaning*. (10th edn) London: Routledge & Kegan Paul.

Osborne, John. 1973. *Four Plays: West of Suez, A Patriot for Me, Time Present, The Hotel in Amsterdam*. New York: Dodd, Mead.

Osgood, Charles E. 1952. The nature and measurement of meaning. *Psychological Bulletin* 49:197-237.

Osgood, Charles E. 1976. *Focus on Meaning. Vol.1: Explorations in Semantic Space*. The Hague: Mouton.

Osgood, Charles E. & J. Kathryn Bock. 1977. Salience and sentencing: some production principles. In Rosenberg (ed.) 1977:89-140.

Osgood, Charles E. & Thomas A Sebeok. 1954. *Psycholinguistics: A Survey of Theory and Research Problems. Journal of Abnormal and Social Psychology* 49. Revised version with 'A survey of psycholinguistic research 1954-64' by A. Richard Diebold, 1965. Bloomington: Indiana University Press.

Osgood, Charles E., George J. Suci, & Percy H. Tannenbaum. 1957. *The Measurement of Meaning*. Urbana: University of Illinois Press.

Palmer, Harold E. 1922. *English Intonation with Systematic Exercises*. Cambridge: Heffer.

Parish, Margaret. 1971. *Come Back, Amelia Bedelia* (I can read book no.83). Tadworth, Surrey: World's Work Ltd.

Partee, Barbara H. 1971. On the requirement that transformations preserve meaning. In Fillmore & Langendoen (eds) 1971:1-21.

Partee, Barbara H. (ed.). 1976. *Montague Grammar*. New York: Academic Press.

Paul, Peter. 1982. Homonyms, semantic divergence and valency. *Lingua* 58:291-307.

Pelletier, Francis J. (ed.). 1979. *Mass Terms: Some Philosophical Problems*. Dordrecht: Reidel.

Perlmutter, David A. 1970. On the article in English. *Progress in Linguistics* ed. by Manfred Bierwisch & Karl Heidolph, 233-48. The Hague: Mouton.

Pike, Kenneth L. 1945. *The Intonation of American English*. Ann Arbor: University of Michigan Press.

Pirsig, Robert M. 1976. *Zen and the Art of Motorcycle Maintenance*. London: Corgi Books.

Plato. *The Sophist*. tr. by Harold N. Fowler, 1921. Loeb Classical Library. London: Heinemann. Also in Jowett (ed.) 1953, Vol.III.

Plato. *Cratylus*. In Fowler (ed.) 1926, also Jowett (ed.) 1953, Vol.III.

Plato. *Phaedrus and The Seventh and Eighth Letters* tr. by Walter Hamilton, 1973. Harmondsworth: Penguin.

Platt, John T. 1980. The relation between accommodation and code-switching in a multilingual society: Singapore. In Giles, Robinson & Smith 1980:345-51.

Pope, Alexander. *Collected Poems* ed. by Ernest Rhys. Everyman's Library No.760, 1924. London: Dent.

Posner, Michael I. 1973. *Cognition: An Introduction*. Glenview: Scott, Foresman.

Postal, Paul M. 1970. On the surface verb "remind". *Linguistic Inquiry* 1:37-120.

Postal, Paul M. 1971a. On coreferential complement subject deletion. *Linguistic Inquiry* 1:439-500.

Postal, Paul M. 1971b. *Cross-Over Phenomena*. New York: Holt, Rinehart & Winston.

Poutsma, Hendrik. 1914. *A Grammar of Late Modern English, Part II, Section IA. Nouns, Adjectives and Articles*. Groningen: Noordhof.

Price, Henry H. 1932. *Perception*. London: Methuen.

Pride, John B. & Janet Holmes (eds). 1972. *Sociolinguistics*. Harmondsworth: Penguin.

Prince, Ellen. 1970. On the given/new distinction. *Papers from the Fifteenth Regional Meeting of the Chicago Linguistic Society*, 267-78.

Prince, Ellen. 1981a. Toward a taxonomy of given-new information. In Cole (ed.) 1981:223-56.

Prince, Ellen. 1981b. Topicalization, focus-movement, and Yiddish-movement: a pragmatic differentiation. *Proceedings of the Seventh Annual Meeting of the Berkeley Linguistics Society*, 249-64.

Quang Phuc Dong. 1971. The applicability of transformations to idioms. *Papers from the Seventh Regional Meeting of the Chicago Linguistics Society*, 200-05.

Quirk, Randolph. 1968. *The Use of English*. (2nd edn) London: Longman.

Quirk, Randolph, Sidney Greenbaum, Geoffrey Leech, & Jan Svartvik. 1972. *A

Grammar of Contemporary English. London: Longman.

Ratcliff, Jan. 1978. An investigation of the plausibility effect. Paper read to the 5th Australian Experimental Psychology Conference, La Trobe University.

Reichenbach, Hans. 1947. *Elements of Symbolic Logic*. London: Macmillan.

Reinhart, Tanya. 1982. *Pragmatics and Linguistics: An Analysis of Sentence Topics*. Bloomington: Indiana University Linguistics Club.

Rescher, Nicholas. 1969. *Many-valued Logic*. New York: McGraw-Hill.

Rey-DeBove, Josette & G. Gagnon. 1981. *Dictionnaire des Anglicismes*. Paris: Le Robert.

Robins, Robert H. 1979. *A Short History of Linguistics*. (2nd edn) London: Longman.

Rochester, Sherry & James R. Martin. 1979. *Crazy Talk: A Study of the Discourse of Schizophrenic Speakers*. New York: Plenum Press.

Rosch, Eleanor. 1973. On the internal structure of perceptual and semantic categories. In Moore (ed.) 1973:111-44.

Rosch, Eleanor, Carolyn B. Mervis, Wayne D. Gray, David M. Johnson, & Penny Boyes-Brame. 1976. Basic objects in natural categories. *Cognitive Psychology* 8:382-439.

Rosenberg, Jay & Charles Travis (eds). 1971. *Readings in the Philosophy of Language*. Englewood Cliffs: Prentice-Hall Inc.

Rosenberg, Sheldon (ed.). 1977. *Sentence Production: Developments in Research and Theory*. Hillsdale: Lawrence Earlbaum.

Ross, John R. 1970. On declarative sentences. *Readings in English Transformational Grammar* ed. by Roderick A. Jacobs & Peter S. Rosenbaum (eds) 1970:222-72. Waltham MA: Ginn.

Ross, John R. 1972. Act. In Davidson & Harman (eds) 1972:70-126.

Sadock, Jerrold M. 1970. *Whimperatives. Studies Presented to Robert B. Lees by his Students*. ed. by Jerrold M. Sadock & Anthony L. Vanek, 223-38. Edmonton & Champaign: Linguistic Research Inc.

Sadock, Jerrold M. 1971. Queclaratives. *Papers from the Seventh Regional Meeting of the Chicago Linguistic Society*, 223-31.

Sadock, Jerrold M. 1974. *Toward a Linguistic Theory of Speech Acts*. New York: Academic Press.

Sag, Ivan & Ellen F. Prince. 1970. Bibliography of works dealing with presupposition. In Oh & Dinneen (eds) 1979:389-403.

Sanctius, F. 1585. *Minerva, seu de Causis Lingue*. Madrid.

Sapir, Edward. 1921. *Language*. New York: Harcourt, Brace.

Saussure, Ferdinand de. 1974. *A Course in General Linguistics* ed. by Charles Bally & Albert Sechehaye, tr. by Wade Baskin. Glasgow: Fontana/Collins. First published 1915.

Schiffer, Stephen R. 1972. *Meaning*. Oxford: Clarendon Press.

Schlick, Moritz. 1936. Meaning and verification. *Philosophical Review* 45:339-69. Reprinted in *Readings in Philosophical Analysis* ed. by Herbert Feigl & Wilfred Sellars (eds) 1949:146-70. New York: Appleton-Century-Crofts. Abridged reprint in Lehrer & Lehrer (eds) 1970:98-112.

Schmerling, Susan F. 1976. *Aspects of English Sentence Stress*. Austin: University of Texas Press.

Schreiber, Peter A. 1972. Style disjuncts and the performative analysis. *Linguistic Inquiry* 3:321-47.

Searle, John R. 1965. What is a speech act? *Philosophy in America* ed. by Max Black, 221-39. London: Allen & Unwin. Reprinted in Searle (ed.) 1971:39-

53, and in Rosenberg & Travis (eds) 1971:614-28.

Searle, John R. 1968. Austin on locutionary and illocutionary acts. *Philosophical Review* 77:405-24. Reprinted in Rosenberg & Travis (eds) 1971:262-75.

Searle, John R. 1969. *Speech Acts*. London: Cambridge University Press.

Searle, John R. (ed.). 1971. *The Philosophy of Language*. London: Oxford University Press.

Searle, John R. 1975a. Indirect speech acts. In Cole & Morgan (eds) 1975:59-82.

Searle, John R. 1975b. A taxonomy of illocutionary acts. In Gunderson (ed.) 1975:344-69. Reprinted in *Language in Society* 4, 1976:1-23.

Searle, John R., Ferenc Kiefer, & Manfred Bierwisch (eds). 1980. *Speech Act Theory and Pragmatics*. Dordrecht: Reidel.

Selkirk, Elizabeth O. 1980a. The role of prosodic categories in English word stress. *Linguistic Inquiry* 11:563-605.

Selkirk, Elizabeth O. 1980b. *On Prosodic Structure and its Relation to Syntactic Structure*. Bloomington: Indiana University Linguistics Club.

Selkirk, Elizabeth O. 1982. *The Syntax of Words*. Cambridge MA: MIT Press.

Seuren, Pieter A.M. (ed.). 1974. *Semantic Syntax*. London: Oxford University Press.

Shakespeare, William. *The Complete Works* ed. by Peter Alexander, 1951. London & Glasgow: Collins.

Shaw, B. 1969. *Visual Symbols Survey: Report on the Recognition of Drawings in Kenya*. London: Centre for Educational Development Overseas.

Siewierska, Anna M. 1983. Choosing between the passive, topicalizations, and left-dislocations in English. Paper read to the Fourth Language and Speech Conference, Monash University, November 1983.

Siewierska, Anna M. 1984. *The Passive: A Comparative Linguistic Analysis*. London: Croom Helm.

Skinner, Burrhus, F. 1957. *Verbal Behavior*. New York: Appleton-Century-Crofts.

Smith, Neil V. 1975. On generics. *Transactions of the Philological Society*, 27-48.

Smith, Neil V. 1982. *Mutual Knowledge*. New York: Academic Press.

Sperber, Dan & Deirdre Wilson. 1981. Irony and the use-mention distinction. In Cole (ed.) 1981:295-317.

Sperber, Dan & Deirdre Wilson. 1982. Mutual knowledge and relevance in theories of comprehension. In Smith (ed.) 1982:61-85.

Steinberg, Danny D. & Leon A. Jakobovits (eds). 1971. *Semantics: An Interdisciplinary Reader in Philosophy, Linguistics, and Psychology*. London: Cambridge University Press.

Stern, Gustaf. 1965. *Meaning and Change of Meaning (with Special Reference to the English Language)*. Bloomington: Indiana University Press. First published 1931.

Stevick, E.W., J.G. Mlela, & F.N. Njenga. 1963. *Swahili Basic Course*. Washington D.C.: Department of State FSI.

Stockwell, Robert. 1972. The role of intonation: reconsiderations and other considerations. *Intonation* ed. by Dwight Bolinger, 87-109. Harmondsworth: Penguin.

Strawson, Peter F. 1950. On referring. *Mind* 59:320-44. Reprinted in Rosenberg & Travis (eds) 1971:175-95.

Strawson, Peter F. 1964. Intention and convention in speech acts. *Philosophical Review* 73:439-60. Reprinted in Rosenberg & Travis 1971:599-614.

Strevens, Peter. 1972. *British and American English*. London: Collier Macmillan.

Sweet, Henry. 1891-8. *New English Grammar*. Oxford: Clarendon Press.

Tannenbaum, Percy H. & Frederick Williamsd. 1968. Generation of active and passive sentences as a function of subject or object focus. *Journal of Verbal Learning and Verbal Behavior* 7:246-50.

Terkel, Studs. 1974. *Working*. New York: Avon Books.

Thomas, David. 1955. Three analyses of the Ilocano pronoun system. *Word* 11:204-8.

Thun, Nils. 1963. *Reduplicative Words in English: a Study of the Types 'Tick-tick', 'Hurly-burly' and 'Shilly-shally'*. Uppsala.

Trager, George L. & Henry L. Smith. 1951. *An Outline of English Structure*. Norman, Oklahoma: Battenberg.

Trier, Jost. 1931. *Der Deutsche Wortschatz im Sinnbezirk des Verstandes: die Geschichte eines Sprachlichen Feldes*. Heidelberg.

Trubetzkoy, Nikolaj S. 1939. Grundzuge der Phonologie. *Travaux du Cercle Linguistique de Prague* 7. Republished as *Principles of Phonology* tr. by Christiane A.M. Baltaxe, 1969. Berkeley & Los Angeles: University of California Press.

Tyler, Stephen A. (ed.). 1969. *Cognitive Anthropology*. New York: Holt, Rinehart & Winston.

Ullmann, Stephen. 1951. *Words and their Use*. London: Frederick Muller.

Ullmann, Stephen. 1957. *The Principles of Semantics*. Oxford: Blackwell.

Ullmann, Stephen. 1962. *Semantics: an Introduction to the Science of Meaning*. Oxford: Blackwell.

Vanderveken, Daniel. 1980. Illocutionary logic and self-defeating speech acts. In Searle, Kiefer & Bierwisch (eds) 1980:247-72.

Varro, Marcus T. *De Lingua Latina* tr. by Roland G. Kent, 1938. Loeb Classical Library Nn.333-4. London: Heinemann.

Vendler, Zeno. 1972. *Res Cogitans*. Ithaca: Cornell University Press.

Vernon, Magdalen D. 1971. *The Psychology of Perception*. (2nd edn) Harmondsworth: Penguin.

Verschueren, Jef. 1980. *On Speech Act Verbs*. Amsterdam: John Benjamins.

Wald, Benji. 1979. The development of the Swahili object marker: a study of the interaction of syntax and discourse. In Givon (ed.) 1979b:505-24.

Walker, David. 1980. *The Oxford Companion to Law*. Oxford: Clarendon Press.

Weinreich, Uriel. 1958. Travels through semantic space. *Word* 14:346-66. Reprinted in Weinreich 1980c:14-36.

Weinreich, Uriel. 1966. Explorations in semantic theory. *Current Trends in Linguistics* 3 ed. by Thomas A. Sebeok, 395-477. The Hague: Mouton. Reprinted in Weinreich 1980c:99-201.

Weinreich, Uriel. 1969. Problems in the analysis of idioms. *Substance and Structure of Language* ed. by J. Puhvel, 23-81. Berkeley & Los Angeles: University of California Press. Reprinted in Weinreich 1980c:208-64.

Weinreich, Uriel. 1980a. Lexicographic definition in descriptive semantics. In Weinreich 1980c:295-314.

Weinreich, Uriel. 1980b. 'Webster's Third' a critique of its semantics. In Weinreich 1980c:361-7.

Weinreich, Uriel. 1980c. *Weinreich on Semantics* ed. by William Labov & Beatrice S. Weinreich. Philadelphia: University of Pennsylvania Press.

Welman, J.B. 1948. *Preliminary Survey of the Freshwater Fishes of Nigeria.* Lagos: Government Printer.

Whitney, William D. 1888. *A Compendious German Grammar.* (6th edn) New York: Holt, Rinehart & Winston.

Whorf, Benjamin L. 1956. *Language, Thought, and Reality: Selected Writings* ed. by John B. Carroll. Cambridge MA: MIT Press.

Wierzbicka, Anna. 1972. *Semantic Primitives.* Berlin: Athenaum.

Wierzbicka, Anna. 1980. *Lingua Mentalis: the Semantics of Natural Language.* Sydney: Academic Press.

Wilkins, John. 1668. *Essay toward a Real Character and a Philosophical Language.* London: Royal Society. Facsimile, 1968. Menston: Scolar Press.

Wilks, Yorick. 1982. Comments on Sperber and Wilson's paper. In Smith (ed.) 1982:113-17.

Wilks, Yorick & Chris Cunningham. Forthcoming. A purported account of semantic relevance.

Wilson, Deirdre. 1975. *Presuppositions and Non-Truth Conditional Semantics.* New York: Academic Press.

Wittgenstein, Ludwig. 1963. *Philosophical Investigations.* Oxford: Blackwell.

Wonderley, William L. 1952. Semantic components in Kechua person morphemes. *Language* 28:366-76.

Woods, Robert S. 1966. *An English-Classical Dictionary for the Use of Taxonomists.* Pomona: Pomona College.

Wright, Walter D. 1978. *A First English Companion.* Digswell Place, Welwyn: James Nisbet. First published 1956.

Wunderlich, Dieter. 1979. *Foundations of Linguistics.* Cambridge: Cambridge University Press.

Yotsukura, Sayo. 1970. *The Articles in English.* The Hague: Mouton.

Zadeh, Lotfi A. 1965. Fuzzy sets. *Information and Control* 8:338-53.

Zadeh, Lotfi A. 1971. Quantitative fuzzy semantics. *Information Sciences* 3:159-76.

Zadeh, Lotfi A. 1972. A fuzzy-set-theoretic interpretation of linguistic hedges. *Journal of Cybernetics* 2:4-34.

Zieglschmid, A.J.F. 1929. Is the use of 'wesan' in the periphrastic actional passive in Germanic languages due to Latin influence? *Journal of English and Germanic Philology* 28:360-5.

Ziff, Paul. 1967. On H.P. Grice's account of meaning. *Analysis* 28:1-8. Reprinted in Rosenberg & Travis (eds) 1971:444-50 and Steinberg & Jakobovits (eds) 1971:60-5.

Zipf, George K. 1949. *Human Behavior and the Principle of Least Effort.* Cambridge MA: Addison-Wesley. Republished, 1965. New York: Hafner.

Index

This index covers both volumes

438   *Index*